FEMINIST
INTERPRETATIONS
OF
IMMANUEL KANT

RE-READING THE CANON

NANCY TUANA, GENERAL EDITOR

This series consists of edited collections of essays, some original and some previously published, offering feminist reinterpretations of the writings of major figures in the Western philosophical tradition. Devoted to the work of a single philosopher, each volume contains essays covering the full range of the philosopher's thought and representing the diversity of approaches now being used by feminist critics.

Already published:

Nancy Tuana, ed., *Feminist Interpretations of Plato* (1994)

Margaret A. Simons, ed., *Feminist Interpretations of Simone de Beauvoir* (1995)

Bonnie Honig, ed., *Feminist Interpretations of Hannah Arendt* (1995)

Patricia Jagentowicz Mills, ed., *Feminist Interpretations of G. W. F. Hegel* (1996)

Maria J. Falco, ed., *Feminist Interpretations of Mary Wollstonecraft* (1996)

Susan J. Hekman, ed., *Feminist Interpretations of Michel Foucault* (1996)

Nancy J. Holland, ed., *Feminist Interpretations of Jacques Derrida* (1997)

FEMINIST INTERPRETATIONS OF IMMANUEL KANT

EDITED BY ROBIN MAY SCHOTT

THE PENNSYLVANIA STATE UNIVERSITY PRESS
UNIVERSITY PARK, PENNSYLVANIA

Library of Congress Cataloging-in-Publication Data

Feminist interpretations of Immanuel Kant / edited by Robin May
    Schott.

      p.   cm.—(Re-reading the canon)
    Includes bibliographical references and index.
    ISBN 0-271-01675-2 (alk. paper)
    ISBN 0-271-01676-0 (pbk. : alk. paper)
    I. Kant, Immanuel, 1724–1804. 2. Woman (Philosophy) 3. Feminist
theory. I. Schott, Robin May. II. Series.
B2798.F35 1997
193—dc21   96-48058
                                            CIP

It is the policy of The Pennsylvania State University Press to use acid-free paper for the
first printing of all clothbound books. Publications on uncoated stock satisfy the
minimum requirements of American National Standard for Information Sciences—
Permanence of Paper for Printed Library Materials, ANSI Z39.48-1992.

To Emil Carl and Maya Rose,
whose entries into the world spanned and prolonged this other labor

Contents

Preface

Take into your hands any history of philosophy text. You will find compiled therein the "classics" of modern philosophy. Since these texts are often designed for use in undergraduate classes, the editor is likely to offer an introduction in which the reader is informed that these selections represent the perennial questions of philosophy. The student is to assume that she or he is about to explore the timeless wisdom of the greatest minds of Western philosophy. No one calls attention to the fact that the philosophers are all men.

Though women are omitted from the canons of philosophy, these texts inscribe the nature of woman. Sometimes the philosopher speaks directly about woman, delineating her proper role, her abilities and inabilities, her desires. Other times the message is indirect—a passing remark hinting at woman's emotionality, irrationality, unreliability.

This process of definition occurs in far more subtle ways when the central concepts of philosophy—reason and justice, those characteristics that are taken to define us as human—are associated with traits historically identified with masculinity. If the "man" of reason must learn to control or overcome traits identified as feminine—the body, the emotions, the passions—then the realm of rationality will be one reserved primarily for men,[1] with grudging entrance to those few women who are capable of transcending their femininity.

Feminist philosophers have begun to look critically at the canonized texts of philosophy and have concluded that the discourses of philosophy are not gender-neutral. Philosophical narratives do not offer a universal perspective, but rather privilege some experiences and beliefs over others. These experiences and beliefs permeate all philosophical theories whether they be aesthetic or epistemological, moral or metaphysical. Yet this fact has often been neglected by those studying the traditions of philosophy. Given the history of canon formation in Western philosophy, the perspective most likely to be privileged is that of upper-class, white males. Thus, to be fully aware of the impact of gender biases, it is imperative that we re-read the canon with attention to the ways in which philosophers' assumptions concerning gender are embedded within their theories.

This new series, *Re-Reading the Canon*, is designed to foster this process of reevaluation. Each volume will offer feminist analyses of the theories of a selected philosopher. Since feminist philosophy is not monolithic in method or content, the essays are also selected to illustrate the variety of perspectives within feminist criticism and highlight some of the controversies within feminist scholarship.

In this series, feminist lenses will be focused on the canonical texts of Western philosophy, both those authors who have been part of the traditional canon, as well as those philosophers whose writings have more recently gained attention within the philosophical community. A glance at the list of volumes in the series will reveal an immediate gender bias of the canon: Arendt, Aristotle, de Beauvoir, Derrida, Descartes, Foucault, Hegel, Hume, Kant, Locke, Marx, Mill, Nietzsche, Plato, Rousseau, Wittgenstein, Wollstonecraft. There are all too few women included, and those few who do appear have been added only recently. In creating this series, it is not my intention to reify the current canon of philosophical thought. What is and is not included within the canon during a particular historical period is a result of many factors. Although no canonization of texts will include all philosophers, no canonization of texts that exclude all but a few women can offer an accurate representation of the history of the discipline as women have been philosophers since the ancient period.[2]

I share with many feminist philosophers and other philosophers writing from the margins of philosophy the concern that the current canonization of philosophy be transformed. Although I do not accept the position that the current canon has been formed exclusively by power relations, I do believe that this canon represents only a selective history of the tradition. I share the view of Michael Bérubé that "canons are at once the location, the index, and the record of the struggle for cultural representation; like any other hegemonic formation, they must be continually reproduced anew and are continually contested."[3]

The process of canon transformation will require the recovery of "lost" texts and a careful examination of the reasons such voices have been silenced. Along with the process of uncovering women's philosophical history, we must also begin to analyze the impact of gender ideologies upon the process of canonization. This process of recovery and examination must occur in conjunction with careful attention to the concept of a canon of authorized texts. Are we to dispense with the notion of a tradition of excellence embodied in a canon of authorized texts? Or, rather than abandon the whole idea of a canon, do we instead encourage a reconstruction of a canon of those texts that inform a common culture?

This series is designed to contribute to this process of canon transformation by offering a re-reading of the current philosophical canon. Such a re-reading shifts our attention to the ways in which woman and the role of the feminine is constructed with the texts of philosophy. A question we must keep in front of us during this process of re-reading is whether a philosopher's socially inherited prejudices concerning woman's nature and role are independent of her or his larger philosophical framework. In asking this question attention must be paid to the ways in which the definitions of central philosophical concepts implicitly include or exclude gendered traits.

This type of reading strategy is not limited to the canon, but can be applied to all texts. It is my desire that this series reveal the importance of this type of critical reading. Paying attention to the workings of gender within the texts of philosophy will make visible the complexities of the inscription of gender ideologies.

Notes

1. More properly, it is a realm reserved for a group of privileged males, since the texts also inscribe race and class biases that thereby omit certain males from participation.

2. Mary Ellen Waithe's multivolume series, *A History of Women Philosophers* (Boston: M. Nijhoff, 1987), attests to this presence of women.

3. Michael Bérubé, *Marginal Forces/Cultural Centers: Tolson, Pynchon, and the Politics of the Canon* (Ithaca: Cornell University Press, 1992), 4–5.

Acknowledgments

Before I acknowledge the articles that are reprinted here by permission, I would like to acknowledge work that is not included here. This anthology is meant as an opening to the field of feminist interpretations of Kant, and as such is necessarily incomplete. There are many outstanding senior scholars whose work is not represented here because, though they have a personal interest in feminist questions, those questions are not central to their own philosophical work. There are many outstanding younger scholars who are working with debates that are introduced in this volume: for example, on Kant's views of women, or on the relation of Kantian ethics to an ethics of care. There are scholars who could not contribute to the anthology because of accidents of timing and the demands of personal life—such as the adoption of a foreign-born child. But the essays included do represent a range of important issues that address both Kant's systematic enterprise and feminist concerns. It is intended to serve as an impetus to continuing work in the area, not as a testament to an already completed project.

The following works included in the volume are reprinted with permission:

Annette C. Baier, "How Can Individualists Share Responsibility?" is reprinted by permission of Sage Publications, Inc., from *Political Theory* 21, no. 2 (May 1993): 228–48. Copyright © 1993 by Sage Publications, Inc.

Cornelia Klinger, "The Concepts of the Sublime and the Beautiful in Kant and Lyotard" is reprinted by permission of Blackwell Publishers from *Constellations: An International Journal of Critical and Democratic Theory* 2, no. 2 (October 1995): 207–24.

Sarah Kofman, "The Economy of Respect: Kant and Respect for Women," from *Le Respect des femmes* (Paris: Galilée, 1982), is reprinted from the English translation by permission of *Social Research* from *Social Research* 49, no. 2 (1982): 383–404.

Adrian M. S. Piper, "Xenophobia and Kantian Rationalism" is reprinted by permission of *Philosophical Forum* 24, nos. 1–3 (Fall–Spring 1992–93): 188–232.

Robin May Schott, "The Gender of Enlightenment" is reprinted by permission of the University of California Press from *What Is Enlightenment? Eighteenth-Century Answers and Twentieth-Century Questions*, edited by James Schmidt. Copyright © 1996. Regents of the University of California.

Sally Sedgwick, "Can Kant's Ethics Survive the Feminist Critique?" is reprinted by permission of Blackwell Publishers from *Pacific Philosophical Quarterly* 71(1990): 60–79.

1

Introduction

This volume presents quite different interpretations of Immanuel Kant's philosophy from a feminist perspective. Some contributors view Kant as having contributed significantly to theories of autonomy, subjectivity, and rationality in ways that can further feminist projects. Other contributors argue that Kant is a preeminent exponent of patriarchal views, and that gender hierarchies are inscribed in the very structure of his theories of morality and aesthetic judgment. How can one understand the coexistence of such competing interpretations? In this introduction, I shall map out the current field of feminist debate in order to focus on both the commonalities and divergences between the authors' views.

First, however, I shall begin with some personal anecdotes that situate myself in relation to the study of Kant's philosophy. My first serious encounter with Kant took place during an honors seminar on the *Critique of Pure Reason* at Swarthmore College in 1975. It was my first and perhaps most intense experience of the pleasures of explication and interpretation, of feeling oneself rise to the challenge of great philosophy. At the same time, it was the occasion for imbibing, as in one's mother's breast-milk, certain assumptions that subsequently became very difficult to question. Along with the exciting concept of the reproductive activity of self-consciousness, I accepted as inevitable the formalism of this activity. Knowledge seemed to me, as Kant argued, necessarily objective and universal, and the particular features of subjective experience that mark the uniqueness as opposed to the universalizability of individual identity seemed without relevance. Later, in graduate school, I experienced the existential need to unlearn these assumptions. If the activity of self-consciousness is formal and universal, the activity of my own consciousness seemed too tainted to meet the demands of such philosophical rigor. It took a good deal of time and anguish for me to be able to comprehend the workings of this ideal. I began to understand how the ideal of a formal, rational self-consciousness functions as an existential ideal, not merely as a method for developing principles of justification. Philosophers often do live in a way that attests to their belief that a "rational" life is independent of the influence of feeling, desire, or subjective interest.

My years in graduate school were also the years in which I began to identify myself consciously as a feminist. Female graduate students of philosophy were still a distinct minority at that time, and my intellectual community was drawn increasingly from women across the disciplines beginning to educate themselves in "women's studies." Kant came to represent for me the masculinist nature of Western philosophy. The Yale seminar on Kant that I attended was filled with men and their smells; as the only woman, I defiantly took out my pocket-watch at the beginning of each session to match the gestures of the professor. Eventually, I wrote a dissertation, and subsequently a book (*Cognition and Eros: A Critique of the Kantian Paradigm*) that thematized the way in which the Western philosophical and religious tradition in general, and Kant in particular, identified the erotic—the sexual, the sensuous, the emotional—with the feminine as a threat to purity and rationality. Now, as editor of this collection of feminist essays on Kant, I am positioned yet again differently in relation to Kant's philosophy. In undertaking to represent responsibly a broad range of feminist interpretations of Kant, I have gone through the process of judging essays that sympathetically appropriate the tools of Kant's philosophy for feminist purposes as convincing as those that give more critical accounts of Kant.

I use a personal voice here in order to thematize some of my concerns that are shared with many feminists. The women's movement that grew in the 1970s, through its early commitment to consciousness-raising and to understanding the personal as political, led to theorizing how knowledge is situated. Women in consciousness-raising groups talked about personal problems (e.g., sexual harassment, frustrations about child care) and discovered that these were social problems that they could protest. We came to the recognition that knowledge is powered not by abstracting from one's situation (as is traditionally taught in philosophy), but by attending to the problems of identity, experience, and context. Feminist philosophers draw on resources within philosophy—existentialism, phenomenology, Marxism, psychoanalysis, and/or post-modernism—to stress that the thinker is embedded, embodied, and engendered in a particular historical matrix. The contributions to this anthology underline the situatedness of knowledge, morality, aesthetics, and politics by focusing on themes of relatedness and embodiment. Instead of prioritizing an abstract moral subject, authors analyze the moral and political dilemmas that face concrete subjects: questions of friendship, collective responsibility, xenophobia, and colonialism. Many feminist philosophers, like Genevieve Lloyd, are critical of the claims of disembodied reason, and argue that it bears the traces of maleness. But contemporary feminist theory also recognizes that however one may resist this philosophical inheritance by analyzing the construction of gender and sexuality, one is never entirely removed from this history.

During the last twenty-five years feminist philosophers have debated heatedly the questions of whether and how to re-read the philosophical canon. On the one hand, some feminists argue for the necessity of feminists' reading, writing, and teaching the history of philosophy for philosophical reasons (feminists have inherited assumptions from this tradition and need to be self-conscious about them, as Elizabeth Spelman points out so convincingly in *Inessential Women*), practical reasons (one cannot reinvent the wheel), and institutional reasons (as the history of philosophy continues to be taught at colleges and universities, the question is how it will be taught). On the other hand, other feminists argue that energy is better directed to creating new beginnings. Rather than interpreting the writings of male philosophers, they argue, it is more fruitful to focus on how women's lives generate radically new ways of thinking and writing that challenge the inherited concepts of philosophical "method."

Today, feminists have increasingly come to the recognition that our task is to be both critical and constructive. As Elizabeth Grosz writes, feminists must continue the antisexist project of resisting philosophical assumptions that define "human" by a masculine model, and define the feminine only in relation to the masculine. If feminists do not analyze the ways sexism has functioned in philosophical theories, then feminist theory risks becoming a utopian alternative that leaves untouched existing forms of thought. But if feminist theory is simply critique, it remains on the very ground that it seeks to contest. Thus, feminist theory must be both critique and construct, and Grosz urges feminists to "apprentice" themselves to patriarchal knowledges in order to understand, "how they function, what presumptions they make, what procedures they rely upon, and what effects they produce."[1] Second, she urges feminists to learn how patriarchal theories function in order to use them against themselves. Though it is impossible for feminists to create something that is entirely new, untainted by the very theories they question, they can critically engage with these methods by focusing on their blind spots, contradictions, and silences. Third, Grosz calls for feminists to take traditional discourses as points of departure in order to create new theories, methods, and values. For example, when women's experience rather than men's selects the objects and methods of investigation, feminists not only can develop new theories, but can also demonstrate that philosophical paradigms are not universal.[2]

In their various ways, the essays in this volume seek to be both critical and constructive. Some contributors appropriate Kant's philosophy to address feminist concerns positively (e.g., Adrian Piper's argument that the Kantian conception of the rational person can counteract xenophobia). Other contributors explore the internal contradictions of Kant's philosophy, the ways in which it fails to meet its own standards (e.g., Hannelore Schröder's discussion of Kant's analyses of the rights of persons and of women). Still others use the tools of Kant's philosophy to go beyond itself (e.g., Jane Kneller's use of Kant's aesthetic theory to reconstruct his concept of moral autonomy). Though some of the authors see the constructive work of feminist theory in departing from Kant, while others invite him along on the voyage, all the contributors bridge the worlds of both Kantian scholarship and contemporary feminist debates.

FEMINIST INTERPRETATIONS

Given Kant's explicit endorsement of the subordination of wives to their husbands, and the exclusion of women from intellectual or political rights, it is no surprise that many feminists consider Kant to be an exemplar of philosophical sexism. Here the tensions between Kantian philosophy and feminist theory are mutual. Kant would consider feminists to be concerned with questions of empirical import, of interest perhaps to a particular group but not relevant to universal questions about ethics or aesthetics, and therefore not properly belonging to the domain of philosophy. Other feminists seek to redefine the ground on which a sympathetic dialogue can take place between Kant and feminism. But there are certain common threads that are present in both these critics and sympathizers. Both groups challenge the accepted topography of Kantian philosophy by which central philosophical concerns are defined as those that are abstract, universal, and transcendental, whereas issues relating to bodily existence, to emotion, or to empirical identity are defined as marginal. Instead, feminists have begun with questions founded in the politics of everyday life to resituate Kantian questions (about the rational self, moral relations, aesthetic judgment, and political rights and responsibilities) in the context of relations between the sexes, races, nations, and between humans and the natural environment.

In other words, although there is no one way of reading Kant from a feminist perspective, there are nonetheless certain features by which one could distinguish "feminist" readings. Since the 1970s, feminism has sought to account for the oppression of women in its "endless variety and monotonous similarity."[3] Although feminist theorizing in the 1970s was characterized by an overgrand invocation of the concept of patriarchy to explain social and psychological structures in universalist terms, in the 1980s and 1990s feminists increasingly have been concerned with localizing differences among women. (Some postmodern feminists like Denise Riley and Judith Butler argue that the term "women" itself is essentialist and should be displaced from its central role in feminist discourse). The current stress on the multiplicity of positions that women inhabit and the complexity of women's identity has arisen from two primary sources. In the 1980s, the women's movement in the United States was forced to grapple with charges of racism. Women of color argued that they were not part of a sisterhood that defined "women's" issues in terms of the concerns of white, middle-class professional women, and ignored, for example, the issue of sterilization abuse. At the same time, feminism became increasingly fueled by French postmodern theories that criticized the Western metaphysical tradition as essentialist and sought to do away with the notions of absolute truth and of a unitary philosophical "subject." These factors have led contemporary feminist writers to stress the differences rather than the commonalities among women, and consequently the diversity of feminist perspectives. Nonetheless, the movements and theoretical strategies that make up contemporary "feminisms" do share certain identifiable features. As Nancy Fraser and Linda Nicholson argue, feminism is still concerned with women's oppression in its "endless variety and monotonous similarity," and hence need not abandon large historical narratives nor analyses of societal macrostructures. But feminist theory should be attuned to the cultural specificity of different societies and periods and to that of different groups within societies and periods.[4] From such a perspective, feminist theory becomes attuned to the complexities of social identity formed by gender, class, race, ethnicity, age, and sexual orientation and forswears a single feminist method or epistemology.

In this anthology, the "feminist" perspectives of the contributors are articulated through their resistance to oppression and discrimination, whether based on gender, race, class, religion, or geographical location. The authors explore the extent to which Kant's philosophy provides reflective tools for resisting discrimination, and the extent to which Kantianism enacts discrimination. Some of the authors focus explicitly on political issues (e.g., Kant's views of women's rights) and some focus on issues that underlie politics (e.g., What is the nature of the community to which the individual is bound? What concept of individuality underlies Kant's discussion of moral or political responsibility?) The contributors discuss individuals and communities in their concreteness by exploring xenophobia, friendship, psychological resistance to loss, and the human relation to nature.

DEBATED THEMES

Four thematic areas emerge in these articles: (1) debates about Enlightenment rationality; (2) debates about an "ethics of care" and autonomy; (3) debates about philosophy's relation to the social world; and (4) debates about the nature of subjectivity. Although the anthology itself loosely follows Kant's own division of philosophy into the categories of rationality, ethics, aesthetics, and political philosophy, with an additional section on Kant's philosophy of nature and human nature, these four themes surface throughout the anthology. For example, debates about a morality of care appear not only in discussions of Kant's ethics but also of his aesthetics, and the relation of philosophy to the social world is discussed in articles on aesthetics as well as in articles on political philosophy. I shall orient the reader about these four areas of debate, before giving brief summaries of the articles.

Enlightenment/Rationality Debates

The Enlightenment claim that progress is possible through the use of reason and the advancement of knowledge is summed up in Kant's dictum, "Have courage to use your own reason!" Kant's phrase epitomizes the Enlightenment belief that the universal principles of rationality mark out the path by which humanity can free itself from an unjust authority. The spirit of Enlightenment typifies not only the philosophical project of the eighteenth century, but lays continuing claims on the present. Debates about Enlightenment rationality continue to divide twentieth-century intellectuals between its defenders and critics. The defenders of Enlightenment conceive of knowledge and scientific progress as based on a unified, rational, self-knowing subject, while its critics challenge these assumptions about subjectivity and truth.

Participants in this debate often respond either positively or negatively to Horkheimer's and Adorno's analysis in *The Dialectic of Enlightenment*. In that work, first published in 1947, Horkheimer and Adorno argued that Kant's definition of Enlightenment, of humanity's stepping out of self-induced tutelage, marked the beginning of the reign of terror of instrumental reason.[5] They argued that Kant, like the Marquis de Sade, displays the dialectic of Enlightenment in which reason's control over nature and human sensuous nature leads to the instrumentalization of reason and eventually to the destruction of civilization itself (as evidenced in Nazism and the Holocaust).

Contemporary scholars are often either inspired by Horkheimer's and Adorno's identification of Enlightenment rationality with an instrumentalizing and dominating power, or are provoked to contradict them, for example, by distinguishing between a "true" and a "false" or reductivist Enlightenment.[6] Jürgen Habermas has been one of the primary defenders of the emancipatory potential of Enlightenment rationality, arguing that the darkest period of German history was caused by the absence of the Enlightenment heritage, not by its presence. French writers such as Lyotard and Derrida have sided with the critics of Enlightenment. In their view, reason's claim to grasp universal truth has precluded an understanding of historicity and particularity.

Feminist theorists have had a particularly embattled relation to the question of Enlightenment. Some feminists argue that the Enlightenment tradition of individual reason, progress, and freedom, is a precondition for the discourse of women's liberation and for the political gains that women have won. They argue that the Enlightenment should be completed by incorporating groups that were historically excluded from this project. On the other hand, theorists like Jane Flax argue that the Enlightenment conception of a universal, rational subject is antithetical to feminist notions that the self is embedded in social relations, that the self is embodied, and is thus historically specific and partial. This controversy resurfaces in feminist debates about rationality. Some feminists defend the Kantian project of defining the universal structures of reason, and view these structures as the precondition for analyzing the empirical and psychological specificity of experiences (e.g., Adrian Piper's argument that Kantian rationalism has the tools within itself for counteracting xenophobia). Other feminists reject such a formalist conception of reason, as it implicitly carries with it the notion of impartiality. Iris Young writes, "Impartial reason must judge from a point of view outside the particular perspectives of persons involved in interaction, able to totalize these perspectives into a whole or general will. This is the point of view of a solitary transcendent God."[7] In stressing that selves and their rationality are historically embedded and partial, not universal and impartial, many feminist philosophers are thus critical of the Kantian project (see my essay, "The Gender of Enlightenment").[8]

Ethics of Care/Autonomy

Feminist debates about an "ethics of care" were inspired originally by Carol Gilligan's book, *In a Different Voice: Psychological Theory and Women's Development*, published in 1982. Gilligan's work touched a nerve in contemporary culture, posing the question of morality in conjunction with the question of sexual difference. In her book she argues that psychological theories of moral development display a distinctly masculine bias by taking boys' moral development as the standard by which girls are measured. In assessing the work of Lawrence Kohlberg she argues that his theory only accounts for one aspect of moral orientation, that which focuses on justice and rights, and does not account for the ethical orientation of care and responsibility so pronounced in women's moral development. She argues that women's moral judgment is typically more contextual than men's, more immersed in the details of relationships, and more able to reveal feelings of sympathy or empathy. These cognitive characteristics should not be seen as deficiencies, but as essential components of adult moral maturity, which views the self as immersed in a network of relationships with others. In the case of decisions, for example, about whether to have an abortion, or whether to leave their parents or partners, Gilligan finds women to be sensitive to the particular context in which their decisions must be made, to be occupied with questions about who will be hurt and who will be helped by their decision.

For many feminist theorists, Gilligan's work has served as a watershed moment in theorizing questions of autonomy, intersubjectivity, and community. It has served as a vehicle to criticize prevailing conceptions of the individual in Western philosophy, which views the autonomous self as disembedded and disembodied. Seyla Benhabib argues that the conception of the individual that has prevailed in thinkers such as Freud, Piaget, Kohlberg, and Rawls is based on the state-of-nature metaphor that has been so powerful for modern consciousness, a metaphor that provides a vision of the autonomous self as a narcissist who sees the world in his own image. She writes, "Yet this is a strange world; it is one in which individuals are grown up before they have been born; in which boys are men before they have been children; a world whether neither mother, nor sister, nor wife exists."[9]

Thus, many feminists have viewed Gilligan's work as enabling a positive development in feminist ethics by recognizing the particularity and situatedness of the "concrete" other. Some seek to anchor feminist ethics exclusively in care ethics, while others seek to integrate the care perspective with the justice perspective. (For example, care and justice perspectives may be simultaneous ways of responding to the same situation; or they may apply to different areas of moral concern; or the concept of the "concrete" other may be necessary for developing a coherent universalizable ethics, as Benhabib argues). Still others, such as Claudia Card, have been critical of the concept of a care ethics, and view it at best as a survival strategy of women under patriarchy, but not as an alternative conception of morality.

Kant has been an obvious figure for debate in the midst of this contemporary feminist interest in ethics. In Kant's view, for an action to be moral it must be wholly motivated by duty, and must exclude the influence of inclination. His account of the moral law is wholly formalistic and is encapsulated in the categorical imperative: "I should never act in such a way that I could not also will that my maxim should be a universal law."[10] Kant prefigures Kohlberg's understanding of moral development in formalistic, rationalist terms, and thus his theory becomes embroiled in contemporary debates about justice and care perspectives in morality. Some contributors focus on how care theorists criticize Kantian morality (e.g., Sally Sedgwick's article, "Can Kant's Ethics Survive the Feminist Critique?"), while others argue that Kant himself contributes to the development of an ethics of care and an understanding of the importance of the "concrete" other (e.g., Herta Nagl-Docekal's article, "Feminist Ethics: How It Could Benefit from Kant's Moral Philosophy"). But writers on both sides of this debate seek to revise the concept of autonomy in order to attend to the ways in which individuals are situated in communities of families or friends or of larger groups that bear collective responsibility for political decision-making.

Philosophy and the Social World

Another group of contributors focus on the relation of philosophy to the social world by examining, among other themes, Kant's views of women's nature. These authors are motivated by the question, How is one to read Kant, or indeed any of the male philosophers in the Western tradition, as a woman?[11] For example, Kant describes the scholarly women who "use their books somewhat like a watch, that is, they wear the watch so it can be noticed that they have one, although it is usually broken or does not show the correct time."[12] Piqued by this comment, the reader might turn to Kant's earlier works and find his view that women's philosophy is "not to reason, but to sense." And, "I hardly believe that the fair sex is capable of principles."[13] No wonder, Kant writes, that under these conditions the woman "makes no secret in wishing that she might rather be a man, so that she could give larger and freer latitude to her inclinations; no man, however, would want to be a woman."[14] What is the reader to do? Should she hold her breath and move quickly over such passages as minor disturbances of understanding the real philosophical significance of Kant's work? Or do Kant's views of the relative merits of the sexes have philosophical significance?

In *The Second Sex,* Simone de Beauvoir examined the significance of philosophical sexism, and thus inaugurated the contemporary wave of feminist philosophy. In the introduction to her book, published originally in 1949, she writes, "In actuality the relation of the two sexes is not quite like that of two electrical poles, for man represents both the positive and the neutral, as is indicated by the common use of *man* to designate human beings in general; whereas woman represents only the negative, defined by limiting criteria, without reciprocity."[15] She adds that whereas woman is deemed to be imprisoned in her own subjectivity because she has glands, man superbly ignores the fact that he has glands and thinks of his body as a direct and normal connection with the world, which he apprehends objectively.

Feminist philosophers in the last quarter-century have explored the significance of Beauvoir's concept of nonreciprocal relations between the sexes for the history of rationality, morality, and aesthetics. For example, Hélène Cixous writes of the dual, hierarchized oppositions, related to "the" couple man/woman: "Activity/passivity, Sun/Moon, Culture/Nature, Day/Night, Father/Mother, Head/heart, intelligible/sensitive, Logos/Pathos."[16] From this point of view, the structures of reason are seen to be imbued with gender hierarchies; reason inheres in a system that subordinates women and all that has traditionally been linked to women: passivity, nature, emotion, bodily processes, and so forth.

In using philosophers' views of women as a lever to pry open philosophical systems, some feminists have drawn on the resources of Marxism and the Frankfurt school of critical theory. Philosophers in this century like Lucien Goldmann, Georg Lukács, Max Horkheimer, and Theodor Adorno, have explicitly theorized the relation between philosophy and the social world. For example, Goldmann views great creative works as those that coherently express on an imaginative or conceptual plane the self-understanding of a social class or group.[17] From this perspective, analyzing the "truths" of particular philosophical theories such as Kant's discloses the "truths" of the world-views that they articulate. Although Marxist and critical theorists have primarily been concerned with power relations between classes, feminists have used these tools to go beyond Marxism in order to analyze sexual relations and ideologies.[18] In this analogy, feminist discussions of philosophy's relation to the social world do not limit themselves to questions of gender and sexuality, but seek to encompass questions of oppression and domination more broadly, including, for example, racism and colonialism.

Theories of Subjectivity

Postmodern theory's challenge to the "philosophy of the subject" has also had an impact on contemporary feminist debates about Kant's theory of the self. Postmodern philosophers doubt the notion of a stable, coherent self, possessing a form of reason capable of privileged insight into its own processes and into the laws of nature. They doubt that reason has transcendental and universal qualities that exist independently of the self's particular bodily, historical experiences, or that freedom or autonomy consists in obeying the laws of a transhistorical form of reason. Similarly, many feminists have been skeptical of the universalizing tendencies of the rational self of modern philosophy. They argue that this notion of the self masks the historical specificity of the self, its embeddedness and dependence upon social relations, and see in transcendental claims of the self a reflection of the experience of white Western males.[19]

From this perspective, Kant's theory of the self seems to epitomize a theory of subjectivity shown to be bankrupt by postmodern critics. Although in Kant's philosophy the activity of subjectivity plays a crucial role in constituting knowledge, these features of subjectivity are understood in formal and universal terms. It is the transcendental unity of apperception that unites the medley of impressions into an object. Kant writes, "It must be possible for the 'I think' to accompany all my representations, for otherwise something would be represented in me which could not be thought at all."[20] The "I think" represents the general and universal features of consciousness; that is, what all representations have in common to be united by one self-consciousness, as well as what all self-consciousnesses have in common. Thus, the constituting activity of the self is confined to the formal, universal feature of consciousness, without any trace of the empirical subject.

However, alternative analyses of the subject have been offered by Nietzsche, Freud, and Lacan, who probe the unconscious, drive, desire, and motivation. These thinkers explore the eroticism, the pain, the loss, the guilt in the subject, who may be blind to the motivations of his or her own desires.[21] In this context, questions concerning the nature and objects of desire, and men's and women's relation to loss and "the law" also enter the orbit of analyses of Kant (see Monique David-Ménard, "Kant, the Law, and Desire"). Many contemporary readers are also fascinated by Kant's theory of imagination in the *Critique of Judgement*. They argue that Kant's aesthetic writing departs radically from the formalist conception of the subject in his metaphysical and moral works, and moves toward a complex theory of the creative processes of the self that has resonance with postmodern concerns.

SYNOPSIS OF ARTICLES

Although the thematic areas mentioned appear in many of the articles, my list can hardly be inclusive of the concerns of all of the contributors. I turn now to an overview of the central concerns of the articles.

Adrian Piper's "Xenophobia and Kantian Rationalism" is the only article that deals explicitly with Kant's analysis of rationality in the *Critique of Pure Reason*. She looks at the concept of personhood in terms of Kant's notion of rational agency in order to understand the phenomenon of xenophobia, which is of particular interest to African-Americans who are treated as objects of xenophobia in white America. She argues that Kant's concept of personhood has both the resources for understanding the phenomenon of xenophobia, and that his theory implies that there are resources within the structure of the rational self for overcoming xenophobic fears in light of new experiences, and even to value human difference positively.

The articles on Kant's ethics are informed by the debates about an "ethics of care." Sally Sedgwick's article, "Can Kant's Ethics Survive

the Feminist Critique?" discusses Kant's notion of moral autonomy and
the moral law in light of feminist criticisms influenced by Carol Gilligan's
work. She argues that these feminist criticisms are founded on a more
general concern about the dichotomy between reason and nature and a
skepticism about an abstract moral law being adequate to the complexities of human life. In this sense, contemporary feminist criticisms echo
earlier philosophical criticisms of Kant, such as those of Schiller and
Hegel. She argues that even the most sympathetic defenses of Kant,
such as that of Barbara Herman, do not put to rest these deeper worries.

In "Feminist Ethics: How It Could Benefit from Kant's Moral Philosophy," Herta Nagl-Docekal also focuses on the relation between Kant's
moral philosophy and an ethics of care. But contrary to Sedgwick, she
argues that Kant has outlined an ethic of care that does not contradict
moral universalism. Nagl-Docekal argues that the formal rule of morality
should be understood as both universalist and radically individualizing,
and claims that Kant's ethics can be an important tool in identifying
moral wrongs to which women are subjected because of their gender.

Jean Rumsey, in "Re-Visions of Agency in Kant's Moral Theory,"
argues that Kant's concept of the moral agent is flawed because it
excludes women from full moral agency, and takes the pattern of
"normal agency" to be that of his contemporary "man." Rumsey analyzes
Kant's discussion of the paired virtues of beneficence and gratitude and
his account of friendship in order to show that Kant's concept of agency
is inadequate to account for the social dimensions of human beings. She
suggests revisioning self-respect so as to include the concrete features of
a self situated in particular relations with others.

Marcia Baron, in "Kantian Ethics and Claims of Detachment,"
defends Kant's ethics against some of the objections raised by Sally
Sedgwick and Jean Rumsey, focusing on objections that involve the
notion of detachment. The detachment that Kantian ethics is said to
involve is generally of one or more of the following sorts: detachment
from other persons, detachment from our projects, and detachment from
our emotions and feelings (the first and third being of greatest interest
to feminists). In evaluating the third sort of detachment, Baron acknowledges that correction is needed in Kant's ethics to give a larger place to
the cultivation of sentiments as part of moral (self-)development.

As the first article on Kant's aesthetics, Jane Kneller's "The Aesthetic
Dimension of Kantian Autonomy," continues the reevaluation of Kant's
philosophy in light of the "ethics of care" debates. She argues that

Kant's concern with aesthetics led him to give greater weight to the role of feelings in moral subjectivity than he did in his ethical writings. In Kneller's view, taking into account the felt and imaginative dimension of subjectivity in Kant's aesthetics can contribute to feminist conceptions of autonomy and freedom.

In "The Concept of the Sublime and the Beautiful in Kant and Lyotard," Cornelia Klinger discusses Kant's aesthetics in a more critical vein. The author contends that the pair of the beautiful and the sublime is part of the inherited dualisms of Western philosophy that imply the dualism of gender, and interrogates the contemporary resurgence of interest in the sublime. She argues that Lyotard brings to light and reinforces the subtext in Kantian aesthetics, in which the experience of the sublime is both gendered and violent.

Marcia Moen, in "Feminist Themes in Unlikely Places: Re-reading Kant's *Critique of Judgement*," argues that Kant's third *Critique* thematizes the loss of the isolated ego, the value of felt connectedness, the significance of embodiment, and the restoration of narrative complexity, in a way that prefigures contemporary feminist concerns. She argues that feminists can appropriate elements of Kant's thought to construct a pluralism that avoids both unrestricted forms of relativism as well as all claims to absolute truth.

Kim Hall's account of Kant's aesthetics, in "*Sensus Communis* and Violence: A Feminist Reading of Kant's *Critique of Judgement*," once again sounds a critical note in reading Kant's aesthetics. She argues that the community that grounds aesthetic judgment in Kant's third *Critique* is founded upon violence. Through Kant's texts she explores his relation to the narratives of colonization written by Columbus and Cortés, and argues that his aesthetics contribute to Western culture's justification of colonial expansion.

The essays dealing with Kant's discussion of political and intellectual rights and responsibilities are also highly critical of Kant. In "Kant's Patriarchal Order," Hannelore Schröder compares Kant's views of women to those of his contemporary Theodor Von Hippel, to show that in his own historical context Kant's views must be deemed to be reactionary. She argues that Kant's failure to accord women equal rights with men undermines the validity of his ethical and political writings.

Annette Baier's "How Can Individualists Share Responsibility?" is critical of the highly individualistic foundations of Kant's version of republicanism. She argues that the Kantian form of individualism that is appropriated by the American tradition cannot account for shared responsibility, and that it provides the basis for rule by an elite rather than for a democratic society.

My article, "The Gender of Enlightenment" takes up the feminist debate about the Enlightenment by considering the questions, What could Kant's conception of Enlightenment have meant to women of the period? How would women's experiences have challenged Kant's formulations? I suggest that it may be necessary for feminists to challenge the primacy of autonomy and focus instead on heteronomy, the interdependence of individuals, as a basis for moral and political theory.

Monique David-Ménard's "Kant, the Law and Desire," opens the section "Philosophy of Nature and Human Nature" by invoking the tools of psychoanalysis to analyze Kant's categorical imperative. She analyzes his concept of morality in terms of the structure of masculine desire (as well as the different forms of "substitutability" of the objects of desire for men and women) in order to compare men's and women's different relation to the moral law.

Sarah Kofman's "The Economy of Respect: Kant and Respect for Women," drawn from her earlier book, *Le Respect des femmes,* also uses psychoanalytic concepts to thematize moral respect between the sexes in Kant's philosophy. She argues that moral respect and the moral law are not "pure" as Kant maintains, but always already contaminated by the original relation of respect—the respect an infant learns in relation to its mother. In Kofman's view, it is the fear of femininity, the need to hold it and all that it represents at a distance, that is the subtext of Kant's morality.

In "Rethinking Kant from the Perspective of Ecofeminism," Holly Wilson analyzes Kant's concept of nature from an ecofeminist point of view. She argues that Kant's treatment of nature as an interconnected system of purposes and his placement of human beings in the context of their natural environment are compatible with contemporary feminist concerns to sustain ecosystems and livelihoods.

This anthology does not seek to decide the case for or against Kant. Rather, it presents a range of analyses written by feminist philosophers, covering many different areas of Kant's philosophy. The contributors themselves are drawn from Europe—Austria, France, the Netherlands—as well as from an American context. This diversity of nationality emphasizes both the wide impact Kant has had on European and

American culture, as well as the international nature of contemporary feminist debates.

If the reader finds herself or himself inclined more sympathetically or more critically to Kant, it may be because of the persuasiveness of the rational argumentation presented by the contributors. But it may also depend on certain predispositions within the reader. Philosophy, like human existence, is not just about rationality—as feminists among others point out. Note, for example, the words I used in describing my own initiation into Kantian philosophy: language relating to pleasure and reproduction. With other philosophical critics, feminists probe the desire, pleasure, and frustration of human existence, and seek to incorporate this dimension into philosophical reflection. The reader might find herself or himself judging Kant on such factors as the triumph and humility of comprehending an elaborate philosophical system, or the desire for a structure or bulwark against the unsettling winds of postmodernism and the uncertainties of contemporary life, or the anger at entrenched misogynist views and at any thinker who gives evidence of such views. Moreover, the reader's own judgment is also enabled by a particular historical context. This historical juncture is marked not only by increasing numbers of women studying at universities, but by the creation of the fields of women's studies and gender studies as academic disciplines. This development over the last quarter-century is the precondition for the current feminist re-reading of the philosophical canon. Although in Kant's own time women were denied access to university education, this education is crucial for women's entering what Kant calls the "public" exercise of reason, defined as the "use which a person makes of it as a scholar before the reading public."[22] When women become scholars, they do not grow beards (as Kant joked), but they do open paths for rethinking the contents and methods of education. It is to this larger project that the present anthology contributes.

Notes

1. Elizabeth Grosz, "Contemporary Theories of Power and Subjectivity," in *Feminist Knowledge; Critique and Construct*, ed. Sneja Gunew (London: Routledge, 1990), 60.

2. Ibid., 61.

3. Gayle Rubin, "The Traffic in Women," in *Toward an Anthropology of Women*, ed. Rayna R. Reiter (New York: Monthly Review Press, 1975), 160.

4. Nancy Fraser and Linda J. Nicholson, "Social Criticism without Philosophy: An

Encounter Between Feminism and Postmodernism," in *Feminism/Postmodernism*, ed. Linda J. Nicholson (New York: Routledge, 1990), 34–35.

5. See John H. Smith's discussion of the Enlightenment debates in "Reading Kant with Sade with Lacan: The Limits and Lost Cause of the Enlightenment," 7ff. Manuscript.

6. Ibid., 10.

7. Iris Young, "Impartiality and the Civic Public: Some Implications of Feminist Critiques of Moral and Political Theory," in her *Throwing Like a Girl and Other Essays in Feminist Philosophy and Social Theory* (Bloomington: Indiana University Press, 1990), 96.

8. In compiling this collection, I noted that although many feminists discuss debates about objectivity (for example, see Linda Alcoff and Elizabeth Potter, *Feminist Epistemologies* [New York: Routledge, 1993]) and many feminists work with Kant, as evidenced both by the articles in this collection and the many fine articles that could not find a home here, relatively few feminists deal with Kant's discussion of knowledge and reason from a feminist perspective. In this volume, see Piper, "Xenophobia and Kantian Rationalism" (Chapter 2). See also the chapter on objectivity in my book, *Cognition and Eros; A Critique of the Kantian Paradigm* (pbk., University Park: Pennsylvania State University Press, 1993).

9. Seyla Benhabib, "The Generalized and the Concrete Other," in her *Situating the Self: Gender, Community and Postmodernism in Contemporary Ethics* (New York: Routledge, 1992), 156–57.

10. Immanuel Kant, *Foundations of the Metaphysics of Morals*, trans. Lewis White Beck (Indianapolis, Ind.: Bobbs-Merrill, 1959), 18.

11. I do not mean to assert there is any single, essential position by which a reader who is also a woman interprets. Rather, I point to the fact that women might be especially disturbed by such passages, just as blacks are especially disturbed by racist comments, and Jews by anti-Semitic ones. Men, of course, may also find such passages disturbing, as many white people also find racist comments deplorable.

12. Immanuel Kant, *Anthropology from a Pragmatic Point of View*, trans. Victor Lyle Dowdell (Carbondale: Southern Illinois University Press, 1978), 221.

13. Immanuel Kant, *Observations on the Feeling of the Beautiful and the Sublime*, trans. John T. Goldthwait (Berkeley and Los Angeles: University of California Press, 1965), 132–33.

14. Kant, *Anthropology*, 222.

15. Simone de Beauvoir, *The Second Sex*, trans. H. M. Parshley (New York: Vintage, 1952), xviii.

16. Hélène Cixous, from "Sorties," *New French Feminisms*, ed. Elaine Marks and Isabelle de Courtivron (Amherst: University of Massachusetts Press, 1980), 90–91.

17. Lucien Goldmann, *The Hidden God: A Study of Tragic Vision in the "Pensées" of Pascal and the Tragedies of Racine*, trans. Philip Thody (London: Routledge and Kegan Paul, 1964) 17.

18. For one example of this, see my *Cognition and Eros.*

19. Jane Flax, "Postmodernism and Gender Relations in Feminist Theory," in *Feminism/Postmodernism*, 41–43.

20. Immanuel Kant, *Critique of Pure Reason*, trans. Norman Kemp Smith (London: Macmillan, 1958), B131.

21. See, for example, Horkheimer's and Adorno's comparison of Kant and the Marquis de Sade in *The Dialectic of Enlightenment*, as well as Jacques Lacan's "Kant with Sade," trans. James B. Swenson Jr. *October* 51 (Winter 1989): 55–104 (originally in *Ecrits II*). See also John H. Smith's manuscript "Reading Kant with Sade with Lacan" for a comparison of these two analyses.

22. Immanuel Kant, "What is Enlightenment?" in *Kant On History*, ed. with an introd. by Lewis White Beck, trans. Lewis White Beck, Robert E. Anchor, and Emil L. Fackenheim (Indianapolis, Ind.: Bobbs-Merrill, 1963), 5.

Part I

Rationalism

2

Xenophobia and Kantian Rationalism[1]

Adrian M. S. Piper

Contemporary Kantian ethics has given a wide berth to Kant's analyses of reason and the self in the *Critique of Pure Reason*.[2] Perhaps this can be ascribed to P. F. Strawson's influential fulminations against Kant's transcendental psychology in *The Bounds of Sense*.[3] Strawson's view was an expression—one of many—of a postwar behaviorist sensibility, for which the best conceptual analysis of interior mental life was no analysis at all. In recent years this sensibility has become increasingly anachronistic, both in ethics and in philosophy of mind, and is in need of reappraisal on these grounds alone.

The neglect by contemporary Kantian ethicists of Kant's first *Critique* has been particularly unfortunate. It forecloses a deeper understanding of Kant's own ethical views, and robs us of valuable resources for addressing contemporary issues in metaethics and applied moral philosophy. It is virtually impossible to understand Kant's conception of the categorical imperative in isolation from his account of reason in the first *Critique*'s Transcendental Dialectic; or his distinction between autonomy and heteronymy in isolation from his inchoate but suggestive formulation of the Two Standpoints Thesis in the solution to the Third Antinomy; or his elaboration of that thesis itself in chapter 3 of the *Groundwork of the Metaphysic of Morals*[4] in isolation from the chapter on Noumena and Phenomena, the Refutation of Idealism, and the Fourth Paralogism in the A edition of the *Critique*. Of course this is not to deny that these concepts can be put to excellent and fruitful use independently of ascertaining what Kant himself meant by them.

Moreover, the first *Critique* offers a developed conception of the self that provides a needed resource for defending Kantian ethics against anti-rationalist criticisms, such as that it is too abstract, alienating, altruistic, or detached from ordinary personal concerns to guide actual human behavior. The conception of the self to be found in the first *Critique* is, to be sure, a thoroughly rationalistic one that no antirationalist would accept. Its virtue, however, is to demonstrate convincingly that in ordinary personal concerns, as well as in the guidance of human behavior, the scope and influence of rationality is inescapable.

Corresponding to these two considerations, the purpose of this discussion is twofold. First, I want to shed some light on Kant's concept of personhood as rational agency, by situating it in the context of the first *Critique*'s conception of the self as defined by its rational dispositions. I hope to suggest that this concept of personhood cannot be simply grafted onto an essentially Humean conception of the self that is inherently inimical to it, as I believe Rawls, Gewirth, and others have tried to do.[5] Instead I will try to show how deeply embedded this concept of personhood is in Kant's conception of the self as rationally unified consciousness.

Second, I want to deploy this embedded concept of personhood as the basis for an analysis of the phenomenon of xenophobia. I focus on this phenomenon for two reasons. First, it is of particular concern for African-Americans. As unwelcome intruders in white America we are the objects of xenophobia on a daily basis. This pervasive fact of our experience conditions all of our social relations, and may itself engender a reciprocal form of xenophobia in self-defense. It is therefore doubly in our interests to understand this phenomenon and the defects in rationality it manifests. Second, Kant's conception of the self affords potent resources for understanding xenophobia as a special case of a more general cognitive phenomenon, namely the disposition to resist the intrusion of anomalous data of any kind into a conceptual scheme whose internal rational coherence is necessary for preserving a unified and rationally integrated self.

I begin by limning the conception of the self as rationally unified consciousness I defend on Kant's behalf. This conception differs from Kant's actual pronouncements in only one respect: I incorporate Strawson's suggestion that, among the candidates for innate concepts in Kant's Tables in the Metaphysical Deduction, only the subject-predicate relation can be understood as what Kant would call a transcendental concept or judgment-form. On this view, all other such concepts are empirical, including that of causality. I then formulate the issue of the relation between transcendental and empirical concepts or categories and its relevance to an analysis of xenophobia. Kant claims that anomalous data that fail to conform to the transcendental concepts of the understanding cannot be experienced by a unified self at all. Xenophobia is fear, not of strangers generally, but rather of a certain kind of stranger, namely those who do not conform to one's preconceptions about how persons ought to look or behave. It is therefore a paradigm case of resistance to the intrusion of anomalous data into an internally coherent conceptual scheme—a threat to the unity of the self defined by it. If a disposition to these preconceptions is innate, then xenophobia is a hard-wired, incorrigible reaction to a threat to the rational integrity of the self. If, on the other hand, a disposition to these preconceptions is the result of empirical conditioning, then xenophobia is corrigible in light of empirical data that may be realistically expected to compel the revision of those concepts.

In section 2 I begin the exegetical part of this project by sifting through Kant's own claims about the relation between transcendental and empirical concepts, and conclude that empirical concepts, on Kant's view, instantiate transcendental ones.[6] In section 3 I locate Kant's concept of personhood relative to the distinction between transcendental and empirical concepts by arguing that this concept has both transcendent and transcendental status for Kant. This implies that Kant's concept of personhood is innate, and not subject to empirical revision. However, the way in which this concept is instantiated or applied is not similarly fixed. On Kant's account, we identify others as persons on the basis of our own self-identification as persons; and Kant insists that the only self to which we have epistemic access is empirical. In section 4 I examine Kant's account of self-knowledge and argue that Kant's distinction between noumenal and empirical selves does not foreclose veridical identification of oneself as a person. I conclude that Kant's transcendent concept of personhood is instantiated by particular empirical exemplars of personhood; i.e, particular persons with particular personalities, among whom each of us necessarily identifies ourself and only contingently identifies others.

In section 5 I then deploy Kant's concept of personhood and his distinction between transcendental and empirical concepts in the service of a detailed analysis of xenophobia. I argue that it is a self-protective reaction to violation of one's empirical conception of people, and involves a cognitive failure to apply the transcendent concept of personhood consistently across all relevant cases. I try to show that racism, sexism, homophobia, anti-Semitism, etc., are pseudorational responses to xenophobia that depend on the mechanisms of rationalization, dissociation, and denial; and on a deep personal investment in the resulting honorific stereotype of the valued group to which one belongs. Derogatory racial, gender, or ethnic stereotyping of others, on this view, is a reciprocally interdependent consequence of honorific stereotyping of oneself.

Finally, in section 6 I recur to the text, in order to settle the question of the cognitive status of xenophobia within Kant's theory. I offer two interpretations of Kant's requirement that all data of experience conform to categories constitutive of the rationally unified self. Interpretation (A) demands that all such data conform both to transcendental and to empirical concepts, whereas interpretation (B) requires that they conform only to the transcendental ones. If (A) is correct, then another who is anomalous with respect to one's empirical conception of people cannot be a person for one at all. So xenophobia is incorrigible. But if (B) is correct, then another might violate one's empirical conception of people but be nevertheless recognizable as instantiating one's transcendent concept of personhood. So it would be possible to recognize the other as a person even though she violated one's empirical presuppositions about what and who people are. In that case, even if a disposition to xenophobia were innate, particular manifestations of it would be the result of conditioning and therefore susceptible to empirical modification. I examine the textual evidence for each interpretation, and conclude that (B) is correct; and that Kant's conception of reason as theory-construction implies resources within the structure of the self for overcoming xenophobia—resources frequently overshadowed, however, by empirical conditioning.

1. KANTIAN RATIONALISM

In the first *Critique*, Kant tells us repeatedly that if a perception does not conform to the fundamental categories of thought that ensure the unity and coherence of the self, they cannot be part of our experience at all (A 112, 122, and B 132, 134).[7] Kant describes these fundamental categories as "*a priori* transcendental concepts of understanding," by which he means innate rules of cognitive organization that any coherent, conscious experience must presuppose. The Table of Transcendental Categories he offers in the Metaphysical Deduction is drawn largely from Aristotle, with considerable additional tinkering by Kant. They include substance, totality, reality, possibility, causality, and community, to name just a few. Some commentators have rightfully concluded that the most significant candidate for this elevated cognitive status is the subject-predicate relation in logic, from which Kant derives the relational category of substance and property in the Table of Categories (Kant regards this as the result of fleshing out the subject-predicate relation or "judgment form" with "transcendental content"; the sensory data our experience presupposes rather than the sensations we perceive as a result of it (A 70/B 95–A 79/B 105)).[8] The idea, then, would be that organizing sensory data in terms of this relation is a necessary condition of experience. On this view, if we do not experience something in a way that enables us to make sense of it by identifying properties of it—for example, in propositions such as,

That car is dark red,

or

I am tired,

we cannot consciously experience that thing at all.

This thesis—call it the *Kantian rationalism thesis*—has the merit of plausibility over the archaic list of categories Kant originally furnished.

It does not seem too controversial to suppose that any viable system of concepts should enable its user to identify states of affairs by their properties, since concepts just are of corresponding properties, and to ascribe a property to an object just is to subsume that object under the corresponding concept. So any system of concepts should enable its user to ascribe to objects those properties of which she has concepts. The Kantian rationalism thesis—henceforth the KRT—is so weak that it may even be defensible in the face of anthropological evidence that languages considerably remote from Indo-European ones evince a cognitive structuring to the user's experience that is so different from our own as to be almost unintelligible to us. It would be an argument in favor of the KRT if it could be shown that the subject-predicate relation held regardless of the other ways in which culturally specific conceptual organizations of experience differed among themselves.

More precisely formulated, then, the KRT says that if we do not experience something in such a way as to allow us to make sense of it in terms of a set of coherent concepts that structure our experience, *whatever those concepts are*, we cannot consciously experience that thing at all. On this thesis the innate capacity would consist in a disposition to structure experience conceptually as such, but not necessarily in accordance with any particular list of concepts,[9] provided that the particular, culturally specific set S of concepts c_1, c_2, c_3, . . . c_n that did so satisfied the following requirements:

(A) S observes the law of noncontradiction, i.e., the members of S are internally and mutually consistent in their application;

(B) Any particular c_i in S is either
  (1) an instantiation of some other c_j in S; or
  (2) instantiated by some other c_k in S; i.e., S is minimally coherent;

(C) for any cognitively available particular p, there is a c_j in S that p instantiates.

The suggestion would be that we can understand a particular state of affairs only if (A) the concepts by which we recognize it are neither internally nor mutually contradictory; (B) those concepts are minimally coherent with one another in that each particular identified by them satisfies the subject-predicate relationship with respect to at least one other of them; and (C) that particular itself instantiates at least one of them. I develop this suggestion at length elsewhere.[10] It says, roughly, that in order for something to register as a conscious experience at all for us, we have to be able to make sense of it in terms of some such concepts in the set; and that if we can't, it won't.

Suppose, for example, that we were to be confronted with some particular such that the concepts it instantiates satisfied (A) but violated (B), i.e., such that we could invoke a concept in identifying it consistently with the application of our other concepts; but that that concept itself bore no instantiation-relation to others in the set (i.e., aside from that of being a concept in the set). In this case, that which we invoked as a "concept" would in fact not be one at all, since the corresponding predicate would by definition denote only the single state of affairs it had been invoked to identify. Since there would be no further concepts in terms of which we might understand the meaning of that denoting term, it could not enter into any analytic truths. In short, this would be like cooking up a special noise to denote only one state of affairs on the single occasion of its occurrence. The enterprises of denotation and meaning themselves would fail.

Alternately, imagine what it would be like to be confronted by a particular such that its concept satisfied (B) but not (A), i.e., such that it enabled us to identify its properties in terms of concepts in the set, but that the application of those concepts themselves was internally or mutually inconsistent. In that event, it would be possible to ascribe to the thing the conjunction of some predicate F and some other one, G, that implied the negation of F.[11] Again the enterprise of identification itself would fail. If we were finally to fail to identify the thing or state of affairs in question as having a consistent set of properties, we would fail to identify it altogether. And then it could not be part of our conscious experience. If such cases characterized all of our encounters with the world, we would have no experiences of it at all and therefore no unified sense of self either.

These are the sorts of failures Kant has in mind when he avers, in the A Deduction, that

> without such unity, which has its rule *a priori*, and which subjects appearances to it, thoroughgoing, universal, and therefore necessary unity of consciousness would not be found in the manifold of perceptions. These would then not belong to any experience,

> therefore would be without object, and nothing but a blind play
> of representations, that is, less even than a dream. (A 112)

Kant is saying that if we do not organize cognitively the data of our senses according to consistent and coherent rules, we cannot be rationally unified subjects. "For otherwise," he adds in the B Deduction, "I would have as many-colored and diverse a self as I have representations of which I am conscious." (B 134) I would, that is, lack a sense of myself as the subject in whose consciousness those representations occur. For a Kantian rationalist, then, the cognitive organization of experience according to consistent and coherent concepts is a necessary condition of being a rationally unified subject.

The KRT as explicated claims that only the subject-predicate relation counts as what Kant would call a transcendental concept or judgment-form; all the rest are empirical. Empirical concepts may differ as to how deeply entrenched in our cognitive dispositions they are. But all empirical concepts, for Kant, apply to and are formed in response to particular empirical contexts, rather than being necessary preconditions of experience itself. However, Kant did not devote sufficient attention to explaining the relation between empirical and transcendental concepts. If empirical concepts are contingent rather than necessary determinants of experience, then presumably we might have a particular experience even though we lacked one particular empirical concept by which to make sense of it—i.e., in the case where we had some other, nonequivalent empirical concept that did the job equally well. And Kant is silent on the question of whether we might have a particular experience that conformed to the transcendental concepts but to none of our empirical concepts—for instance, of an empirical state of affairs for the evident properties of which we could find absolutely no fitting predicates at all. Is the formation of empirical concepts itself a necessary precondition of experience? Or is it as contingent on circumstance as those empirical concepts themselves are? Nor does Kant explain how susceptible to change our empirical concepts are, in light of their relation to transcendental ones on the one hand and to new or anomalous empirical data on the other.

These issues are central to the topic of this essay. Thomas Kuhn has documented the inherent impediments to paradigm shift in the natural sciences—their conservatism and constitutional insensitivity to the significance of new data, and their resistance to revising deeply entrenched theories in light of experiment anomaly.[12] Elsewhere I have argued that the resistance to integrating anomaly is a general feature of human intellection that attempts to satisfy a Kantian requirement of rational self-preservation.[13] I have also offered elsewhere a Kantian analysis of a certain brand of xenophobic resistance to anomaly that finds typical expression in racism, sexism, anti-Semitism, class elitism, and homophobia, among other types of discrimination.[14] The question at issue here is whether a Kantian conception of the self explains xenophobia as a necessary or a contingent attribute of the self; i.e., whether it is a hard-wired disposition to defend the self against attacks on its internal integrity that is impervious to modification, or whether a xenophobic fear of strangers as violating one's conceptual presuppositions about persons is contingent on such empirical conditions as upbringing, degree of exposure to diversity or integration, and peer-group reinforcement—and therefore revisable in light of new experience. Ultimately I think Kant's view implies the latter; I will try to show this in what follows.

2. TRANSCENDENTAL AND EMPIRICAL CONCEPTS

Kant says many things about the relation between transcendental and empirical concepts, most of which are inconclusive. He says that empirical concepts are based on transcendental ones (A 111), that they are grounded in transcendental ones (A 113), that they are subject to them (B 163), that they must agree with them (B 164), and that their source is in them (A 127). None of this is precise enough to shed light on the actual relation between them. A more specific but fallacious account of the relationship is suggested by Kant's assertion that empirical concepts are a consequence of transcendental ones (A 114). Regardless of whether by "consequence" Kant means "causal consequence" or "logical consequence," he clearly should not have said this: causality as itself a transcendental concept is not a relation that can be maintained to hold between transcendental and empirical concepts, and transcendental concepts cannot be supposed to imply empirical concepts (indeed, Kant as much as acknowledges this when he says later that empirical laws cannot derive their origin from transcendental concepts [A 128, B 165]). Nor is the extended account of the reproductive imagination in the A

Deduction at A 119–24 and in the B Deduction at B 152 helpful in ascertaining exactly in what the relationship consists.

Surprisingly, Kant does admit the existence of "derivative pure *a priori* concepts." These are derived by combining the transcendental ones with one another or with "modes of pure sensibility," i.e., our innate disposition to structure our experience spatiotemporally. Whatever the character of this latter process of combination, it cannot be identical to or even very much like that involved in schematizing the categories in time, since this, Kant tells us, is what gives the transcendental concepts applicability to our sensory and spatiotemporal experience (A 140/B 179–A 142/B 181); it does not engender any derivative ones. Among these derivative necessary concepts are those of action, passion, and force, derived from the transcendental concept of causality; and the concept of presence and resistance, derived from that of community (A 82/B 108). The concepts of action and passion are of particular interest for understanding the role of human agency and inclination in Kant's moral philosophy, and it is useful to see them identified as necessary preconditions of experience so early on in the first *Critique*.[15] But Kant defers the project of enumerating all of these additional transcendental concepts to another occasion, and says nothing more about the nature of their process of derivation.

More helpful is Kant's assertion, in both the A and B Editions of the first *Critique*, that empirical concepts depend on the transcendental ones (A 114, B 164). This implies that transcendental concepts are a necessary but not sufficient condition of empirical ones, i.e., that transcendental ones make the empirical ones possible without ensuring any particular set of them. Earlier, in the Transcendental Logic, Kant had explained why transcendental concepts alone (i.e., in their corresponding logical forms of judgment) cannot furnish a sufficient condition of empirical truth. Although they do furnish criteria of logical truth,

> [t]hese criteria . . . concern only the form of truth, that is, of thought in general; and in so far they are quite correct, but not sufficient. For although our knowledge may be in complete accordance with logical form, that is, may not contradict itself, it is still possible that it may be in contradiction with the object. (A 59/B 84)

Here Kant observes that the fact that a proposition may satisfy logical requirements does not by itself determine its content; indeed, it may happen that a system of propositions may satisfy these requirements, yet its content might be "contradicted," i.e., conclusively disconfirmed by the objective states of affairs it purports to denote (also see B 190, A 155–57).

The sufficient condition for the veracity of empirical concepts—i.e., that which ensures the consistent and coherent application of at least one specifiable *kind* of empirical concept rather than any other to a particular ("rabbit" or "gavagai" rather than "H_2O" to small furry entities with long ears, for instance)—is given by the source of their transcendental content. That transcendental content itself is what Kant calls the manifold, and he thinks that the process of synthesizing or unifying the manifold under concepts is what specifies their content:

> Synthesis of the manifold (whether empirical or a priori) is what first produces a cognition, which certainly may be crude and confused at first and therefore in need of analysis. But synthesis alone is what actually collects the elements into a cognition, and unifies them into a particular content. (B 103/A 78)

The crucial missing link in these remarks is an answer to the question of whether a randomly chosen element of the manifold has attributes that lead us to collect it under one concept rather than another (i.e., whether natural kinds exist), or whether its attributes are conferred solely by the concepts that subsume it. Here Kant is silent on which account of transcendental content is correct, but later relies on the latter possibility to justify the need for a Schematism of the Pure Understanding (B 177/ A 138). This latter possibility implies that any datum could be subsumed under any concept arbitrarily, and therefore that there is no systematic relation between our capacities of cognitive organization and the particular data we organize—hence the need for time as a schema that mediates between them. By contrast, the former implies that these data carry markers or clues to the concept that most appropriately subsumes them, and therefore that there is at least some minimal correspondence between the way we organize the world and the elements of the world that we organize. Kant furnishes no unambiguous evidence for this possibility (but see note 17, below).

And what about the source of this transcendental content? Its nature and ontological plausibility is a point of endless debate among Kant scholars. Here I will simply state (but not defend) the view that this source is what Kant describes, in a passage in the Schematism willfully mistranslated by Kemp Smith, as "the transcendental matter of all objects as things in themselves" (A 143/B 182;[16] also see A 20, A 28, A 30/B 46, B 60, B 75, B 125, B 145, A 168, A 223, A 372, A 375, A 385, B 422a–423, A 581).[17] This is to suggest that first, in addition to our innate capacities for cognitive organization, a multiplicity of objects that are ontologically independent of us must provide us with the sensory data we organize, in order for empirical experience to occur; and second, if these objects provide such data, and our cognitive capacities are in good working order, systematically related empirical experience will occur.

This suggestion does not imply that the systematic relation we detect among empirical objects is identical to any relation that might obtain among ontologically independent objects that are by definition inaccessible to our empirical experience. Nor does it imply that the relation between these two sets of relations is one of causality as we now understand that term (although of course it might be). But it does imply that we are justified in thinking of the systematic coherence we discover in the empirical world we experience as at least a clue to the character of the coherence that may be presumed to actually exist among ontologically independent states of affairs as they are in fact. Indeed, in the "Regulative Employment of the Ideas of Pure Reason" Kant himself concedes this when, in arguing that the unity in nature we discover by exercising our rational capacities in inquiry and research is a necessary precondition of experience rather than a contingent outcome of it, he says,

> In fact it is hard to see how there can be a logical principle of the rational unity of rules, unless a transcendental principle is also presupposed, through which such a *systematic unity is* a priori *assumed to be necessarily attached to the objects themselves.* . . . The law of reason which requires us to seek this unity is a necessary law, since without it we would have no reason at all, and without this no coherent use of the understanding, and in the absence of this no *sufficient criterion of empirical truth. So in reference to this criterion we must necessarily presuppose the systematic unity of nature as objectively valid and necessary throughout.* (A 650/B 678–A 651/ B 679; emphasis added)

Kant's point is that we are required, by the fact that reason and understanding must unify all of our experience under increasingly inclusive concepts in order for us to have experience at all, to conceive of all the possible objects of experience thus unified—i.e., the empirical world of nature in toto—as an ontologically independent system that is necessarily unified as well. Kant is not claiming that we detect that objective system in our necessarily limited experience of the natural world as it appears to us. He is not even claiming that we can infer any veridical characteristics of it from the areas of systematic structure we do empirically detect. He is claiming only that we must rationally conceive the totality of the natural world as an ontologically independent, systematically unified whole in order to experience any empirical part of it coherently; and the passages cited earlier demonstrate his own thinking as an example of this requirement.

The sufficient condition for the veracity of empirical concepts then— that which prevents conclusive disconfirmation (or "contradiction") of our explanatory theories by the objects we experience—is the natural world conceived as an ontologically independent phenomenon, unified under a maximally inclusive explanatory theory that can account for them, which we must presuppose in order to experience any of its natural objects at all. This assumption explains why, although an explanatory theory of the natural world might undergo revision in light of new empirical data, it can never be conclusively disconfirmed or "contradicted" by that data all at once. The more inclusive and sophisticated the theory becomes, the more anomalous data offer the challenge of revising and extending that theory into an even more powerful one that can integrate them, and the less susceptible the theory becomes to conclusive disproof by piecemeal anomalous evidence.[18] Only relatively primitive or provincial explanatory theories are vulnerable to the kind of attack Kant describes. I consider some in greater detail in section 5 below, and argue elsewhere that the dogmatism with which such a theory is maintained is an index of its explanatory fragility.[19] The external natural world, then, conceived as an ontologically independent, systematically unified, and fully explicable whole, supplies the sufficient condition of empirical truth for Kant.

But now conjoin this suggestion to Kant's further claim that any conscious experience we have must conform to the transcendental concepts (B 162), and that empirical concepts are "special determinants" of transcendental ones (A 126, A 128). From this latter claim we can infer that an experience that conforms to empirical concepts thereby conforms in content to the transcendental ones that determine them. Now Kant does not say whether by the word "determine" he means "designate" or "ascertain" or "specify," nor does the German (*bestimmen*) enlighten us on this question.[20] I will assume that by "determine," when used in this context, Kant means "specify" since it is a broader term that can be used more or less synonymously with either "designate" or "ascertain" in most contexts. Kant is then saying, in the above-cited passages, that empirical concepts specify more precisely some of the same content that is structured by transcendental ones and initially generated by systematically related things in themselves.

Again this does not give us direct access to the nature of things in themselves, since the content of a more inclusive concept can be specified in a variety of nonequivalent ways by less inclusive ones. But the specification relation between transcendental and empirical concepts preserves relevant content from systematically interrelated things in themselves through transcendental and then empirical concepts that give it cognitive structure. And we can think of the specification relation as for present purposes equivalent to the instantiation relation described in section 1 such that

(A) c_i specifies c_j if and only if c_i instantiates c_j.

On this reading, empirical concepts instantiate transcendental ones, and the more inclusive properties corresponding to transcendental ones may be ascribed to the less inclusive properties corresponding to empirical ones—as, for example, the property of being a cause of change may be ascribed to a behavior, which in turn may be ascribed to an action. This reading accords with the KRT, according to which each (empirically contingent) concept within a subject's experience instantiates the (transcendentally necessary) subject-predicate relation or judgment-form relative to some others.

3. THE CONCEPT OF PERSONHOOD

The question of whether a Kantian conception of the self contains the resources for explaining and reforming xenophobia now can be reformulated more precisely as the question of whether an instantiation interpretation of the relation between concepts necessary for experience and those contingent to it can explain the phenomenon of xenophobia with respect to its degree of conceptual entrenchment and corresponding amenability to rational correction. Since xenophobia involves withholding recognition of personhood from those perceived as empirically different or anomalous, part of the answer to our question will turn on ascertaining the cognitive status of the concept of personhood in Kant's epistemology. To do this we first need to understand Kant's conception of the relation between transcendental and transcendent concepts.

Kant regards the "transcendental judgment-forms" as having two separate functions. The first, already discussed, is to structure cognitively the sensory data that unified experience presupposes. In that role Kant calls them "transcendental concepts" or "categories." But these logical forms—which under the KRT reduce to the subject-predicate relation— have a second function as well. This is to reason, construct syllogisms and hypotheses, formulate theories, and make deductive inferences at increasingly abstract and inclusive conceptual levels from the unified experience thus structured. In this way these judgment-forms not only unify experience according to certain innate cognitive patterns, but unify the resulting multiplicity of unified experiences themselves under more abstract concepts and theories according to the same basic cognitive patterns:

> Understanding may be considered a faculty of the unity of appearances by means of rules, and similarly reason is the faculty of the unity of the rules of understanding under principles. Accordingly, reason never applies directly to experience or to any object, but to understanding, in order to give its manifold cognitions a unity *a priori* through concepts, a unity which may be called the unity of reason, and which is of a very different kind from that which can be accomplished by the understanding (A 302/B 359). . . . In fact multiplicity of rules and unity of principles is a requirement of reason, in order to bring the understanding into thoroughgoing coherence with itself. . . . But such a principle . . . is merely a subjective law for the management of the resources of our understanding, in order to reduce their general use to the smallest possible number through comparison of its concepts. . . . (A 305/B 362–A 306/B 363)

In this second function, Kant refers to the transcendental judgment-forms as "*transcendent* concepts" or "ideas" of reason. Whereas the term "transcendental" refers to the necessary preconditions of experience, "transcendent" refers to that which exceeds or surpasses the limits of experience. Kant's notion is that abstract theories (whether moral, psychological, theological, or cosmological) that unify all the relevant data under a minimum of explanatory principles necessarily transcend in scope of application the contingent and piecemeal data that empirically confirm them. Thus the difference between transcendental concepts of the understanding and transcendent concepts or ideas of reason is ultimately a difference in degree of abstraction from experience rather than a difference in kind. (Compare Kant's account of judgment as knowledge by subsumption at A 68/B 93–A 70/B 95 with his account of knowledge from principles at A 300/B 357; also see A viii, A 302/B 359, A 311/B 368, A 329/B 386, A 409, A 643/B 671–A 644/B 672, A 651/B 679.)

As a transcendent concept (or idea), the concept of personhood gives coherence to our occasional, particular empirical experiences of these characteristics of human behavior by unifying them under this more abstract and inclusive notion that surpasses in scope of application under any particular instance of human behavior that conforms to it. It thereby contributes to a standing expectation that other human beings will regularly behave as persons no matter how frequently this expectation is violated in fact.[21] As a transcendental concept, by contrast, it is what makes our particular empirical experiences of these same characteristics of human behavior possible. It is what enables us to recognize particular occurrences of consciousness, thought, rationality, and action for what they are. Whereas the transcendent concept of personhood supplies us with a higher-level *conception* of what being a person involves—a standing conception to which particular individuals may or may not conform on any given occasion, the transcendental concept of personhood enables us to recognize those occasions on which they do.

Kant clearly regards transcendent ideas of reason, like the transcendental categories of the understanding, as innate in the sense that reasoning beings are inevitably led to them by virtue of the categories of reasoning they use. But according to the KRT, only the subject-predicate relation, and so the substance-property transcendental category that corresponds to it, is a necessary condition of experience. From this it follows that only that transcendent idea of reason which is generated by the subject-predicate relation is similarly rationally inevitable, if any of them are.

Kant thinks the subject-predicate relation engenders the transcendent idea of a rationally unified, temporally continuous self as the content of the concept of personhood. His explanation in the Paralogisms of why he thinks this is not the most convincing argument available. What he could have said is just that the "I think" accompanies all our other concepts and therefore is instantiated in them, whereas it itself instantiates only the yet more inclusive substance-property concept. Being rationally inevitable, it is either just as innate conceptually as is that relation for Kant, or else is at least very deeply entrenched. This would be to suggest something like a hard-wired disposition to recognize others of our own (human) kind.

Because unified consciousness and thought presuppose cognitive structuring by rational categories, and because Kant believes reason can be motivationally effective, the concept of *personhood* also may be supposed to include, in addition to rationally coherent and persisting consciousness, the capacity for action. This departs from Kant's usage in the first *Critique* somewhat, where he uses that term in discussing only the former properties. But in the *Groundwork* his characterization of a person as a rational being (Ac. 428) makes explicit the first *Critique*'s connection between consciousness, rationality, and agency. Now there is no obstacle to conceiving of a being who has these properties but does not know that she does; indeed, Kant claims that this is precisely the human predicament, since genuine experiential knowledge of this topic is foreclosed to us. In order to prove the inevitability and so the transcendental necessity of this concept for human experience, Kant must show that we are disposed to identify ourselves as persons on the basis of evidence from which we cannot but infer that we are.

Kant has plenty to say about each of the properties of personhood, and there is plenty of textual support for assigning the concept of personhood a transcendental as well as a transcendent status. For example, in the opening sections of the Transcendental Dialectic Kant treats the concept of virtue, which for him is part of the concept of a perfectly rational being (A 315/B 372, A 569/B 597) as a necessary practical idea of reason (A 317/B 374–A 319/B 376)—i.e., one that can motivate action. This implies a corresponding concept with transcendental status. This implication is strengthened by Kant's explicit assertion, in his discussion of the Platonic forms, that no human being coincides with the idea of what is most perfect in its kind, but neverthe-less carries it—i.e., the idea of humanity—"in his soul as the archetype of his actions" (A 318/B 375). In the Ideal of Pure Reason Kant explicitly describes an "idea of perfect humanity" at A 568/B 596.

Similarly, Kant's treatment of the unity of the thinking subject as a transcendental concept or idea of reason that engenders the Paralogisms of Pure Reason implies transcendental status for the corresponding concept of the understanding, for example, in the second paragraph at A 365. Indeed, he explicitly assigns that concept to the list of transcen-dental ones at A 341/B 399, and says of it,

> One quickly sees that this is the vehicle of absolutely all concepts, and therefore also of transcendental ones, and so is always conceived along with all of these, and therefore is itself equally transcendental.

A concept that is "always conceived along with" other concepts is instantiated by those other concepts. Therefore, empirical concepts instantiate more inclusive transcendent ones, and those, in turn, instan-tiate the most inclusive, highest-order transcendent concept of the thinking subject; and all of these instantiate the most inclusive transcen-dental concept of the substance-property or subject-predicate relation. This is just another way of suggesting—as Kant repeatedly does in the A and B Deductions—that the thinking self or "I" (as predicate) must be able to accompany (i.e., must be ascribable to) any experience (A 116–117a, A 123, B 131–36, B 140; note, however, that he never explicitly acknowledges that the "I" would have to denote a property, not a substance). All of these passages taken together provide especially compelling support for the KRT.

Moreover, in the A Paralogisms Kant denies that the concept of a unified thinking subject can come from any empirical source when he declares,

> Now I cannot have the slightest representation of a thinking being through any outer experience, but only through self-consciousness. So these sorts of objects are nothing more than the transference of this consciousness of mine to other things, which can be represented as thinking beings only in this way. (A 347/B 406)

He reiterates this at A 357, in the Second Paralogism. So he thinks that the concept of a unified thinking being is one I derive from the property of first-personal self-consciousness—a requisite, remember, for unified selfhood—and then ascribe to certain external empirical objects.

But which ones? How do I manage to ascertain which, among the array of available empirical objects, actually has that property, since I can find no empirical representation of it? Kant provides an answer to this question in the Solution to the Third Antinomy. There he first develops at length the thesis that the behavior of actual human beings is subject to empirical laws of causality in the natural world, such that our behavior from a third-personal, observational perspective is entirely predictable: "[I]f we could exhaustively investigate all the appearances of the human power of choice," he tells us, "there would not be found a single human action which we could not predict with certainty . . . if, that is to say, we are merely *observing*, and, as happens in anthropology, want to investigate physiologically the motive causes of someone's actions" (A 550/B 578).

But he also says that the situation is different from a first-personal perspective:

> Only a human being, who knows all of nature otherwise solely through the senses, also knows himself through pure appercep-tion, and, indeed, in acts and inner determinations which he cannot class with impressions of the senses. . . . [W]hen we consider the same actions in relation to reason . . . in so far as reason is the cause *producing* them . . . we find a rule and order altogether different from the order of nature. (A 546/B 574; A 550/B 578)

That is, it is different from the rule and order of rationality, of reasoning and deliberating about actions and goals, of forming generalizations and making inferences, and of reaching conclusions about what is the case and what to do that move us to act accordingly. From the first-personal perspective, then, we are not just objects of empirical investigation, determined by causal forces, but thinking and reasoning persons, deter-mining our own actions through rational intention and will.

Thus the rule and order of rationality "shows, in its effects in appearance, a rule in accordance with which we may surmise rational motives and the kind of degrees of actions themselves, and judge subjective principles of the power of choice" (A 549/B 578). So Kant's solution to the problem of other minds, that is, of how we can distinguish those third-personally observed objects who are similarly thinking subjects from those which are not, is to point out that although the behavior of all such objects satisfies the laws of causality, only that of some also may satisfy the laws of rationality. Only some external objects, that is, exhibit the capacity for rational *action*. The concept of a unified thinking being is, then, a transcendent and a transcendental concept we apply to those external empirical objects whose behavior gives evidence of being governed by the same laws of rationality we first-personally experience as governing our own.

4. SELF-KNOWLEDGE

Now Kant does not think such "acts" of first-personal introspection give us knowledge of ourselves as we are in ourselves (i.e., as noumena) but only as we appear to introspection. Moreover, Kant warns us about the dangers of transcendental illusion inherent in the use of reason when he says,

> in our reason (considered subjectively as a human faculty of knowledge) there are basic rules and maxims of its use, which have all the look of objective principles, and through which it happens that the subjective necessity of a particular connection of our concepts is, to the advantage of the understanding, taken for an objective necessity in the determination of things in themselves. (A 297/B 353)

Kant is cautioning us against trusting our own, inescapable inference to the objective validity of our rational principles from their seeming necessity and universality. Our innate susceptibility to both of these conceptual traps raises the questions of whether our ascription of personhood to ourselves and others on the basis of our first-personal experience of the rule and order of rationality can have anything more than a contingent empirical foundation; and whether the concept of personhood itself can therefore claim any more validity than that.

Moreover, even if this concept should turn out to be necessary, it does not follow that we are necessarily justified in applying it to ourselves: if all we can know of ourselves is the way we appear to ourselves rather than the noumenal selves we are in actual fact, then the first-personal appearance of personhood may, for all we know, lack any basis in actual fact. Kant's distinction in Paragraph 25 of the B Deduction between what we can know (namely that of which we have empirical experience) and what we can consciously think or conceive (namely that about which the categories of thought enable us to reason, regardless of the extent to which it can be confirmed by experience) provides an answer to these questions.

Kant argues that it is the act of introspection (or—Kant's term—self-intuition (B 68–69, 153–56, 157–58a)) that enables one's self to appear to one at all. In the Transcendental Aesthetic Kant describes time as "the way in which the mind is affected through its own activity, namely by this situating (Setzen) of its representation [in temporal relations], and so is affected by itself." This, he says, identifies time as an inner sense (B 68). Kant's idea here is that the mind's cognitive process of forming and organizing representations itself causes the mind to situate those representatives in temporal succession; he elaborates on this idea at greater length in the Transcendental Deduction. A temporal succession of mental representations, however, is a property of the subject's interior consciousness, not of the external world; this is why Kant calls time an inner rather than an outer sense.

In the same passage, Kant goes on to say that the subject is itself the object of inner sense. What he means is that the temporal succession of mental representations that is a property of the subject's interior consciousness is identified by the subject as the subject's self when the subject turns its attention to it (cf. also B 140). This succession of mental representations is the appearance of the self that Hume found when he looked within and searched in vain for the enduring soul or substance that had been supposed to unify these representations. Kant calls it the empirical self, in contradistinction to (A) the underlying noumenal self that does the appearing; and (B) the transcendental subject that both undergoes those cognitive processes and also has such properties (we will suppose (A) and (B) to be materially equivalent for purposes of this discussion). The empirical self is the self as it appears to one when one looks for it. It is therefore the product rather than the presupposition of these cognitive processes (cf. also B 152–53, 155–56, 407). We can think of Kant's empirical self as equivalent to what I have elsewhere called one's *self-conception*. [22] Kant describes this as an appearance of the self because, he claims, the very act of looking for it is what causes it to appear:

> If the faculty of becoming self-conscious is to seek out (apprehend) what lies in the mind, it must affect the mind, and only in this way can it engender an intuition of itself . . . it then intuits itself, not as it would immediately and self-actively represent itself, but rather in accordance with the way in which it is internally affected, and so as it appears to itself, not as it is. (B 69)

However, Kant later warns us at least twice about investing too much credence in our empirical selves, or self-conceptions, as a source of self-knowledge. The first time is in the Solution to the Third Antinomy. There he maintains that "[t]he real morality of actions (merit and guilt), even that of our own conduct . . . remains entirely hidden from us. Our imputations can be referred only to the empirical character" (A 551/B 579a). This warning is echoed in chapter 2 of the *Groundwork of the Metaphysic of Morals* in Kant's remarks on the perniciousness and ubiquity of the "dear self." There he cautions us that

> it often happens that in the keenest self-examination we find absolutely nothing except basic moral duty that could have been powerful enough to move us to this or that good action and so to greater sacrifice. But it cannot be ruled out with certainty that in fact some secret impulse of self-love, under the mere pretense of this idea, has been the actual, determining cause of the will. For this we gladly flatter ourselves, by falsely appropriating a nobler motivational basis. But in fact even the most strenuous probing of our hidden motives yields absolutely nothing, because when the issue is moral worth, it is not about the actions one sees, but rather about their internal principles one does not see. (Ac. 407; also see 419)

These caveats follow from Kant's previous remarks on the contingency and epistemic unreliability of the empirical self as a source of information about the transcendental subject to whom the empirical self appears. Here Kant is simply extending his remarks to cover the case of specifically moral self-knowledge as well. Thus the impossibility of knowing the noumenal self through acts of introspection would seem to foreclose reliance on first-personal consciousness, thought, rationality, and action as conclusive evidence of authentic personhood in both first- and third-personal cases.

Kant also distinguishes sharply between the active spontaneity of the act of introspection, and the empirical self that is caused by this act to appear. He thus rules out direct and unmediated knowledge of oneself as an active and spontaneous intellect. A *fortiori*, he rules out direct experience of oneself as initiating the processes of reasoning and cogitation that would conclusively identify one as a person (the terms "experience" and "knowledge" for Kant are usually synonymous). Indeed, Kant's description in the *Groundwork* of the imperfect human will as one which, on the one hand, "is determined by reason," but on the other, "is not necessarily obedient to it by nature" or "subjective condition" (Ac. 413), suggests that reasoning and intellection are processes we experience ourselves as passively and sometimes resistantly undergoing rather than as actively initiating.

But Kant does acknowledge the possibility that a subject may nevertheless *represent* or conceive herself as an active, spontaneously reasoning and thinking subject (recall that this was the alternative he discarded in his account of self-intuition at B 69). The basis for this self-conception would not be the direct experience of active and spontaneous intellection. Instead it would be the apparently spontaneous, uncompelled character of the content of those mental "acts and inner determinations" themselves. As Kant puts it,

> I cannot determine my existence as a self-active being, but rather I represent to myself only the spontaneity of my thought, that is, of the determining, and my existence always remains sensibly determinable, that is as the existence of an appearance. But this spontaneity is why I call myself an intelligence. (B 158a)

Kant is, on the one hand, denying that I can ascertain my self-activity as a fact; but acknowledging, on the other, that I can conceive my thought as spontaneous in virtue of the autonomous character of my attempts cognitively to ascertain or specify things: it seems to me, that is, that my disposition to conceive and analyze are themselves self-initiated rather than externally caused or compelled (also cf. *Ground-*

work, Ac. 448). Although I can ascertain my existence only through empirical means, and therefore as an appearance, it is because I try to ascertain or determine things cognitively at all that I identify myself as an intelligent being.

So although the subject cannot know herself as an active intelligence, she can still represent herself as one, on the evidence of the autonomous quality of her thought. And she can include this representation among those constitutive of her empirical self-conception. Thus a subject may at least reliably conceive herself as having the properties that identify her as a person, even if she cannot experience herself as having them.

But Kant's distinction between what can be known and what can be thought or conceived is not only useful in formulating our self-conception as persons. It is also useful in formulating the evidence on which that self-conception depends. "The use of reason," he tells us, "is not always directed to the determination of the object, therefore to knowledge, but also to the determination of the subject and of its volition" (B 166a). Following the suggestion in section 2 that we translate *bestimmen* by the broad term "specify," Kant would then be saying that, in addition to ascertaining the nature of objects of knowledge, reason also can be used to shape the subject and its volition in certain specific ways. That is, reason can fix the form and specific content of the intentional object of the subject's will. It can fix the form of that intentional object in that it conceives the action that is its content as a valid conclusion of deductive and inductive reasoning. And reason can fix the content of that intentional object in that this reasoning process identifies a particular course of action as the rational one to pursue. This interpretation conforms to the instantiation interpretation of the relation between transcendental and empirical concepts offered in section 2. So although reason alone may not yield knowledge of the true nature of the self, it may yield a precise and recognizably rational formulation of the subject's particular deliberations, resolutions, and intentions. Although this would not count as self-knowledge in Kant's technical sense, it certainly would constitute evidence for one's self-conception as a reasoning subject.

Further support for this reading can be gleaned from Kant's characterization of reason in the Solution to the Third Antinomy as atemporal and unaffected by empirical states, but as itself nevertheless a determining influence on them (A 556/B 584). First, he describes the "appearances" of reason as "the ways in which it manifests itself in its effects."

Presumably these effects are the particular, spatiotemporally specific instances of reasoning in accordance with the nonempirical canons of rationality. That Kant does not mean to identify the "effects" of pure reason with empirical action itself is clear from his assertion earlier in the same section that "the action, so far as it is to be ascribed to a way of thinking as its cause, does not thereby follow from it in accordance with empirical laws, that is, so that the conditions of pure reason precede it, but rather only so that their effects in the appearance of inner sense do" (A 551/B 579). If action is preceded by the effects of the conditions of pure reason in inner sense, it obviously cannot be identical with those effects. The only effects of pure reason in inner sense that can plausibly precede action are particular processes or occurrences of reasoning about what action to take. These empirical instances of valid reasoning specify the form and content of the intentional object of the will, as well as contribute to the motivational force of that will itself.

Second, at A 556/B 584 Kant also says of reason that it "is present in all human actions in all temporal circumstances and is always one and the same, but is not itself in time, nor falls somehow into a new state in which it was not before; it is determining, but not determinable in regard to this."[23] Here the idea is that the abstract canons of theoretical rationality themselves are not spatiotemporally local to any particular empirical action or situation, but are nevertheless locally instantiated by reasoning subjects who apply them to each such situation in such a way as to affect the action taken. The effect of reason on action cannot be merely to nudge it into existence causally as an occurrence. Instead it must affect action by specifying or fixing the form and intentional content of the action relative to universal and necessary rationality requirements that the subject applies to all actions.

Third, Kant maintains that "when we say that in spite of his whole previous course of life the liar could have refrained, this means only that the lie is directly under the power of reason, and reason in its causality is not subordinated to any conditions of appearance or the passage of time." This means that an agent who is assumed to have been capable of doing otherwise is supposed not to have been handicapped in doing otherwise by intervening causal variables that might have obstructed the effect of reason on her action. This does not conflict with Kant's earlier claim that reason manifests itself in empirical appearances, if we understand by this that the abstract canons of reason are instantiated in particular, empirical occurrences of reasoning. Rather, it merely denies that there are any other internal empirical processes—such as inclinations or emotions—that might interfere with the subject's ability to recognize what reason abstractly requires of a specific instance of reasoning, or obstruct the effect of that specific reasoning process on action.

Finally, Kant concludes this paragraph by asserting that "although difference of time can indeed make a big difference in the relations among appearances . . . it can make no difference to the action in relation to reason." By this Kant means that irrespective of when the action occurs, and when the particular reasoning process that ought to precede it occurs, the action itself is nevertheless subject to evaluation in terms of rational criteria. This is something that the agent can recognize in so far as there are no cognitive obstructions to the "direct power of reason" to fix the form and content of her particular reasoning process.

Taken together, these passages contribute to an explanation of why conscious subjects who think, reason, and act are inevitably led to identify themselves as bona fide reasoning and acting persons, even though they can have no knowledge of themselves as such. Centrally required for such identification is the subject's conception of reason as independent of and instantiated by particular empirical occurrences of reasoning that aspire to conform to it. This requirement is satisfied by the passages just considered. These provide evidence for adding the following to the conjunction of mental representations that constitute the empirical self:

1. the representation of the form and intentional content of one's deliberations and intentions as fully specified by abstract canons of theoretical reason (from B 166a);
2. the representations of particular empirical occurrences of reasoning as instantiations of these abstract canons of reason (from A 556/B 584);
3. the representation of these abstract canons of rationality as thereby causally affecting subsequent action (from A 546/B 574, A 550/B 578, A 556/B 584); and
4. the representations of (1)–(3) as evidence for one's self-conception as an active and spontaneous intellect (from B 158a).

Conjointly these identify any subject who finds them in introspection as a conscious subject, thinking, reasoning, and acting in accordance with the same rationality requirements that unify the self. Since those rationality requirements are innate, our capacity to identify these properties of personhood would be similarly innate, or at least very deeply entrenched. Under these circumstances, it would, indeed, be difficult to avoid including these properties in one's self-conception.

Notice the explanatory elegance and simplicity of Kant's account of personhood, under the assumption of the KRT: structuring our experience according to the subject-predicate relation gives it a basic consistency and coherence that extends to the particular set of contingent empirical concepts thus structured. Satisfying this structural requirement, in turn, is a necessary condition of a rationally unified self. A self that satisfies this rationality requirement thereby generates the cognitively inevitable concept of a reasoning and acting person, which it then applies, first to its own first-personal representations of unified rational agency; and second to those external empirical objects whose behavior exhibit similar adherence to rationality requirements. The concept of rational personhood thereby supplies simultaneously the principles of cognitive organization, self-identification, and recognition of other rational persons in Kant's system. To be a person is to be a self-consciously rational and unified self that manifests its rationality in action.[24]

Recalling the interpretation of the relation between transcendental and empirical concepts as one of instantiation, the proposal would then be that the transcendental concept of a unified rational person is instantiated by particular empirical exemplars of personhood, among whom each of us necessarily and first-personally counts herself, and inferentially and third-personally counts others. We each necessarily conceive of ourselves as persons, and then use this concept as a criterion for identifying others similarly.

5. XENOPHOBIA

In what follows I will use the terms *person* and *personality* to denote particular, empirical instantiations of personhood as analyzed above. These terms correspond closely to the nontechnical use of the terms. Thus when we refer to someone as a person, we ordinarily mean to denote at the very least a social being whom we presume—as Kant did—to have consciousness, thought, rationality, and agency. The term "person" used in this way also finds its way into jurisprudence, where we conceive of a person as a rational individual who can be held legally and morally accountable for her actions. Relative to these related usages, an individual who lacks to a significant degree the capacities to reason, plan for the future, detect causal and logical relations among events, or control action according to principles applied more or less consistently from one occasion to the next is ascribed diminished responsibility for her actions, and her social and legal status as a person is diminished accordingly.

Similarly, when we call someone a "bad person," we communicate a cluster of evaluations that include, for example, assessing her conscious motives as corrupt or untrustworthy, her rationality as deployed for maleficent ends, and her actions as harmful. And when we say that someone has a "good personality" or a "difficult personality," we mean that the person's consciousness, thought, rationality, and agency are manifested in pleasing or displeasing or bewildering ways that are particular to that individual. We do not ordinarily assess a being who lacks any of these components of personhood in terms of their personality at all. Persons, then, express their transcendent personhood in their empirical personalities.

With these stipulations in place, I now turn to an analysis of the concept of xenophobia based on the foregoing interpretation of Kant. Xenophobia is not simply an indiscriminate fear of strangers in general: it does not include, for example, fear of relatives or neighbors whom one happens not to have met. It is more specific than that. Xenophobia is a fear of individuals who look or behave differently than those one is accustomed to. It is a fear of what is experientially unfamiliar, of individuals who do not conform to one's empirical assumptions about what other people are like, how they behave, or how they look. Ultimately it is a fear of individuals who violate one's empirical conception of persons and so one's self-conception. So xenophobia is an alarm reaction to a threat to the rational coherence of the self, a threat in the form of an anomalous other who transgresses one's preconceptions about people. It is a paradigm example of reacting self-protectively to anomalous data that violates one's internally consistent conceptual scheme.

Recall that on the KRT, if we cannot make sense of such data in terms of those familiar concepts, we cannot register it as an experience at all. I have argued elsewhere[25] that *pseudorationality* is an attempt to make sense of such data under duress, i.e., to preserve the internal rational coherence of the self, when we are baldly confronted by anomaly but are not yet prepared to revise or jettison our conceptual scheme accordingly. It is in the attempt to make sense of anomalous data in terms of empirically inadequate concepts that the mechanisms of pseudorationality—rationalization, dissociation, and denial—kick in to secure self-preservation. But they succeed in preserving only the appearance of rational coherence. In *rationalization*, we misapply a concept to a particular by distorting its scope, magnifying the properties of the thing that instantiates the concept, and minimizing those that fail to do so. So, for example, conceiving of a slave imported from Africa as three-fifths of a person results from magnifying the properties that appear to support this diminished concept of personhood—the slave's environmental and psychological disorientation, lack of mastery of a foreign language, lack of familiarity with local social customs, incompetence at unfamiliar tasks, etc.; and minimizing the properties that disconfirm it—her capacity to learn, to forge innovative modes of communication and expression, to adapt and flourish in an alien social environment, to survive enslavement and transcend violations of her person, etc. In *dissociation*, we identify something in terms of the negation of the concepts that articulate our theory: identifying Jews as subhuman, blacks as childlike, women as irrational, gays as perverts, or working-class people as animals, for example, conceives of them as lacking essential properties of personhood, and so are ways of defining these groups of individuals out of our empirical conceptions of people. In *denial*, we suppress recognition of the anomalous particular or property altogether, by ignoring it or suppressing it from awareness. For example, ignoring a woman's verbal contributions, or passing over a black person's intellectual achievements, or forgetting to make provisions at a Christmas celebration for someone who is a practicing Jew are all ways of eradicating the anomalous other from one's domain of awareness.

Thus xenophobia engenders various forms of discriminatory stereotyping—racism, sexism, anti-Semitism, homophobia, class elitism—through the pseudorational mechanisms of rationalization and dissociation, by reducing the complex singularity of the other to a set of oversimplified but manageable properties that invariably diminish our full conception of personhood. For the xenophobe, this results in a provincial self-conception and conception of the world, from which significant available data is excluded—data the inclusion of which would significantly alter the scope and content of the theory. And this provincial theory is sustained with the aid of denial, by enforcing those stereotypes through such tactics as exclusion, ostracism, scapegoating, tribalism, and segregation in housing, education, or employment.[26] My thesis is that xenophobia is the originating phenomenon to which each of these forms of discriminatory stereotyping is a response. The phenomenon of xenophobia is a special case of a perfectly general human intellective disposition to literal self-preservation; i.e., preservation of the internal rational coherence and integrity of the self against anomalous data that threaten it.

Nevertheless, to say this much is not to answer the question of how deeply entrenched xenophobia is in our cognitive scheme. Even if it is true that we are innately cognitively disposed to respond to any conceptual and experiential anomaly in this way, it does not follow that our necessarily limited empirical conception of people must be so limited and provincial as to invite it. A person could be so cosmopolitan and intimately familiar with the full range of human variety that only an "alien" would rattle her. On the other hand, her empirical conception of people might be so limited that any variation in race, nationality, gender, sexual preference, or class would be cause for panic. How easily one's empirical conception of people is violated is one index of the scope of one's xenophobia; how central and pervasive it is in one's personality is another. In what follows I will focus primarily on cases midway between such extremes: for example, of a white person who is thoughtful, well-rounded, and well-read about the problems of racism in the United States, but who nevertheless feels fearful at being alone in the house with a black television repairman. In all such cases, the range of individuals in fact identifiable as persons is larger than the range of individuals to whom one's empirical conception of people apply. In all such cases, I will argue, xenophobia can be understood in terms of certain corrigible cognitive errors, only the last of which constitutes full-blown xenophobia.

A. The Error of Confusing People With Personhood

Xenophobia is fueled by a perfectly general condition of subjective consciousness, namely the same first-/third-person asymmetry that, as we saw in section 3, led Kant to propose rational action as a basis for inferring another's personhood. Although I must identify myself as a person because of my necessary, enduring first-personal experience of rationally unified selfhood, my experience of you as a person, necessarily lacking that first-personal experience, can have no such necessity about it:

> Identity of person is . . . in my own consciousness unfailingly to be found. But when I view myself from the standpoint of another (as object of his outer intuition), this external observer considers me first and foremost in time. . . . So from the I, which accompanies all representations at all times in my consciousness, and indeed with full identity, whether he immediately concedes it, he will not yet conclude the objective continuity of my self. For because the time in which the observer situates me is not the same as that time to be found in my own, but rather in his sensibility, similarly the identity that is necessarily bound up with my consciousness, is not therefore bound up with his, i.e., with the outer intuition of my subject. (A 362–63)

Kant is saying that the temporal continuity I invariably find in my own consciousness is not matched by any corresponding temporal continuity I might be supposed to have as the object of someone else's consciousness. Since I am not always present to another as I am to myself, I may appear discontinuously to her consciousness in a way I cannot to my own. And similarly, another may appear discontinuously to my consciousness in a way I cannot to my own.

This is one example of how it can happen, on a Kantian conception of the self, that a necessary concept is instantiated by contingent ones: although personhood is a necessary concept of mine, whether or not any other empirical individual instantiates it is itself, from my point of view, a contingent matter of fact—as is the concept of that particular individual herself. Though you may exhibit rationality in your behavior, I may not know that, or fail to notice it, or fail to understand it. Nor can you be a necessary feature of my experience, since I might ignore or overlook you, or simply fail to have any contact with you. In any of these cases, you will fail to instantiate my concept of personhood in a way I never can. Because the pattern of your behavior is not a necessary and permanent, familiar concomitant of my subjectivity in the way my own unified consciousness and ratiocinative processes are, I may escape your personhood in a way that I cannot escape my own. For me the transcendent idea of personhood is also a transcendental concept that applies necessarily to me, but, from my perspective, only contingently and empirically to you.

Hence just as our empirical experience of the natural world is limited relative to the all-inclusive, transcendent idea of its independent unity, similarly our empirical experience of other persons is limited relative to our all-inclusive, transcendent idea of personhood. But there is an important disanalogy between them that turns on the problem of other minds and the first-/third-person asymmetry earlier described. For any empirical experience of the natural world we have, we must, according to Kant, be able to subsume it under the transcendent concept of a unified system of nature of which it is a part, even if we do not know what that system might be. By contrast, it is not necessarily the case that for any empirical experience of other people we have, we must be able to subsume them under the transcendent idea of personhood. This is because although they may, in fact, manifest their personhood in their personality, we may not be able fully to discern their personhood through its empirical manifestations, if those manifestations fall outside our empirical conception of what people are like.

Suppose, for example, that within my subculture, speech is used to seek confirmation and promote bonding, whereas in yours it is used to protect independence and win status;[27] and that our only interpersonal contact occurs when you come to fix my TV. I attempt to engage you in conversation about what is wrong with my TV, to which you react with a lengthy lecture. To you I appear dependent and mechanically incompetent, while to me you appear logorrheic and socially inappropriate. Each of us perceives the other as deficient in some characteristic of rationality: you perceive me as lacking in autonomy and basic mechanical skills, whereas I perceive you as lacking in verbal control and basic social skills. To the extent that this perceived deficit is not corrected by further contact and fuller information, each of us will perceive the other as less of a full-fledged person because of it. This is the kind of perception that contributes to one-dimensional stereotypes, for example, of women as flighty and incompetent or of men as aggressive and barbaric, which poison the expectations and behavior of each toward the other accordingly.

Or take another example, in which the verbal convention in my subculture is to disclose pain and offer solace, whereas in yours it is to suppress pain and advert to impersonal topics; and that our only interpersonal contact occurs when I come to work as your housemaid. Again each of us perceives the other as deficient in some characteristic of rationality: you perceive me as dull and phlegmatic in my lack of responsiveness to the impersonal topics you raise for discussion, whereas I perceive you as almost schizophrenically dissociated from the painful realities that confront us. Again, unless this perceived deficit is corrected by further contact and fuller information, each of us will perceive the other as less of a person because of it, thereby contributing to one-dimensional stereotypes of, for example, blacks as stupid, or of whites as ignorant and out of touch with reality, that similarly poison both the expectations and the behavior of each toward the other.

In such cases there are multiple sources of empirical error. The first one is our respective failures to distinguish between the possession of rationality as an active capacity in general, and particular empirical uses or instantiations of it under a given set of circumstances and for a given set of ends. Because your particular behavior and ends strike me as irrational, I surmise that you must be irrational. Here the error consists in equating the particular set of empirical behaviors and ends with which I am familiar from my own and similar cases with unified rational agency in general. It is as though I assume that the only rational agents there are are the particular people I identify as such. Kant might put the point by saying that each of us has conflated her empirically limited conception of people with the transcendent concept of personhood.

B. The Error of Assuming Privileged Access to the Noumenal Self

But now suppose we each recognize at least the intentionality of the other's behavior, if not its rationality. Since each of us equates rational agency in general exclusively with the motives and actions of her own subculture in particular, each also believes that the motives and ends that guide the other's actions—and therefore the evidence of conformity to the rule and order of rationality—nevertheless remain inaccessible in a way we each believe our own motives and ends not to be inaccessible to ourselves. This third-personal opacity yields the distinction between the appearance and the reality of the self: you, it seems, are an appearance to me behind which is hidden the reality of your motives and intentions, whereas I am not similarly an appearance that hides my own from myself. The less familiar you are to me, the more hidden your motives and intentions will seem, and the less benevolent I will assume them to be.

Of course whom we happen to recognize as familiar determines whose motives are cause for suspicion and whose are not. There is no necessary connection between actual differences in physical or psychological properties between oneself and another, and the epistemic inscrutability we ascribe to someone we regard as anomalous. It is required only that the other seem anomalous relative to our familiar subculture, however cosmopolitan that may be, in order to generate doubts and questions about what it is that makes her tick. Stereotypes of women as enigmatic or of Asians as inscrutable or of blacks as evasive all express the underlying fear of the impenetrability of the other's motives. And someone who conceives of Jews as crafty, blacks as shiftless, or women as devious expresses particularly clearly the suspicion and fear of various third-personal others as mendacious manipulators that is consequent on falsely regarding them as more epistemically inaccessible to one than one is to oneself.[28]

Thus our mutual failure to identify the other as a person with the same status as oneself is compounded by skepticism based on the belief that each of us has the privileged access to her own personhood that demonstrates directly and first-personally what personhood really is. The inaccessibility and unfamiliarity of the other's conception of her own motives to our consciousness of her may seem conclusive justification for our reflexive fear and suspicion as to whether her motives can be trusted at all.

Now we have already seen in section 14 that Kant thinks the belief in privileged access is erroneous. From the first-personal relation I bear to my empirical self-conception which I lack to yours, it does not follow that my actual, noumenal motives are any more accessible to me than yours are. Therefore, regardless of how comfortable and familiar my own motives may seem to me, it does not follow that I can know that my own motives are innocuous whereas yours are not. In fact it is difficult to imagine how I might gain any understanding of the malevolent motives I reflexively ascribe to you at all, without having first experienced them in myself. Of course this is not to say that I cannot understand what it means to be the victim of maleficent *events* without having caused them myself. But it is to say that I must derive my understanding of the malevolent *intentionality* I ascribe to you from my own firsthand experience of it. Therefore your epistemic opacity to me furnishes no evidence for my reflexive ascription to you of malevolent or untrustworthy motives, although that ascription itself does furnish evidence for a similar ascription of them to myself. Thus Kant might put this second error by saying that we have been fooled by the first-/third-person asymmetry into treating the ever-present "dear self" as a source of genuine self-knowledge on the basis of which we make even faultier and more damaging assumptions about the other.

C. The Error of Failing Rationally to Conceive Other Minds

These two errors are interconnected with a third one, namely our respective failures to imagine each other's behavior as animated by the same elements of personhood that animate our own (i.e., consciousness, thought, and rationality). Our prior failure to recognize the other's behavior as manifesting evidence of these properties—a failure compounded by conceptual confusion and misascription of motives—then further undermines our ability to bridge the first-/third-person asymmetry by imagining the other to have them. Since, from each of our first-personal perspectives, familiar empirical evidence for the presence of these properties is lacking in the other, we have no basis on which to make the ascription, and so no basis for imagining what it must be like from the other's perspective. Our respective, limited empirical conceptions of people, which are the consequence of ignorance of others who are thereby viewed as different, delimit our capacity for empathy. This is part of what is involved in the phenomenon feminists refer to as objectification, and what sometimes leads men to describe some women as self-absorbed. Kant might put this point by saying that by failing to detect in the other's behavior the rule and order of rationality that guides it, we fail to surmise or imagine the other's motives and intentions.

This error, of failing to conceive the other as similarly animated by the psychological dispositions of personhood, is not without deleterious consequences for the xenophobe herself. Elsewhere I have described the self-centered and narrowly concrete view of the world that results from the failure to imagine empathically another's inner states, and its interpersonal consequences.[29] From the first-personal perspective, this error compounds the seeming depopulation of the social environment of persons and its repopulation by impenetrable and irrational aliens. This is to conceive one's social world as inhabited by enigmatic and unpredictable disruptions to its stability, to conjure chimeras of perpetual unease and anxiety into social existence. Relative to such a conception, segregation (assuming no relations of interdependence preclude it) is no more effective in banishing the threat than is leaving on the nightlight to banish ghosts, since both threats arise from the same source. Vigilance and a readiness to defend oneself against the hostile unknown may become such intimately familiar and constitutive habits of personality that even they may come to seem requisites of personhood.

D. The Error of Equating Personality With Personhood

The three foregoing errors involve cognitive failures for which a well-intentioned individual could correct. For example, someone who regularly confuses people with personhood might simply take a moment to formulate a general principle of rational behavior that both applies to all the instances with which she is familiar from her particular community and has broader application as well; and remind herself, when confronted by anomalous behavior, to at least try to detect the operation of that principle within it. Similarly, it does not require excessive humility on the part of a person who falsely assumes privileged access to the noumenal self to remind herself that our beliefs about our own motives, feelings, and actions are exceedingly fallible and regularly disconfirmed; and that it is therefore even more presumptuous to suppose any authority about someone else's. Nor is it psychologically impossible to gather information about others' inner states—through research, appreciation of the arts, or direct questioning and careful listening, so as to cultivate one's imaginative and empathic capacities to envision other minds.

Thus it is possible for someone to exhibit these failures without being a xenophobe, just in case she has no personal investment in the defective empirical conception of people that results. A person has a *personal investment* in a conception or theory if (1) that theory is a source of personal satisfaction or security to her; (2) to revise or reject it would elicit in her feelings of dejection, deprivation, or anxiety; and (3) these feelings are to be explained by her identification with this theory. She *identifies with* this theory to the extent that she is disposed to identify it as personally meaningful or valuable to her.[30] A person could make the first three cognitive errors without taking any satisfaction in her provincial conception of people ("Is this really all there is?" she might think to herself about the inhabitants of her small town), without identifying with it (she might find them boring and feel ashamed to have to count herself among them), and without feeling the slightest reluctance to enlarge and revise it through travel or exploration or research.

What distinguishes a xenophobe is her personal investment in her provincial conception of people. Her sense of self-preservation requires her conception to be veridical, and is threatened when it is disconfirmed. She exults in the thought that only the people she knows and is familiar with (whites, blacks, WASPs, Jews, residents of Waco, Texas, members of the club, etc.) are persons in the full, honorific sense. This is the thought that motivates the imposition of pseudorational stereotypes, both on those who confirm them and those who do not.

To impose a *stereotype* on someone is to view her as embodying a limited set of properties falsely taken to be exclusive, definitive, and paradigmatic of a certain kind of individual. I will say that a stereotype

(a) equates one contingent and limited set of valued properties that may characterize persons under certain circumstances with the universal concept of personhood;

(b) restricts that set to exclude divergent properties of personhood from it;

(c) withholds from those who violate its restrictions the essential properties of personhood; and

(d) ascribes to them the essential, disvalued properties of deviance from it.

Thus a stereotype identifies as persons those and only those who manifest the valued properties in the set ((a) and (b))—call this set the *honorific stereotype*—and subsidiary ones consistent with it (such as minor personality quirks or mildly idiosyncratic personal tastes). And reciprocally, the honorific stereotype by implication identifies as deviant all those who manifest any properties regarded as inconsistent with it ((c) and (d))—call this second set of disvalued properties the *derogatory stereotype*. So, for example, an individual who bears all the valued properties of the honorific stereotype as required by (a) may be nevertheless disqualified for membership according to (b), by bearing additional disvalued ones as well—being related by blood or marriage to a Jew, for example; or having bisexual inclinations; or, in the case of a black person, an enthusiasm for classical scholarship. In virtue of violating (b), one may then fail to qualify as a full-fledged person at all (c), and therefore may be designated as deviant by the derogatory stereotype according to (d). The derogatory stereotype most broadly includes all the disvalued properties that fall outside the set defining the honorific stereotype (i.e., "us versus them"), or may sort those properties into more specific subsets according to the range of individuals available for sorting.

A stereotype generally is therefore distinguishable from an inductive generalization by its provincialism, its oversimplification, and its rigid imperviousness to the complicating details of singularity. Perhaps most important, a stereotype is distinguishable from an inductive generalization by its function. The function of an inductive generalization is to guide further research, and this requires epistemic alertness and sensitivity to the possibility of confirming or disconfirming evidence in order to make use of it. An inductive generalization is no less a generalization for that: it would not, for example, require working-class blacks living in the Deep South during the 1960s to dismantle the functionally accurate and protective generalization that white people are dangerous. What would make this an inductive generalization rather than a stereotype is that it would not preclude recognition of a white person who is safe if one should appear. By contrast, the function of a stereotype is to render further research unnecessary. If the generalization that white people are dangerous were a stereotype, adopting it would make it cognitively impossible to detect any white people who were not.

Thus Kant might describe the reciprocal imposition of stereotypes as the fallacy of equating a partial and conditional series of empirical appearances of persons with the absolute and unconditioned idea of personhood that conceptually unifies them. Whereas the first error—of confusing one's empirical conception of people with the transcendent concept of personhood—involves thinking that the only persons there are the people one knows, this fourth error—of equating personality with personhood—involves thinking that the kind of persons one knows are all there can ever be. So unlike inductive generalizations, the taxonomic categories of a stereotype are closed sets that fundamentally require the binary operation of sorting individuals into those who fall within them and those who do not.[31]

As a consequence of her personal investment in an honorific stereotypical conception of persons, a xenophobe has a personal investment in an honorific stereotypical self-conception. This means that that self-conception is a source of personal satisfaction or security to her; that to revise or disconfirm it would elicit in her feelings of dejection, depriva-tion, or anxiety; and that these feelings are to be explained by her identification with this self-conception. In order to maintain her honor-ific self-conception, a xenophobe must perform the taxonomic binary sorting operation not only on particular groups of ethnic or gendered others, but on everyone, including herself. Since her self-conception as a person requires her and other bona fide persons to dress, talk, look, act, and think in certain highly specific and regimented ways in order to qualify for the honorific stereotype, everyone is subject to scrutiny in terms of it.

This is not only prejudicial to someone who violates these require-ments and thereby earns the label of the derogatory stereotype. It is also prejudicial to someone who satisfies them, just in case there is more to her personality than the honorific stereotype encompasses and more than it permits. Avoidance of the negative social consequences of violating the honorific stereotype—ostracism, condemnation, punish-ment, or obliteration—necessitates stunting or flattening one's personal-ity in order to conform to it (for example, by eschewing football or nightclubs and learning instead to enjoy scholarly lectures as a form of entertainment because one is given to understand that that is the sort of thing real academics typically do for fun); or bifurcating one's personality into that part which can survive social scrutiny and that "deviant" part which cannot (as, for example, certain government officials have done who deplore and condemn homosexuality publicly on the one hand while engaging in it privately on the other). One reason it is important not to equate personality with personhood is so that the former properties can flourish without fear that the latter title will be revoked.

Truncating one's personality in order to conform to an honorific stereotype in turn damages the xenophobe's self-esteem and also her capacity for self-knowledge. Someone who is deeply personally invested in the honorific stereotype but fails fully to conform to it (as everyone must, of course) views herself as inherently defective. She is naturally beset by feelings of failure, inferiority, shame, and worthlessness which poison her relations with others in familiar ways: competitiveness, dishonesty, defensiveness, envy, furtiveness, insecurity, hostility, and self-aggrandizement are just a few of the vices that figure prominently in her interpersonal interactions. But if these feelings and traits are equally antithetical to her honorific stereotype, then they, too, threaten her honorific stereotypical self-conception and so are susceptible to pseudorational denial, dissociation, or rationalization. For example, a xenophobe might be blindly unaware of how blatantly she advertises these feelings and traits in her behavior; or she might dissociate them as mere peccadilloes, unimportant eccentricities that detract nothing from the top-drawer person she essentially is. Or she might acknowledge them but rationalize them as natural expressions of a Nietzschean, übermenschliche ethic justified by her superior place in life. Such pseudorational habits of thought reinforce even more strongly her personal investment in the honorific stereotype that necessitated them, and in the xenophobic conception of others that complements it. This fuels a vicious downward spiral of self-hatred and hatred of anomalous others from which it is difficult for the xenophobe to escape. Thus the personal disadvantage of xenophobia is not just that the xenophobe devolves into an uninteresting and malevolent person. She damages herself for the sake of her honorific stereotype, and stunts her capacity for insight and personal growth as well.

A sign that a person's self-conception is formed by an honorific stereotype is that revelation of the deviant, disvalued properties provokes shame and denial, rather than a reformulation of that self-conception in such a way as to accommodate them. For example, a family that honorifically conceives itself as white Anglo-Saxon Protestant may deny that its most recent offspring in fact has woolly hair or a broad nose. Similarly, a sign that a person's conception of another is formed by a derogatory stereotype is that revelation of the other's nondeviant, valued properties provokes hostility and denial, rather than the corresponding revision of that conception of the other in such a way as to accommodate them. For example, a community of men that honorifically conceives itself in terms of its intellectual ability may dismiss each manifestation of a woman's comparable intellectual ability as a fluke.[32]

These two reactions are reciprocal expressions of the same dispositions in the first- and third-personal cases respectively. Shame involves the pain of feeling publicly exposed as defective, and denial is the psychological antidote to such exposure: for example, if the purportedly WASP offspring does not have negroid features, there is nothing for the family to feel ashamed of. So a person whose self-conception is defined by an honorific stereotype will feel shame at having disvalued properties that deviate from it, and will attempt to deny their existence to herself and to others. By contrast, hostility toward another's excellence is caused by shame at one's own defectiveness, and denial of the excellence is the social antidote to such shame: for example, if the woman is not as intelligent as the men are purported to be, then there is no cause for feeling shamed by her, and so none for hostility toward her. So a person whose self-conception is formed by an honorific stereotype will feel hostility toward a derogatorily stereotyped other who manifests valued properties that violate that derogatory stereotype, and will attempt to deny the existence of those valued properties in the other to herself and to others.

In the first-personal case, the objects of shame are disvalued properties that deviate from one's honorific stereotypical self-conception. In the third-personal case, the objects of hostility are valued properties that deviate from one's derogatory stereotypical conception of the other. But in both cases the point of the reactions is the same: to defend one's stereotypical self-conception against attack, both by first-personal deviations from it and by third-personal deviations from the reciprocal stereotypes this requires imposing on others. And in both cases, the reactions are motivated in the same way: the properties regarded as anomalous relative to the stereotype in question are experienced by the xenophobe as an assault on the rational coherence of her theory of the world—and so, according to Kant, on the rational coherence of her self.

Indeed, left untreated, all four of these cognitive errors—the conflation of the transcendent concept of personhood with one's provincial conception of people that another happens to violate; the ascription to the other of malevolent motives on the basis of an epistemically unreliable self-conception; the inability to imagine the other as animated by familiar or recognizably rational motives; and the equation of personality with personhood inherent in the imposition of reciprocal stereotypes—combine to form a conception of the other as an inscrutable and malevolent anomaly that threatens that theory of the world which unifies one's experience and structures one's expectations about oneself and other people. If this were an accurate representation of others who are different, it would be no wonder that xenophobes feared them.

6. XENOPHILIA

Now recall once more Kant's original claim about the structure of the self (the KRT). He said that if a perception failed to conform to the categories of thought that unified and structured the self, it could not be experienced by that self at all. Also recall that we detected an ambiguity in Kant's claim: it was unclear whether a perception would have to conform to (A) both the transcendental and the empirical concepts that unified the self, or (B) only the transcendental ones, in order to be minimally an object of experience. Suppose (A) is correct, and perceptions must conform both to the transcendental and to the empirical concepts that structure the self and its experience. Then these sets of concepts are materially equivalent: something is a person if and only if it falls under one's empirical conception of people. Then someone must conform not only to my transcendental concept of personhood, but also to my empirically contingent and limited concept of what persons are like (i.e., of people) in order for me to recognize her as a person. Therefore, (A) implies that an anomalous other who violates my limited conception of people thereby violates my transcendental conception of personhood as well.

We have already seen in section 3 that even if the concept of personhood is transcendental as well as transcendent according to Kant, this concept is at best an instantiation of the transcendental substance-property relational category. Since my transcendental concept of personhood is not equivalent to the transcendental concept of a thing or substance in general, my failure to recognize the other's personhood does not imply a failure to recognize her as an object with properties altogether. I may recognize another who is anomalous with respect to my concept of personhood as consistent with my concept of objects in general. However, if the other must conform to my limited conception of people in order to conform to my concept of personhood but does not, then from my perspective, an object is all that she can ever be. In this case, xenophobia is a hard-wired cognitive disposition that is impervious to empirical modification.

But suppose instead that (B) furnishes the correct account of the relation between transcendental and empirical concepts, such that perceptions need conform only to the transcendental concepts and not necessarily to the empirical ones, in order to be part of one's coherent experience. (B) leaves open the possibility that a person might have an empirically limited conception of people yet fail to be a xenophobe, just in case she acknowledges as a matter of principle that there must be other ways to do things and other ways to live besides those with which she is familiar; and just in case she is able to put this principle into practice when confronted by some of them. This is the case described in section 5.D, of the individual who commits cognitive errors A–C, but has no personal investment in the defective empirical conception that results.

(B) also leaves open the possibility that one could be a xenophobe in the sense discussed in section 5.D, yet be corrigible in one's xenophobia. For (B) acknowledges the possibility that even though the xenophobe equates her limited conception of people with her transcendental concept of personhood, someone might conform to her transcendental concept of personhood without conforming to her empirical conception of people. That is, in this case it is cognitively possible to introduce into her range of conscious experience a new object the behavior of which satisfies the rule and order of rationality even though it fails to satisfy her honorific stereotype of personhood. And it is possible for her to recognize in this conceptually anomalous behavior the rule and order of rationality, and so the personhood of another who nevertheless violates that honorific stereotype.

Since recognition of the existence of such an anomaly constitutes a counterexample to her honorific stereotype of personhood, the xenophobe has two options according to (B). Either she may, through the mechanisms of pseudorationality, seek some strategy for explaining this anomaly away; or else she may revise her stereotypic and limited conception of people in order to accommodate it. Thus (B) suggests that it is in theory possible for the xenophobe to reformulate and reform that conception in light of new data that disconfirms it, and so to bring her reciprocal stereotypes closer to open-ended inductive generalizations.

Of course whether or not this occurs, and the extent to which it occurs, depends on the virulence of her xenophobia; and this, in turn, on the extent of her personal investment in her honorific, stereotypical self-conception. But if (B) is correct, and one can discern the personhood of someone who violates one's limited conception of people, then pseudorational dismissal of the stranger as a person is not a viable option. By hypothesis the properties that constitute her identity as a person cannot be denied. Attempts to dissociate them (i.e., to dismiss them as insignificant, alien, or without value) have unacceptable implications for one's own, which similarly must be pseudorationalized out of the picture.[33] Moreover, attempts to rationalize them as flukes or mutations or illusions or exceptions to a rule undermine the universality of the rule itself. As in all such cases, pseudorationality does not, in fact, preserve the rational coherence of the self, but only the appearance of coherence in one's self-conception, by temporally dismissing the anomaly that threatens it. In the event that a xenophobe is confronted with such a phenomenon, xenophobia conflicts with the requirements of literal self-preservation and finally must be sacrificed to it. So finally, the only way for the xenophobe to ensure literal self-preservation against the intrusion of an anomalous person is to revise her reciprocal stereotypes of herself and others accordingly so as to integrate her.

There is evidence in the text of the first *Critique* that supports (B) as Kant's preferred alternative. These are in those introductory, explicative sections of the Dialectic in which Kant maintains that it is in the very nature of transcendent concepts of reason to have a breadth of scope that surpasses any set or series of empirical experiences we may have; indeed, to provide the simplest unifying principle for all of them and more. Thus, for example, he tells us that "the principle peculiar to reason in general, in its logical use, is: to find for the conditioned cognitions of the understanding the unconditioned whereby its unity is brought to completion." (A 307/B 364) By the "conditioned," Kant means those experiences and rules that depend on an inferential relation to other, more inclusive principles that explain them. And by the "unconditioned," Kant means those principles, concepts, or ideas of reason that are not themselves dependent on any further ones but rather provide the explanation of all of them. What he is saying here is that rationality works interrogatively for us: given some datum of experience we understand, we reflexively seek to enlarge our understanding by searching for further data by which to explain it.

Kant then goes on to say in the same passage that this logical principle becomes a transcendent one through our assumption that if dependent explanatory rules and experiences are given, then the whole series of them, ordered in relations of subsumption of the sort that characterize a covering-law theory, must be given as well; and that this series is not itself dependent on any further explanatory principles.[34] Kant's point is that we assume that any limited explanation of experience we have is merely part of a series of such explanations that increase in generality and inclusiveness, up to a maximally inclusive explanation of all of them. Thus we regard each such partial experience of the world we have as one among many, all of which are unified by some higher-level theory. And later he says that

[t]he transcendental concept of reason is none other than that of proceeding from a totality of conditions to a given conditioned. Now since only the unconditioned makes the totality of conditions possible, and conversely the totality of the conditions is itself always unconditioned; so a pure concept of reason in general can be explained through the concept of the unconditioned, so far as it contains a basis of the synthesis of the condition (A 322/ B 379). . . . Concepts of pure reason . . . view all experiential knowledge as determined through an absolute totality of conditions. (A 327/B 384; also see A 311/B 368, B 383–85, A 409, A 509)

What he means is that we regard any particular phenomenon as embedded in a systematically unified series of such phenomena, such that if we can explain some partial series of that kind, then there is an entire series of which that partial series is a part that we can also explain; and such that that more inclusive explanation explains everything there is about the phenomenon to explain. So Kant is saying that built into the canons of rationality that structure our experience is an inherent disposition to seek out all the phenomena that demand an inclusive explanation, and to test its inclusiveness against the range of phenomena we find.

These remarks support (B) because they imply that the innate cognitive concepts that structure and unify our experience invariably, necessarily outstrip our empirical conceptions of it. Kant is saying that it is in the nature of our cognitive limitations (i.e., that we can only have knowledge of sense-based experience) that the explanatory scope of the innate concepts that structure and unify it necessarily exceeds that sensory basis itself. This means that we view any experience in implicit relation to other possible experiences of its kind, and finally in relation to some systematic explanation that makes sense of all of them. So no single experience, or series of experiences, can ultimately satisfy our appetite for conceptual completeness, because the scope of the higher-level concepts we invoke to explain them necessarily outstrips the limited number of those experiences themselves. There will always be a lack of fit between our innate rational capacity and the empirical theories it generates, because they will always appear limited in scope in a way our innate capacity for explanation itself does not. So no matter how much sensory data we accumulate in support of our empirical theories of ourselves or the world, we are so constructed intellectually as to be disposed to feel somewhat dissatisfied, inquisitive, restless about whether there might not be more to explain, and to search further for whatever our search turns up.[35]

But this means that we are disposed reflexively to regard anomalous data as more than mere threats to the integrity of our conceptions of the world and ourselves, for the disposition to inquire further and to seek a more inclusive explanation of experience remains, even when literal self-preservation has been achieved. We also are disposed to regard those data as irresistible cognitive challenges to the scope of our conceptions, and as provocations to reformulate them so as to increase their explanatory reach. Because, according to Kant, we are always seeking the final data needed to complete the series of experiences our conceptions are formulated conclusively to explain, it could even be said that we are disposed actively to welcome anomalies, as tests of the adequacy of the conceptions we have already formulated.

When applied specifically to the transcendent idea of personhood, this disposition to welcome anomaly as a means of extending our understanding amounts to a kind of xenophilia. That is, it amounts to a positive valuation of human difference as intrinsically interesting and therefore worthy of regard, and a disvaluation of conformity to one's honorific stereotypes as intrinsically uninteresting. It dismantles the assumption that there is any cause for self-congratulation or self-esteem in conforming to any stereotype at all, and represents anomalous others as opportunities for psychological growth rather than mere threats to psychological integrity. It implies an attitude of inquiry and curiosity rather than fear or suspicion, of receptivity rather than resistance toward others; and a belief that there is everything to be gained, and nothing to be protected, from exploration of another person's singularity.[36] We often see this belief expressed in the behavior of very young children, who touch, poke, prod, probe, and question one without inhibition, as though in knowledge of another there were nothing to fear. What they are lacking, it seems, is contingent empirical evidence to the contrary.

Notes

1. Work on this paper was supported by an NEH Summer Stipend and a Woodrow Wilson International Scholars' Fellowship. Portions are excerpted from chapter 7 of a manuscript in progress, *Rationality and the Structure of the Self*. It has benefited from presentation to the

Wellesley Philosophy Department Faculty Seminar and also from the comments of Anita Allen, Alison MacIntyre, John Pittman, and Kenneth Winkler.

2. Immanuel Kant, *Kritik der Reinen Vernunft*, ed. Raymund Schmidt (Hamburg: Felix Meiner, 1976). All references to this work are parenthesized in the text. Translations from the German are my own. Connoisseurs will find my translations to be generally more literal than Kemp Smith's and (I think) more accurate in conveying not only the substance of Kant's claims but his manner of expression. Despite Kant's tendency to indulge in run-on sentences, he is by and large a plain speaker with a fondness for the vernacular, not the stilted, pretentious Prussian Kemp Smith makes him out to be. But the major objection to Kemp Smith's translation is that he obscures important philosophical issues by overinterpreting Kant so as to resolve them before the monolingual English reader can become aware that there is anything to dispute. This is particularly evident in the debate about transcendental content (see below, section 2 and notes 16 and 17).

3. P. F. Strawson, *The Bounds of Sense* (London: Methuen, 1968).

4. Immanuel Kant, *Grundlegung zur Metaphysik der Sitten*, ed. Karl Vorlander (Hamburg: Felix Meiner, 1965). All references to the Academy Edition are parenthesized in the text. Translations from the German are my own.

5. John Rawls, *A Theory of Justice* (Cambridge: Harvard University Press, 1971), chaps. 3 and 7; Alan Gewirth, *Reason and Morality* (Chicago: University of Chicago Press, 1978), chap. 2; Thomas Nagel, *The Possibility of Altruism* (Oxford: Oxford University Press, 1975), pt. 2. I discuss Rawls's recent transition away from a Humean model of rationality in "Personal Continuity and Instrumental Rationality in Rawls's Theory of Justice," *Social Theory and Practice* 13, no. 1 (Spring 1987): 49–76, and Nagel's and Gewirth's reliance on a Humean model of motivation in chaps. 2 and 3 respectively of my *Rationality and the Structure of the Self*.

6. My exegetical remarks in this paper should not be mistaken for a defense of the extended overall interpretation of Kant they clearly presuppose. I defend this interpretation against the canonical views in Kant's *Metaethics* (in progress).

7. This thesis may be viewed as the resolution of a *Gedankenexperiment* Kant earlier conducts at A 89–91, in which he entertains the possibility of unsynthesized appearance. In any case, his ultimate commitment to this thesis is clear. See Robert Paul Wolff, *Kant's Theory of Mental Activity* (Cambridge: Harvard University Press, 1968), for a discussion.

8. See, for example, Strawson, *The Bounds of Sense*, chap. 2. In hindsight Kant himself grudgingly admits that hypothetical and disjunctive syllogisms contain the same "matter" as the categorical judgment, but he refuses to budge on their essential difference in form and function. See Kant's *Logic*, trans. Robert Hartman and Wolfgang Schwarz (New York: Bobbs-Merrill, 1974), paras. 24–29, 60 n. 2, especially pp. 111 and 127.

9. This thesis is elaborated in the contemporary context by Gerald M. Edelman, *Neural Darwinism: The Theory of Neuronal Group Selection* (New York: Basic Books, 1987) and *The Remembered Present: A Biological Theory of Consciousness* (New York: Basic Books, 1989). See the review of Edelman and others by Oliver Sacks in "Neurology and the Soul," *New York Review of Books* 37, no. 18 (22 November 1990): 44–50.

10. "Rationality and the Structure of the Self," excerpted from *Rationality and the Structure of the Self* and delivered to the Association for the Philosophy of the Unconscious, American Philosophical Association Eastern Division Convention, Boston, Mass., 1986.

11. "Rationality and the Structure of the Self."

12. Thomas Kuhn, *The Structure of Scientific Revolutions* (Chicago: University of Chicago Press, 1971), chaps. 6–8.

13. A. M. S. Piper, "Two Conceptions of the Self," Philosophical Studies 48, no. 2 (September 1985): 173–97, repr. in *Philosopher's Annual* 8 (1985): 222–46; also see A. M. S. Piper, "Pseudorationality," in *Perspectives on Self-Deception*, ed. Amelie Oksenberg Rorty and

Brian P. McLaughlin (Berkeley and Los Angeles: University of California Press, 1988), 297–323.

14. "Higher-Order Discrimination," in *Identity, Character, and Morality: Essays in Moral Psychology*, ed. Owen Flanagan and Amelie Oksenberg Rorty (Cambridge: MIT Press, 1990), 285–309; reprinted in condensed form in the monograph series Studies on Ethics in Society (Kalamazoo: Western Michigan University, 1990).

15. Kant definitively identifies human desires and inclinations as empirical concepts at A 15/B 29. In the following sections I shall offer an interpretation of the relation between transcendental and empirical concepts as one of instantiation. This would treat the empirical concepts of desires and inclinations as instantiations of the transcendental concept of passion, and the empirical concept of intentional human behavior as an instantiation of the transcendental concept of action.

16. The German sentence runs as follows: "Da die Zeit nur die Form der Anschauung, mithin der Gegenstände, als Erscheinungen, ist, so ist das, was an diesen der Empfindung entspricht, die transzendentale Materie aller Gegenstände, als Dinge an sich (die Sachheit, Realität)."

17. Kant's statement here of course makes a great deal of trouble for his doctrine of transcendental idealism and therefore is not developed significantly in the first *Critique*. The Refutation of Idealism, for instance, provides no conclusive evidence either of his acceptance or rejection of such a view. However, there are other passages and problems in the first *Critique* and *Prolegomena* that furnish evidence of Kant's underlying commitment to it.

Specifically, the view that the sufficient condition for the correct application of empirical concepts is given by the transcendental matter of things in themselves answers a question regarding the status of what Kant entitles the "matter of appearance" that remains unanswered through both editions of the first *Critique*. In both editions, Kant clearly wants to say that the form of appearance is spatiotemporal intuition, which inheres innately in the transcendental subject and is empirically real. And in both editions he contrasts the form of appearance with its matter, which is "that in the appearance which corresponds to sensation" and is given a posteriori (A 20/B 34). But exactly where and to what the sensation is given, and what exactly is the nature of the correspondence, remains unclear. Kant defines sensation as "the effect of an object upon the faculty of representation, so far as we are affected by it" (A 19/B 34). Here he is clearly referring to the transcendental subject's faculty of representation. And since empirical objects are the consequence of that subject's cognitive activity, they cannot be supposed to exert causal influence on it. So by "an object" (*Gegenstand*), Kant must mean a nonempirical object, i.e., a thing in itself. So he is claiming that there is a nonempirical object that, by affecting the transcendental subject's faculty of representation, causes that subject to feel sensations.

Kant also denies that there is any "subjective representation, referring to something *outer*, which could be called objective *a priori*" (A 28/B 44). So, in particular, sensation (a subjective representation that, by corresponding to the matter of appearance, presumably refers to it) cannot be empirically real. Therefore, although sensation is the causal effect of an object on the transcendental subject, and although it refers to something outer, namely the matter of appearance, it is also a posteriori subjective representation that, unlike intuition, is not empirically real.

If sensation is a posteriori, one would expect to find it in the empirical world of appearance, and this is exactly where Kant locates it in the A Edition. There Kant's justification for assigning this status to sensation is that tastes, for example, belong to the "special constitution of sense in the subject that tastes it," and colors similarly are not properties of the objects we see, "but only modifications of the sense of sight, which is affected in a certain manner by light." By contrast with space, which is a necessary part of appearances, "[t]aste and colors are . . . connected with the appearances only as effects accidentally added by the particular constitution of the sense organs . . . grounded in sensation, and, indeed, in the case of taste, even upon feeling (pleasure and pain) as an effect of sensation" (A 28–29). So colors are effects of sensation, and taste is an effect of feeling, which in turn is an effect of sensation. And what is it that affects the sense organs, so as to give rise to the sensation that in turn causes one to perceive, say, colors? Kant tells us that it is light.

But light is itself an appearance, just as the sense organs are among the appearances of the empirical self and not part of the transcendental subject to whom the empirical self appears. So the secondary qualities of appearances such as color and taste must result from the effect of some of those appearances, such as light, on other appearances, such as the empirical self's sense organs. This explains how the empirical self comes to experience the secondary qualities of appearances: it experiences them as sensory effects of empirical appearances on its sense organs. But the mere spatiotemporal *form* of an appearance cannot be supposed to have such causal efficacy. If anything about an appearance does, it must be its *matter*. So the matter of appearances cannot be supposed to be identical to the secondary qualities it may cause the subject to generate. So although these appearances have matter, they do not have secondary qualities except insofar as these are ascribed to them by a sensing empirical subject. Thus when Kant describes sensation as "corresponding" to the matter of appearance, he seems to be suggesting a three-place causal relation: the matter of appearance causes the empirical subject's sensation, which in turn causes the empirical subject to perceive the secondary qualities she ascribes to it.

Locating sensations in causal relations between the empirical self and the natural world of objects accords well with empirical psychology. The problem is that without explaining the connection between empirical sense organs and transcendental sensibility, this account obscures Kant's claim that sensations are the effect of a nonempirical object on the representational ability of the transcendental self. For since empirical objects are the product of transcendental cognitive activity, they cannot themselves engender the activity that produces them. And since things in themselves are supposed to be beyond our cognitive capacity to understand, Kant is not entitled to assert their effect on the subject, either.

What Kant should do is break his own rule of silence on what things in themselves can and cannot do, just this once. He should say that sense organs may be the way transcendental sensibility appears to the introspecting transcendental subject (see below), just as empirical objects such as light may be the way things in themselves appear to that subject. That way the "*transcendental* matter of things in themselves" (A 143/B 182) could causally affect the subject's sensibility such that it then generated sensations, and so the secondary qualities of empirical objects. This would make sense of the sentence at A 143/B 182 that Kemp Smith mistranslates. It would stipulate a simpler, two-place causal relation between sensation and the transcendental matter that corresponds to it, namely that the latter causes the former.

Moreover, it would make sense of Kant's claim at A 20/B 34 about the matter of appearance corresponding to sensation. For if appearances could be the way things in themselves appear to the transcendental subject, and sensations occur in the transcendental subject, which itself appears as the empirical subject, then one way for both the matter of appearance and the transcendental matter of things in themselves to correspond to sensation would be if these two kinds of matter were, so to speak, materially equivalent. In this case, the causal relation of transcendental matter to the transcendental subject's sensations would appear as a causal relation between the matter of appearance and the empirical subject's sense organs.

Another benefit of this interpretation for the present discussion would be that it would supply detailed support for my suggestion, immediately following, that an instantiation relation between transcendental and empirical concepts preserves relevant content from systematically related things in themselves, through the transcendental and finally empirical concepts that structure that content. The material equivalence of transcendental and empirical matter would offer some evidence of what that content might be, and how increasingly specific conceptualizations of cognitively available particulars might preserve it.

This interpretation would only require Kant to revise the doctrine of transcendental idealism, not necessarily to abandon it. In particular, it would require him to revise his claim in the A Paralogisms, that

> in fact, when one regards outer appearances as representations, which are effected in us by their objects as existing things in themselves outside us, it is not possible to see how one can know their existence otherwise than through the inference from the effect to the cause, relative to which it must always remain doubtful whether the latter is in us or outside us. One can, indeed, concede that there may be something which is, in the transcendental sense, outside us and is the cause of our outer intuitions, *but this is not the object that we understand under the representations of matter and corporeal things; for these are merely appearances, i.e. mere types of representations, which are to be found only in us,* and whose reality is based on immediate consciousness, just as is the consciousness of my own thoughts. (A 372; emphasis added)

Consistent application of Kant's strictures about the unknowability of things in themselves would require Kant to replace the italicized passage, which makes a positive, substantive claim about what things in themselves cannot be, with one that admits our inability to *know whether or not* the "something which is in the transcendental sense outside us and is the cause of our outer intuitions" is "the object that we understand under the representations of matter and corporeal things." Kant is entitled to say that such an object is at least an appearance to be found in us. He is also entitled to say that, by hypothesis, we can know nothing about such an object beyond its appearance to us. But he is not entitled to deny that it might, in fact, accurately represent the nature of things in themselves as well.

This interpretation would, however, require Kant to jettison his allegiance to the traditional distinction between primary and secondary qualities. Since both would now be generated a priori by the subject's innate faculty of sensibility, and both would refer to something "outer"—respectively, the form and matter of appearance—the asymmetry between them would be far less striking. But Kant could still maintain that secondary qualities vary from person to person (i.e., to the extent that the transcendental subject's senses do) whereas primary ones do not; and so continue to insist that secondary qualities are not, unlike space and time, empirically real.

In the B Edition Kant moves closer to such a view. Here his argument for denying that sensations are empirically real is that "they belong merely to the subjective constitution of our *manner of sensibility*, for instance, of sight, hearing, touch, as in the case of the sensations of colors, sounds, and heat, which, since they are mere sensations . . . do not of themselves yield knowledge of any object" (A 28/B 44; emphasis added). On the next page Kant goes on to deny that colors and tastes can "be rightly regarded as properties of things, but only as changes in the subject, changes which may, indeed, be different for different people [and] with reference to color, can appear differently to every eye" (B 45; the passage in German runs, "jedem Auge in Ansehung der Farbe anders erscheinen kann." Kemp Smith *again* willfully mistranslates this passage as "in respect of its color, can appear differently to every observer"). In this version of the argument Kant ascribes the five senses, and eyes in particular, to the subject's transcendental sensibility. Clearly this is a strategic error: Kant should not ascribe apparent properties of empirical objects, such as the sense organs human beings happen to have, to the transcendental subject to whom these properties empirically appear. But the interest of this faux pas is the evidence it provides of Kant's actual view. It clearly implies that he does think transcendental subjects have senses even if he shouldn't say so.

And it supports the above suggestion that these senses can be understood as appearing empirically as sense organs to empirical observation or introspection.

What remains is to provide at least some textual evidence that the transcendental subject's sensations are caused by things in themselves. We have just seen that sensations cannot come from the empirical objects that are their consequences, as the A Edition suggests. Either they are self-generated by the subject or they come from something else. Now Kant insists that sensibility is a purely receptive capacity for "receiving representations through the way in which we are affected by objects" (A 19/B 33). Moreover, he later identifies and discusses that class of representations he thinks are actively generated by the mind's effect on itself (B 68–69; see section 4, below). So we can infer that he doesn't think sensations can be actively self-generated. If they come from something else, this can only be from things in themselves. The above remarks, imploring Kant to speak up about the behavior of things in themselves, offers a possible account of this behavior that would square nicely, not only with A 143/B 182, but with A 19/B 34 as well.

Now for Kant actually to state this in the *Critique* would constitute a commitment to causal realism that conflicted with his strictures that we can know nothing of things in themselves, and in particular cannot assert the applicability of the categories to them. So Kant refrains from any such claim in the first *Critique*. Luckily for us, by the time he writes the *Prolegomena* he is ready to tip his hand. There Kant states quite clearly, in contrasting his own view with that of the idealist:

> I, on the contrary, say that things as objects of our senses existing outside us are given, but we know nothing of what they may be in themselves, knowing only their appearances, *that is, the representations which they cause in us by affecting our senses. Consequently I grant by all means that there are bodies without us, that is, things which, though quite unknown to us as to what they are in themselves, we yet know by the representations which their influence on our sensibility procures us.* (Immanuel Kant, *Prolegomena to Any Future Metaphysic*, trans. Lewis White Beck [New York: Bobbs-Merrill, 1950], Ac. 288, emphasis added)

Surely Kant's considered commitment to causal realism (i.e., to things in themselves as causal sources of the appearances they effect in us by impinging on our senses, a commitment achieved with intellectual and temporal distance from the many ambiguities and confusions of the first *Critique* could not be any clearer than this.

18. Scientific paradigm shifts needn't invalidate Kant's insight, since a "gavagai" doesn't stop being a "gavagai" when we consider that it is "really" a perturbation in the electromagnetic field. I discuss the requirement of inclusiveness at greater length in "Seeing Things," *Southern Journal of Philosophy* 21, suppl. vol. (1990): 29–60.

19. Piper, "Pseudorationality."

20. The use of *bestimmen* can also mean to decree or ordain someone to do something; but it cannot mean merely to cause something. *Bestimmen* always carries the connotation of shaping some idea or event by cognitive means. Therefore it does rule out "cause" as a synonym for "determine." Kant's usual words for causality are *Kausalität* or *Ursache*. So *Selbstbestimmung* would refer to the cognitive activity of resolving to be or act in a certain way, not to that of merely causing oneself to do so. The tendency to think of Kant's concept of self-determination on analogy with that of causal determination should be resisted at all costs.

21. I develop this claim at greater length in "The Meaning of 'Ought' and the Loss of Innocence," invited address delivered to the American Philosophical Association Eastern Division Meeting, Atlanta, Georgia, December 1989. Abstracted in the *Proceedings of the American Philosophical Association* 63, no. 2 (October 1989): 53–54.

22. Piper, "Two Conceptions," and "Pseudorationality."

23. Lest I be charged with the same fault I ascribe to Kemp Smith, I note the ambiguity of the German: "Sie die Vernunft, ist allen Handlungen des Menschen in allen Zeitumständen gegenwärtig und einerlei, selbst aber ist sie nicht in der Zeit, *und gerät etwa in einen neuen Zustand*, darin sie vorher nicht war; etc." (emphasis added). A literal translation of this passage would make the meaning incoherent, so I infer that Kant was expressing himself ungrammatically.

24. Now in the *Groundwork*, Kant claims that "the human being and in general every rational being *exists* as end in himself, *not merely as means* for arbitrary use by this or that will, but rather must be viewed as *at the same time an end* in all of his actions, whether directed to himself or to other rational beings. . . . [R]ational beings are called *persons* because their nature distinguishes them as ends in themselves, i.e. as something that must not be used merely as means, and thus so far restricts all power of choice (and is an object of respect)" (Ac. 428). Besides an immediately preceding paragraph that introduces these concepts with definitions of them, there is little in the *Groundwork* of an explicit nature to have prepared the reader for these remarks on personhood as an end in itself, so it may seem that Kant has simply pulled these intuitively appealing ideas out of a hat. Moreover, Kant does not explain in the *Groundwork* why it is that personhood or rational nature deserves to be regarded as an end in itself, or even what he thinks an end in itself is.

The explanations of Kant's claims lie, rather, in the first *Critique*. There Kant characterizes an end as a species of idea (A 318/B 375). As we have seen, an *idea* is for Kant a technical term that denotes a final outcome of the rational disposition to generalize inclusively from lower-level to higher-level concepts, principles, and theories. He also describes the peculiar sphere of reason as an order of ends which is at the same time an order of nature, and human beings as the only creatures in nature who can contain the final end of this order in themselves and also exempt themselves from it through morality (B 425). So the sphere of rationality is one in which all of our experience is systematically organized and unified according to inclusive theoretical concepts in the manner already discussed. Human beings both contain the final end of this natural order within themselves and also can transcend it through moral conduct. In the Canon of Pure Reason, Kant tells us what this final end is: it is the idea of a natural world made moral, in which the free power of choice of rational beings "has, under moral laws, thoroughgoing systematic unity as such, as much with itself as with the freedom of every other" (A 808/B 836). In this moral world, the supreme good is happiness as directly apportioned to moral worth by a Supreme Reason that rules according to moral law, and we are rationally compelled to envision this world as the outcome of our efforts to achieve moral worthiness to be happy (A 809/B 837–A 811/B 839, A 813/B 841–A 816/B 844). The ultimate end, Kant tells us, is the entire vocation of man, and this is treated by moral philosophy (A 840/B 868). So Kant says in the *Groundwork* that personhood is an end in itself because a person has the capacity rationally to represent to herself, as a final end of her moral conduct, a divinely just moral order in which she participates as an equal member. This is the same vision that lies behind Kant's obscure remarks about membership and lordship in the kingdom of ends (Ac. 433–34).

25. Piper, "Two Conceptions" and "Pseudorationality."

26. Piper, "Higher-Order Discrimination."

27. This is the main thesis of Deborah Tannen's fascinating *You Just Don't Understand: Women and Men in Conversation* (New York: William Morrow, 1990), a popularization of her research in linguistics on gender differences in language use.

28. I chart the systematic use of such disvaluative properties in "Higher-Order Discrimination."

29. "Impartiality, Compassion and Modal Imagination," *Ethics* 101, 4: Symposium on Impartiality (July 1991), 726–57.

30. The concept of personal investment is discussed in my "Moral Theory and Moral Alienation," *Journal of Philosophy*, 84, no. 2 (February 1987): 102–18. Also see notes 13 and 14.

31. I am indebted to Rüdiger Bittner for pressing this question in discussion of my "Higher-Order Discrimination," although I was unable to address it properly in that context.

32. See note 14 for a fuller discussion.

33. A case study of this phenomenon might be the postmodernist attitude of mourning over the loss of value and meaning in contemporary creative and intellectual products of "Western civilization" at just that historical moment when the long-standing contributions to it by women and people of color are gaining recognition.

34. I argue that Kant's moral theory is a descriptive, explanatory theory that fits the deductive-nomological model in "The Meaning of 'Ought' and the Loss of Innocence."

35. This idea of theoretical rationality and theory-building as an innate disposition is given some support by Robin Horton's cross-cultural work. See his "African Traditional Thought and Western Science," in *Rationality*, ed. Bryan Wilson (Evanston, Ill.: Harper and Row, 1970), 131–71. As I understand Horton's conclusions, the main difference between Western scientific theories and the cosmologies of traditional societies is that the latter lack the concept of modality, i.e., recognition of the conceptual possibility that the favored and deeply entrenched explanation may not be the right one or the best one. They therefore lack the attitude of epistemic uncertainty that leads in the West to the joint problems of skepticism and solipsism. To this extent the stance of intellectual dissatisfaction I am attributing to Kant's epistemology may be culturally specific.

36. Thus xenophilia in the sense I am defining it should be distinguished from a superficially similar, but in fact deeply perverse form of xenophobia, in which the xenophobe reinforces her honorific, stereotypical self-conception by treating the other as an exotic object of research, whom (like a rare species of insect) it is permissible to examine and dissect from a superior vantage point of inviolate disingenuousness. By contrast, the xenophile acknowledges the disruption and threat to the integrity of the self caused by the other's difference, and seeks understanding of the other as a way of understanding and transcending the limitations of her own self-conception.

Part II

Ethics

3

Can Kant's Ethics Survive the Feminist Critique?[1]

Sally Sedgwick

As is well-known, Kant is not much loved by feminist philosophers. He has come under attack not only because on his view women are passive by nature and determined more by inclination than reason (and therefore cannot be legitimate citizens, equal partners in marriage or, even, capable scholars), but also because there is something supposed to be deeply androcentric built into the theoretical assumptions of his Critical philosophy. Very roughly, there is something about this conception of "pure reason" and its purported independence from but also capacity to determine and order the realm of nature that is taken to exclude the experience of women.

In this essay I consider Kant's ethics and two particularly important kinds of feminist criticisms directed against it. Each reveals the influence that Carol Gilligan's reflection on various Kantian components of Lawrence Kohlberg's theory of moral development has had on moral philosophers.[2] The first concerns Kant's notion of moral autonomy. Because moral agency on his view is a function of acting from reason rather than from feeling, it is said to reflect features more of male than of female identity. Autonomy on the Kantian model seems to be something achieved not in the course of cultivating our relationships, but rather in weakening their hold. In acting from pure reason, the moral subject raises itself above the needs of its affective nature and is free in its willing of its contingent connections to others.

The second objection addresses features of Kant's supreme moral law. In that what the categorical imperative tests is whether or not a maxim or action is universalizable, it is argued that its application requires that we abstract the object of our moral assessment from its particularity. What we lose if we are Kantians in moral theory is a sense of the uniqueness of persons and their contexts and histories, or a sufficiently informed and compassionate standpoint from which to judge them. The Kantian moral agent views its objects "thinly"—with an eye merely to their possible subsumability under some abstract rule. In so doing, its judgments are taken to reflect an orientation foreign to the experience of women, an orientation that is "anti-care."

If we abstract from these criticisms their specifically feminist content and formulate them more generally, what we are left with is, on the one hand, a concern about the tenability and costs of the dichotomy between reason and nature upon which Kant's conception of moral autonomy rests, and, on the other, a skepticism with regard to his claim to derive from an abstract law of practical reason particular duties adequate to the complexities of human life. Formulated in this way, the objections should strike a familiar chord, because they have been given various forms of expression from diverse philosophical orientations since the time of Kant's contemporaries Schiller and Hegel.[3] While to my knowledge the specifically feminist critique has not yet occasioned a strong line of response on the part of those sympathetic to the Kantian position, the criticisms construed more broadly have. And in view of the success of recent efforts on the part of Anglo-American philosophers to cast Kant's ethics in a new, more defensible light,[4] it is far from clear that there is anything remaining of these objections worth taking seriously, or that the feminist version of them has anything of a plausible case against Kant to make.

In sections 1 and 2 of what follows I lay out the above two criticisms in greater detail and present what I take to be the strongest representations of recent responses to them. In sections 3 and 4, I argue that while these defenses of Kant correct many misinterpretations of his moral theory, they fail in the end to put to rest the deeper worries of both the more general as well as the specifically feminist formulations of the objections. This, on my view, is because they leave his groundwork for a metaphysics of morals fully intact.

1

The possibility of morality, Kant argues, depends upon there being a nonempirical or noumenal basis of motivation; it depends upon our being moved not just by laws of nature, but by laws of freedom as well. If morality is not a chimera, it must be possible that pure reason has a practical employment; it must issue forth laws that are determining for my phenomenal nature without themselves being laws of nature.

Two problems arise from this account of moral agency, both of which are consequent upon the dichotomy it requires between phenomenal and noumenal aspects of the self. First, the dichotomy seems to be necessarily disharmonious. If my maxims are to have moral content, they must have as their ground practical reason and not natural inclination; they must be determined by that capacity in me which is independent of the influence of my empirical desires, needs, and motives—or by that part of myself which is productive of a noumenal versus phenomenal form of causality. But if the laws governing my empirical nature can never be sufficient to determine me to act morally, it would appear that the requirements of duty and of inclination must always be at odds.

This is the feature of Kant's account of moral agency responsible for those representations of his view as involving a permanent tug-of-war between the two sides of the self. What duty requires, it is objected, is something that can never be integrated into my nature as a phenomenal subject. This is why we find in Hegel, for example, the criticism that the Kantian moral ought can never become an is. Practical reason commands actions or maxims of me that I as an empirical being can never in fact perform. As one contemporary philosopher has put it, theories such as this, which insist upon driving a gap between moral reasons or justifications and our natural motives, force upon us a kind of "schizophrenia."[5] What they seem to ask as the price for morality is that we give up integrity.[6]

The second problem revolves around the fact that on Kantian moral theory the empirical self is not only split off from its noumenal counterpart, but also clearly subordinated to it. It is not just that a harmony between inclination and duty cannot be achieved because each issues forth unique kinds of laws originating from distinct aspects of the self; from the point of view of the possibility of morality, inclination seems either to drop out of the picture altogether, or to be of relevance only insofar as it is a hindrance to practical reason—something that has to be brought under practical reason's legislation or control. Kantian morality is for this reason criticized for degrading the significance of the feeling, affective side of our natures.

One of the strongest recent defenses of Kant against these kinds of objections can be found in the work of Barbara Herman. In her essay "Integrity and Impartiality," she argues that it is a mistake to understand Kantian moral theory either as posing a threat to the integrity of the self or as entailing the exclusion of feeling from morality.[7] The portrayal of the Kantian moral subject as always on the lookout for occasions to realize impartial value, as having successfully suppressed or denied its own empirical nature and personal interests in the service of duty, represents as Herman sees it a distortion of Kant's view. While it is true that emotions cannot serve as the ground of morality according to Kant, his position does not entail that acting in the absence of or in opposition to emotions is necessarily desirable from a moral standpoint. As Herman points out, insofar as the cooperation of emotions diminishes psychological obstacles to acting from duty, it is from Kant's perspective something to be encouraged.[8] He furthermore urges that we cultivate in ourselves sympathetic feelings as a means of being better prepared to recognize those situations that call for a helping response.[9]

On Herman's reading, duty according to Kant must always be present as a "limiting condition," but this does not mean that it must function in every instance as our "primary motive." There may be cases in which whatever occasions our response (for instance, to save the life of a loved one) is nothing other than our emotional attachment to that person. This kind of spontaneous, natural reaction that affirms the special character of our relationships to others is not ruled out by the Kantian conception of moral agency—as long as our responses are subjected to the check of duty as a limiting condition. Our actions are more often than not over-determined; it is not Kant's view that moral subjectivity has no other interests, desires, or ends than the realization of duty. But if our actions or maxims are to have moral content, the motive of duty, as Herman puts it, "must be by itself sufficient to bring about whatever is morally required."[10]

To those convinced that even on this reading something of a human response is still absent from Kant's account of moral agency in that impartial reason and not feeling is supposed to function as the final determination of moral worth, Herman replies by drawing out the Kantian point that emotions can never serve as the foundation of morality. Emotions in themselves, she tells us, are morally indifferent. The person who by nature possesses a kind heart and sympathetic temperament toward others, while deserving praise, has no moral worth on Kant's view, because in Herman's words, "nothing in what motivates him would prevent his acting in a morally impermissible way if that were helpful to others." "[I]t is to be regarded as a bit of good luck," she continues, "that he happens to have the inclination to act as morality requires."[11]

But again, that emotion cannot serve as the ground of morality by no means implies that as Kantians we opt for a cold and unfeeling moral theory. Although it is true that in those cases in which our personal projects and desires happen to conflict with morality it is morality that must win the upper hand, this does not mean that we are thus forced to compromise a human standpoint for an inhuman one. What it does mean is that we let the needs and interests that define us as individuals submit to the regulating influence of the needs and interests we share with others as members of humanity. We let personal feeling be checked by a feeling that is not emotion-based but is known "a priori."[12] We trade a self-centered for what might be called a human-centered point of view.[13] One might even say, on this interpretation, that Kant's ethics is a morality of care in the broadest possible sense. The requirement that morality be grounded in practical reason and not in feeling expresses his conviction that insofar as our maxims and actions are determined solely by our personal interests and projects, we fall short of recognizing ourselves as members of a human community and of acknowledging the consequences our behavior has for that community at large. That the moral point of view from the Kantian standpoint demands that we perform an act of abstraction in testing our personal ("subjective") ends against the ("objective") ends of humanity in this way is on this reading a mark not against it, but clearly in its favor.[14]

2

We now turn to criticisms directed against Kant's supreme moral law or categorical imperative. As an abstract law of practical reason, it is said to lack in any of its formulations sufficient content to give rise to particular duties nonarbitrarily and in a manner that reflects adequate sensitivity to the complexity and variety of our experience. Kant's discussion of the four duties in the *Groundwork*, for example, has time and again occasioned the objections that his own applications of the moral law involve the uncritical introduction of additional content and are rigoristic in nature.

In Kant's defense, commentators have pointed out that he does not intend that out of the categorical imperative alone we should be able to deduce or generate specific duties. Its application, in other words, is on his own admission dependent on various facts and assumptions, the nature of which is in part determined by his level of analysis. At first glance, we might be tempted to interpret what looks like his sweeping condemnation of suicide in the *Groundwork*, for example, as consequent upon the misguided assumption that mere reflection on the formal requirements of the moral law in the absence of any consideration of actual cases is sufficient to determine its concrete application. But on closer inspection and after comparing his treatment of suicide in that text with some of his other discussions, it becomes clear that it is not the taking of one's life as such that Kant thinks the categorical imperative absolutely rules out, but the taking of one's life in the service of self-love or inclination. There will be occasions, he admits, in which self-sacrifice may not be only morally permissible, but morally required (if, for example, I am called upon to defend my country).[15] Properly described, this kind of case is not a violation of duty, because it is not a form of self-murder as a "means to an arbitrary end." The duty of self-preservation is therefore not unconditional on Kant's view; as this example illustrates; it can be overridden in cases of moral conflict.[16]

But why are these kinds of subtleties left out of the discussion in the *Groundwork*? And why does Kant give us no acknowledgment there that duties can sometimes conflict? There are good reasons for this deriving from architectonic features of his moral theory and from the aims he sets out to accomplish in the *Groundwork* in particular. As he takes pains to emphasize in his preface, his chief concern in that text is not to consider concrete applications of the moral law, but to establish its a priori foundation. We are therefore mistaken if we understand his treatment of the four duties there as an exercise in applied ethics. Kant's aim is rather both to demonstrate in a preliminary way that an appeal to the requirements of practical reason is sufficient to justify the four distinct *kinds* of duties, and to convince us that those requirements never allow of exception in the interest of inclination. This latter point he can argue without introducing into his discussion any close consideration of concrete applications of the moral law, because it follows from the nature of duty as he has defined it.

A more precise determination of which acts of self-sacrifice in fact count as "arbitrary" self-murder and treatment of cases of possible moral conflict occurs in Kant only once he has left the project of a groundwork. Once he makes this transition, the charge that his derivation of individual duties suffers from rigorism and insensitivity becomes more difficult to defend. Again, because his chief concern in the *Groundwork* is to argue that morality rests on an a priori foundation and can never be overridden by inclination, he is not interested in that text to sort through a variety of cases to determine which instances of self-sacrifice are morally permissible and which are not, or—to cite another example—which utterances of falsehoods count as lies. But the *Groundwork* is Kantian moral theory in its most abstract form. This does not mean that Kant thinks that the validity of the categorical imperative as the supreme principle of morality can be established purely formally or without the help of *any* factual assumptions or content. The moral law only appears to us in the form of a command, he tells us, because of the fact that we are determined not just by reason but by inclination as well. So even at this level Kant's argumentation depends on the introduction of content; but the nature of the content admitted is limited by the *Groundwork*'s specific task.

It is not until the *Metaphysics of Morals* where he focuses directly on the problem of applying the moral law that Kant gives us some acknowledgment of the relevance of variations in context in our assessment of moral worth. Because his interest in that text is to consider duties valid for humanity as such versus duties valid for particular individuals in particular situations, however, the content introduced as necessary to determine the appropriate application of the categorical imperative is still highly abstract because it is restricted to facts about human nature as such. That most specific level of analysis (which takes into account differences in the circumstances and relations of individuals to one another and requires an empirical classification of the facts proper to particular cases) belongs, he tells us, not within the scope of a metaphysics of morals, but as an appendix to the system.[17]

Kant of course never gives us this part of his system. But we are mistaken if we interpret the *Groundwork* as well as the *Metaphysics of Morals* as if he had, and charge him with rigorism because he does not enter into those discussions a consideration of the kind of content appropriate to the level of an applied ethics.[18] We are further mistaken, as we have seen, if we think that he presumes that the derivation of particular duties can proceed by way of reflection on the formal requirements of morality alone. Rather than generate duties out of itself analytically, the moral law is intended by Kant as a test by means of which we assess either the moral fitness of some content specified in an individual's maxim, or the legal fitness of some content specified in the description of a given action.[19] The determination of precisely what content is relevant from the point of view of our evaluation of moral or legal fitness is something not specified by the categorical imperative itself, but decided on his view by human judgment. As is clear from our discussion above, one factor that must be taken into account is our level of analysis. It won't do to ignore a person's history, her relationships, the contingencies of her situation, if what we are interested in assessing is the maxim of that person as a unique individual—if, that is, we are working at the level of an applied ethics. Nor need we build into the description of our object under investigation more information than is morally relevant—the fact, for example, that in willing to help his neighbor, the man wore blue suede shoes. Since what the categorical imperative tests is the *universalizability* of a maxim or action, we furthermore need to ensure that the content we admit as relevant not be so agent- or action-specific as to defeat the purpose of carrying out the test. Kant unfortunately provides little guidance specifying just where that line should be drawn; but with reference to the few indications he does give us of how his moral philosophy would proceed were it carried out at the applied level, we can at least say that he thinks that features individuating an agent or her actions to *some* degree constitute at that level morally relevant content.[20] That even at this level of specificity an act of abstraction is required if the universalizability test is to be properly applied is in any case taken by those sympathetic to the Kantian position to be a small price to pay for the determination of moral worth.[21]

Given these considerations, we can see why it is argued that there is nothing built into the mechanism of Kant's moral theory that warrants the criticism that it requires any significant negation or denial of the uniqueness of our objects of moral judgment. There is nothing about the categorical imperative test that requires us to regard others "thinly," or necessitates that, in the words of one critic, we place "a prepared grid upon conduct and upon a person's activities and interests" and see the pieces of that person's conduct and life "as they are divided by lines on the grid."[22] According to the reading of Kant's moral philosophy I have presented here, the proper application of the categorical imperative calls on the contrary for sensitivity on the part of human judgment in deciding precisely what features of an individual case are to figure into our procedure of moral assessment. On this interpretation, there is no reason to conclude that—when carried out at the applied level—Kantian moral theory lacks any of the essential ingredients of a morality of care.

3

The above defenses of Kant place his moral theory in what I think is its best possible light. They demonstrate what is wrong with the portrayal of the Kantian subject as blindly obedient to unyielding commands and as having successfully eliminated its spontaneous, feeling responses in the service of duty. With reference to architectonic features of his system, they explain its apparent inattention to differences among persons and to contingencies of circumstance. Insofar as the two general objections I have considered depend on ignoring important features of Kant's position, they clearly go too far; but we would be mistaken if we concluded from this that they have nothing to offer by way of pointing to inadequacies in his underlying conception of moral agency.

Even Herman admits that the fact that the Kantian model allows feelings to function as "primary" motives is not likely to satisfy those troubled by the insistence that it is practical reason that ultimately must decide moral worth.[23] While Kant may not be so blind in his understanding of human psychology as to underestimate the significance of our empirical motives, he nonetheless awards those motives no moral weight. Although he is not committed to the view that acting in the absence of emotions is morally desirable, he does insist that it is practical reason alone that determines duty.

As we have seen, Herman's defense of this model of agency is contingent upon her acceptance of the Kantian argument that emotions cannot serve as the ground of morality.[24] The possibility of the moral ought, according to Kant, requires principles that command conduct universally and necessarily, principles fit to serve as "laws" and not merely as "practical precepts."[25] Since generalizations based on our observations of the realm of nature or of human behavior can never give rise to such principles, morality cannot rest on empirical facts about human nature but rather must be grounded on the a priori requirements of practical reason.

In her response to critics of the corresponding account of moral motivation, Herman's tactic is therefore to fall back on a restatement of the Kantian party line: "[I]f it is rational to prefer the emotion-based action over the dutiful one," she says, "then we . . . have to conclude that it is not always desirable to do a dutiful action in a morally worthy way."[26] If critics want to urge, that is, that a response motivated and not just influenced by feeling is on some occasions morally appropriate, then as Herman sees it, they also have to accept that such a response can have no moral worth. While she argues that even a Kantian can recognize that sometimes the best way to extend a helping hand is to act out of ("pathological") love rather than duty, what this means on her analysis is that it will sometimes be morally necessary that morality step aside.[27]

We get a sense here of the kind of background assumptions that support Herman's defense, and they are of course assumptions that can be challenged. What is called into question is not just whether our motives can ever in *fact* be determined by reason alone. Kant himself suffered from no illusions about this; on the contrary, he expressed a sober realism in his estimation of the very imperfect capacity of human nature to realize morality.[28] The objections arise out of what are more serious doubts about his insistence that our morally worthy motives are necessarily and exclusively those that are reason-based.

This is the deeper thrust of the criticism that his various applications of the moral law presuppose the uncritical introduction of additional content. The objection need not merely be taken to rest on the mistaken supposition that he thought that specific duties could be generated out of the categorical imperative analytically, and that he therefore neglected to take into consideration variations in the contexts in which it could be applied. As we saw above, the defense of Kant against that charge depends on pointing to his own acknowledgment that content must indeed be introduced via some maxim or via some description of the action under investigation. The objection can be raised, however, even given this corrective interpretation; what it challenges is the Kantian claim to have captured in his moral theory a conception of practical agency "valid for the will of every rational being."[29]

Kant himself admits that even in its most abstract formulation as a test of universalizability or as the requirement that we respect the dignity of ourselves and of others, the validity of the categorical imperative depends on the introduction of material assumptions: the fact, for example, that we have practical reason; and the fact that since we are also determined by inclination, we have to be commanded in morality. But, at least in its abstract formulation, it is difficult to discover in the moral law any presence of the kind of underlying assumption that might compromise its status as a principle legislating over rational human nature as such; nothing that suggests, for example, that it has greater validity for one sex over the other. As Hegel saw, however, it is also true that formulated in this abstract way, the categorical imperative has little or no "content": In the absence of further specification of just what is supposed to count as the "dignity" of humanity or of what it means to treat oneself and others always as ends, it either provides no clear practical guidance at all, or reduces in its formulation as a test of universalizability to nothing more than the requirement that we consistently will any maxim we please.[30]

Kant certainly meant more than this by his supreme moral law. We know this because he did take care to fill in for us what he thought lies at the basis of human dignity. It is of course not simply consistency that is the criterion of moral worth, on his view, but respect for self and others in the name of the capacity of free or rational choice. It is by virtue of this capacity to be determined by laws that we ourselves make that we are "persons" as opposed to mere "things," and as such, subject to moral imputation.[31] Thus for Kant, autonomy in the sense of self-legislation whereby reason and not nature is determining for our will serves as the "ground" of the categorical imperative.[32] A maxim or action has moral content only if it is motivated by respect for the autonomy of ourselves or of others. And because autonomy is a capacity that is supposed to be attributable to rational human nature as such, it can furthermore serve as the basis of practical laws that are universally and necessarily binding.

What of this portrayal of moral agency is objectionable, given Herman's corrective defense? The answer may be taken from what was said above about her strategy for treating arguments in favor of the appropriateness, in some cases, of an emotion- versus duty-based response. While as she points out, emotions may indeed function as "primary motives," they are in themselves "morally indifferent" on the Kantian account; as such, they must so far as morality is concerned always be subject to the regulating influence of practical reason.

This is indeed the Kantian view; but it is not difficult to see why its underlying conception of agency might still be thought of as impoverished or "schizophrenic" even in light of Herman's sympathetic portrayal of it. So long as our affective natures are allowed no *constitutive* role in the forming of the strictly moral component of personality, that part of ourselves from the moral point of view will have to drop out on the Kantian model as simply irrelevant. No matter how great an influence Kant admits feelings to have in preparing us for the proper moral response, he nonetheless takes them to be in themselves ill-suited to determine the morally permissible maxim or the right course of action. The side of the self he does suppose to be fit to determine duty is motivated by practical reason alone. It is also the side of the self that has few recognizably human features. Its identity is formed outside time and in isolation from any particular culture or worldview. It has no relations to others or ends that it can call its own. Its defining form of self-expression is its autonomy, and this is taken to consist exclusively in its capacity to free itself of the causal forces of its empirical ends and to legislate its own moral laws.

Not only do Kant's critics find uncompelling his insistence that a sharp line can be drawn between our empirical and noumenal natures or between our faculties of inclination and reason; as I understand them, they challenge Kant's motive for setting up such a model as an ideal as well. Why should what one critic has called a "disembedded" and "disembodied" self be taken to represent the kind of agency required in determining duty?[33] Why should we accept the Kantian view that our empirical natures tend to stand in the way of our ability to judge impartially and cut us off from access to the moral point of view?

As I noted above, the specifically feminist critique finds troublesome these same features of the Kantian conception of agency and in addition discovers in them evidence of gender bias. At the most obvious level, women are excluded by Kant's moral theory because he finds them lacking in that quality which constitutes human dignity; they are thus on his view imperfect members of humanity, or only imperfectly human. While he tells us that all rational human nature possesses the capacity to be determined by practical reason, women turn out to possess this capacity to a lesser extent since they are as he sees it guided in judgment for the most part by feeling. The wisdom of women, he remarks in part 3 of his 1764 essay "Observations on the Beautiful and the Sublime," has to do not with what is rational, but with feeling. "Women will avoid what is evil not because it is unjust," he says, "but because it is ugly; and for them virtuous actions are those that are morally beautiful."[34] As he notes in his *Metaphysical Elements of Justice*, women are not fit to be "active" or voting members of a commonwealth because they depend for their "subsistence and protection" "on arrangements by others." They thus have no right, "to guide the state, to organize, and to work for the introduction of particular laws."[35] And that women are "dependent" is not simply a contingent historical fact, on Kant's view, but a permanent feature of their nature. When it comes to running the household, men have a "naturally grounded right to command," women to obey— precisely because while it is man's nature to be governed by understanding, women are governed by inclination. The man, he says in his *Anthropology*, "will be like a minister to his monarch who thinks only of amusement."[36] It is no wonder, then, that in his essay on the "Old Saw" Kant lists as a "necessary qualification" for citizenship the "natural one of not being a child or woman."[37] This of course amounts not just to a denial to women of citizenship, but of equality as well. Natural laws of freedom and the "equality which accords with this freedom," he says in the *Elements of Justice*, require that everyone be able to work up from passive to active or voting status. But since this is just what a woman by virtue of her nature cannot do, she has no reason ever to expect on the basis of Kantian morality equality under the law.[38]

In Kant's defense we would like to be able to say when we read his denial to women of the right to citizenship and equality that he is simply laboring under a faulty or antiquated anthropology, and that all that needs correction is his grasp of the facts. We would like to say that there is nothing about the questionable assumptions that make up his moral anthropology that need cause any worry about the validity of the supreme moral law itself. While he may have been ideologically misled or empirically mistaken, his moral *groundwork* on this interpretation remains safely intact. Following this line of defense, we might then go on to argue that one fact that indeed needs correcting is his assumption that it is the *nature* of women to be more determined by inclination than by reason. In light of what we know about the socio-historical forces that have confined them to the home and hindered their participation in the public domain, we might claim that women have simply been deprived of the opportunity to exercise their rational faculties to the extent that men have. And this is surely a correction that can be made without requiring any adjustment in our guiding principle.

This is the line Herman takes in her article "The Practice of Moral Judgment" with regard to the problem of eliminating the presence of racist or sexist bias in our rules for applying the categorical imperative. In the name of acknowledging the full moral status of blacks and women, she says, any prejudices that infect our rules will of course call for correction; and such correction or revision is the kind of thing she imagines "instituting a practical adjustment in the concept of 'person as an end-in-himself.' " But while Herman argues that it is entirely compatible with Kantian theory that such "practical adjustments" be made from time to time to ensure the proper determination of duty, she implies that none could ever be so critical as to challenge Kant's conception of agency itself. In fact, she thinks that we can or must draw from that conception the "terms of criticism" by means of which we assess and revise our rules of application.[39] She assumes on the one hand that a clear line can be drawn between the underlying conception or agency that serves as the ground of Kant's categorical imperative and our rules for applying it, and on the other that any ideological bias or factual error will undermine the adequacy of the latter alone.

It should by now be clear that the point of the objections I have raised above challenges both these assumptions. It is not enough to say that Kant simply got his facts about women wrong and was therefore blinded from recognizing their true potential as rational agents. Following Gilligan's critique of Kohlberg, the worry is rather that Kant's judgments about women reflect not just his failure to properly apply the categorical imperative, but also a bias in the categorical imperative itself or in the model of agency upon which it is based.

4

I turn in this final section to evaluate more closely the specifically feminist critique of the two general objections I have presented above, looking first at Kant's conception of autonomy and then at his test of universalizability. I do not include in my discussion an exact summary of Gilligan's reflections on moral theory; instead, I reformulate her criticisms in a way that poses the deepest challenge to Kant. As I understand it, her view is neither that the differences in male and female identity development outweigh the similarities, nor that none of the features of a Kantian ethics have as much validity for women as they do for men. Nonetheless, the arguments she and others put forward in favor of incorporating a "different voice" into moral theory do seem to demand that Kant's metaphysical groundwork be given up.

What of the Kantian portrayal of moral subjectivity mirrors male more than female identity and thus leaves women and their experience out? That the affective sides of our natures can play no constitutive role in the making of the strictly moral side of our characters may be a problem, Gilligan suggests, for those who place special value on and confidence in their capacities to feel, and who experience feeling as an integral part of and aid to judgment. While Kant does not believe that we are by virtue of our emotional lives narrowly selfish and necessarily ruthless in our treatment of others, he does cast doubt on the reliability and depth of our most well-meaning empirical motives. He admits that there are individuals (like the do-gooder in the much-discussed passage in the *Groundwork*) who out of generous temperament are naturally inclined to look out for the welfare of others.[40] But such cases of kindheartedness do not on his view provide a solid enough foundation from which to derive duty. As effects of natural causation, inclinations of any kind can never as he sees it serve as grounds for moral imputation. There is also the possibility that behind every apparently altruistic motive lurks the "dear self"—looking out, in however a discreet and indirect way, for nothing but its own interests.[41] And finally, emotion-based motives are bound to be morally indiscriminate. The do-gooder will be inclined to spread her goodness, Kant thinks, no matter what, no matter to whom. It is not that his view is that emotions as such necessarily blind or distort our moral vision. This is only true for those emotions or "passions" that have become so powerful as to no longer be susceptible to the guidance of reflection. While the "man who *loves* can still remain quite clear-sighted," he tells us in the *Anthropology*, the man who is "*infatuated* inevitably becomes blind to the faults of his beloved."[42] Whether calm or passionate, however, Kant does think that emotions in themselves lack discrimination and judgment. In this way, his moral psychology mirrors his conception of the household division of labor: the woman must submit to the command of her "minister" if her actions or motives are to be properly governed or directed. Reason and feeling, like man and woman, form a hierarchy in Kant—with reason very clearly on the top.

When we turn to the discussions in the *Doctrine of Virtue* of the various kinds of ends obligating us, this hierarchy shows up again. We have the duty to cultivate our own powers, the highest of which, Kant says, "is understanding, the power of concepts and so too of those concepts that belong to duty." "[T]his duty," he continues, "includes the cultivation of one's will (moral attitude) to fulfill every duty as such." We are obligated, then, to raise ourselves above the "crude state" of our empirical nature or "animality" and develop in ourselves "moral feeling" by virtue of which the moral law serves as the "motive as well as the norm" for our actions.[43] Suicide is a violation of duty on this account because it requires the destruction of practical reason, of that part of ourselves which constitutes our "humanity." In the same way, intemperance is morally impermissible insofar as we reduce ourselves by its means to a mere animal state. As for our obligations to others: the ground of the duty of "practical love" or "benevolence" and of the "respect" that it requires us to show others as well as ourselves is, again, the "dignity of humanity," the capacity of rational choice.[44] In the name of best being able to respect this capacity we furthermore have the duty to cultivate in ourselves the kind of sympathetic feelings that enable us to "participate actively in the fate of others."[45]

These obligations are only applications of the thesis Kant argues in the opening paragraphs of the first section of his *Groundwork* that the basis of human dignity and morality is the goodwill or the faculty of practical reason. Strictly speaking, our affective natures are of no moral significance; they enter into consideration only because they can possibly hinder or aid our capacity to respect duty. What is essential about us, the only thing about us that has unconditional worth, is this capacity.

What the feminist critique challenges is not the importance of human judgment and self-determination, but their supposed independence from and priority over the affective side of our natures. As we have seen, the emotions are generally viewed by Kant with suspicion: both because even the most other-regarding variety may serve as a front behind which the "dear self" hides, and because unless emotions are regulated by practical reason, they are apt on his view to be untrustworthy in their discernment of duty. The only candidate for moral agency is the subject who is able to free herself of their determining influence.

But why should we embrace this conception of practical agency? Why assume that the sole form of human autonomy adequate to support our moral theory is one that an agent can achieve only in isolation from her contingent ends, her culture, history, and relations to others? What is ruled out on this model is the possibility that out of our social and personal attachments can evolve a kind of respect for self and others that reflects discrimination and is more than just a disguised form of self-love. The Kantian picture of agency seems to presuppose a context of distrust. My autonomy and identity as a moral subject is made to depend on my severing my ties to my community and relationships, because these are thought to endanger my capacity of self-determination and to interfere with my ability to be impartial in the face of competing self-interest. Left solely to the devices of inclination, I am a threat to my moral self and I threaten to neglect or infringe upon the moral selves of others. This is why practical love according to Kant must be commanded. It cannot be expected to be truly integrated into an agent's material ends in a sustained and reliable way.

Since our empirical motives are not to be trusted, they also cannot be included among the ingredients of human dignity. Suppose that the "adversities and hopeless sorrow" of the man contemplating suicide in Kant's *Groundwork* example refer to his deep personal loneliness or to the loss of his capacity to love.[46] None of this could possibly add up to a moral defense of suicide, because none of it threatens the destruction of his "dignity" or "humanity" as Kant has defined them. The only consideration that needs to be taken into account in determining the moral status of his proposed course of action is the possible harm he may do to his capacity of rational choice.

To those for whom identity formation involves community and connectedness to others in an essential way, the Kantian conception of autonomy is obviously problematic. According to Gilligan, it is not so much self-determination and independence that figure as the central ingredients of female identity, but empathy, cooperation, and trust. Or, these become virtues of a different kind of self-determination—one that places far less emphasis on detachment as a necessary condition. The other is experienced not so much as a potential threat as someone to be understood and someone through whom I may come to understand or know myself. For female identity on Gilligan's understanding, it is not in isolation but in connection with others that my autonomy as a moral agent as well as my moral obligations themselves first take form; and this connection requires the coordination of competing conceptions of the moral point of view. Because the real needs and interests of the members of my community—like the real contexts in which our choices are made—are subject to change, so will be the agreed-upon vision of morality. For those following Gilligan, there will thus be no guarantee that what is identified as the ground of duty or of human dignity will be beyond revision. There will on this account be no a priori metaphysical foundation.[47]

In important respects, the self that emerges out of Gilligan's observations of girls and women seems to resemble more a communitarian than a Kantian model of moral agency.[48] Because for Gilligan female identity development essentially involves community rather than detachment, the values associated with cooperation will rival in importance that of rational choice. Human autonomy will signify on the basis of the female's experience something in addition to practical reason; it will stand as well for the capacity to care for and connect with others. Because moral ends on this model emerge in the course of real-world relationships, the agent will find foreign the suggestion that those ends are antecedently fixed, and inhabit a noumenal or transcendent side of the self.

Because Kant's account of autonomy excludes the "difference" Gilligan discovers in female identity, his moral theory furthermore neglects to consider the special motivational problems that have burdened women more than men. Too willing to lose themselves in attending to the needs of others, women require not so much a check on self-love as on their propensity for self-denial. As Sandra Bartky, Cheshire Calhoun, and Alison Jaggar have suggested, for the sake of their own moral development, women need to allow their personal ends and desires to determine their behavior not less but more.[49] This does not mean that they are the more virtuous sex. It is intended only to point out another way in which Kantian morality fails to address women's experience.

What, finally, about the categorical imperative as a test of universaliza-bility? Given what was said above about the architectonic features of Kant's moral theory, how can the criticism be defended that his proce-dure for assessing moral worth is "anti-care" because it abstracts from particularity? Since Kant never fills in his moral theory for us at the applied level, we are reduced to guesswork when it comes to determining precisely where to draw the limits on the degree of specific content that should be considered part of an individual's maxim or part of the description of some action. For this reason, it is not clear that the objection that the categorical imperative test requires an excessive level of abstraction is valid. What *is* clear is that testing a maxim for universalizability, according to Kant, does *not* require (as so many critics have assumed) that we abstract away from the particularities of the given case.[50]

Two further versions of the feminist critique of the universalization procedure derive from some of the worries about Kant's conception of agency I mentioned above. The first challenges the particular vision of humanity Kant urges us to universalize or to realize in our "kingdom of ends." We test for universalizability because we want to ensure impartial-ity, ensure in other words that no case be given privileged treatment without warrant over others. In determining whether a maxim is univer-salizable, we ask whether it could be willed by all rational human agents or is compatible with the ends of rational human nature as such. If, however, our operative conception of rational human nature is itself biased in any way, then so will be the test devised to honor that conception. For those following Gilligan, as we have seen, there are reasons for skepticism about Kant's claim to have provided a model of practical agency that is valid universally. If Gilligan is right, there are reasons for revising that model to include a different voice.

The second version challenges what could be referred to as Kant's Cartesianism about human subjectivity. What is rejected is the concep-tion of agency required as a condition of the applicability of the universalization test. That a maxim has moral content (as is at least morally permissible) only when it can be willed as universal law by all rational agents means for Kant that it has moral content only when it is at least compatible with ends agents *qua* rational hold in common. There would be no point in testing for the universalizability of a maxim; in other words, could we not assume that there are ends we share not merely generally, but universally as rational agents? For those feminists who see their feminism closely allied to the project of "deconstructing" the very idea of a unified subject, however, there can be no demonstrably universal rational ends. This amounts to a rejection of Kant's conception of the nonempirical subject whose a priori laws condition the possibility of both our theoretical and practical experience. It is a line of criticism that, if successfully argued, would undermine the foundation not only of Kant's moral theory but of his epistemology as well.[51]

Notes

1. This essay originally appeared in the *Pacific Philosophical Quarterly* 71 (1990): 60–79. I owe thanks to the editors of that journal for their permission to reprint it here. At the suggestion of the editor of this volume I have added a few more comments in section 4 about feminist criticisms of the categorical imperative's test of universalization. I have also made minor (and for the most part, only stylistic) changes in other sections of the paper. The original version of this paper was written some eight years ago; I cannot say that I am willing now to embrace all of the views I defended then.

2. *In a Different Voice* (Cambridge: Harvard University Press, 1982). For discussions of the importance of the Gilligan-Kohlberg debate for moral theory, see Owen Flanagan and Kathryn Jackson, "Justice, Care, and Gender: The Kohlberg-Gilligan Debate Revisited," *Ethics* 97 (April 1987): 622–37; and Lawrence A. Blum, "Gilligan and Kohlberg: Implications for Moral Theory," *Ethics* 98 (April 1988): 472–91.

3. For example, the "virtue" critiques of Aristotelians like Alasdair MacIntyre and Charles Taylor; what might be called the "integrity" critiques of Bernard Williams, Lawrence M. Hinman, and Michael Stocker; and representing the Humean tradition, the objections raised by Annette Baier (references to individual works follow).

4. Here I have in mind as representative examples the Kant interpretations of Karl Ameriks, Barbara Herman, Christine Korsgaard, Onora O'Neill, and J. B. Schneewind among others (again, specific references follow).

5. Michael Stocker, "The Schizophrenia of Modern Ethical Theories," *Journal of Philosophy*, 73, no. 14 (August 1978): 454.

6. For other expressions of this kind of criticism, for example, see Susan Wolf, "Moral Saints," *Journal of Philosophy* 79, no. 8 (August 1982): 419–39; Lawrence M. Hinman, "On the Purity of Our Moral Motives: A Critique of Kant's Account of the Emotions and Acting for the Sake of Duty," *Monist* 66, no. 2 (April 1983): 251–67; Bernard Williams, "Persons, Character and Morality," in his collection *Moral Luck* (Cambridge: Cambridge University Press, 1981).

7. Barbara Herman, "Integrity and Impartiality," *Monist* 66, no. 2 (April 1983): 233–50.

8. Ibid., 237.

9. Herman cites as evidence Kant's *Doctrine of Virtue*, AK[456]. For further discussion of these points see also Herman, "On the Value of Acting from the Motive of Duty," *Philosophical Review* 90 (1981): 363–66; and Karl Ameriks, "The Hegelian Critique of Kantian Morality," in *New Essays on Kant*, ed. Bernard den Ouden and Marcia Moen (New York: Peter Lang, 1987).

10. "Integrity and Impartiality," 237. Marcia Baron makes the same point in "The Alleged Moral Repugnance of Acting from Duty," *Journal of Philosophy* 81, no. 4 (April 1984): 212.

See also Ameriks, "The Hegelian Critique of Kantian Morality," 197: "We are not obliged by Kant to hold only to what strict duty enjoins, nor need we have the thought of such duty foremost in our mind at the time of our action. But what moral worth does require is some implicit sensitivity to not being so immediately helpful that one would be willing to act at the cost of violating what is clearly owed as a matter of strict duty."

11. "On the Value of Acting From the Motive of Duty," 377. The passage Herman has in mind in the *Groundwork* is AK[398].

12. For example, *Critique of Practical Reason*, AK[73].

13. In "Integrity and Impartiality," 244, Herman puts this point the following way: "For Kant . . . commitment to impartial morality acknowledges the respect owed other persons. In his willingness to shape and limit his projects so that they do not conflict with the principles of respect for others, the moral person expresses his conception of himself as a member of a community of equal moral persons."

14. Other commentators who draw out this aspect of Kantian theory include Onora O'Neill, "Kant After Virtue," *Inquiry* 26 (1983), esp. 399; Thomas E. Hill, "The Importance of Autonomy," in *Women and Moral Theory*, ed. E. Kittay and D. Meyers (Totowa, N.J.: Rowman and Littlefield, 1987), esp. 132f.; J. B. Schneewind, "The Use of Autonomy in Ethical Theory," in *Reconstructing Individualism: Autonomy, Individuality, and the Self on Western Thought*, ed. T. Heller, M. Sosna, and D. Wellberg (Stanford: Stanford University Press, 1986), esp. 72f.

15. *Doctrine of Virtue*, AK [422]. Here, it is true, Kant presents the example in the form of a casuistic question. But in other discussions he makes it clear that he does not think that the duty of self-preservation is unconditional. See "On the Old Saw: That May Be Right in Theory but It Won't Work in Practice," where he tells us that the duty to preserve one's life is unconditional provided that in doing so one does not commit a crime. AK VIII [300n], translated by E. B. Ashton (Philadelphia: University of Pennsylvania Press, 1974), 68n. And in his *Lectures on Ethics*, he says that "if a man cannot preserve his life except by dishonouring his humanity, he ought rather to sacrifice it." Menzer edition [283f.], trans. Louis Infield (Indianapolis, Ind.: Hackett, 1963), 156.

16. *Doctrine of Virtue*, AK [421f.].

17. Ibid., AK [467f.]. See also his remarks in the preface to his *Metaphysical Elements of Justice* regarding the distinction between "metaphysical elements of justice" and the "empirical practice of law."

18. For a thorough discussion of the significance of these architectonic considerations, see Mary J. Gregor, *Laws of Freedom: A Study of Kant's Method of Applying the Categorical Imperative in the "Metaphysik der Sitten"* (Oxford: Basil Blackwell, 1963), esp. chap. 1. For a discussion of these architectonic considerations with reference to Kant's views on being, see my "On Lying and the Role of Content in Kant's Ethics," *Kant-Studien* 82, no. 1 (1991): 42–62.

19. This interpretation of the categorical imperative test is defended by Barbara Herman, esp. in "The Practice of Moral Judgment," *Journal of Philosophy* 82, no. 8 (August 1985); and by Onora O'Neill in "Kant After Virtue," esp. 392ff.

20. See again *Doctrine of Virtue*, AK [467f.]. As I said, Kant himself gives us little indication of precisely how much content can be built into an individual's maxim or into the description of an action if we are to properly carry the categorical imperative test out. In "Integrity and Impartiality," 247, Herman defends the view that in order to evaluate an individual's maxim, individuating features do need to be taken into account. This interpretation seems to me compatible with Kant's remarks in the *Doctrine of Virtue* regarding the content that would have to be included in an "appendix" to a metaphysics of morals. For an alternative interpretation of maxims as general and "indeterminate," however, see Onora O'Neill, "Kant After Virtue," 392ff.

21. See again O'Neill in "Kant After Virtue," 399; and Schneewind in "The Use of Autonomy in Ethical Theory," 72f.

22. Stuart Hampshire, "Public and Private Morality," in *Public and Private Morality*, ed. Stuart Hampshire (Cambridge: Cambridge University Press, 1978), 40. Quoted by Herman in "Integrity and Impartiality," 246.

23. See in "Integrity and Impartiality," 235.

24. "Integrity and Impartiality," esp. 234–38. Marcia Baron and Karl Ameriks follow the same line of argument in their above-cited essays.

25. *Critique of Practical Reason*, AK [33f.].

26. "Integrity and Impartiality," 238.

27. In Herman's words, 239: "it is no longer obvious [that is, given her corrective interpretation of Kantian theory] that the Kantian must prefer the beneficent (morally worthy) action to the helping action done from a nonmoral motive."

28. See, for example, *Groundwork for a Metaphysics of Morals*, AK [407f.].

29. *Critique of Practical Reason*, AK [19].

30. See G. W. F. Hegel, *Philosophy of Right*, esp. §§133–135. Here I am arguing against the interpretation of Hegel's critique of Kant's ethics I presented in "Hegel's Critique of the Subjective Idealism of Kant's Ethics," *Journal of the History of Philosophy* 26, no. 1 (January 1988): 89–105, and in "On the Relation of Pure Reason to Content: A Reply to Hegel's Critique of Formalism in Kant's Ethics," *Philosophy and Phenomenological Research* 49, no. 1 (September 1988): 59–80.

31. See Kant's Introduction to his *Metaphysics of Morals*, AK [222], and his *Groundwork*, AK [428].

32. *Groundwork*, AK [428].

33. Seyla Benhabib, "The Generalized and the Concrete Other: The Kohlberg-Gilligan Controversy and Feminist Theory," in *Feminism as Critique: Essays on the Politics of Gender in Late-Capitalist Societies*, ed. Seyla Benhabib and Drucilla Cornell (Cambridge: Polity Press, 1987), 81.

34. AK II [231] (my translation).

35. §48.

36. From "The Character of the Sexes" in Kant's *Anthropology From a Pragmatic Point of View*, trans. Mary J. Gregor (The Hague: Martinus Nijhoff, 1974). See also *Metaphysical Elements of Justice*, §§24–26.

37. AK VIII, Part II [295].

38. For a discussion of Kant's political philosophy and the status of women, see Susan Mendus, "Kant: An Honest but Narrow-Minded Bourgeois?" in *Women in Western Political Philosophy: Kant to Nietzsche*, ed. Ellen Kennedy and Susan Mendus (Hempstead, Great Britain: Wheatsheaf Books, 1987). See also Kant's *Metaphysical Elements of Justice*, §46. For a more general discussion of Kant on feeling, see Robin M. Schott, "Kant's Treatment of Sensibility" in *New Essays on Kant*, ed. Bernard den Ouden and Marcia Moen (New York: Peter Lang, 1987). See also esp. chaps. 8 and 9 of Schott's *Cognition and Eros: A Critique of the Kantian Paradigm* (University Park: Pennsylvania State University Press, 1988).

39. See in "The Practice of Moral Judgment," 429–31.

40. AK [398].

41. AK [407f.].

42. *Anthropology From a Pragmatic Point of View*, §74.

43. AK [386]. I use Mary Gregor's translation of *The Doctrine of Virtue* (Philadelphia, University of Pennsylvania Press, 1964).

44. AK [448].

45. AK [456].

46. AK [398]. Here I use Robert Paul Wolff's translation, *Foundations of the Metaphysics of Morals* (Indianapolis, Ind.: Bobbs-Merrill Educational Publishing, 1969).

47. This discussion owes a great deal to Annette Baier's excellent "Trust and Antitrust," *Ethics* 96 (January 1986): 231–60.

48. Here I have in mind Michael J. Sandel's critique of the Rawlsian moral subject in *Liberalism and the Limits of Justice* (Cambridge: Cambridge University Press, 1982).

49. See Bartky's "Feeding Egos and Tending Wounds: Deference and Disaffection in Women's Emotional Labor," in her collection *Femininity and Domination: Studies in the Phenomenology of Oppression* (New York: Routledge, Chapman and Hall, 1990); Cheshire Calhoun, "Justice, Care, and Gender Bias," *Journal of Philosophy* 85, no. 9 (September 1988), esp. 459; Alison M. Jaggar, *Feminist Politics and Human Nature* (Totowa, N.J.: Rowman and Allanhead, 1983), esp. 44–48.

50. The idea that Kant's emphasis on universalizability requires that we abstract from difference or particularity in our acts of moral assessment shows up in much feminist criticism. In *Feminine and Feminist Ethics* (Belmont, Calif.: Wadsworth, 1993), 64, Rosemarie Tong seems to assume, for example, that because "Kantians bid us to have equal respect and consideration for persons simply because they are persons," we are not allowed to attend to those features which distinguish persons, or to "favor our loved ones' interests over those of strangers."

In section 3 of her essay "The Generalized and the Concrete Other: The Kohlberg-Gilligan Controversy in Moral Theory" (cited above), Seyla Benhabib expresses a similar worry. Kant's noumenal agent, like the self behind Rawls's "veil of ignorance," on her characterization, is "disembedded and disembodied." In other words, it has no individuating features. But a self that has no individuating features, she argues, cannot carry out the universalization procedure properly. The universalization test (on the Kantian formulation) requires that I ask myself whether my maxim could be willed by all rational agents. But, Benhabib asks, "Can moral situations be individuated independently of our knowledge of the agents involved in these situations, of their histories, attitudes, characters and desires? . . . While every procedure of universalizability presupposes that 'like cases ought to be treated alike' . . . , the most difficult aspect of any such procedure is to know what constitutes a 'like' situation or what it would mean for another to be exactly in a situation like mine. Such a process of reasoning, to be at all viable, must involve the viewpoint of the concrete [vs. "generalized"] other."

While Benhabib raises interesting and important criticisms of Kant in this essay, I believe that this particular objection is based on a mistake. It is of course in some sense true that the Kantian noumenal subject is the key player in his moral theory. If the self did not "belong" to the noumenal as well as to the phenomenal realm, in his view, we could not account for the possibility of its freedom from laws of nature. We could therefore also not account for the possibility of moral imputation. But this does not mean, as Benhabib suggests, that it is the noumenal ("disembodied . . .") subject that formulates and tests maxims. Doing so on Kant's account requires precisely the kind of sensitivity and judgment that Benhabib tells us the Kantian practical agent necessarily lacks. Kant does insist upon the importance of carefully formulating our maxims, and that means carefully attending to the particularities of the given case. To do this, we have to rely on imperfect human judgment; we have to rely on the understanding of behavior and motivation we have gained *through experience*. Our noumenal subjectivity only comes in as a condition of the possibility of testing a maxim's moral status. Then we ask whether the maxim is compatible with ends rational agents share universally—ends we have as members of the noumenal realm. As I have mentioned, feminists may have good reasons for wanting to reject Kant's insistence that our phenomenal or empirical selves cannot be constitutive of our moral agency, strictly speaking. But I believe that Benhabib is wrong to suggest that it is the noumenal subject who goes about the mundane business of formulating and testing maxims (regarding Kant's views on formulating maxims, see note 20 above).

Finally, for a good discussion from a feminist standpoint of the impartialist/partialist controversy, see Marilyn Friedman's "The Social Self and the Partiality Debates," in *Feminist Ethics*, ed. Claudia Card (Lawrence: University Press of Kansas, 1991), 161–79. Friedman correctly points out that "only a few moral impartialists" (and she does not mention Kant here) assume that impartiality requires that, in the name of "equal treatment," we ignore the special demands of particular relationships.

51. For an expression of this position, see, for example, Iris Marion Young, "The Ideal of Community and the Politics of Difference," in *Feminism/Postmodernism*, ed. Linda J. Nicholson (New York: Routledge, Chapman and Hall, 1990).

4

Feminist Ethics: How It Could Benefit from Kant's Moral Philosophy

Herta Nagl-Docekal
Translated by Stephanie Morgenstern

In this essay I shall show that Kant's moral philosophy contains distinctions that can be of relevance to feminist ethics. The recent debate on some core concepts of care ethics has led to problems that call for a renewed reading of Kant. In particular, I shall expose the dilemma that, while care ethics claims to offer an alternative to a universalist conception of morality, it tacitly presupposes precisely such a conception. Kant's theory of a formal universalism can be instrumental for dissolving this dilemma and for redefining feminist ethics in a way that no longer restricts it to the question of whether or not there exists a specifically feminine mode of moral reasoning.

Before taking up this task, however, it is necessary to address the fact that Kant was convinced women were incapable of acting in accordance with what he described as the ideal type of morality. Only men, in his view, could act out of respect for the moral law; only men could do good out of a sense of duty. With regard to women, Kant wrote: "I hardly believe that the fair sex is capable of principles."[1] This view, which Kant first put forward in his *Observations on the Feeling of the Beautiful and Sublime,* is not one I have any intention of glossing over here. Nor do I suppose that the Kant of the *Groundwork of the Metaphysic of Morals* had distanced himself from the ideas on gender difference that he had been expressing in the period before he wrote the *Critique of Pure Reason.* On the contrary, a remark in the *Groundwork* suggests that we should postulate a continuity in Kant's assessment of women's moral action.[2] Further support for such a continuity theory comes from his later work, notably in the *Anthropology from a Pragmatic Point of View,* where Kant took up his early thinking on gender difference once again.[3]

The present essay addresses a different issue. Here I propose to discuss not Kant's theories regarding the morality of women but rather the question of whether the basic categories of Kantian moral philosophy contain elements that, irrespective of their author's view on gender differences, admit to a feminist appropriation.

Some authors will of course object to the very question. Lawrence Blum provides a paradigm of the way of thinking that entails a fundamental objection to my project. To begin with, Blum notes that men and women have different virtues attributed to them. Where men are expected to develop "rationality, strength of will, adherence to universal principle and duty," women are supposedly distinguished by "sympathy, compassion, human concern, kindness, and emotional supportiveness."[4] He goes on to contend that "moral rationalism" (his use of the term embraces the moral philosophies of both Kant and Hegel) elevates the male virtues as the ideal type of morality: "In this way the rationalist's moral ideals are a kind of morally idealized projection of the typical gender characteristics of males in a male-dominated society" (296). At the same time, Blum maintains the qualities that typify women are neglected; consequently, the moral rationalist finds it "natural . . . to ignore or underplay the female qualities as they are found in his society" (297). In light of this assessment, any attempt to adopt Kant's moral philosophy within a feminist framework appears contradictory. From Blum's point of view, such an attempt would suggest that women should in fact themselves devalue their qualities and take their cue from male ideals.

However, Blum's concept of "moral rationalism" fails to reflect precisely enough the structure of Kant's argument. (This is not the place to debate the validity of his interpretation of Hegel.) The starting point of Kant's theory of morality is the question of which ideal we all—that is, women as well as men—have in mind when we use the term "good" in a moral sense. The very first sentence of the *Groundwork* indicates that it was this question Kant focused on: "It is impossible to conceive anything at all in the world, or even out of it, which can be taken as good without qualification, except a good will" (61). Kant's primary objective is therefore to clarify the term "moral" generally, and only secondly does he examine the question of who is capable of obeying the moral law. In the context of this subordinate question, Kant not only expresses his doubts about the competence of women to act out of respect for the moral law; he notes as well that "principles . . . are also extremely rare in the male."[5] Moreover, he stresses that even with regard to one's own actions, one is not able to state with certainty whether duty or some private interest constituted the crucial motive (*Groundwork*, 74–75). In short, Kant's definition of the "good will" formulates an ideal that proves difficult for everyone to implement. From this perspective, Blum's suggestion that Kant's concept of morality coincides with "the typical gender characteristics of males in a male-dominated society" lacks plausibility. It rather seems adequate, as a reading strategy, to take seriously Kant's claim that his analysis of morality presents an ideal of general validity. One matter that needs to be discussed in this context is that what may be problematic about Kant's concept of morality, from a feminist point of view, is not its claim to be of relevance to all of us, but rather the way in which it is, in a second step, linked to a patriarchal construction of gender difference. (Space does not permit me, however, to take up the issue here.) This issue raises a further consideration: As long as Kant's claim to generality is not invalidated, it cannot be ruled out as inadmissible to inquire whether Kant's moral philosophy might have some contribution to make to feminist ethics.

Before undertaking this inquiry, I shall address some doubts that readers are likely to have in mind. Many authors who contributed to the development of feminist ethics conceived of it as a counterpoint to Kant's moral philosophy. This is the case particularly with those for whom the object of feminist ethics consists in the analysis of a specifically feminine way to deal with moral dilemmas. (However, as will be explained below, this is not the only possible project for a feminist ethics.) The concept of "caring," which was introduced to characterize the mode of moral thinking typical of women, is usually defined in contradistinction to any kind of ethics associating morality with a universally binding rule. "Caring" is commonly described as attending to the specific needs of individual others, and this attitude is perceived as precluding the logic of universalization, as it is analyzed in Kant's theory of the categorical imperative. (I shall discuss the notion of "caring" in more detail later.) Annette Baier's writings offer a paradigm here. Baier is concerned with whether or not the tradition of moral philosophy provides the means to specify the form of moral thinking that characterizes women. The title of her essay, "Hume, the Women's Moral Theorist,"[6] indicates her conclusion. In this essay, Baier interprets the morality of women with the aid of Hume's concept of "sympathy." From this point of view, she takes up the controversy between Hume and Kant. She rejects Kant's concept of universality, blaming it for misrepresenting morality as obedience to a "book of rules."[7] She argues: "To become a good fellow-person one doesn't consult some book of rules, but cultivates one's capacity for sympathy, or fellow feeling" (40). (As I shall explain below, the prime issue to be discussed regarding this argument is not whether women are indeed "Humeans rather than Kantians" (40), but whether or not this way of reading Kant's moral philosophy is correct.)

To examine this version of feminist ethics, a step-by-step procedure is required. First, I shall point out that care ethics in fact addresses two different issues that are conjoined and need to be distinguished clearly. At one level, the core concern is the detection of gender differences in moral reasoning; at the other level, the issue is a juxtaposition of two philosophical concepts of morality assumed to be mutually exclusive: the concept grounding morality on a universal law versus the concept focusing on care (i.e., on particularity).

As regards the first level, theories such as Gilligan's, which I shall term "duality theories," distinguish two gender-specific types of moral reasoning. These have been met in recent years with many challenges, a number of which I find convincing. Because I gave a more comprehensive account elsewhere,[8] I shall only summarize a few of these arguments here. One objection claims that the duality theory is not supported empirically. Gertrud Nunner-Winkler and Rainer Döbert, for instance, found in their empirical studies that sensitivity to context does not depend on feminine gender identity but on the degree of personal involvement.[9]

Other critics pointed out that the material used by Gilligan could just as well have allowed for a different, nondualistic interpretation.[10] Another reservation to the duality theory questions its normative pretensions. Critics such as Claudia Card,[11] Barbara Houston,[12] and Sarah Lucia Hoagland[13] argue that attributing high value to the virtues traditionally associated with women risks obscuring the fact that those virtues evolved in conditions of patriarchal domination and result in women's (self-)exploitation. Discussing this problem, Alison Jaggar concludes that theories which recommend that women cultivate virtues commonly classified as feminine do not address the genuine concern of feminism. She therefore suggests a wider definition of the project of feminist ethics, one that would include addressing the manifold subordination of women as a moral problem.[14] (I shall return to this topic later.)

My opinion regarding the duality theory is this: It can certainly not be denied that women and men (in Western culture, at least) behave, and are expected to behave, in typically different ways. Virtues, for instance, that rank highly in public esteem if displayed by a woman may discredit a man, and vice versa. This does not prove, however, that there exist in fact two types of *moral* reasoning. I suggest a distinction here between custom and morality. The specific virtues attributed to women and men respectively enforce the gender relations that are customary in a certain culture. Yet to act in accordance with these expectations does not necessarily mean to act morally. As the reflections of Card, Houston, Hoagland, and Jaggar mentioned above indicate, it may sometimes prove necessary, from a moral perspective, to break with virtues sanctioned by custom, as is the case when patriarchal habits need to be overthrown. Speaking more generally, in spite of the obvious gender differences in behavior, it cannot be ruled out that women and men draw upon shared categories where morality proper is concerned (this issue will be taken up again below). Support for the distinction between custom and morality I am suggesting here is provided by the fact that—the divergent behavior patterns of women and men notwithstanding—empirical studies such as Nunner-Winkler's and Döbert's do not discover significant gender differences in the reasoning on issues that the test subjects perceived as genuinely moral.

Due to the number of problems that were exposed, the duality theory has been losing ground in the recent debate. One characteristic demand is Marilyn Friedman's call for a "de-moralization of gender,"[15] suggesting that the concept of a division of labor between women and men with regard to moral competence should be dropped. This demand signals a move toward what was above called the second level of the discourse on care ethics. The core concern at this level is no longer gender difference but the search for the most adequate understanding of morality. Discussing this issue, a number of authors claim superiority for care ethics; they argue that the behavior called "caring" implies a model of morality relevant to men as well as women. In this sense, Nel Noddings states that her notion of caring is intended to "achieve an ultimate transcendence of the masculine and feminine in moral matters."[16] Carol Gilligan also notes, especially in more recent publications, that the perspective of care is not necessarily restricted to women.[17] In her view, a caring attitude is most promising when applied to the crises of the present; this "promise . . . lies in the fact that human survival, in the late twentieth century, may depend less on formal agreement than on human connection."[18]

This quotation indicates the method that is usually applied in this context. Two models of morality are set up for comparison: the care perspective is confronted with what Gilligan called the justice perspective. When defining the latter, many authors refer to Kant's concept of the moral law.[19] Then, in view of this juxtaposition, it is concluded that in order to explain the achievements of the model of caring, it is necessary to claim its superiority over the moral philosophy of Kant. I intend to challenge the presupposition that the care perspective and the perspective of the moral law are, in fact, mutually exclusive.

DUCK VERSUS RABBIT—AN IMAGE OF MORAL THEORY?

One basic premise of the theory to be discussed here is that every moral dilemma can be solved in two possible ways: either in the mode of justice or in the mode of care. Carol Gilligan and Grant Wiggins illustrate this proposition with Jastrow's jumping image, as used in Gestalt psychology, which may be seen either as a duck or as a rabbit.[20] Stressing the meaninglessness of asking which is the "right" way to see it, they note "an irreducible sense of ethical ambiguity" ("Origins," 128). (If they then nevertheless describe the care perspective as superior, they do so only with reference to the specific background of relationships behind each of the "two logics," but more on that later.) However, the argument based on placing the two perspectives side by side turns out to have flaws that ultimately make it untenable.

Let us look at the perspective of justice first. How is this perspective described by the authors opting for an ethics of care? Summarizing the definitions that seem to be widely accepted, what is meant by the logic of justice is a way of thinking that presupposes a contract between autonomous, equal partners[21] and that sees other people not as individuals in their particularity but as "generalized others"[22]—that is to say, from the viewpoint of "an abstract rational nature in virtue of which we are all alike."[23] This way of thinking is further characterized by its reliance upon "a host of narrow and rigidly defined principles"[24] that are understood as possessing universal validity and are "rigidly applied to a situation" ("Origins," 134). with the principles of "noninterference" and "impartiality"[25] constituting the foundation. Certainly, there are some differences in the definitions of the justice perspective provided by individual authors, but this is not my concern here. By outlining a general profile of the justice perspective, as it is seen and dismissed from the viewpoint of care ethics, I intended to prompt the question, Can this profile really claim to reflect a *moral* stance? What is described here certainly does not correspond to what anyone has in mind, in everyday life, when the term "moral" is used. Moreover, neither one of the definitions just cited can claim to render accurately the way in which morality was characterized by Kant (as will be explained below). Rather, this profile comprises elements of what is discussed in philosophy of law. The discourse on care ethics shows a want of sophistication here in that it fails to distinguish the spheres of law and morality.

Since the concept of a contract between autonomous equal partners or the principle of noninterference were not intended by the philosophers of the Enlightenment to define morality in the first place, it is wrong to criticize them for reflecting a lack of moral sensibility. Rather, they are components of a theory of the modern state. That they continue to be indispensable is shown not only by such contemporary studies on democratic theory as those of John Rawls and Jürgen Habermas, but also by a series of publications on feminist legal theory.[26] (Of course, present-day conceptions of the state also go beyond the theoretical elements just assembled. The latter are derived from the original liberalist model and leave the development of welfare-state concepts out of consideration. It is in this sense that Friedman complains of Gilligan having not taken on board the discourse about welfare law.[27] Generally speaking, one focus of contemporary legal discourse in many countries is on how legislation can take account of special needs, for example, needs pertaining to the specific situation of women on the labor market.)[28]

My point here is that the duck-rabbit image, as used by care theorists, is misleading. It may indeed be the case that one and the same practical conflict admit different solutions, depending on whether it is seen as a legal or as a moral question. However, there is no duplication of morality involved. The very essay in which Gilligan introduces the ambiguous figure of Gestalt psychology illustrates this point. Where Gilligan explains the difference between the two orientations, she characterizes the justice perspective as "judging the conflicting claims of self and others against a standard of equality or equal respect (the Categorical Imperative, the Golden Rule)."[29] But what makes her think that this procedure of judgment marks a form of moral orientation? Gilligan fails to show where Kant, in his characterization of morality, would employ the notion of mutuality that obviously informs the standard to which she refers. And this evidence could hardly be produced. Kant's concept of morality is strictly asymmetrical: I am obliged to respect and do good to others, regardless of how they treat me.[30] Gilligan also does not acknowledge that Kant has made it quite clear that the categorical imperative is not to be confused with the Golden Rule (Groundwork, 97). One topic discussed above might be taken up here once more: It may well be the case that men, given that they have customarily been assigned to the public sphere, are more likely than women to be predisposed to viewing conflicts from a legal perspective; but this does not prove the existence of gender differences in moral reasoning. To illustrate this point, it is again possible to use one of Gilligan's own examples. As is well known, Gilligan refers to the short story "A Jury of Her Peers," written by Susan Glaspell, emphasizing that the male and female characters are portrayed as reacting differently to a murder case. But she fails to address the fact that the male figure whose mode of thinking she considers representative of the masculine form of morality is a sheriff who deals with the crime from the perspective of this occupation.[31]

Why do care theorists tend to run together the levels of law and morality? I think this has to do with imprecise handling of the term "universalism." On the one hand this term is identified with the liberalist concept of citizenship that operates with the notion of equal and "generalized" subjects; on the other, it is used to refer to the philosophies that define being moral as obeying a general law. One context in which this ambiguity becomes apparent—and where it results in a number of problems—is the interpretation of Kant favored by care theorists. This interpretation neglects the following fact: liberalist conceptions are indeed to be found in Kant's philosophy—but in his theory of the state and in his philosophy of history, not in his moral philosophy. While, for instance, the principle of noninterference is an essential element of Kant's reflections on the right of every citizen to free self-development, this principle is not, as Kant underscores, an equivalent to the categorical imperative (*Groundwork*, 97).

The failure of care theorists to apprehend these differentiations in Kant's practical philosophy is shown by the way many of their statements claiming to be criticisms of the universalism of Kantian moral philosophy make no reference to the detailed explanations Kant gave of the meaning of the categorical imperative. I shall cite but one example (apart from Gilligan's assumption just mentioned, that the categorical imperative amounts to a concept of mutuality). In her essay "Hume, the Women's Moral Theorist," Baier praises Hume for starting from the bond between parents and children: "This relationship, and the obligations and virtues it involves, lack three central features of relations between moral agents as understood by Kantians and contractarians—it is intimate, it is unchosen, and is between unequals."[32] Baier then criticizes the Kantian approach for getting "into obvious trouble both with duties of young children to their unchosen parents, to whom no binding commitments have been made, and of initially involuntary parents to their children" (45). She fails to take into account, however, that the concept of the social contract, albeit one of the foundations of Kant's political philosophy, is not a defining element of Kant's understanding of morality. Consequently, the problem Baier claims to detect is not actually present in Kant's writings; on the contrary, Kant discusses the moral obligation of parents and children toward one another at several occasions.[33] (Generally speaking, a deplorable split seems to have evolved in the current debates on Kant. On the one hand, there are authors such as Barbara Herman and Onora O'Neill who investigate the inner structure of Kant's moral philosophy in a very elaborate manner—O'Neill also explaining how moral issues brought to the fore by feminist activists could be theoretically clarified on the basis of distinctions provided by Kant.[34] On the other hand, there are care theorists criticizing Kant without taking into account the results of those investigations.) In the following section of this paper, I shall try to show that the ambiguity surrounding the concept of "universalism" leads to a deadlock in the current debate on care ethics.

(By the way, the problem of ambiguity also surrounds the term *autonomy* as it is commonly understood in the current debate, not only on care ethics but also on feminist theory in general. It has become a widely accepted view that Kant, in introducing this concept, is suggesting—and needs to be criticized for suggesting—that we perceive human beings as isolated and detached. Yet such an understanding fails to recognize the different meanings the term *autonomy* has been endowed with in psychology and in philosophy. For instance, whereas object relations theory employs this concept to describe the way boys seek detachment from their mothers, autonomy is not used as a psychological category by Kant.[35] Instead, the term is introduced in his writings in the course of the discussion of what it means to be morally responsible.)

CARING AS THE MORAL NORM FOR ALL?

Let us turn now to morality, as a sphere distinct from the sphere of justice. As several authors have postulated that the care model should have the same relevance for men and women, the debate culminates in the question, Can the care theory really claim superiority over universalist moral conceptions? It is therefore important to analyze the individual elements of the care theory more closely. In essence, as we have seen, there are three characteristics by which care is usually defined: it is sensitive to context, it is guided by relationships, and it is governed by feelings. Each of those features will be shown to have universalist implications that have not as yet been clarified.

First, the call for individuals to be perceived and supported in their particularity and in their specific situation is certainly compelling. For instance, if somebody refuses to help others in fulfilling their personal needs although assistance could easily be given, he or she can hardly claim to be acting morally. This is part of our daily experience: someone standing in front of a vending machine asks us to change a bill; someone is lost and asks for directions, and so forth. To deny such requests, without any necessity to do so, is certainly not what we normally call moral behavior. At the same time, of course, one must bear in mind that the call for sensitivity to context itself has no particularist character. What makes us think that others should be helped in situations such as those just sketched? Obviously, we are guided by a principle like this: "I have the duty to assist others, insofar as this is possible, where they are unable to pursue their self-chosen ends on their own." As will be shown later, this principle is identical with one of the elements Kant claims are contained in the categorical imperative. At this point a dilemma becomes apparent: while care theorists claim to offer an alternative to moral universalism, they introduce the "particularity-is-to-be-respected" concept, which, on closer inspection, turns out to be a universal moral principle.

A further point may be useful to illustrate this dilemma. There are repeatedly cases where the moral requirement appears to be precisely that we should not comply with individual wishes we are asked to fulfill. Such situations arise daily in education. As Noddings points out, a "sort of conflict occurs when what the cared-for wants is not what we think would be best for him."[36] In response to this problem, she defines the concept of caring in a way that includes the maxim to do "what we think would be best for . . . the cared-for." What exactly does this mean? How do adults who take their responsibility seriously proceed if, let's say, a young child wants to play in a street with heavy traffic? Clearly, their actions will be guided by the conviction that what matters more than granting the wish the child actually expresses is protecting the safety and health of the child. Our common notion of morality also requires us to act in this manner in cases where we see a child in danger whom we are not in charge of, nor even acquainted with. But what is the basis for our conviction that to act morally means to provide protection in such a case? There must be a principle like this involved: "It is my duty to help others, wherever I can, to become or to remain human beings who are as fully as possible in command of their capacities, and thereby to enable them to pursue their self-chosen ends." This principle again corresponds with Kant's explanation of the meaning of the categorical imperative. In other words, our caring for this particular child in this specific situation of danger is grounded in a universal moral principle. Thus, we are confronted once more with the dilemma pointed out above: focusing on particularity, care theorists invoke precisely the kind of universality they claim to reject.

Second, as for the theory that human attachments must have relevance for moral behavior, two versions are to be found. One is related to the "addressees," the other to the "agents" reflecting their morality. In the former case, what matters is the principle of seeing others not as isolated individuals but in terms of the networks of relationships in which they are embedded. This principle became explosively important, for example, in the context of feminist discussions of the regulation normally governing divorce in the United States. Feminists criticized the fact that decisions about who should be granted custody of the children are often made in accordance with abstract criteria: for example, giving greater consideration to the income of each spouse than to the attachment of each to the children.[37] As these practical applications indicate, the demand to take emotional ties into account is thoroughly plausible. Yet a further differentiation is needed here. There are cases where we would consider it immoral to support an existing relationship. Examples are found plentifully again within the area of education. Where teenagers get involved in circles of drug addicts or in cliques performing terrorist attacks, we are convinced that our moral duty is not to support these ties but to help the youngsters to develop alternative attachments. Here the question arises, How do we decide which relationships deserve our support and which do not? If we do not wish to end up with arbitrary decisions—in which case we would not be able to call our actions moral—a criterion is needed. In order to justify our decision, however, we must refer to the same universal principle that was shown to form the basis for protective measures. But this means that we are confronted once again with the dilemma exposed above.

The second version consists in seeing attachments as the source of morality. It too has been subject to a twofold interpretation. On the one hand, morality has been understood as the spontaneous attentiveness in which close emotional bonds find expression. In this case, however, moral behavior remains restricted to small groups. In her argument with Noddings, Claudia Card, among others, sets this out as a serious shortcoming. She complains that the theory referring to group solidarity "threatens to exclude as ethically insignificant our relationship with most people in the world,"[38] and she reminds us on this matter that "we can affect drastically, even fatally, people we will never know as individuals" (103). What she obviously has in mind are problems such as those caused by radioactive waste, which poses a health risk for people who are not yet born. Hoagland makes a similar reproach when she writes: "An ethics that leaves starving people in a distant land outside the realm of moral consideration is inadequate."[39]

On the other hand, the attachment argument has been propounded in such a way that the behavior typical of relationships grounded in love (e.g., the caring relationship between mother and child) is seen as the starting point for a more widely apprehended morality. It is in this sense that Gilligan and Wiggins underline the importance of early childhood experiences: "The experience of attachment profoundly affects the child's understanding of human feelings and how people should act toward one another. The moral implications of attachment relationships have generally been overlooked in theories of moral development. . . . Yet the experience of attachment generates a perspective on relationships that underlies the conception of morality as love" ("Origins," 115). For them, this is also where the ultimate superiority of caring becomes clear. Gilligan and Wiggins conclude that, whereas the justice approach comes about through a process of detachment in which "norms and rules become reified as 'self-chosen principles,' removed from the relational contexts which give them life and meaning" (134), the caring perspective consists in transferring the ability to relate to others acquired through early attachments to someone "who is otherwise a stranger" (137). "Moral immaturity may consist not in an absence of general moral knowledge but in an absence of the attachments necessary for making moral notions moral insights" (134).

The moral requirement here involves acting toward other people *as if* a close attachment existed. To achieve this, a process of generalization is called for. This may not always be done in a reflective manner; nevertheless, it is necessary first to abstract from the distinctive character of the caring relation experienced in early childhood, to focus on the basic pattern of caring, and then to transfer this pattern to the level of our actions toward persons to whom we are not attached, including anyone "who is otherwise a stranger." But why should we apply the pattern of caring to everyone who might be affected by our actions? It becomes apparent once more that the care ethic, albeit unintentionally, rests on a universal moral principle. Nel Noddings, at one point, concedes this herself as she writes: "My first and unending obligation is to meet the other as one-caring."[40]

Turning now to the third characteristic feature of care ethics, namely the proposition that emotions rather than reason are operative in actions that truly qualify as moral, further tensions need to be exposed. On the one hand, the importance of emotion is obvious. Noddings, for instance, certainly makes a convincing point when she writes (in reference to

Kierkegaard) "to be touched, to have aroused in me something that will disturb my own ethical reality, I must see the other's reality as a possibility for my own."[41] On the other hand, numerous reservations have been expressed to an ethics basing morality on emotion. In this context, although space does not allow me, it would be appropriate to discuss the objections advanced throughout the history of moral philosophy to attempts to outline an ethics of feeling (that of Hume, for instance). There are also feminists expressing misgivings with regard to such attempts. The salient claim in their reservations is that feelings can also have damaging consequences for others, and therefore require reflective control. It is in this sense that Hoagland notes the "conflict . . . between resentment and tenderness" that characterizes the emotional state of mothers, mentioning, among other things, the problem of child abuse.[42] Drawing upon similar arguments, Friedman points out that close attachments condition a susceptibility to emotional injury such as can never arise in less personal relationships. She accuses Gilligan of leaving out of account the potential for violence and suffering latent in intimate relationships.[43] Such reservations suggest that an intention to act morally calls for critical reflection on one's own emotional reactions rather than blind reliance on them. This raises the question of the criteria to be applied in that kind of critical reflection. What is required here is a principle such as this: "I am not to act out emotions that entail my doing harm to others." The basis for such a principle apparently is a universal concept of human dignity and respect for others. Given that such a control of emotional impulses is needed, it seems no longer plausible to assume that feeling, rather than the universal principle that guides critical reflection on it, forms the actual basis of morality. This was clearly the direction taken by some of the experimental subjects whose statements were evaluated for *In a Different Voice*. Some of the women formulated a universal principle, though Gilligan did not take this up. One of the women, for example, tackling Heinz's dilemma, argued as follows: "Heinz should steal the drug, whether or not he loves his wife, 'by virtue of the fact that they are both there.' Although a person may not like someone else 'you have to love someone else. . . . That other person is part of that giant collection of everybody.' "[44]

An ethics of feeling also has relativist implications. The imperative to follow one's own emotions leads to the question of how morality is to be determined at all, if not in terms of "do what feels good."[45] Jaggar, who has discussed this question, points out that it is also not possible, on the basis of such an approach, for feminist criticism to have any binding force: "Such a view would seem to preclude feminist moral criticism of the domination of women, where this is an accepted practice, and even to entail that only feminists are bound by feminist ethics."[46] (I shall return below to the problem Jaggar identifies here.)

FEMINIST ETHICS

It has now become clear in various ways that the debate thus far has led to the following paradoxical situation: In care ethics, as it is commonly defined, a universalist conception of morality is rejected and at the same time required or, rather, tacitly presupposed. In my opinion, the reason for this is that the afore-mentioned ambiguity of the concept of "universalism" has remained largely unnoticed. Therefore, there seems to be a need to recall the variant of this concept that is proper to moral philosophy, as distinct from the liberalist and jurisprudential variant. The focus here is on the formal universalism elaborated by Kant and transformed and further developed by discourse theory and transcendental pragmatics. However, in taking up this theoretical tradition, my prime concern is not with the history of philosophy; rather, I am interested in demonstrating that a reconstruction of that kind of universalist moral philosophy may help to resolve the tiresome paradox.

The crucial point is precisely that formal universalism does not amount to "a host of narrow and rigidly defined principles."[47] On the contrary, its core concept is only one formal rule, which Kant called "the categorical imperative." According to the third of the formulations set out in the *Groundwork of the Metaphysic of Morals*, this imperative demands that we respect humanity in every human being (i.e., both in my own person and in every other person) (96). Commenting on this formulation, Kant highlights two elements. According to his explanation, the categorical imperative implies on the one hand a prohibition that says people must never be used "simply as a means," that is, instrumentalized against their will. On the other hand, it embodies the precept that humanity must always be valued "as an end in itself"; in other words, it must be acknowledged that to be a person means to be competent to determine one's ends for oneself.

In the present context, it is chiefly this precept (i.e., the second of the two elements) that needs to be examined more closely. It turns out to express a more demanding concept of morality than does the element of prohibition, as it entails additional duties. From the viewpoint of the prohibition alone, actions seem morally unproblematic as long as they do not use people "simply as means," whereas from the viewpoint of the precept to acknowledge the faculty of self-determination in every person, it is not enough, for someone who intends to act morally, simply to refrain from doing any harm to others. What exactly is Kant's argument here? His starting point is the observation that, while people are equal as regards the faculty of self-determination as such, it is precisely through that faculty that the differences between them develop. Their practical decisions are shaped individually. Kant uses the term "happiness" in this context (*Groundwork*, 98). As he explained earlier in the *Groundwork*, while the search for happiness is a "natural end," each person looks for happiness in her or his particular way. Happiness cannot be defined in a manner that has general validity (85). One consequence is this: The requirement to acknowledge the faculty of self-determination in every person, which is implied in the one moral law, means that it is a duty insofar as it is possible (and insofar as it is consistent with morality) to support others in the pursuit of their individual ideas of happiness. Kant states: "Now humanity could no doubt subsist if everybody contributed nothing to the happiness of others but at the same time refrained from deliberately impairing their happiness. This is, however, merely to agree negatively and not positively with humanity as an end in itself unless everyone endeavors also, so far as in him lies, to further the ends of others. For the ends of a subject who is an end in himself must, if this conception is to have its full effect on me, be also, as far as possible, my ends" (98).

We now see the significance of the fact that the categorical imperative is formal and not abstract. As the comments provided by Kant make clear, the categorical imperative is precisely *not* restricted to the demand of seeing other people merely as "generalized others,"[48] that is, from the viewpoint of "an abstract rational nature in virtue of which we are all alike."[49] The requirement is not to disregard the peculiarities of the individual but, on the contrary, to further them.[50] In this connection Kant also introduces the notion of "duties of kindness" (or rather "duties of love," as would be the more adequate translation for the German term *Liebespflichten* used by Kant). He employs this notion in the course of his explanation of why the categorical imperative must not be confused with the "golden rule," that is, with the "do-as-you-would-be-done-by" principle. Kant argues that, among other shortcomings, this principle does not contain the reason for the "duties of kindness to others," "for many a man would readily agree that others should not help him if only he could be dispensed from affording help to them" (*Groundwork*, 97). Onora O'Neill is among those who have elaborated upon this aspect of Kant's moral philosophy. Outlining an anthropology that stresses the fact that human beings are vulnerable and in many ways unable to pursue their ideas of happiness on their own, she maintains that Kant's concept of the "duties of kindness" is a particularly relevant element in his ethics. She notes: "vulnerable, finite beings do not treat one another as ends merely by leaving each other an appropriate 'space.' . . . Failures of love also occur when the other's ends are indeed respected . . . yet no positive encouragement, assistance or support for their pursuit is given."[51]

At this point, a striking parallel becomes apparent: On the one hand, as indicated above, the concept of "care" is commonly defined by a concern for the needs of individuals in their specific situation; on the other, such a concern is, as Kant's explanations make clear, implied in the categorical imperative. In view of this parallel, it appears we can conclude that Kant has outlined an ethics of care. But is this not too hasty a move? Is not Kant's understanding of love that informs his concept of *Liebespflichten* entirely different from the kind of sympathy contemporary care theorists have in mind? Does not the very idea of a duty to love indicate this difference? In my opinion, questions such as these imply misunderstandings. One has to bear in mind the following differentiations. First, Kant does indeed distinguish between love in an emotional sense—which he calls "pathological" and which he considers unfit to ground morality—and love in the sense of a practical commitment to support others where they are unable to pursue their ideas of happiness on their own, as is required by the moral law. "Kindness done from duty—although no inclination impels us, and even although natural and unconquerable disinclination stands in our way—is practical, and not pathological, love" (*Groundwork*, 67). Second, this distinction is to be found in care ethics as well. As indicated earlier, there are basically two ways to understand the element of feeling that is implied in the concept of care. One option is to define caring as being guided by immediate emotional attachment; yet this concept of morality is vulnerable to objections such as those raised by Card, Friedman, and Hoagland, as summarized above. It should not go unnoticed that those objections argue, although no explicit references are made, in a manner similar to Kant's criticism of pathological love. Where, for instance, Hoagland complains that a theory defining morality by emotional attachment "leaves starving people in a distant land outside the realm of moral consideration,"[52] her critique is obviously grounded in the idea that it is our duty to help, in cases where we have the means to do so, even if we are not emotionally "stirred by the need of others" (*Groundwork*, 66), as Kant phrased this argument. The alternative option is to define caring as acting toward everybody *as if* a close attachment existed; in this case, love is no longer understood as a form of immediate emotionality but in the sense of a universal principle such as the one suggested by Noddings: "My first and unending obligation is to meet the other as one-caring."[53] This principle is in perfect accordance with Kant's concept of the "duties of kindness."

In view of this congruence it does indeed seem legitimate to state that Kant has outlined an ethic of care. There is one important difference, though: the concept of care advanced by Kant does not contradict moral universalism. It now becomes clear how the impasse of particularism versus universalism dogging the current debate might be resolved: the one formal rule suggested by Kant is both strictly universalist (it applies to all people equally)[54] and radically individualizing (it requires that one perceive and support the specific needs of others).

The course of the debate so far has led from an empirical investigation of "female virtues" to a conception of morality that has equal relevance for women and men, according to which caring attention to individuals is demanded in the form of a universal law. This development has made it possible to shift the focus of feminist ethics. Its core concern is no longer—or, at least, no longer exclusively—to investigate whether women deal with moral dilemmas in a specific way; rather, it is to make clear that the discrimination against women still prevailing all over the world is morally wrong. As Alison Jaggar pointedly writes: "While feminist ethics may begin with feminine ethics, it cannot end with it."[55] Jaggar calls for an ethical theory capable of demonstrating that the social practices amounting to a subordination of women pose a problem not only to women, or to feminist activists, but to everyone who intends to act morally. From this viewpoint, she stresses that feminist ethics should not be understood as "ethics for feminists—only" (161), referring in this connection to "feminism's concern that its moral critique of the practices (and theory) of the larger society—and perhaps even the practices (and theory) of other societies—should be objectively justified" (163).

Guided by such an interest in a *moral* critique of discriminating practices and in the justification of that critique, one project for future research should be, in my view, a thorough exploration of the hitherto seriously underestimated potential of formal universalism.[56] The categorical imperative provides a valuable tool for identifying moral wrongs in the treatment that women are normally subjected to because of their gender. To develop this potential more fully, it is necessary to bring formal universalism to bear on the position of women in all spheres of present-day life.

What I am suggesting here—and what I can only briefly sketch in this final part of the present essay—is that we adopt, as critical categories, both elements shown by Kant to be implied in the moral law: the prohibition that says people must never be used "simply as a means," and the precept defined by the notion of "duties of kindness." The first category allows us to expose as immoral the many ways in which women are exploited. Crucial themes to be considered in this connection are, for instance, the international modus operandi of prostitution, the various forms of sexual harassment and of violence against women, and the moral problems raised by pornography. The extent to which national legislation permits, or even facilitates, such modes of harm done to women[57] also warrants further analysis.

The instrumentalization of women also exists in veiled forms. It has become such a common practice that many of its aspects have been rendered unrecognizable even to those affected by it. A great number of women as well as men in Western countries, for instance, do not perceive as oppressive the traditional gender division of labor. Applied in this context, the prohibition against using others "simply as a means" proves to have an enlightening effect: it requires us to ask not only whether people—in this case, women—feel incapacitated, but also whether in fact they are. In this connection, studies like Susan Moller Okin's analysis of the "vulnerability by marriage"[58] gain relevance for locating a moral problem. The gender division of labor typical of Western culture in the modern age, which assigns women to the domestic sphere, has led, she argues, to women being generally associated, as a matter of course, with unpaid work. Okin points out that this also affects women who are unmarried and have no children, because they are viewed as potential wives and mothers. In this widespread way of perceiving women, she sees the roots of women's remarkably weaker position in the labor market. Thus, Okin's analysis helps to reveal that the traditional understanding of gender roles is morally questionable although it is widely considered morally unproblematic.[59] Generally speaking, the point is this: Where formal universalism is used as a critical tool, gender asymmetries can no longer be viewed merely as a matter of specific interest groups in the political sphere but must be acknowledged as moral problems concerning everyone.

The second element which, as Kant explains, is contained in the universal moral law, requires that we ask to what degree women find support in their individual search for happiness. Here the main topic for discussion must be that women are often not perceived as individuals in the way men are. An opinion expressed in Hegel's theory of gender difference seems still prevalent today: according to Hegel, only men are capable of developing individuality, whereas women share the traits characteristic of their gender.[60] In the present-day world, a similar perception seems to be operative where women, because of the gender roles assigned to them, are presented with limited options. For example, women, unlike men, frequently find themselves having to choose between career and family.[61] Another problem for discussion in this context is that formal equality of rights often proves an insufficient guarantee that women in fact have the same chances as men to pursue their individual ends. The question here is, What can be done to enable women to seize de facto the opportunities (e.g., in terms of educational, occupational, and political equality) that are accessible to them de jure? To emphasize the crucial point once more: Applying the categorical imperative to concrete gender asymmetries renders apparent the moral character of problems otherwise likely to be regarded merely in terms of conflicts of interest. This perspective entails, for instance, that measures such as programs for affirmative action and quota regulation may claim to be morally grounded, as attempts at ending a situation in which women are denied moral treatment in the sense of support for their self-chosen ends.[62]

To summarize: feminist ethics could benefit from Kant's moral philosophy in two ways. First, this philosophy offers a critical tool for revealing, in the manner just outlined, that the subordination of women is morally wrong. Second, Kant's thinking contains an anticipatory component as well; it has far-reaching practical consequences—politically, legally, and otherwise—because it gives rise to the following question: What changes are needed in the common perception of gender, and in the practices informed by this perception to enable women as well as men to find the sympathy and support of others on their chosen roads to happiness?

Notes

1. Immanuel Kant, *Observations on the Feeling of the Beautiful and the Sublime* (Berkeley and Los Angeles: University of California Press, 1965), 81.

2. Kant notes there that some people do good out of personal pleasure rather than any sense of duty: "there are many spirits of so sympathetic a temper that, without any further motive of vanity or self-interest, they find an inner pleasure in spreading happiness around them and can take delight in the contentment of others as their own work. Yet I maintain that in such a case an action of this kind, however right and however amiable it may be, has still no genuinely moral worth. It stands on the same footing as other inclinations" (*Groundwork of the Metaphysic of Morals* [New York: Harper and Row, 1964], 66; hereafter cited as *Groundwork*). This description tallies with the way in which Kant characterizes the "beautiful virtues" of women in *Observations*: "They (i.e., women) do a thing only because they like doing it, and the skill lies in so ordering things that they like only what is good" (231ff.). It may therefore be assumed that, in the passage from *Groundwork* quoted above, Kant had women in mind (or that women were at least among those he had in mind). For a discussion of this passage, see also Robin May Schott, *Cognition and Eros: A Critique of the Kantian Paradigm* (University Park: Pennsylvania State University Press, 1990), 139.

3. For the overall development of the philosophy of gender relations in Kant, see Ursula Pia Jauch, *Immanuel Kant zur Geschlechterdifferenz: Aufklärerische Vorurteilskritik und bürgerliche Geschlechtsvormundschaft* (Vienna: Passagen, 1988 and 1993).

4. Lawrence Blum, "Kant's and Hegel's Moral Rationalism: A Feminist Perspective," *Canadian Journal of Philosophy* 2, no. 2 (1982): 294.

5. Kant, *Observations*, 81.

6. Annette Baier, "Hume, the Women's Moral Theorist," in *Women and Moral Theory*, ed. Eva F. Kattay and Diana T. Meyers (Totowa, N.J.: Rowman and Littlefield, 1987), 37–55.

7. See also Annette Baier, "The Need for More Than Justice," in *Science, Morality and Feminist Theory*, ed. Marsha Hanen and Kai Nielsen, *Canadian Journal of Philosophy*, suppl. vol. 13 (1987): 41–58.

8. See Herta Nagl-Docekal, "Jenseits der Geschlechtermoral: Eine Einführung," in *Jenseits der Geschlechtermoral: Beiträge zur feministischen Ethik*, ed. Herta Nagl-Docekal and Herlinde Pauer-Studer (Frankfurt am Main: Fischer, 1993), 9–16.

9. Gertrud Nunner-Winkler, "Gibt es eine weibliche Moral?" in *Weibliche Moral: Die Kontroverse um eine geschlechtsspezifische Ethik*, ed. Gertrud Nunner-Winkler (Frankfurt am Main and New York: Campus, 1991), 147–61; Rainer Döbert, "Männliche Moral, weibliche Moral," in ibid., 121–46.

10. See for instance Debra Nails, "Social-scientific Sexism: Gilligan's Mismeasure of Man," *Social Research* 50 (1983): 643–63.

11. Claudia Card, "Caring and Evil," *Hypatia* 5, no. 1 (1990): 101–8.

12. Barbara Houston, "Caring and Exploitation," *Hypatia* 5, no. 1 (1990): 115–19.

13. Sarah Lucia Hoagland, "Some Concerns about Nel Noddings' Caring," *Hypatia* 5, no. 1 (1990): 109–14.

14. Alison M. Jaggar, "Feminist Ethics: Some Issues for the Nineties," *Journal of Social Philosophy* 20 (1989): 91–107.

15. Marilyn Friedman, "Beyond Caring: The De-Moralization of Gender," in *Science, Morality and Feminist Theory*, ed. Hanen and Nielsen, 87–110.

16. Nel Noddings, *Caring: A Feminine Approach to Ethics and Moral Education* (Berkeley and Los Angeles: University of California Press, 1984), 6.

17. Carol Gilligan, "On 'In a Different Voice': An Interdisciplinary Forum," *Signs* 11, no. 2 (1986): 327.

18. Carol Gilligan and Grant Wiggins, "The Origins of Morality in Early Childhood Relationships," in *Mapping the Moral Domain: A Contribution of Women's Thinking to Psychological Theory and Education*, ed. Carol Gilligan, Jenny Victoria Ward, and Jill McLean Taylor (Cambridge: Harvard University Press, 1988), 128; hereafter cited as "Origins."

19. See, for instance, Annette Baier's way of proceeding, as summarized above.

20. Carol Gilligan, "Moral Orientation and Moral Development," in *Women and Moral Theory*, ed. Kittay and Meyers, 19–33; see also Gilligan and Wiggins, "Origins."

21. See Annette Baier, "Need For More Than Justice," 47.

22. Seyla Benhabib, "The Generalized and the Concrete Other: Visions of the Autonomous Self," *Praxis International* 5, no. 4 (1986): 402–24.

23. Marilyn Friedman, "Beyond Caring," 108.

24. Nel Noddings, *Caring*, 25.

25. Iris M. Young, "Impartiality and the Civic Public. Some Implications of Feminist Critiques of Moral and Political Theory," in her *Throwing Like a Girl and Other Essays in Feminist Philosophy and Social Theory* (Bloomington: Indiana University Press, 1990), 92–113.

26. A select bibliography entitled "Feminist Jurisprudence and Legal Theory" appeared in the *Newsletter on Philosophy and Law*, published by the American Philosophical Association, vol. 90, no. 1 (1990): 159–61; see also Ute Gerhard, *Gleichheit ohne Angleichung: Frauen im Recht* (Munich: Beck, 1990).

27. Marilyn Friedman, "Beyond Caring," 104.

28. See for instance the chapter "Equality in Form and Equality in Fact: Women and Work," in *Justice and Gender: Sex Discrimination and the Law*, by Deborah L. Rhode (Cambridge: Harvard University Press, 1989), 161–201; also Beate Rössler, ed., *Quotierung und Gerechtigkeit: Eine moralphilosophische Kontroverse* (Frankfurt am Main and New York: Campus, 1993).

29. Gilligan, "Moral Orientation," 23.

30. For a careful analysis of this aspect of Kant's moral philosophy see Barbara Herman, *The Practice of Moral Judgment* (Cambridge: Harvard University Press, 1993), 45–72.

31. Carol Gilligan, "Moral Orientation," 29ff.

32. Annette Baier, "Hume, the Women's Moral Theorist," 44.

33. See for instance Immanuel Kant, *The Doctrine of Virtue* (New York: Harper and Row, 1964), pt. 2, "On the Duty of Gratitude"; and Immanuel Kant, *Über Pädagogik*, in Kant, *Werke in sechs Bänden*, ed. Wilhelm Weischedel (Darmstadt: Wissenschaftliche Buchgesellschaft, 1964), 691–746.

34. Onora O'Neill, *Constructions of Reason: Explorations of Kant's Practical Philosophy* (Cambridge: Cambridge University Press, 1989); for a discussion of problems such as sexual coercion and paternalism see the chapter "Between Consenting Adults," 105–25.

35. Jaggar provides a summary of the objections to the concept of "autonomy" that were raised in the context of care ethics. This summary also reveals, although this is not Jaggar's main focus, that the Kantian sense of the term was blended uncritically with its psychological sense in this debate. See Jaggar, "Feminist Ethics," 100–101.

36. Nel Noddings, *Caring*, 18.

37. See Iris M. Young, *Justice and the Politics of Difference* (Princeton: Princeton University Press, 1990), esp. chap. 1, "Displacing the Distributive Paradigm," 15–38.

38. Claudia Card, "Caring and Evil," 102.

39. Sarah Lucia Hoagland, "Some Thoughts About 'Caring,' " in *Feminist Ethics*, ed. Claudia Card (Lawrence: University Press of Kansas, 1991), 260–61.

40. Nel Noddings, *Caring*, 17.

41. Ibid., 14.

42. Sarah Lucia Hoagland, "Some Thoughts About Caring," 253.

43. Marilyn Friedman, "Beyond Caring," 104.

44. Carol Gilligan, *In a Different Voice: Psychological Theory and Women's Development* (Cambridge: Harvard University Press, 1982), 57. See also Lawrence Blum, "Gilligan and Kohlberg: Implications for Moral Theory," *Ethics* 98 no. 3 (1988): 473; and Will Kymlicka, *Contemporary Political Philosophy: An Introduction* (Oxford: Clarendon Press, 1990), 271. Eva-Maria Schwickert points out that the two moral perspectives compared and contrasted by Gilligan can be run together into one. She states that "universalism does not preclude pluralism but makes it possible"; see her "Gerechtigkeit und Fürsorge," *Ethik und Sozialwissenschaften* 3, no. 4 (1992): 569.

45. See Alison M. Jaggar, "Feminist Ethics: Projects, Problems, Prospects," in *Denken der Geschlechterdifferenz: Neue Fragen und Perspektiven der Feministischen Philosophie*, ed. Herta Nagl-Docekal and Herlinde Pauer-Studer (Vienna: Wiener Frauenverlag, 1990), 161ff. Gilligan's characterization of moral maturity in terms of a "contextual relativism" is emphasized by Hubert L. Dreyfus, "Was ist moralische Reife? Eine phänomenologische Darstellung der Entwicklung ethischer Expertise," *Deutsche Zeitschrift für Philosophie* 41, no. 3 (1993): 435–58.

46. Alison M. Jaggar, "Feminist Ethics: Projects, Problems, Prospects," 162ff.

47. Nel Noddings, *Caring*, 25.

48. See Seyla Benhabib, "The Generalized and the Concrete Other."

49. Marilyn Friedman, "Beyond Caring," 108.

50. Jean Grimshaw also stresses that universal principles, unlike special rules, do not in fact call for abstraction from the concrete circumstances of a situation; see her *Philosophy and Feminist Thinking* (Minneapolis: University of Minnesota Press, 1986), 207ff.

51. Onora O'Neill, *Constructions of Reason*, 121.

52. Sarah Lucia Hoagland, "Some Thoughts About 'Caring,' " 253.

53. Nel Noddings, *Caring*, 17.

54. The relevance of Kant's universalism from the viewpoint of feminist concerns is stressed by Joan Tronto, "Beyond Gender Difference to a Theory of Care," *Signs* 12, no. 4 (1987): 644: "Whatever the weakness of Kantian universalism, its premise of the equal moral worth and dignity of all humans is attractive."

55. Allison M. Jaggar, "Feminist Ethics: Projects, Problems, Prospects," 161.

56. In the spirit of this requirement, Susanne Lang outlines a "discourse ethics of solidarity" intended to serve "the strategic objective of overthrowing the existing gender order and its concrete as well as structural injustices"; see Susanne Lang, "Feministische (Diskurs-)Ethik? Überlegungen zu Ansatz und Gegenstand feministischer Ethik und Ethikkritik," in *Ethik und Politik: Diskursethik, Gerechtigkeitstheorie und politische Praxis*, ed. Walter Reese-Schäfer and Karl-Theodor Schuon (Marburg: Schüren, 1991), 85ff.

57. For analyses of this kind see for instance Catharine A. MacKinnon, *Toward a Feminist Theory of the State* (Cambridge: Harvard University Press, 1989); Susan Moller Okin, *Justice, Gender, and the Family* (New York: Basic Books, 1989; and Deborah L. Rhode, *Justice and Gender: Sex Discrimination and the Law.*

58. Susan Moller Okin, *Justice, Gender, and the Family*, 134–69.

59. I am not suggesting here that Moller Okin views her research as a contribution to feminist ethics; my intention is rather to show how her work can be used to shed light on an otherwise unrecognized moral problem.

60. Georg Wilhelm Friedrich Hegel, *The Phenomenology of Mind* (New York: Harper Torchbooks, 1967), chap. "The Ethical World: Law Divine and Human: Man and Woman," 464–82.

61. As Drucilla Cornell notes: "As long as the gender hierarchy is in place, it will be impossible for women to be recognized as individuals"; see Cornell, *Transformations: Recollective Imagination and Sexual Difference* (New York: Routledge, 1993), 168.

62. For a discussion of the moral relevance of the concept of quota regulation see Rössler, ed., *Quotierung und Gerechtigkeit*.

5

Re-Visions of Agency in Kant's Moral Theory[1]

Jean P. Rumsey

Feminists tend to question the very features of Kant's moral theory that have been influential on contemporary thinkers such as Alan Donegan and Alan Gewirth: the authority of reason, the importance of general rules, and the methodology of considering rational beings abstracted from cultural and social contexts. For instance, Annette Baier questions the Kantian assumption that at the heart of ethics is something called "the moral law" or "the moral rules," and quotes Alan Donegan to show Kant's influence: "The Theory of Morality is a theory of a system of laws or precepts binding upon rational creatures as such, the content of which is ascertainable by human reason." She urges her readers to abandon this rationalist, law-centered tradition in moral philosophy, and instead to try a Humean approach, of which the key features are its nonrationalism and its positing of an intimate relationship between moral philosophy and "the actual human practices in which appeals to moral judgments are made and in which morality makes a difference to what is done, thought and felt."[2]

In general, feminist ethics focuses on the embodied agent, emotional as well as rational, socially and culturally specific. For these reasons a feminist might choose to turn from Kant's *Groundwork* to his empirical works, to see the implications of his view for actual agents and practices. However, when one does so, one finds that the views he expresses in the *Sublime* and the *Anthropology* on women's supposed "nature" and "purpose" are vulnerable to criticism by feminists and others. He claims, for instance, that women are "naturally" beneficent and complaisant, that they are incapable of understanding principles, and that their typical "virtues" are merely social rather than moral excellences. Two thoughts here intercept hasty criticism: first, it would be distinctly odd for feminists, committed to a view of the enculturated, embodied agent, to expect Kant to rise magically above his own society, holding views on women that were radically different from those of his neighboring Königsbergers. A responsible critic should consider the possibility that this view of women can be somehow separated from his theory as a whole. Perhaps these views could just be bracketed, and women considered as basically rational beings, in the way that one working with Aristotle's ethics need bracket his view of women's reason.

However, an examination of Kant's application of his theory of rational agency to the human species, in the *Religion*, reveals a problem that stems from his gendered perception of human nature, one that infects his entire theory. I shall show that Kant's conception of the moral agent is flawed, because, excluding women from full moral agency, Kant then takes the pattern for "normal agency" to be that of the man of his place and time.[3]

While women are enmeshed in the interdependencies of social life, Kant holds in the *Anthropology* that the strongest passion in the heart of *man* is for independence. I shall here argue that Kant's gendered conception of human nature does not support an adequate conception of agency because it fails to account for the social dimension of human beings. After examining Kant's conception of human nature I shall examine the consequences of this view for his analysis of the paired virtues of beneficence and gratitude, and for his account of friendship.

On the basis of my argument above, I shall hold that productive feminist work in Kantian theory will lie primarily in re-visioning Kant's conception of agency, and in working to show connections between his fundamental theory and the moral lives of nonideal, embodied agents. To support this claim I shall turn, in conclusion, to the recent work of Onora O'Neill, in expanding Kant's conception of agency; of Barbara Herman, in constructing Rules of Moral Salience, to serve as a middle theory connecting high theory with application; and of Robin Dillon, in revising the important Kantian concept, self-respect, in its relation to moral agency.[4]

KANT'S READING OF HUMAN NATURE

Three central assumptions underlying Kant's conception of human nature are that (1) each human being is an isolated, atomistic individual; (2) the natural motivation of the agent is egoism, prior to any moral understanding, and (3) the species is bifurcated into two genders, having different natures, capacities, and purposes. I shall not argue that the view of human nature following from these assumptions is false, in part because I am not certain what it would be like for a theory of human nature to be falsifiable. Nor would I wish to deny the reality of egoistic motivation, alienation, and isolation in human experience. Instead I shall argue for a weaker claim, that Kant's theory of human nature is inadequate as a basis for his moral theory, because of its strong emphasis on autonomy and individuality, and corresponding neglect of human propensities to cooperation and affiliation.

Kant's view of premoral human nature can be intuitively grasped by attending to the following quotation from Dostoevsky's "White Nights": "People are alone in the world. That's what is so dreadful. 'Is there a living man on the plain'? Cries the Russian legendary hero. I, too, echo the same cry, but no one answers."[5] Kant holds that human beings are isolated in their egoism, and learn to be devious in hiding: "From the day a human being begins to speak in terms of 'I,' he brings forth his beloved self wherever he can, and egoism progresses incessantly. He may not show it (for the egoism of others checks him); but it progresses secretly, at least, so that his apparent self-abnegation and specious modesty will give him a better chance of being highly esteemed by others."[6] Though it should be noted, in fairness, that Kant recognizes variations from egoism in his theory of temperaments, the "dear self first" serves as the standard for the premoral human. Additional evidence for Kant's belief in egoistic motivation comes from his exposition of the duty of beneficence, the duty to adopt into one's character the steady maxim of making another's happiness one's own end. Kant tells us that this duty goes against nature, contrasting this moral injunction with the maxim persons naturally follow, absent morality: "the maxim 'Every man for himself, God (fortune) for us all' seems to be the most natural one."[7]

In the *Religion*, the darker side of this egoism is spelled out as a consequence of the propensity to evil in human nature. Kant writes of a

> secret falsity even in the closest friendship, so that a limit upon trust in the mutual confidence of even the best friends is reckoned a universal maxim of prudence in intercourse; of a propensity to hate him to whom one is indebted, or of a hearty well-wishing which yet allows of the remark that "in the misfortune of our best friends there is something which is not altogether displeasing to us."[8]

It should be noted that distrust and ingratitude, though omnipresent in the species, are here regarded not as natural qualities, but as qualities that can be grafted onto the propensity for evil by choices of the agent. Corresponding to this evil propensity is a predisposition to the good, whereby, for example, the virtue of beneficence can be acquired through the exercise of reflective choice. This predisposition provides a needed bridge across the chasm Kant posits between egoistic human nature and rational morality. Yet we may well inquire, with Philippa Foot, whether this chasm was of Kant's own making.

In her article "Morality as a System of Hypothetical Imperatives," Foot questions Kant's claim that the true moral imperative must be categorical. Hypothetical imperatives are contingent on some end, and Foot argues that there are some ends humans might simply possess. Did those who endured the siege of Leningrad do so solely from the thought of duty, or from their loyalty and devotion to the city? She argues that persons may just care about the sufferings of others, and want to help if they can, and implies that the thought of duty in such cases might be one thought too many. She claims that Kant cannot understand this, because of his psychological hedonism, "and this faulty theory of human nature was one of the things preventing him from seeing that moral virtue might be compatible with the rejection of the categorical imperative."[9]

Kant's further analysis of human nature in the *Religion* makes clear his view of persons as isolated individuals. Elements in the "fixed character and destiny (*Bestimmung*)" of the species are three function-based divisions of the predisposition to the good. The first is the predisposition to animality (biological); the second to humanity (rational, in the sense of technical or prudential reason); the third is the predisposition to personality (practical reason, moral and accountable) (21). Kant's exposition of the first two categories reveals his denigration of the biological and social dimensions of human beings.

First, the social impulse, or impulse for community with other persons, is wholly subsumed within the category of animality. Kant holds it to be the third of three nonrational impulses following that for self-preservation and for the preservation of the species. It is important to note that he includes here not only the sexual impulse, but the institution of the family itself ("the care of offspring so begotten"). The predisposition to animality is one of a "physical and purely mechanical self-love," and therefore requires no reason.[10] Because reason does not enter into this predisposition, the impulse for community with others is nonrational and blind.

The second predisposition, to humanity, is to the individual's happiness; it is "a self-love which is physical and yet compares" (for which reason is required) (*Religion*, 22). The "reason" involved here, however, is mere prudence and shrewdness, not practical reason. (Kant tells us in the *Anthropology* that this is the sort of reason women possess [306/169].) This difference in the kind of reason is what primarily distinguishes this predisposition from that of morality, a point that will become important later.

Kant's explanation of the predisposition to humanity is couched mainly in terms of power over others rather than of reason or the agent's happiness. For instance, the legitimate desire for equality with others is held to lead inexorably to the "unjustifiable craving" to win superiority over others: "Upon this twin stem of *jealousy* and *rivalry* may be grafted the very great vices of secret and open animosity against all whom we look on as not belonging to us . . . inclinations, aroused in us by the anxious endeavors of others to attain a hated superiority over us, to attain for ourselves a measure of precaution and for the sake of safety such a position over others" (*Religion*, 22). Perhaps more telling than the Hobbesian passage above is the question of what Kant might have overlooked or omitted in explaining this predisposition to humanity. One might expect, for example, that it might lead to corresponding good, as well as evil qualities; what we might call "virtues of community." By this phrase I mean to include such phenomena as cooperation, to achieve individual or collective ends, along with the trust and fellow feeling that underlie the ability to work with others, even to envision shared purposes. So if such phenomena exist, onto what part of human nature, as Kant conceives it, could these be grafted?

Kant cannot connect them to the human social impulse, nor to the institution of the family, for it has been relegated to the nonrational domain of biological urges. Yet one might object that the purpose and significance of the human family is not limited to the biological needs of the offspring, but includes the early education and socialization of the young. Minimally, a basic lesson is that the child is not alone, but is a member of a group that shares at least the common purpose of survival. Had Kant, like Hume, taken as morally central the family with its possibilities for, and sometimes realized practices of trust and cooperation, rather than the isolated and self-seeking (adult) individual, he might have noticed the significant neglect of the virtues of community in his account.

WOMEN'S NATURE AND PURPOSE

Having sketched Kant's general account of human nature, it is now time to argue for my claim that Kant's conception of human agency deriving from that account is damaged by his exclusion of women's experience from his theory. I argue that one reason for this exclusion is a perceived difference in women's nature, particularly in their reason and emotions; a second is that Kant holds that women are morally encumbered by being the specific agents of nature's purposes. Their function is to continue and to civilize the race, while males are not similarly hostage to ends that they have not themselves chosen.

First, women are characterized in both the *Observations* and the *Anthropology* as creatures led by their emotions and incapable of grasping principles; as naturally sympathetic, benevolent, and complaisant, pos-

sessing feminine virtues complementary to those of men (having patience rather than tolerance, being sensitive rather than responsive,
saving rather than acquiring).[11] Kant's view of the "natures" of men and
women is encapsulated in his statement that the principal object in
growing old is that "the man should become more perfect as a man, and
the woman as a wife" (Observations, 95).

The difference between women's and men's reasoning is seen not only
in Kant's claim that women are unable to grasp principles, but in Kant's
praise of women's "precocious shrewdness" (Anthropology, 306/169).
Women are indeed rational animals, in that they possess a kind of
reason, but it is the reason described in the predisposition to humanity—
pragmatic, shrewd, and subject to being overridden by the emotions.
Lacking a basis in principle, it falls short of the practical reason
demanded by the predisposition to morality.

Women's second moral liability is that they are held to be co-opted to
nature's purposes: to perpetuate and civilize the race. In order to carry
out this first task, Kant holds that nature has implanted fear and timidity
in women, through which they require men to be their protectors.
They are, furthermore, in civil tutelage to their husbands, dependent,
timorous, without political standing (Anthropology, 306/169). Their
second task, the civilizing of the race, is important, for Kant holds that
civilizing is a necessary prerequisite for its moralization. However,
women are here simply a means to an end. Important though these tasks
are to the progress of civilization, Kant denigrates women's skills in the
appendix to the Doctrine of Virtue: courtesy, sociability, affability, and
gentleness (in disagreeing without quarreling) are not considered virtues.
They are merely the "outworks of by-products which present a fair
illusion of something like virtue, an illusion which deceives no one"
(472/175).

Women, then, are in Kant's view less than (if not other than) full
moral agents. He takes as his model for full moral agency the adult male,
described not in the section of the Anthropology entitled "On the
Character of the Sexes" (which he devotes to explaining the anomalies
of human female), but in the subsequent "On the Character of the
Species." Women's characteristics have been described as a variation
from an assumed norm of masculinity—as a second sex, if you will. For
Kant, the human species, per se, is represented by an asocial creature
whose "self-will is always ready to break faith in hostility toward his
neighbors, and always presses him to claim unconditional freedom,

not merely *independence* of others but even *mastery* of other beings (*Anthropology*, 323/188). Kant thus leaves behind the perceived dependency, emotionalism, complaisance, and limited rationality of the female. He then models the moral agent on the male-identified qualities of his patriarchal world: autonomy, rationality, independence, detachment, courage, and strength.

The following section will examine the implications of this conception of agency for other aspects of his theory, in particular the paired virtues of beneficence and gratitude and for his account of friendship.

INCOMPLETE AGENCY:
AUTONOMY-AS-INDEPENDENCE

In the *Groundwork* Kant defines autonomy as "the property the will has of being a law to itself"; it is this capacity that enables humans to be moral agents.[12] However, when Kant turns from these foundational arguments to his account of empirical character, he holds that a different sense of autonomy is paramount to embodied persons. Although Kant's phrase for this is "outer freedom," I believe that "autonomy-as-independence" captures its sense more fully, because it positions the agent in relation to others, showing his norm-sanctioned isolation. In the *Anthropology* Kant writes that "the inclination to freedom is the most vehement of all inclinations in natural man," and the constant warfare of the savage is explained as a means "to keep others as far away from him as possible and to live scattered in the wilderness." Kant holds that this is justified in order to keep him from falling into submission or dependence (*Anthropology*, 268/135). Freedom from domination by others is essential if the agent is to maintain his autonomy-as-independence, which, as Kant argues in the religion, is continually threatened by the vices growing rankly over the natural human desire for equality.

While external forces such as rivalry, competition, and warfare threaten this precarious independence, the inability of humans to understand, much less successfully promote, the ends of others make it even more essential. Kant asserts, "A man whose happiness depends upon *another* man's choice (no matter how benevolent the other may be) rightly considers himself unfortunate. For what guarantee has he that his powerful neighbor's judgment about his well-being will agree with his own?" (*Anthropology*, 323/188). Kant makes a related point in his exposition of the duty of beneficence, where he asserts that "I cannot do good to anyone according to *my* concept of happiness (except to young children and the insane."[13] Given the isolation of the Kantian agent, it is difficult to escape the conclusion that no human being is able to make good judgments about (much less promote) the well-being or happiness of anyone save himself.

But we do know that good friends often do help each other wisely; by exchanging tokens of friendship (just the right hammers for Ethan's dulcimer, sharing concerns with Andy, finding that out-of-print book Elizabeth has been wanting); by giving or withholding advice, when hard choices are to be made; by commiserating, when nothing can be done. (And surely the friend who regularly sent him the turnips knew Kant's desires well). Further, the mere existence of intimate friendships and kin groupings would seem to cast doubt on Kant's view of the unqualified value and strength of the human passion for independence.

One would not wish to deny the moral significance of the human desire for independence, connected as it is with the development of autonomy in its moral sense and of integrity. However, it seems clear that an adequate view of human agency would also admit of a natural impulse for affiliation (with its accompanying dread of isolation from others) as well as of independence (with its accompanying dread of domination by others). Onora O'Neill holds that the balance between dependence and independence in the conception of the agent is crucial, for "a complete erosion of capacities for independent action destroys plurality and with it the context of justice; a complete erosion of dependence privileges an ideal of the person whose relevance to human life is wholly unestablished."[14]

In more concrete terms, David Hume, by contrast, takes as his starting point human dependence, grounded in the experience of personal connection: "[the human's] very first state and situation may justly be esteem'd social."[15] Supporting this view of the importance of human interdependence are friendships, kinship groups, and voluntary associations of all kinds. Further evidence of the importance of human connection is the effective use of ostracism or shunning as punishment, from the ancient Greeks to the modern-day Amish.

In defense of his position, Kant might argue that some degree of autonomy-as-independence is a prerequisite to the development of autonomy in its primary sense of self-legislation. For this reason Kant criticizes the dependency of tutelage (in its broad sense of guardianship and protection) at length, holding that many otherwise capable persons escape responsibility for their own agency by submitting to the guidance of others. However, we must consider different purposes of tutelage, and distinguish between global and partial dependencies. When we wish to master a subject or develop a talent we place ourselves in the hands of those who can help us achieve this end. The decision to apprentice to a silversmith, to take bassoon lessons, or to study philosophy, is a decision to become dependent upon others, in certain limited respects, for a period of time. Through such tutelage persons develop their talents and deepen their understandings. One's motivation in entering into such unequal relationships can hardly be described as the evasion of moral responsibility, since the development of one's talents is a Kantian duty. Autonomy-as-independence is here at odds with Kant's injunction that persons should strive to develop such talents as they possess.

BENEFICENCE AND GRATITUDE

Let us now examine the way in which Kant's conception of the moral agent gives rise to difficulties in explaining these paired virtues. Like Cinderella's slipper, they fit awkwardly on the isolated agent. An ordinary understanding of these virtues implies that the one who is benefited is grateful to his benefactor, but this is not necessarily true for Kant. Acceptance of another's beneficence may threaten this agent's self-respect; he may come to hate his benefactor, or despise himself for accepting that aid. This unhappy fact leads the Kantian benefactor into tangles of deception; he is enjoined to "carefully avoid any appearance of intending to put the other under obligation," so as not to "humble the other in his own eyes." However, since his beneficence in fact does put the other under an obligation, the best way to circumvent this problem is "to practice his beneficence in complete secrecy" (*Doctrine of Virtue*, 453/21 and 453/117).

Let us suppose that Smith wishes to give a musically gifted, impoverished young man a grand piano. Let us further suppose that Smith manages to have this piano delivered in such a way that the young man does not know who sent it. Not knowing the identity of his benefactor might be a heavier burden than if Smith had declared herself. For the obligation is inevitable, according to Kant: "By the fact that I fulfill a duty of love to someone I obligate the other as well. I make him indebted to me" (*Doctrine of Virtue*, 449/117).

The metaphor of "debt" or "owing" in relation to a duty of love may seem inappropriate, as does the duplicity enjoined above. But for Kant it is indeed more blessed to give than to receive, because of the moral discomfort in accepting what is given by another person. The recipient is saddled with an obligation he can never fulfill: "one cannot, by any requital of a kindness received, rid oneself of the obligation to this kindness, since one can never win away from the benefactor his *priority* of merit; the merit of having been the first in benevolence" (*Doctrine of Virtue*, 454/123). The recipient must then, literally, be eternally grateful to the person who has, with the best of motives, unwittingly done him great moral harm.

Although the use of the phrase "much obliged" to thank a benefactor testifies to the component of obligation in gratitude, Kant's view here is difficult to reconcile with the duty of mutual aid. For if it is good to give to those in need, and if we all understand that as finite human beings we might by turns be either benefactor or recipient, then why is it not good to accept such aid, at those times when we are in need?

A simple answer to this question would be that the duty of mutual aid applies only to narrowly defined needs, such as rescue. Any assistance beyond the level of survival would be excessive, and should be rejected in order to keep one's moral ledger balanced. But surely the young musician does need a piano, and the worried friend a sympathetic ear. Surely, one might argue, people help each other not only in order that they might survive, but that they might live well.

The underlying problem here seems to be that the Kantian agent is not characterized by the trust in himself and his fellows that would enable him to give and accept freely the daily tokens of human affection and interdependence. Although Kant does officially recognize this interdependence in the duty of mutual aid, and advises the agent "not to avoid places where we shall find the poor who lack the most basic essentials, but rather to seek them out; not to shun sickrooms and debtors' prisons" (*Doctrine of Virtue*, 455/124), he seems also to urge any agent worth his salt to flee from anyone—teacher, grandmother, friend, or even the Guggenheim foundation—who threatens to become his benefactor.

FRIENDSHIP, INDEPENDENCE,
AND SOCIAL UNION

Let us now turn to Kant's account of friendship, in which the tension between independence and social union is most acute. The problem, stated succinctly, is that "man is a being made for society (though he is also an unsociable one)." Although isolate and self-interested by nature, and desirous of independence, he feels the need for union with others. He is torn between the strong "need to reveal himself to others (even with no ulterior purpose)" and the fear that others would misuse his disclosures, or would respect him less "if he revealed his failings while the other person concealed his own." From this reading of the human situation Kant concludes that the greatest value of moral friendship is that one is not, as in his natural state, alone. To a true friend he can "reveal himself with complete confidence, he can then air his views. He is not completely *alone* with his thoughts, as in a prison" (*Doctrine of Virtue*, 471/143–44).

However, Kant warns us that these moral friendships are vulnerable in the following three ways: (1) they are extremely difficult to build and preserve; (2) each person's autonomy is threatened by the relationship; and (3) even when established, they can be criticized on the grounds that the relationship is not universal, but narrow and particular.

The difficulty with moral friendship arises from the requirement that the relationship must be free of any taint of self-interest, between noble persons who are equal in the respect due each other. In contrast, echoing Aristotle's conception of the friendship of utility, Kant holds that most ordinary human friendships are aimed at promoting the self-interest of one or both participants in the relationship. Kant holds that even when this kind of "pragmatic friendship" is motivated by love, it is an inferior form (*Doctrine of Virtue*, 471/144). True friendship must not be aimed at mutual advantage but must be instead a "pure moral" friendship, wherein each is concerned to bear the other's burden, but where this should not, in fact, happen. If it did, Kant holds, the precarious balance of love and respect that defines this highest form of friendship would be destroyed.

Kant holds that any inequality between love and respect threatens the autonomy of each agent, which is integral to his self-respect. When one friend does a favor for the other (carnations, a short-term loan) the relationship can become unequal. The recipient may lose respect, for with friend as well as stranger, "he sees himself obviously a step lower insofar as he is under obligation without being able reciprocally to impose obligation" (*Doctrine of Virtue*, 470/172). Kant states this problem clearly in the *Lectures on Ethics:* "A friend who bears my losses becomes my benefactor and puts me in his debt. I feel shy in his presence and cannot look him boldly in the face. The true friendship is canceled and friendship ceases."[16] If one simply imposes his worries upon the other, without receiving any sort of favor, the relationship may still become unequal, and Kant holds that such an "imposition" would not occur at all if both partners to the friendship were truly noble. Friends *do* want to help each other, from a "heartfelt benevolence," but a benevolence "which should not be put to the test because it is always dangerous (*Doctrine of Virtue*, 470/142). We must recall here that the effort to form such friendships is a duty of the Kantian agent, and that "the adoption of this ideal in men's attitudes to one another contains their worthiness to be happy" (*Doctrine of Virtue*, 468/140). But we have seen that this duty is strewn with traps internal to Kant's theory. When anything happens to alter the delicate balance of love and respect in moral friendship, the friendship does not survive. If fortune brings trouble to one partner, the other, out of respect, can only help him on pain of dissolving the friendship. Thus, paradoxically, the agent is enjoined to form friendships to transcend his natural solitary state, but the execution of his duty is virtually impossible for the isolated Kantian agent.

The third problem even with true friendship, from Kant's perspective, is that it is particular rather than universal. He claims that friendship should ideally include, if not all moral beings, at least the "all-inclusive circle of those who, in their attitude, are citizens of the world" (*Doctrine of Virtue*, 472/145). But what would that be like? Who among us is capable of such a vast and yet intimate friendship, with those we have not even met? And, if this were possible, would this measure up to Kant's high standards for personal friendships, or would it be something quite other (say an expanded conception of civic friendship)?

Kant admits that this universality is an extraordinary demand, not recognized by the common moral consciousness of his time. While he admits that "it is not man's way to embrace the whole world in his good-will; he prefers to restrict it to a small circle," he believes that when human beings become civilized this may change, for "civilized man seeks universal pleasures and a universal friendship, unrestricted by special

ties; the savage picks and chooses according to his taste and disposition."[17] But friendship just is a special tie between one person and
another, or among some few persons. It is particular, and although it
may of course originate in or be supported by principle (e.g., friendships
that arise among those committed to a political or aesthetic movement),
it is always personal. While Kant's conception of universal friendship
may well be significant in the context of international relations, a world
in which it would replace, or be coeval with, "special ties" is hard to
imagine. While we should heed Kant's warning here that the danger of
particular friendships is that of "shutting out from our hearts all who are
not within our charmed circle,"[18] the corresponding danger of universal
friendship is that the agent would never allow any particular individual
into the perfect circle of his own ego.

To comment on the discussion in this section: in order for the duty of
friendship to be practically possible, and for beneficence and gratitude
to be unencumbered virtues, Kant need not have held that human
beings are basically good. He need only have held that they are social
beings, with strong desires and needs for both independence and connection, autonomy and affiliation, and purposes that are not always merely
their own. I have argued that he viewed human beings as natural egoists,
normatively independent, because he took his culture's gendered conception of masculine human nature as a model for moral agency, considering
the experience and "nature" of women to be morally irrelevant.

If the interpretation above is sound, it would point to the need for
serious re-visioning of Kant's conception of moral agency, based on the
full spectrum of human moral experience. This would at the same time
help us understand how Kantian moral theory can be applied to embodied beings, and how it can help guide moral inquiry and judgment in
contexts somewhat different from that in which it arose.

KANTIAN CONSTRUCTIVISM AND
FEMINIST REVISIONS

In her *Constructions of Reason*, Onora O'Neill sets herself the task of
explaining two related Kantian notions: that of using someone, and of
treating others as persons. She argues that in order to understand others
as persons, they must be viewed not abstractly, "but as particular men

and women with limited and determinate capacities to understand or to consent to proposals" (105). Her secondary aim is to give a reading of some of Kant's central claims that "does not depend on an inflated view of human cognitive and volitional capacities; does not generate implications that are rigorously insensitive to variations of circumstances and is not tied to a strongly individualistic assumption of agency" (106; emphasis added).

Because the individualism of Kant's conception of agency has been amended, O'Neill is able to argue forcefully for its centrality in the moral life. She argues therefore for an imperfect obligation to block or avoid such agency-threatening phenomena such as coercion, deception, violence, and hunger (233). This argument would not go through for unspecified rational agents, but it does for embodied humans, vulnerable to illness, death, coercion, and deceit, needing regular nourishment and at times the assistance of others. O'Neill points out that these are not merely simply biological or arbitrary needs, but prerequisites for the exercise of moral agency. In rejecting individualism she argues that human beings are not only "distinct rational beings," but claims that human rationality and their mutual dependence constitute the very basis of their agency (198).

Barbara Herman sees Kant's theory in need of supplementation as well as of reconstruction. She attempts to provide missing connections between the two parts of Kant's theory—the rational capacity for agency, and its actualization or thwarting in situated human agents. In her words, she is working to provide the missing "middle theory," lying "between the high value of theory and the low theory of application."[19]

An important example of Herman's middle theory is the construction of Rules of Moral Salience, guides for the agent's moral perceptions in actual communities. These make it clear who counts as an agent, the conditions of agency for ends-in-themselves, and ways in which agents are vulnerable. These rules are not timelessly true, but are subject to criticism, as when agency is denied to some group whose members otherwise meet the society's criteria for agency (e.g., slaves, women) (83–93). Like O'Neill, and unlike Kant, Herman's concerns focus on situated agency: a central aim is to "articulate the contingent structure of rational agency" and to investigate "the contingent empirical situation" of human agents to understand how some circumstances, primarily those involving dependency or other power relations, can undermine agency (233–34).

Of particular relevance to my essay is Herman's defense of Kant's account of friendship. She is particularly concerned with refuting charges that Kantian impartiality precludes friendship, or that for Kant morality preempts personal relations. Her argument proceeds through the use of her concept of an agent's "deliberative field." She claims that if friendship is a moral relationship, "then there will be alterations in one's deliberative field as one has friends. . . . If among the moral features of friendship is a more stringent duty of mutual aid, then the needs of one's friends will occupy higher ground in the deliberative field" (180). That is, those obligations will be more compelling. This argument might show the way to avoid some of the traps that I have argued are internal to Kant's account of friendship.

Herman's argument for Kantian friendship may or may not be Kantian, or may not even seem Kantian, to Kant scholars generally or to feminists. Nonetheless, Herman's pragmatic answer to this objection is worth noting by anyone with an interest in moral theory: "In the end, we may not be able to claim this elaborated theory as Kant's, or not all of it; but that seems all right if what we get by proceeding in this way is sufficiently interesting and of some use" (212).

When we turn to explicitly feminist work deriving from Kant, we can see both Kant's significance for feminist work and those features of his theory that are unacceptable to many feminists. Robin Dillon's work on the key Kantian concept of respect extends that concept to that of self-respect in the moral life of embodied agents.[20] Her basic claim is that Kant regards self-respect as the subjective basis of morality, and that the categorical imperative commands respect for all persons, including oneself (65).

Dillon argues that self-respect is essential to moral agency, and politically important in empowering women to change institutions and practices that threaten or deny full agency to women, and which "work to stunt our sense of worth." She then argues that self-respect, as conceived in our philosophical tradition, is a male-based "neo-Cartesian model of the moral self, disembodied, rational, autonomous, separate, isolated, indistinguishable from every other self" (53 and 56). What Dillon finds objectionable about this conception is that it abstracts from all particularities, substituting respect for the moral law, moral rights, or moral capacity for respect for the actual person. Under this abstract conception of self-respect, the agent's circumstances, and particularly "the subordinating circumstances of women's lives" must go unnoticed.

Furthermore, conceiving persons in this way separates and distances us from each other.[21]

Dillon points out how this dominant conception of self-respect constrains women's moral choices. First, if this concept is antithetical to feminist goals, then women must choose between maintaining our self-respect (thus defined), or transforming ourselves toward liberation. Or second, we may mold ourselves to fit this conception's model of a disembodied, separate self.

Her revision of self-respect (not necessarily the only feminist one, as she reminds us) can be sketched as follows. On this conception the self is situated, fully specific and concrete, and therefore constituted at least in part by its relationships with others. While self-respect does involve valuing oneself in one's concrete particularity, Dillon claims that this valuing is not myopic or egocentric; "in appreciating myself, I appreciate the others with whom I am connected and on whom I depend. . . . Indeed it may be that for some individuals the way to develop or strengthen self-respect is to focus on others with whom one is connected than on oneself" (61).

The primary value of this reconstructed conception is that it is empowering personally and politically to the agent in whatever community or circumstances agents find themselves. Women and men who possess this important moral quality may unite to thwart practices and beliefs that threaten their moral agency. This claim is related to the point that Kant makes at the close of the *Anthropology* (albeit in a grander, more abstract context): solutions to moral problems are not to be found through individual effort or even individual virtue alone, but in community (*Anthropology*, 333/193).

Beginning from a basis of Kantian concern with self-respect as a prerequisite for moral agency, Dillon's robust conception of self-respect might help to correct a purported deficiency in the ethic of care. According to Carol Gilligan, Nell Noddings, and others, women's experience causes them to value affiliation and caring over autonomy and justice. But if this is true, and if the moral worth of the one caring lies wholly in her ability to care for others, then she is valued only as a means. Thus it can be argued that the "ethic of care" valorizes women's altruism while denying her autonomy, thus underwriting her oppression. Dillon's claim is that women are to be valued in themselves: because self-respect is "the appreciation of my intrinsic worth, it says I may and ought to take care of myself, not only or primarily so that I am better able to take care of others, but . . . because I matter in my own right" (62). I take this an important corrective to some theories of care; it is the Kantian point that human beings are not to be valued only as causal levers that can produce the greatest amount of good in the world, but for themselves as rational, purposive beings.

Dillon, like O'Neill and Herman, is concerned with the general conditions that thwart or promote moral agency. However, as a feminist, she is particularly concerned with the agency of women in what she calls the subordinating circumstances of women's lives. More important, her essay is not simply concerned with forwarding a more adequate moral theory; it is particularly concerned with the moral and physical survival of women. Another feminist, Ruth Ginzberg, expresses this same concern: "We must conceive of ethics as a part of our survival. We have no choice. For as long as we don't take that step, we are still doing androcentric philosophy with a 'feminist twist.' "[22]

Does Ginzberg's warning mean that feminists should refrain from approaching moral theory by using the master's tools? I think not. I think that the work of O'Neill, Herman, and Dillon shows the value of building on, though doubtless distorting and extending it in ways in which the master might not have recognized, much less approved. Further, feminist theory is not monolithic; there is room for a rich variety of approaches that do not rely on the great moral philosophers of the past, approaches that are yielding fruitful theories.[23] Commenting on the future of feminist ethics, Alison Jaggar adds a pragmatic warning against a feminist's rejection of the Western philosophical canon: "even if these are sometimes inadequate for feminist purposes it would hardly be conceivable, let alone prudent, for feminists [or anyone else] to resolve to start from scratch and reinvent everything."[24]

In conclusion, I agree that it is important for feminists, and other serious moral theorists, to continue carefully examining, revising, and extending Kantian theory, as we work toward a more adequate understanding of the moral life. Barbara Herman's reinterpretation of Kant's conception of friendship is an important example of fruitful work. Whether or not it can be classed as Kant's theory, in whole or in part, it certainly derives from Kant, and, as Herman says, "that seems all right if what we get in this way is sufficiently interesting and of some use" (112).

Notes

1. I thank Marcia Baron, John Vollrath, and Robin Schott for their helpful criticisms and especially Claudia Card for her long work with men on Kantian ethics.

2. Annette Baier, *Postures of the Mind: Essays on Mind and Morals* (Minneapolis: University of Minnesota Press, 1985), 235–36.

3. Two earlier essays of mine deal with this general problem: "The Development of Character in Kantian Moral Theory," *Journal of the History of Philosophy* 27 (April 1989): 257–65; and "Agency, Human Nature and Character in Kantian Theory," *Journal of Value Inquiry* 24, no. 2 (April 1989): 109–21.

4. Onora O'Neill, *Constructions of Reason: Explorations of Kant's Practical Philosophy* (Cambridge: Cambridge University Press, 1989); Barbara Herman, *The Practice of Moral Judgment* (Cambridge: Harvard University Press, 1993); and Robin Dillon, "Toward a Feminist Conception of Self-Respect," *Hypatia* 7, no. 1 (Spring 1992): 56–69.

5. Fyodor Dostoevski, *The Best Short Stories*, ed. David Magarshack (New York: Modern Library, n.d.), 293.

6. Immanuel Kant, *Anthropology from a Practical Point of View*, trans. Mary J. Gregor (The Hague: Martinus Nijhoff, 1974), 129/10.

7. Immanuel Kant, *The Doctrine of Virtue*, trans. Mary J. Gregor (New York: Harper and Row, 1964), 542/120.

8. Immanuel Kant, *Religion Within the Limits of Reason Alone*, trans. Theodore M. Green and Hoyt H. Hudson (New York: Harper and Row, 1960), 28–29.

9. In her *Virtues and Vices and Other Essays in Moral Philosophy* (Berkeley and Los Angeles: University of California Press, 1978), 165.

10. *Religion*, 21 and 22. This denigration of the biological has been criticized by such feminists as Hilda Lindemann Nelson and James Lindemann Nelson; see their "Cutting Motherhood in Two: Some Suspicions Concerning Surrogacy," in *Feminist Perspectives in Medical Ethics*, ed. Helen Bequaert Holmes and Laura M. Purdy (Bloomington: Indiana University Press, 1992), 256–65. They write: "Instead of starting with the facts of human biology, liberal theory has started with 'abstract individualism'—a model of autonomous self-interested entities interacting contractually in pursuit of their own goods. These individuals, untouched by any particular language, culture, or socialization, seem woefully inadequate to the facts of biological existence" (42).

11. Immanuel Kant, *Observations on the Feeling of the Beautiful and the Sublime*, trans. John T. Goldthwait (Berkeley and Los Angeles: University of California Press, 1960), 79–81. *Anthropology*, 303/166 and 310/173.

12. Immanuel Kant, *The Groundwork of the Metaphysic of Morals*, trans. H. J. Paton (New York: Harper and Row, 1953), 440/108.

13. *Doctrine of Virtue*, 453/122. Marcia Baron has suggested, in private correspondence, that Kant's statements here may have more to do with the special problems of patronage than with ordinary social relations.

14. O'Neill, *Constructions of Reason*, 213.

15. David Hume, *Treatise*, ed. L. A. Selfly-Bigge (Oxford: Clarendon Press, 1955), 493.

16. Immanuel Kant, *Lectures on Ethics*, trans. Louis Infield (New York: Harper Torchbooks, 1963), 207.

17. Ibid., 206. Also see the conception of cosmopolitan citizenship in Kant's *Perpetual Peace*.

18. *Lectures on Ethics*, 206.

19. Barbara Herman, *Practice of Moral Judgment*, 233.

20. Dillon, "Toward a Feminist Conception of Self-Respect," 52–69.

21. Ibid., 56 and 57. Throughout this discussion, Dillon makes it clear that she is discussing the fundamental "recognition respect" rather than "appraisal respect," a point I omitted for the sake of brevity.

22. Ruth Ginzberg, "Philosophy Is Not a Luxury," in *Feminist Ethics*, ed. Claudia Card (Lawrence: University of Kansas Press, 1991), 126–45; quotation on 130.

23. An excellent example is the work of Maria Lugones; see her "On the Logic of Pluralist Feminism," in *Feminist Ethics*, ed. Card, 35–44.

24. Alison Jaggar, "Feminist Ethics: Problems, Projects, Prospects," in *Feminist Ethics*, ed. Card, 78–104; quotation on 87.

6

Kantian Ethics and Claims of Detachment

Marcia Baron

Feminist criticisms of Kant's ethics often meet with the following reply: Clearly, Kant's own views on women are deplorable. This has been amply documented (see, for example, Robin Schott's essay in this anthology).[1] But as is sometimes the case with brilliant thinkers, his theory was way ahead of him. It contains in it the basis for a challenge to positions, such as his own, that give women a subordinate moral and political status. All that needs altering, on this view, are Kant's disturbing "anthropological" remarks about women, and his claims about their moral and political status that rest on those "observations." Challenging this line of defense, Sally Sedgwick articulates it as follows in her contribution to this collection.

In Kant's defense we would like to be able to say when we read his denial to women of the right to citizenship and equality that he is simply laboring under a faulty or antiquated anthropology, and that all that needs correction is his grasp of the facts. We would like to say that there is nothing about the questionable assumptions that make up his moral anthropology that need cause any worry about the validity of the supreme moral law itself. While he may have been ideologically misled or empirically mistaken, his moral *groundwork* on this interpretation remains safely intact. Following this line of defense, we might then go on to argue that one fact that indeed needs correcting is his assumption that it is the *nature* of women to be more determined by inclination than by reason. In light of what we know about the sociohistorical forces that have confined them to the home and hindered their participation in the public domain, we might claim that women have simply been deprived of the opportunity to exercise their rational faculties to the extent that men have. And this is surely a correction that can be made without requiring any adjustment in our guiding principle.[2] (Chapter 3)

In other words, we would correct Kant by saying that women are not by nature inferior to men in their moral and cognitive abilities, and that if by chance it is more common among women than among men to be blinded by emotion, to be morally weak, or to have "impure wills,"[3] this could easily be explained by the fact that girls and women are taught in a myriad ways that females *are* more emotional than men and that any female who isn't, is highly suspect (as are emotional men).[4] As John Stuart Mill put it,

In the case of women, a hot-house and stove cultivation has always been carried on of some of the capabilities of their nature, for the benefit and pleasure of their masters. Then, because certain products of the general vital force sprout luxuriantly and reach a great development in this heated atmosphere and under this active nurture and watering, while other shoots from the same root, which are left outside in the wintry air, with ice purposely heaped all round them, have a stunted growth, and some are burnt off with fire and disappear, men, with that inability to recognise their own work which distinguishes the unanalytic mind, indolently believe that the tree grows of itself in the way they have made it grow, and that it would die if one half of it were not kept in a vapour bath and the other half in the snow.[5]

I endorse a very qualified version of the reply. I do think that Kant's theory was *much* more progressive than he was. I deplore much of what he wrote regarding women but I do not think that it impugns his theory.[6] I also think that feminists have reason to look favorably on his moral theory, principally because of its egalitarianism. At the same time, however, I think that Kant's ethics needs more reform than what is suggested in the view that Sedgwick limns above. In addition to recognizing the effects of socialization on women, we recognize its effects on men: men haven't had adequate encouragement (and thus, opportunity) to develop their emotional and affectional capacities. The correction needed, in relation to gender, is not merely to say, with Mary Wollstonecraft, that women are just as rational as men—or can be, with comparable educational and professional opportunities (including encouragement). Kant, who presumably has men and not women in mind much of the time when he speaks of generic persons, doesn't consider the possibility that proper moral development might involve more cultivation of feeling than he supposes. So, it seems to me, a further correction needed to Kant's ethics is to give a larger place to the cultivation of sentiments as part of moral (self-)development. And this is tied to the feminist point that insofar as generic humans are thought of as male, what is seen as virtuous tends to favor qualities of character traditionally associated with men.

In this essay I develop and assess a set of criticisms of Kant's ethics that are often, though by no means always, developed as feminist objections, and that are presented by those feminists who are sharply critical of Kant's ethics as reasons for thinking that not just Kant's own views, but his entire ethics, are deplorable. Because the same points are often made by those who flag them as feminist as well as by those who do not, I shall not generally try to sort out the feminist from the nonfeminist claims, but I shall at some points assess the claim that a particular objection draws sustenance from feminism. What I have to say on this will not be novel, however, and so I shall not belabor it; all it amounts to, in a nutshell, is that the disagreements regarding the objections to Kant's ethics that are presented as feminist objections reflect differences among feminists regarding feminism. Feminists who find Carol Gilligan's "other voice" a feminist voice, or at least a voice very congenial to feminism, find the criticisms more compelling than I do. As Robin Schott observes at the end of her essay in this anthology (Chapter 13), feminists have responded in various ways to Gilligan's work, and I think the differences show up plainly in the sharply divergent stances we take regarding Kant's ethics. It is striking that so many contemporary Kant scholars and/or Kantians today are women (many if not most of them women who regard themselves as feminists). Although I have not made a systematic study of it, my impression is that despite Annette Baier's advertisement for Hume as "the women's moral theorist" (and her very firm denunciation of Kant), there are no more women working on Hume's ethics than on Kant's. Nor, I believe, is the population of philosophers who work on Hume more predominantly female (or less predominantly male) than are the philosophers who work on Kant.[7] As someone who has worked on both Hume and Kant, I certainly do not see Hume's ethics as more congenial to feminism. Humean—and, for that matter, Aristotelian—ethics may count as more feminist than Kant's ethics because they give feeling a much larger positive role in ethics (and in Aristotle's case, because of the attention to and value assigned to *philia*), and because they seem to attend more than Kant's ethics does to human life as it is actually lived (at least in the times and places that they know best). But to my mind a more important feminist consideration is the resources and, better yet, impetus provided by the theory for social change—social change that brings about (among other things) full recognition of women as moral and political equals. Kant's strongly egalitarian moral philosophy provides both (despite Kant's own views regarding women and despite the limits of his egalitarianism in the *Doctrine of Right*). Placing far more value on social conventions than is appropriate, Hume's and Aristotle's ethics make it very difficult to challenge the status quo. Whether feminists should prefer a theory that gives feeling a prominent and positive role and that accords importance to the concrete, to "particulars," is less certain than that we should favor a theory that provides the resources for social change.

The criticisms of Kantian ethics that I shall be examining all involve the notion of detachment. The detachment that Kantian ethics is said to involve is of the following three sorts: detachment from other persons, detachment from our own projects, and detachment from our emotions and feelings.[8]

DETACHMENT FROM OTHER PERSONS

Here is one statement of the first criticism, again from Sedgwick's "Can Kant's Ethics Survive the Feminist Critique?" (Chapter 3): "The Kantian picture of agency seems to presuppose a context of distrust. My autonomy and identity as a moral subject are made to depend on my severing my ties to my community and relationships, because these are thought to endanger my capacity of self-determination and to interfere with my ability to be impartial in the face of competing self-interest." I don't see any reason for thinking that on a Kantian view ties to community and relationships endanger one's capacity of self-determination. It is not as if we are supposed to avoid being influenced by others. What is true is that we are to think for ourselves, and not ask others to direct our lives for us. But this hardly seems objectionable; indeed, it seems to me much more congenial to feminism than, say, the conventionalism of Hume's ethics. (I'm thinking here of the expectation, in connection with Hume's artificial virtues such as justice and charity, that we will follow the conventions without giving them much thought, and in particular, without giving them any critical thought.)

The other reason indicated for thinking that on a Kantian view my "autonomy and identity as a moral subject is made to depend on my severing" ties to others, is that these ties are thought to "interfere with my ability to be impartial." Although strong attachments to others could make it harder for us to be impartial in certain circumstances where impartiality is called for, certainly no Kantians (Kant included) would take this to be a reason for severing ties to others. Severing ties would, first of all, be a drastic solution. Drastic not only in the eyes of feminists and most other contemporary readers, who place great value on friendships and other personal ties, but also in Kant's view.[9] Friendship, he says, is a duty.[10] Presumably severing a friendship is not something we should do lightly. But in addition, this would be an un-Kantian approach to the problem for a different reason. Central to Kant's theory is the position that we are capable of acting from duty alone. It is not as if we are supposed to rid ourselves of contrary impulses in order to facilitate acting from duty. The same point applies regarding ties to others. Ties to others may occasionally make it harder for me to act morally—since morality requires that I not make exceptions for my friend—but this is no reason to sever ties to others. What is needed is a firm commitment to putting morality first, no matter what the competing considerations.

It should also be noted that on a Kantian view (and on any sensible view) partiality to those dear to me—temptation to make an exception for them to morality's requirements—is no greater a temptation to act immorally than is partiality to myself. So, severing attachments to others would be a silly approach; I would cease to be partial to certain others but would still (maybe even more intensely) be partial to myself. Moreover, strong attachment very likely makes it easier for me to act morally: it heightens my appreciation of others, helping me to be more sensitive and more aware of their needs, thus more able to help others, and it is likely to deepen the respect I have for others as beings who set ends for themselves (i.e., as rational beings). If I were to sever my ties to others, I would, among other things, be cutting myself off from important avenues for improving my character and helping others. Clearly, the moral loss would be far greater than the moral gain, and the moral gain needn't be pursued by this route anyway. Better to address the problem head-on. I am capable of doing what morality requires, and if I find it hard, the solution isn't to remove temptation by not having close friends (a foolish route in any event) but to strengthen my commitment to acting morally.[11]

But my reply to the objection contains the seeds of another objection. If Kantian ethics doesn't require severing ties to others, it might be replied, it surely mandates that we be somewhat detached from them. Kant may say that friendship is a duty, but what he takes friendship to be must be rather chilly.

It is true that our attachments to others have to be tentative or qualified on a Kantian view. "I'm yours!" is a tad problematic on a Kantian view. For the most part I think that the truth is salutary and more congenial to feminism-as-I-see-it than is the take on attachments to others endorsed by Carol Gilligan and many, probably most, Gilligan-ians. I'll say more about this shortly; first, I spell out in what way our attachments to others have to be tentative or qualified on a Kantian view. What qualifies our attachments is, of course, moral constraints.

No relationship, no attachment to another, justifies acting immorally (either toward another or toward oneself). Should there be a conflict between the wants and needs of another, or of a relationship, and the requirements of morality, morality is supposed to win. This is one way in which Kantian ethics might plausibly be said to require a certain detachment in one's ties to others. One cannot be unconditionally committed to doing whatever is best for one's loved one, for moral constraints circumscribe what one may do. This seems to me to be just as it should—though only, I might add, insofar as the requirements of morality are reasonable requirements. That commitments to others be subject to moral constraints is problematic, I think, just insofar as the moral constraints are dubious—extreme, silly, fastidious, or too coarse-grained. Let me explain the last worry—that moral constraints are too coarse-grained, or too blunt—as it is the one that is most often raised in connection with Kant's ethics.

The suspicion is that on Kant's ethics, moral requirements are blunt rules that disregard the particular circumstances (never lie; never steal; and so forth). Although there is some textual basis for the worry, it has been amply shown by Barbara Herman and Onora O'Neill, among others, that this is not an accurate picture of Kant's ethics.[12] Consider his (in)famous examples in the Groundwork. One is of suicide committed out of self-love, when the agent's life threatens more evil than it promises happiness; another is of someone who, finding himself in comfortable circumstances, chooses not to develop his talents and instead to "give himself up to pleasure."[13] The circumstances and the reason for the action or policy clearly are treated as significant. This is even more apparent in the Doctrine of Virtue, where casuistical questions are posed: May I kill myself if I've been bitten by a rabid dog and feel dementia coming on? By killing myself I prevent the otherwise imminent dementia, in which I am likely to inflict serious harm on others (MM 424.)

Failure to recognize the moral relevance of the particulars, on Kant's view—or believing that when Kant does treat them as relevant, he must be cheating—is due, I suspect, to supposing that because the Categorical Imperative abstracts from all empirical facts, the duties that are based on it must also abstract from them. The inference is not warranted. Whether they must abstract from particular empirical facts depends on the particular facts. Some are relevant; others are not. Surely there is no problem here, or indeed anything out of the ordinary.[14] Problems would arise only if relevant particulars were required by Kant's ethics to be treated as irrelevant (for instance, if the fact that someone is related to me had to be regarded as morally irrelevant). I see no reason for thinking that this is the case. It is okay for me to treat as morally relevant the fact that this is my sister if it is okay for anyone to treat as morally relevant, in relevantly similar circumstances, the fact that the person is his or her sister. Preferences for or exceptions for those close to us are not as such prohibited, but they must be permissible for anyone if they are to be permissible for me.[15]

In short, I see no reason for thinking that Kantian moral constraints are too coarse-grained (or otherwise silly, fastidious, or unreasonable), and therefore see nothing lamentable in the position that our commitments to others are not unconditional, but are circumscribed by moral constraints.

Not only is it not lamentable; I think it is salutary. It seems to me better for the purposes of overcoming oppression that people put fairness before helping out those nearest and dearest to them. The "old buddy system" thrives on people thinking that they should put helping those they are close to, or "their kind," ahead of "impersonal" fairness. And the worst-off people are much more likely to be aided by justice than by partiality. Partiality is good for those with friends in a position to do them good turns, and this is more typically the situation of those who are well off already than of those who are not.[16]

A word about "impersonal." Sometimes it is supposed that impartiality is, or requires, being impersonal, impersonal in the sense of ignoring anything that distinguishes that person from other persons.[17] Impartiality might thus be thought to require that when I grade my students' papers, I penalize each late paper equally, rather than taking into account that one student's paper was late because she had a miscarriage and was deeply distressed, while another student's paper was late because she was very busy with sorority "rush." But impartiality doesn't require this. It requires that I treat like cases alike, but does not dictate which cases are like. I do not violate the demands of impartiality if I regard the two cases just described as not alike, and choose to penalize only the paper of the second student for lateness.

Impartiality does not demand that I ignore the personal circumstances of my students. There is another way in which impartiality is sometimes thought to require that one act impersonally. It is claimed that to act impartially, I must remove myself from my particular standpoint and judge from a wholly impersonal standpoint: from the viewpoint of no one and nowhere. But "impartial" doesn't entail "impersonal." Sometimes the best way to keep from being biased—for example, in voting for or against promotion for a candidate whom I particularly do (or don't) like—indeed is to try to detach my reflections about the person's work from my personal perspective on this person. Sometimes it isn't clear whether I should so detach, simply because it isn't clear that the considerations that lead me to like or dislike the person are irrelevant. But often it is, and I may need to adopt an impersonal stance. At any rate, it is not part of the notion of impartiality that one think or judge or act impersonally. Doing so is simply one way of eliminating bias and thus being impartial, and it is not always the best way.[18]

But there is another reason for thinking that Kant's ethics requires that our attachments to others be highly attenuated. Love, he holds, has to be tempered. Indeed, moral beings are bound together by attraction and repulsion.

> In speaking of laws of duty (not laws of nature) and, among these, of laws for men's external relations with one another, we consider ourselves in a moral (intelligible) world where, by analogy with the physical world, *attraction* and *repulsion* bind together rational beings (on earth). The principle of **mutual love** admonishes men constantly to *come closer* to one another, that of the **respect** they owe one another, to keep themselves *at a distance* from one another, and should one of these great moral forces fail, "then nothingness (immorality), with gaping throat, would drink up the whole kingdom of (moral) beings like a drop of water" (if I may use Haller's words, but in a different connection). (MM 449)

Love needs to be checked by a proper sense of boundaries. Loving concern for one's friend—and here I have in mind genuine concern, not a desire to control the person—easily becomes paternalistic and heavy-handed. In addition—and here we see a desire to control the loved one—love too often involves a jealous desire that the loved one's attention be more fully (if not exclusively) focused on oneself. Fondness for and intimate conversations with others—even a strong attachment to a pet—is found threatening. (The father of one of my childhood friends found some pretext for having their dog "put to sleep," apparently because he couldn't stand his wife's fondness for the dog.)

Love may involve possessiveness, paternalism, and protectiveness. There are other risks, too, some of which infect not only love but also (simple) interests in another's welfare and a desire to help. Consider the zealous do-gooder, eagerly offering to do favors for her neighbors. She calls me with an offer to babysit my child; on another occasion, she offers to shop for me when she goes to an outlet store in Chicago that, she informs me, has terrific children's clothes at unusually low prices. On another occasion she calls to say that she made too much casserole, and would I like some? As it happens, she is not one of my favorite people. Accepting her favors puts me into a closer relationship than I would like. Turning any one of them down is feasible, turning most of them down is very awkward, and will no doubt seem rude to her. (This is due in part to her manner in offering to do favors: she argues with me when I try to decline; she also calls the next time she is going to the outlet store to repeat the offer, despite my having declined it the first time.) Now that I am, thanks to having accepted some of her offers, more closely linked to her, she invites me to her dinner parties. The dilemma again arises: accept and be more closely linked; decline and offend her. Accepting her favors puts me under an obligation to her. When she needs a babysitter, she of course thinks of me. Having accepted some of her many dinner invitations, I should invite her to my home for dinner, too.

Too often, the motivation for doing favors and offering advice includes a desire to shape another person's life, to influence another, to be able to claim credit for something the other person is or does. These desires need not involve any malevolence or even go quite so far as to count as desires to control another, and they are not only compatible with a fondness for the other person, but are some people's way of expressing fondness or of trying to develop a friendship with another. That they are common constitutes a strong reason in favor of a sort of moral caution: a recognition of the need to respect others as separate persons.

Kant sees friendship not as perfect love, but as the perfect blend of love and respect. In his words, it is "the union of two persons through equal mutual love and respect" (MM 469).[19] It is not only in cases such as that of the do-gooder, where the objects of one's would-be benefaction are not close friends, that respectful distance is in order. Within close relationships people (usually) learn that they should not always offer advice, and that there are times when it might be more considerate not to offer help. When one does offer help, it matters how one does it. Such offers, like helpful advice, sometimes convey the sense that the other person is not fully competent. "Here, I'll take that" can be said in such a way as to convey only that one wants to help out, to share the burden, but it can also come across as "It's easy for me and hard for you, given that I am strong and muscular and you're delicate and frail."

Keenly aware that accepting favors may undermine self-respect and a sense of equality with others, Kant stresses that we should render aid sensitively, taking care not to burden others with our favors and in particular, not to make them feel inferior to us. We "acknowledge that we are under obligation to help a poor man; but since the favor we do implies that his well-being depends on our generosity, and this humbles him, it is our duty to behave as if our help is either merely what is due him or but a slight service of love, and to spare him humiliation and maintain his respect for himself" (MM 448–49).

The approach Kant urges might seem singularly dishonest. If our help is not due him, why act as if it really is? But Kant points out that the wealthy person may well be mistaken if he thinks that his aid to the needy counts as doing a favor rather than as giving the needy their due.

> Having the means to practice such beneficence as depends on the goods of fortune is, for the most part, a result of certain men being favored through the injustice of the government, which introduces an inequality of wealth that makes others need their beneficence. Under such circumstances, does a rich man's help to the needy, on which he so readily prides himself as something meritorious, really deserve to be called beneficence at all? (MM 454)

Respect, in short, entails taking care not to make people feel inferior and (I add to Kant's points) not to force our favors on them, particularly if doing so puts them into a relationship with us with which they are uncomfortable. An unsympathetic reader will point out that one way of not forcing favors on others is never to help others at all. But this is of course not an option for a Kantian. We have a duty to render aid; more broadly, to promote others' happiness. Nonbeneficence is not an option. The "maxim of common interest, of beneficence toward those in need, is a universal duty of people, just because they are to be considered fellow humans, that is, rational beings with needs, united by nature in one dwelling place so that they can help one another" (MM 453).[20]

Kant's remarks about how to understand others' happiness further illustrate the need for respect to check love. In promoting another's happiness, are we to promote what we, who seek to help, take the other person's happiness to be? Or should we promote what the person whom we want to help takes her happiness to consist in? With some qualification, the second option is the one that Kant takes. The duty to promote others' happiness is the duty to help them to realize their ends (MM 388). The qualification is that we are only to promote their permissible ends. We are not to "give a lazy fellow soft cushions so that he [can] pass his life away in sweet idleness," nor "see to it that a drunkard is never short of wine and whatever else he needs to get drunk" (MM 481). Apart from this qualification, we must not override the other person's conception of her happiness. This is yet another way in which respect shapes and constrains love.

Kant's construal of "promoting others' happiness" reflects his staunch opposition to paternalism and his almost as staunch opposition to moralism in our interactions with others. The latter is also reflected in the fact that our second obligatory end (the other obligatory end being others' happiness) is one's own perfection—and only one's own. We have no obligation to perfect others.

Both his construal of others' happiness as their-happiness-as-they-see-it and his denial that we have a duty to promote others' perfection have come in for criticism. Citing his claim that "I cannot do good to anyone according to my concept of happiness (except to young children and the insane)" (MM 454), Jean Rumsey observes, "it is difficult to escape the conclusion that no human being is able to make good judgments about (much less promote) the well-being or happiness of anyone besides himself."[21] Because we have a duty to promote others' happiness—to promote their ends—this would be a peculiar view to attribute to Kant. Moreover, it does not follow from the claim that Rumsey cited ("I cannot do good . . .") The idea is simply that in seeking to promote another adult's happiness, I am to make use of her concept of her happiness, not mine (if mine is different). Rumsey continues by pointing out that "good friends often do help each other wisely . . . surely the friend who regularly sent him the turnips knew Kant's desire well." But that is just the point: the friend knew Kant's desires. He didn't judge that whatever Kant really did like, he should like carrots. He didn't try to turn Kant into something he wasn't. The point here is that there is no reason to infer from Kant's admonition to seek to promote the other's (permissible) ends, rather than promote what we think her ends should be, the conclusion that no humans (or even few humans) are able to promote the happiness of others. It merely takes care and forbearance. We have to learn what the other's ends (and tastes) are, and we have to resist the temptation to turn (would-be) beneficence into an opportunity to transform the other.

Is there reason to regard this—or Kant's claim that we have a duty to perfect others—as antithetical to feminism? Only if we suppose that it is part of feminism to oppose the degree of individualism, and the emphasis on agency and respect for persons as agents, that we find in Kant's ethics. But what we find is a less extreme individualism than some critics (e.g., Rumsey) claim. The Kantian idea is not that we cannot help others; indeed, it is very much our duty to help others. But we should do so in a way that does not diminish them as agents: does not invade their privacy or foist on them unwanted favors that will leave them with a sense of being beholden to us, and does not substitute for *their* conception of their happiness our own.[22]

What about the duty to perfect only oneself, not others? This too will sound objectionable to those feminists (and others) who believe that the boundaries of the self are more porous than is usually supposed. And indeed if Kant meant, in denying any obligation to perfect others, that it is inappropriate or impossible to help someone other than oneself to improve his or her character, I too would find his view highly objectionable. That this is not his view is indicated by his assertion that it is a duty to point out one's friend's faults to him (MM 470). So one can, and should, sometimes help another to improve. But there is a marked difference between what goes on when one seeks to help one's friend improve and what goes on when one seeks to improve oneself. One is providing the friend with information that the friend can make use of or not as he will, depending on his view of his own self-perfection. One can provide assistance to one's friend, but cannot do the improving for him. This is the point of denying a duty to perfect another, and I see no reason for feminist opposition to it, and much reason for feminist approval.[23]

In sum, to the limited extent that our attachments to others are supposed, on a Kantian view, to be attenuated and conditional, I see no cause for feminist opposition. Again, this reflects my particular feminist commitments; feminists (e.g., Gilliganians) who believe that ethical theories should reflect the outlook—if there is one—that seems (traditionally) to be that of most women will take a different stand. That love needs to be tempered with respect (which of course includes self-respect) is something that I think feminists should endorse.[24]

DETACHMENT FROM PROJECTS

In his "Persons, Character, and Morality," Bernard Williams extended his criticisms of utilitarianism to include Kantian ethics, claiming that Kantian ethics doesn't fare much better than utilitarianism despite its claim to respect persons. As Williams puts it, "the question arises, of whether the honourable instincts of Kantianism to defend the individuality of individuals against the agglomerative indifference of Utilitarianism can in fact be effective granted the impoverished and abstract character of persons as moral agents which the Kantian view seems to impose."[25] That Kantian ethics has a severely impoverished notion of character is evident, Williams thinks, when we consider that it, no less than utilitarianism, requires us to abandon our projects if they are in conflict with impersonal morality. Central to having a character is having projects, some nexus of which gives one's life meaning. The project or nexus of projects that provides "the motive force that propels him into the future, and gives him a reason for living" Williams calls a "ground project." If Kantian ethics forces us to treat our ground projects as expendable, as something we must be ready to give up if impersonal morality demands us to, it asks us not to take ourselves and our lives seriously.

This is not a particularly feminist objection to Kantian ethics. I bring it up because reflection on it supports the thought that Kantian ethics is considerably more congenial to feminism than are at least some of the views suggested by (and some of the bases for) a rejection of Kantian ethics.

Williams's point has some force with respect to consequentialism. Although there are consequentialist moves to deflect the charge, it does indeed seem that insofar as we are morally required to maximize impersonal good, we shall not be able to take our own projects very seriously. They will have to be assessed by reference to impersonal good and jettisoned, if giving them up maximizes impersonal good (even if it makes the agent miserable). Of course the cost to the agent of giving them up weighs in, and it might be argued that more impersonal good is promoted if people are allowed to pursue their projects (within very modest moral constraints) than if they are required to subject them to consequentialist evaluation. I shall not evaluate that line of response, as my concern is with Kantian ethics.[26]

The problems that arguably accrue to consequentialism don't afflict Kantian ethics, precisely because it doesn't require that we maximize. What it requires is less drastic, and distinctively egalitarian: if pursuit of a project is part of having a character, as Williams claims, then assuming that we are all equally entitled to have a character, everyone's pursuit of a project should be subject to the constraint that it not keep anyone else from pursuing a project. Our pursuits of our projects have to be circumscribed in such a way as to avoid its being the case that one person's pursuit of a project prevents others from having or pursuing a project. This is to use Williams's terminology to express a very Kantian idea. We are all rational beings; that is, we are all beings who set ends for ourselves, and my pursuit of my ends must not undercut others' capacity to set and pursue their ends. To expect others to shape their lives around my ends, without doing likewise myself, is to fail to respect them as rational beings. The notion that Kantian ethics is in trouble because it might require giving up or modifying one's project in the name of impersonal morality could gain a foothold only if one either (a) failed to understand that what Kantian ethics would demand is fairness or (b) rejected egalitarianism (perhaps on Nietzschean grounds).

There is a more general point to make here. Many of the objections to Kantian ethics reflect a sort of romanticism—about projects, relationships, and feelings—that is, in my view, considerably more at odds with feminism, and indeed with the task of overcoming any form of oppression, than is anything in Kantian ethics. The reason is simple: such romanticism tends to block recognition of the seriousness of injustices. It tends to put fairness and respect rather low on the scale of values. It encourages the perpetuation of something we are all too familiar with: regarding one person's ambitions and projects as so very important that others—in particular, the person's wife—are expected not to form their own ambitions and projects, but simply to submerge them into his. Being his muse, or his helpmate, is supposed to be project enough for her. Or to take a different, less extreme scenario: The wife is "allowed" to form her own projects, but they are expected to be sharply circum-scribed by his, while his projects are not supposed to be circumscribed by hers. It seems to me that the sort of detachment that Kantian ethics asks us to take regarding what Williams calls our "projects" is detachment that we *need* to take if we are to overcome inequalities—sexual inequali-ties among others. By contrast, opposition to such detachment, insis-tence that it is part of having a character that one not have to give up one's projects in the name of "impersonal morality," demotes fairness, and suggests (both to those who reap the benefits of the unfairness and to the losers) that concern with fairness is petty and small-minded. Not only does it encourage complacency among those who benefit from the status quo, it also encourages those who suffer from it to look beyond the unfairness, to focus on something "loftier"—the fact that the man to whom she is devoted loves (needs, depends on) her, to the beauty of self-sacrifice, to the pleasure (or the nobility) of giving without asking anything in return. It encourages, moreover, turning a blind eye in intimate relationships to ill-treatment and the absence of respect, provided, of course, that the relationship is sufficiently romantic.

DETACHMENT FROM FEELING

I argued above that Kant's ethics doesn't require detachment from other persons and from one's own projects except in a way that is not objectionable and is congenial to feminism—at least insofar as the chief concern of feminism is to overcome oppression. To those who see the celebration of (the lives of) women as they are and as they traditionally have been as more central to feminism than I do, Kant's ethics will seem less congenial to feminism. I am less concerned with seeing women's traditional domain given its due than I am troubled by ethical theories and approaches that (inadvertently) invite men to continue to exploit women and invite women to continue to submerge their interests in those of their men, to view their own role to be that of helpmate, and to make large personal sacrifices to men without expecting sacrifices of comparable magnitude to be made for them. Although some critics have claimed that Kant's ethics is ill-suited to address the fact that women (as we know them) tend to be "too willing to lose themselves in attending to the needs of others" and thus "require not so much a check on self-love as on their propensity for self-denial," I think the opposite is true.[27] Kant's ethics is somewhat unusual in that it doesn't regard self-love or selfishness as the one serious motivational obstacle to acting morally[28] and recognizes that self-sacrifice can go too far. One's own happiness must count too. ("Since all *others* with the exception of myself would not be *all*, so that the maxim would not have within it the universality of a law . . . the law making benevolence a duty will include myself, as an object of benevolence" [MM 451].) Servility is a vice; respect for humanity involves respect for oneself as well as for others, and servility is at odds with this. So while Kant (who, after all, was not J. S. Mill) almost certainly was not thinking about women and the moral outrageousness of the roles into which they traditionally have been cajoled or forced, his ethical theory is far more able to provide the tools for challenging those roles than many other theories (including, notably, care ethics).

But whereas I do not believe that Kant's ethics requires objectionable detachment from other persons and from one's projects, the claim that it requires objectionable detachment from one's emotions, feelings, and other affects does pose a more formidable challenge. Feminists and others are right to question the acceptability of Kant's ethics for anyone who doesn't regard feeling and emotion as primarily a moral hazard and who thinks that ethics is in part about proper feeling. In responding to the criticism, I want first to correct some misconceptions and thereby to argue that even though emotional agitations and passions are viewed in Kant's ethics primarily as moral hazards, not all affect is. But although this dispels some objections, there are lingering problems that are not so easily resolved. I do not hope to resolve them here, but I can at least isolate the more serious problems from the ones based on error.

The misconceptions I particularly want to dispel are that on Kant's view, (1) everything affective is bad, (2) all affect is "on a level,"[29] and (3) it is a matter of moral indifference, on Kant's ethics, what (or how) we feel. I use "affect" broadly to encompass inclinations, passions, emotions, feelings, and so forth.

Kant's most vehemently negative remarks about affects concern passions (*Leidenschaften*). They are, he says, "without exception *evil*" (A 267). Emotional agitations (*Affekten*) fare only slightly better. Some *Affekten* "can be healthful, provided they do not reach the point of enervating" the body.[30] Already I have said enough to show that (1) and

(2) are false. But the striking contrast is not between *Leidenschaften* and *Affekten*, which admittedly are viewed as primarily (though in the latter case not only) moral hazards, but between these and other, milder affects. Marking his disagreement with the Stoics, Kant writes in *Religion:* "Natural inclinations, *considered in themselves*, are good, that is, not a matter of reproach, and it is not only futile to want to extirpate them but to do so would also be harmful and blameworthy. Rather, let them be tamed and instead of clashing with one another they can be brought into harmony in a wholeness which is called happiness" (R 58/5).[31]

The reason why inclinations come in for so much more positive an assessment isn't hard to find: passions and emotional agitations are a threat to freedom and self-mastery, while inclinations—unless they get out of control, turning into passions and emotional agitations—are not. "In an emotional agitation we are taken unawares by feeling, so that the mind's self-control is suspended" (A 252). An "emotional agitation . . . rises swiftly to a degree of feeling that makes reflection impossible" (A 252).[32] Both passions and emotional agitations "exclude the sovereignty of reason" (A 251), but emotions tend to be short-lived whereas passions "tend to get themselves rooted and can co-exist even with subtle reasoning" (A 266). Kant is contrasting passions to emotional agitations when he says, after noting that Socrates wondered whether it would not be good to get angry at times, "On the other hand, no one wishes to have passions. For who wants to have himself put in chains when he can be free?" (A 253).

I turn now to (3), the claim that it is a matter of moral indifference, on Kant's ethics, how we feel. Of course how people feel is morally relevant in at least one way. We cannot both embrace as an end others' happiness and regard as of no importance others' feelings. The duty to promote others' happiness entails that how people feel is morally relevant. Those who hold (3) probably realize this; their focus is on the feelings of the agent, not the recipient. Their idea, I take it, is that all that matters morally, on the Kantian picture, is our actions and our maxims; how we feel toward others, in helping them, and so forth, is morally irrelevant. Kant's emphasis in the *Groundwork* and the *Critique of Practical Reason* on the unsuitability of sentiment to serve as a foundation for ethics understandably leaves readers with the impression that sentiment is, in his view, of no moral significance.[33] But it is clear from the work to which the *Groundwork* is the groundwork, the *Metaphysics of Morals*, that Kant does indeed think it matters what sentiments we have (and by the same token, that [1] and [2] are false). Consider his remarks about arrogance: "*Arrogance* (*superbia* and, as this word expresses it, the inclination to be always on top) is a kind of *ambition* (*ambitio*) in which we demand that others think little of themselves in comparison with us. It is, therefore, a vice opposed to the respect that every man can lawfully claim" (MM 465). Notice that the vice does not seem to be one of doing something—for example, convey-ing to others a demand that they think little of themselves—but rather of having a particular inclination (to be always on top) and a particular attitude toward others.

Consider too his remarks about malice, which he lists as a vice of hatred for men (MM 458):

> It is indeed natural that, by the laws of imagination (namely, the law of contrast), we feel our own well-being and even our good conduct more strongly when the misfortune of others or their downfall in scandal is put next to our own condition, as a foil to show it in so much the brighter light. But to rejoice immediately in the existence of such *enormities* destroying what is best in the world as a whole, and so also to wish for them to happen, is secretly to hate men; and this is the direct opposite of love for our neighbor, which is incumbent on us as a duty. (MM 460)

And many other examples could be provided to show that Kant thinks it does matter how we feel toward others, and that it is a duty to feel as one should. We have a duty not to feel envy or ingratitude, for these, like malice, are "vices of hatred" where the hatred is "not open and violent but secret and veiled" (458). Envy is "a propensity to view the well-being of others with distress, even though it does not detract from one's own" (458). Ingratitude "stands love of man on its head . . . and degrades absence of love into an authorization to hate the one who loves" (459).

Of course these are examples of sentiments and attitudes that we are not to have, the having of which constitutes a vice on Kant's ethics; and so while they refute (3), they may only add further fuel to the view that when feelings are morally significant, they matter only negatively. But (as the last sentence of the quote above on malice indicates) Kant attributes moral significance to feelings that we should have, not only to those which it is a vice to have. He says, for instance, that "it is a duty to sympathize actively in [the] fate [of others]" and to this end it is a duty to "cultivate the compassionate . . . feelings in us" (MM 457).

Having spoken in Kant's defense by arguing against the views that affects are for Kant, all on a level, that they are all bad, and that it doesn't matter, morally, what or how we feel (i.e., that only our actions and our maxims matter), I now indicate what I think *is* disturbing about his view of affect. And that is best done by quoting a passage that occurs just two paragraphs before the line quoted above, in which Kant says it is a duty to sympathize actively in the fate of others.

> It was a sublime way of thinking that the Stoic ascribed to his wise man when he had him say, "I wish for a friend, not that he might help *me* in poverty, sickness, imprisonment, etc., but rather that I might stand by *him* and rescue a man." But the same wise man, when he could not rescue his friend, said to himself, "What is it to me?" In other words, he repudiated imparted suffering. (MM 457)[34]

There are various points to make that render the passage slightly more palatable. Although Kant says "rescue," suggesting that if one can't cure one's friend's fatal illness, one might as well turn coldly away, in the sentence that follows the paragraph quoted above, he says "help," as he does in a very similar passage elsewhere.[35] And of course helping encompasses much more than rescuing does, including simply being with one's friend, sitting at her bedside in the hospital while she dozes. It's also worth pointing out that although "What's it to me?" may suggest "I'll worry about my own problems; to hell with hers," that isn't the idea at all; Kant is endorsing the Stoic ideal of not letting oneself be troubled by anything beyond one's control (be it one's own problems or someone else's). But, this said, the passage remains disturbing. What if I really cannot help in any way (perhaps because my friend is comatose—or has just died)? Is it really preferable that I feel no sadness?[36]

The passage suggests that Kant values a sort of disengagement from affect. We are to cultivate our sympathetic impulses, but we cultivate them in such a way that they are completely under our control. Up to a point this doesn't strike me as objectionable; it is important to be able to temper or moderate one's emotion. We need to be able to carry on even when grief-stricken—if not to go to work, keep appointments, and so forth, at least to cancel appointments; and if we have children or other dependents, we cannot simply ignore them or stash them away until we feel more able to cope. Rescue workers and people tending their dying companions cannot help very well unless they moderate their emotion. But moderation is one thing; "shutting it off" is another (although, interestingly, shutting off emotion does not seem at all objectionable if the agent is in the midst of a demanding task—rescuing victims from a bomb explosion, performing emergency surgery—particularly if the people she's helping are strangers to her or mere acquaintances). The passage seems to reflect too little appreciation of the value of affect and to advocate (what to non-Stoics is) excessive self-control.

More work is needed to locate our disagreement with Kant.[37] Perhaps the problem is this: we don't believe that someone can be a real friend, or even have others' happiness as one of her ends, if, when she can't help her friend, she thinks "What's it to me?" If so, our disagreement could be about the nature of friendship and what it is to care about others' happiness or about the nature of emotion and the extent to which it is subject to self-control—or about all of these. Our disagreement may also be normative: we may disagree with Kant not (only) about the extent to which it is possible to turn off our emotions, but the extent to which it is desirable (morally and, if this is different, for the agent's well-being). We think it possible and desirable for a rescue worker or a medical practitioner trying to resuscitate accident victims to be able to shut off her emotions while immersed in her work; but we also think less of such a person (and are perplexed) if she never feels emotional distress about the plight of the victims whose lives were lost. We think—but of course we may in years to come revise our opinion—that if she never feels (never "lets herself feel") emotional distress about an acute crisis (say, the bombing of the federal building in Oklahoma City in 1995) she will later suffer more distress. (One thinks here of reports of war veterans who never grieved the loss of their buddies and fifteen years later were, to their great puzzlement, devastated by the death of a pet.) I suspect that our disagreement with Kant involves more than one of these elements: we disagree about the desirability of shutting off emotion for a suffering friend when one cannot help, and we think less of someone who never feels sympathetic sadness in such circumstances.[38]

The degree of detachment that Kant thinks desirable bears an obvious connection to his attitudes toward women. His assumptions about gender roles and the proper relations between men and women color his views about emotion and self-control. He observes that if a compassionate man "were to weep, he would offend against his own sex and, because of his effeminacy, would not fulfill his role of protecting the weaker sex; but if he were not moved at all, he would not show the compassion toward the other sex that his masculinity makes his duty—the duty, namely, of taking her under his protection" (A 263). Add to this the tendency to equate male virtue with generic human virtue and it is hardly surprising that we do not find among the qualities that it is a duty to cultivate in oneself the qualities of being nurturing, affectionate, tender, loving, and expressive—qualities that have traditionally been expected of women but not (or not to the same degree) of men. And there are many other qualities that are expected of women much more than of men: being patient, being good listeners, having a sense of humor (crucial for anyone who spends much time with young children), being peaceable. (I omit those that I do not think belong in the catalog of virtues, but that have traditionally been asked of women: being compliant, submissive, meek, eager to please.) Kant's picture of traits we should cultivate in ourselves and of proper affect would be different if he pictured women along with men as prototypical virtuous persons.[39] Thus I don't entirely agree with the view sketched (and rejected) by Sedgwick, quoted at the opening of my paper: the problem isn't only that Kant didn't recognize that women are full-fledged rational beings, but also that he has too narrow—too "masculine"—a picture of the virtuous person. I do not think that this shakes his theory at the very foundations, however, as his theory is in no way based on a conception of the virtuous person. I see no incompatibility between accepting much of Kantian ethics while taking issue with some aspects of Kant's stance on affect (along with much that he says about women).[40]

Notes

1. Although I do not present this reply in my own voice, this is a good place to note that I don't believe that Kant's views were *quite* so deplorable as critics make them out to be. For example, while he says, as Schott cites, "I hardly believe that the fair sex is capable of principles," he adds that "these are also extremely rare in the male" (Immanuel Kant, *Observations on the Feeling of the Beautiful and Sublime*, trans. John T. Goldthwait [Berkeley and Los Angeles: University of California Press, 1960], 232/81; hereafter abbreviated as OBS). Note: if I provide just one page number, it is to the Academy edition. For translations, such as OBS, that do not provide the Academy page number, I cite the page number of the translation, as well.

Moreover, though Kant certainly is disdainful of scholarly women his objection is not that they are *incapable* of good scholarship, but that (God forbid!) it undermines their charm. "Laborious learning or painful pondering, even if a woman should greatly succeed in it, destroy the merits that are proper to her sex, and because of their rarity they can make of her an object of cold admiration; but at the same time they will weaken the charms with which she exercises her great power over the other sex" (OBS 229/78).

(It should be borne in mind that whether or not it reflects Kant's "mature" view of women, OBS certainly does not reflect his mature ethical theory. Written in 1763, it presents a rather different moral picture than the works of the 1780s and 1790s. For this reason we should be cautious about conjoining his remarks in OBS about women with his mature ethical view (unless, of course, they are repeated in *Anthropology*), as Jean Grimshaw does in her *Philosophy and Feminist Thinking* [Minneapolis: University of Minnesota Press, 1986], 42–45.)

2. Sedgwick's essay was originally published in *Pacific Philosophical Quarterly* 71 (March 1990). It should be noted that Sedgwick no longer holds some of the positions that she took in her essay.

3. That is, to seek incentives for doing what is morally required rather than taking the fact that it is morally required as a decisive reason for acting accordingly. See *Religion Within the Limits of Reason Alone*, trans. Theodore M. Greene and Hoyt H. Hudson (New York: Harper Torchbooks, 1960), 29–30/25; hereafter cited as *R*.

4. I shall not, in the course of this paper, challenge the assumption that Kant holds that women are by nature inferior to men in their moral and cognitive abilities. But as noted above there are reasons for questioning it. To be sure, he does speak of nature's purposes. In "devising the female sex," nature had two ends: "the preservation of the species" and "the cultivation of society and its refinement by woman" (*Anthropology from a Pragmatic Point of View*, trans. Mary Gregor [The Hague: Nijhoff, 1974], 306; hereafter abbreviated as A. "Nature entrusted to woman's womb its dearest pledge, the species, in the form of the foetus" and to safeguard the fetus, and thus the species, "implanted . . . fear in the face of physical harm and timidity in the face of physical dangers . . . in woman's nature" (A 306). "Through this weakness woman rightfully demands that man be her protector" (A 306). In connection with the second end, nature, wanting "to instil the more refined feelings that belong to culture—the feelings, namely, of sociability and decorum . . . made woman man's ruler through her modesty and her eloquence in speech and expression" (A 306). So far there is no suggestion that nature gave women inferior moral or intellectual capacities. Moreover, as noted above, he recognizes that women may greatly succeed in "laborious learning," and this suggests that he does not think that we are naturally incapable of such pursuits (though of course he might hold that it is only female freaks of nature who are good scholars). But one might see the second end of nature as explaining at least some of the alleged female inferiority: if, as Kant says, it *is* inconsistent with charm to be a brilliant scholar, perhaps nature did see to it that women (the exceptions, of course, being freaks) would neither wish to be scholars nor be any good at it if they tried. It's harder to trace a connection between charm and the other alleged forms of female inferiority. I shall not try to resolve these questions here; I want only to point out that although I'm assuming, for purposes of discussion that Kant's views of women are as critics have depicted them, there is some reason for questioning the critics' claims.

5. John Stuart Mill, *The Subjection of Woman* (Indianapolis: Hackett, 1988), 22–23.

6. His treatment of Maria von Herbert is also disturbing. See, in addition to Kant's letters to and about von Herbert and her letters to him, Rae Langton's "Duty and Desolation," *Philosophy* 67 (1992): 481–505. The letters are available in English in Arnulf Zweig, ed. and trans., *Kant: Philosophical Correspondence, 1755–99* (Chicago: University of Chicago Press, 1967).

7. At least in the English-speaking world.

8. The criticisms are of course intertwined. Because among the projects dearest to most of us will be our relationships with and the well-being of those we love, each of the first two forms of detachment will usually (though not always) involve the other. Detachment from our emotions and feelings is likely to entail detachment from other persons and from our own projects—at least it will mean that we are emotionally detached from both, though we might pursue both from a sense of commitment.

9. For a detailed discussion of Kant on personal relations, see Christine Korsgaard, "Creating the Kingdom of Ends: Reciprocity and Responsibility in Personal Relations," *Philosophical Perspectives* 6 (1992): 305–32.

10. Immanuel Kant, *Metaphysics of Morals*, trans. Mary Gregor (Cambridge: Cambridge University Press, 1991), 469. Hereafter abbreviated as MM.

11. I can't help thinking that I must be missing something, however, given how often one encounters the objection, and given how astute most of Sedgwick's article is. See also Schott's claim that "to privilege the autonomy of the individual as the primary factor in moral thinking makes human separateness and detachment morally normative" (Chapter 13). For a more in-depth discussion of Kantian autonomy than I provide, see Jane Kneller's defense of Kantian autonomy in her contribution to this volume (Chapter 7).

12. See Mary Gregor, *Laws of Freedom: A Study of Kant's Method of Applying the Categorical Imperative in the "Metaphysik der Sitten"* (Oxford: Basil Blackwell, 1963), chap. 1; Barbara Herman, *The Practice of Moral Judgment* (Cambridge: Harvard University Press, 1993), chap 2; Onora O'Neill, *Construction of Reasons: Explorations of Kant's Practical Philosophy* (Cambridge: Cambridge University Press, 1989), p. 2; and Sally Sedgwick, "On the Relation of Pure Reason to Content: A Reply to Hegel's Critique of Formalism in Kant's Ethics," *Philosophy and Phenomenological Research* 49 (September 1988): 59–80.

13. Immanuel Kant, *Groundwork of the Metaphysics of Morals*, trans. H. J. Paton (New York: Harper and Row, 1964), 423. Hereafter cited as G.

14. As Onora O'Neill points out, abstraction is both innocuous and unavoidable. It is silly to speak as if certain approaches to ethics involve abstractions while others do not. (As she suggests, the underlying confusion may be between idealization, which can be objectionable, and abstraction, which isn't.) See her "Kant's Ethics and Kantian Ethics," in her *Bounds of Justice* (Cambridge: Cambridge University Press, forthcoming).

15. I treat this more fully in my "Impartialism and its Critics," unpublished.

16. See Marilyn Friedman, "The Practice of Partiality," *Ethics* 101 (July 1991): 818–35.

17. This seems to be a background assumption in Robin Schott's essay (Chapter 13), particularly in the last pages, and in the work she cites by Iris Young.

18. See Margaret Urban Walker, "Partial Consideration," *Ethics* (July 1991): 758–74.

19. Unfortunately, Kant speaks of unions of two people rather differently when he turns to the subject of marriage. "If a union is to be harmonious and indissoluble . . . one party must be *subject* to the other and, reciprocally, one must be the *superior* of the other in some way, in order to be able to rule and govern him. For if two people who cannot dispense with each other make *equal* claims, self-love produces nothing but wrangling" (A 303; see also A 309–10).

20. I have altered Gregor's translation, translating *Menschen* as "people" rather than as "men" and *Mitmenschen* as "fellow humans" rather than as "fellow men." *Mensch*, unlike "man," is gender-neutral. In many passages there is nonetheless reason to believe that Kant had only men in mind when he used *Menschen*, but I see no reason for thinking that is the case in this instance.

21. Rumsey, Chapter 5, this volume. I should note that she is using a different translation from the one that I am using. I've quoted MM 454 the way she does.

22. Though as noted, we may, indeed should, seek to promote only those ends that we believe to be permissible.

23. I would not want to endorse everything that Kant says regarding the need for respect to temper love. In his discussion of friendship in *The Doctrine of Virtue* he says that "the principle of respect requires [friends] to stay at a proper distance from each other." This wouldn't have to be objectionable; the point could be that even within close friendships we need to respect the other's need for privacy, not press to know her innermost thoughts if she seems reluctant to voice them, and so forth. But Kant goes on to explain that this "limitation on intimacy" expresses "the rule that even the best of friends should not make themselves too familiar with each other" (MM 470), and this is not something I would endorse.

24. That Kant's ethics provides a good basis for criticizing subservient roles, such as that of the deferential wife, has been pointed out in Thomas Hill Jr., "Servility and Self-Respect" in (among other places) his *Autonomy and Self-Respect* (Cambridge: Cambridge University Press, 1991). See also Marilyn Friedman, "Moral Integrity and the Deferential Wife," *Philosophical Studies* 47 (1984): 141–50, and my "Servility, Critical Deference and the Deferential Wife," *Philosophical Studies* 48 (1985): 393–400.

25. Bernard Williams, "Persons, Character and Morality," in his *Moral Luck: Philosophical Papers, 1973–1980* (Cambridge: Cambridge University Press, 1981), 4–5.

26. This line of defense is developed by Peter Railton in "Alienation, Consequentialism, and the Demands of Morality," *Philosophy and Public Affairs* 13 (1984): 134–71, and by Philip Pettit and Geoffrey Brennan in "Restrictive Consequentialism," *Australasian Journal of Philosophy* 64 (December 1986): 438–55. See too William Wilcox's reply to Railton in "Egoists, Consequentialists, and their Friends," *Philosophy and Public Affairs* 16 (1987): 73–84.

27. The quote is from Sedgwick, Chapter 3. Cheshire Calhoun makes a similar claim regarding Kant's ethics in her "Justice, Care, and Gender Bias," *Journal of Philosophy* 58 (September 1988): 459.

28. I say "motivation" advisedly: most ethicists recognize that foolishness, short-sightedness, and the like are obstacles to acting morally. What is rather unusual is to recognize the perils Kant recognizes, namely, the perils of love untempered by (self-) respect.

29. Robin Schott cites approvingly Iris Young's claim: "Since all desiring is equally suspect, we have no way of distinguishing which desires are good and which bad"; see Schott, Chapter 13. Julia Annas makes a similar claim in her "Personal Love and Kantian Ethics in *Effi Briest*," *Philosophy and Literature* 8 (1984): 15–31, repr. in *Friendship: A Philosophical Reader*, ed. Neera Kapur Badhwar (Ithaca: Cornell University Press, 1993). I reply to Annas's article in my "Was Effi Briest a Victim of Kantian Morality?" *Philosophy and Literature* 12 (1988): 95–113, also reprinted in *Friendship*.

30. Kant, "On Philosophers' Medicine of the Body," trans. Mary J. Gregor. In *Kant's Latin Writings: Translations, Commentaries, and Notes*, ed. Lewis White Beck in collaboration with Mary J. Gregor, Ralf Meerbote, and John A. Reuscher (New York: Peter Lang, 1986), 228–29. Page reference is to the translation. Kant also says that laughing and weeping are agitations "by which nature promotes health in a mechanical way" (A 262).

31. Readers may wonder how this passage is to be squared with the following: "Inclinations themselves, as sources of needs, are so far from having an absolute value to make them desirable for their own sake that it must rather be the universal wish of every rational being to be wholly free from them" (G 428) and "Inclinations . . . are . . . always burdensome to a rational being, and, though he cannot put them aside, they nevertheless elicit from him the wish to be free of them" (*Critique of Practical Reason*, trans. Lewis White Beck [Indianapolis: Bobbs-Merrill], 118). The second quote is easier to reconcile: since (as Kant noted in the *Groundwork*) our inclinations grow and multiply as we indulge them, and since they become more demanding, sometimes becoming passions, we're bound to feel at times that life would

be better without them. Nonetheless, this is futile and wrongheaded. The first quote is more jarring. I take it to be a hyperbolic version of what he says in the second quote. It might be claimed that Kant's view simply changed, that he took a more positive view in the 1790s than in the 1780s. But I think the difference is mainly one of emphasis. Given the projects of the second *Critique* and the *Groundwork*, Kant is concerned to stress how unsuited sentiment is to serve a foundational role in morality. In those works he is seeking to show that moral motivation does not require the aid of inclination and that the supreme principle of morality can and must have a purely nonempirical foundation. *Religion, Anthropology*, and the *Doctrine of Virtue* build on the earlier works and are not primarily concerned with foundations, so there is little need to emphasize the unsuitability of sentiment to play a foundational role.

32. I have substituted "emotional agitation" for "affect" in Gregor's translation of *Affekt*. I do so for two reasons: first, I want to use "affect" as a generic term, covering passions, emotional agitations, inclinations and so on; second, Gregor is not consistent in her translation of *Affekt*—translating it sometimes as "emotional agitation" and sometimes as "affect"—and I think consistency is important here.

33. Except, of course, insofar as the fact that an action done from inclination precludes its having moral worth. For a discussion of Kant on moral worth, see chap. 5 of my *Kantian Ethics Almost Without Apology* (Ithaca: Cornell University Press, 1995).

34. I have substituted "repudiated imparted suffering" for Gregor's "rejected compassion" as a translation for *verwarf die Mitleidenschaft*. "Repudiated imparted suffering" is the way Gregor put it in her 1964 translation, and I think it is preferable because it helps to bring out the fact that what the sage rejects is catching or being infected by another's pain. For a more extensive discussion of this passage, see chap. 6 of my *Kantian Ethics Almost Without Apology*.

35. Kant, *Lectures on Ethics*, trans. Louis Infield (Indianapolis: Hackett, 1981), 200 (page reference is to the English translation).

35. Interestingly, Kant does acknowledge that unrestrained, unmoderated grief can be healthy. Under the heading "On Emotional Agitations By Which Nature Promotes Health Mechanically," he writes: "Weeping—inhaling with sobs (convulsively), when it is combined with a gush of tears—is likewise one of nature's provisions for health, because of the soothing effect it has; and a widow who, as we say, refuses to be comforted—that is, will not hear of stopping the flow of tears—is taking care of her health without knowing it or really wanting it" (A 262).

37. In using "our" rather than "my" I am assuming that most contemporary readers of Kant find this passage disturbing, and I am trying to figure out just what it is that we find disturbing.

38. In thinking about these matters, I've been helped by comments from Lara Denis on another paper of mine, and from reading Thomas Hill Jr., "Moral Dilemmas, Gaps, and Residues," *Moral Dilemmas and Moral Theory* ed. Eugene Mason (Oxford: Oxford University Press, 1996).

39. I don't mean to suggest that he doesn't think of women as virtuous; he certainly does. He notes the differences between feminine and masculine virtue: "Feminine and masculine virtue or lack of virtue are very different from each other, more as regards their incentive than their kind. —She should be patient; he must be tolerant. She is sensitive [*empfindlich*]; he is reponsive [sic] [*empfindsam*]" (A 307–8). Interestingly, he sees the merit of (at least some of) the feminine virtues to be contingent on the social role into which women are cast, not on the nature of women; see A 308.

40. It is based on the goodwill, but that is different.

41. I am grateful to Jane Kneller, Robin Schott, and Sally Sedgwick for comments on an earlier draft and to Martha Pellegrino and Christine Korsgaard for discussion of some of the issues raised in this paper.

Part III

Aesthetics

7

The Aesthetic Dimension of Kantian Autonomy

Jane Kneller

Recent interest in the Kantian notion of autonomy among feminists was sparked by the "ethics of care" debate arising out of the work of Carol Gilligan. The contrast between an ethics of care and an ethic of autonomy was precipitated by Gilligan's landmark criticism of Kohlberg's work on moral psychology and the "Kantian" notion of autonomy enshrined therein.[1] Kohlberg's hierarchical account of the stages of moral development placed considerations of care and sympathy below the "higher" stage approaches oriented around more abstract principles of justice, impartiality, and autonomy.[2] Because moral thinking that is characteristically defined by appeal to universal principles and impartial duty is associated with Kant's, and because, as Gilligan's early work pointed out, this a prioristic approach is empirically associated with men and not with women, Kantian notions of moral autonomy have often been presumed guilty of masculinist bias.[3] In what follows I shall argue that Kant's concerns with aesthetic theory led him to reevaluate the importance of the role of feelings in a way that allows for a reconstruction of Kantian autonomy that could be valuable to feminist theorists. I shall argue that the conception of autonomy usually associated with Kant is something of a caricature, and briefly discuss two important works, by Hannah Arendt and Onora O'Neill, that have to some extent corrected that picture by adding a social dimension to it. I shall then argue that even these fall short of developing a full-blown account of Kantian autonomy because they fail to take into account aesthetic elements of moral development that Kant himself theorized.

AUTONOMY AND THE MORAL HERO

The ability to stand up for oneself and to be in some sense self-determining has typically been labeled "autonomy" in the history of modern social philosophy, and the notion has a venerable place in the history of emancipation movements. However else it may be characterized, the capacity to think and act on one's own has been held up over and over by modern social theorists as definitive of liberated subjectivity. Kant's 1784 essay on Enlightenment is a classic statement of the modernist call to social progress through autonomous thought: "Have the courage to serve your *own* understanding!" is the campaign slogan of the Enlightener, for Kant. Those wishing enlightenment will trade their comfortable dependence on the authority of others for a more challenging state of rational autonomy.[4] For Kant every human being, so far as he or she is rational, may attain this autonomy if only he or she has the courage and industry to do so. (It is worth noting, of course, that "courage" for Kant is a "masculine" virtue, and he finds indolence typically associated with the "fair sex."[5] Some are going to be better candidates for autonomy than others!)

In spite of the emancipatory rhetoric of the "Enlightenment" essay, the "Kantian" view of autonomy has come to be associated with a questionable sort of figure: a moral superstar alone on a rock of rational will power, removed from the individuals whose humanity this will requires him (Kant's hero is clearly conceived as male by Kant himself) to respect, relying only on himself, with no "taint" of love or emotion spoiling his moral glory. This picture, however, is a caricature due in large part to Kant's own formulations in what was intended as a popular introduction to his ethical theory, *The Foundations of the Metaphysics of Morals*. This work has often left readers with the impression that the fully developed moral human being is typified by a moral-heroic subject who stands alone and independent of determination by "alien causes," having a will that is characteristically "a law to itself."[6] The moral superhero devoid of compassion but committed to principles and the duties that follow therefrom is understandably unappealing to those, including feminists, who see an important place for care and sympathy in the nature of moral character.[7] Given such a portrait of the autonomous being, it is no wonder that feminists have objected to the very concept of autonomy. Autonomy, some argue, is premised on an abstract individualism that portrays the paradigm moral agent as isolated, nonsocial, and ahistorical. It is thus often seen to be a thoroughly masculinist ideal.[8]

Still, for many feminists (often the very same ones who criticize this particular conception of autonomy) there is a lingering sense that we need, or at least should not too quickly dispose of, *some* concept of autonomy as necessary to genuine political dialogue and to the development of oppositional consciousness.[9] What is needed is an account of autonomy that is not predicated on an isolationist individualism, and that recognizes the importance of the individual's being situated within a community of others as an essential part of her autonomy. Thus it is important to recognize that even if the picture just drawn bears some resemblance to Kant's account of moral subjectivity in the ethical writings, Kant himself came to believe that there is more to say about human subjectivity than can be accounted for simply by an individualistic account of "pure practical reason." To find this further account one must also turn as Arendt and O'Neill have done to the third *Critique*.

Arendt and O'Neill: The Social Dimension of Kantian Autonomy

Hannah Arendt's published lecture notes on Kant's political philosophy are perhaps the most famous example of an attempt to find more than a "critique of taste"—that quaint-sounding eighteenth-century occupation—in the *Critique of Judgement*. Arendt argues that this work goes far beyond an inquiry into taste and that the *Critique of Judgement* contains the germ of Kant's political theory. It is not a theory of political agency, she argues, but of political *assessment and evaluation*, and it is precisely this critical function that makes Kant's politics emancipatory. The ability to judge the past, to pronounce it good or bad, just or unjust, is what allows us to "reclaim our human dignity, win it back as it were, from the pseudo-divinity named History of the modern age."[10] What follows this introduction to her lectures is, in the words of one eminent Kant scholar, "an informal mixture of sketchiness, paradox, and profundity,"[11] and I shall not attempt to pull the many provocative and illuminating aspects of her lectures together here. Rather, I will focus only on her argument that Kant's aesthetic theory, especially his theory of taste, lays the conceptual groundwork for a theory of human political freedom, i.e., for an autonomy that will make possible "a better kind of life," a life of humans in community with other humans (*Lectures*, 25).

Arendt accepts the standard "heroic" view of Kantian moral autonomy, so she argues that in the first two *Critiques*, "Man" is identified with a "reasonable being, subject to the laws of practical reason which he gives to himself, autonomous, an end in himself." But in the third *Critique* this notion of autonomy is contrasted with a more political portrait: "Men" (she uses the plural) are identified in the "Critique of Aesthetic Judgment" with "earthbound creatures, living in communities, endowed with common sense, *sensus communis*, a community sense; *not autonomous*, needing each other's company even for thinking" (*Lectures*, 27; emphasis added). Even though she labels this new picture as lacking a vision of autonomy, she later rightly points out that "political freedom is defined quite unequivocally and consistently through [Kant's] work as "to make public use of one's reason at every point."[12] In other words, Arendt recognized that for Kant, to be fully autonomous, self-determining "earthbound" human beings require community:

> Kant's view of this matter is . . . that the very faculty of thinking depends on its public use; without "the test of free and open examination," no thinking and no opinion-formation are possible. Reason is not made "to isolate itself but to get into community with others . . . unless you can somehow communicate and expose to the test of others, either orally or in writing, whatever

you may have found out when you were alone, this faculty exerted in solitude will disappear. In the words of Jaspers, truth is what I can communicate. (*Lectures*, 40)

Thus for Arendt, community, or what comes to the same thing, publicity, is necessary for critical thought, which is *definitive* of political autonomy. What seems surprising, in hindsight perhaps, is that she did not conclude that this aspect of Kant's philosophy must profoundly affect the interpretation of Kantian moral autonomy as well. What is moral autonomy, after all, but the ability to think for oneself, free of "alien" determination? Why may it not also be the case that moral autonomy requires "getting into community with others"? She herself points out that

> To think critically applies not only to doctrines and concepts one receives from others, to the prejudices and traditions one inherits; it is precisely by applying critical standards to one's own thought that one learns the art of critical thought.
>
> And this application one cannot learn without publicity, without the testing that arises from contact with other people's thinking . . . *impartiality* is obtained by taking the viewpoints of others into account; impartiality is not the result of some higher standpoint that would then actually settle the dispute by being altogether above the melée. (*Lectures*, 42)

She points out that Kant's notion of impartiality is really the maxim of enlarged thought of the *Critique of Judgement* "to put ourselves in thought in the place of everyone else." Kant says: "[It] indicates a man with a *broadened way of thinking* if he overrides the private subjective conditions of his judgment, into which so many others are locked, as it were, and reflects on his own judgment from a universal standpoint (which he can determine only by transferring himself to the standpoint of others)" (*CJ* AK V 295). By drawing attention to this aspect of Kant's work in the third *Critique*, Arendt makes possible a reevaluation of other parts of Kant's doctrine of moral autonomy. "Transferring oneself to the standpoint of others" here is held up as a necessary condition of achieving a "universal standpoint," which perspective is itself a condition of moral thought, for Kant. Clearly, it is only a short step from Arendt's insights into publicity and "enlarged thought" as conditions of political autonomy to an understanding of Kantian autonomy with a social dimension, one that involves membership in community, rather than isolation.[13]

Seen in this context, Onora O'Neill's Kantian social constructivist account of morality is very much in the tradition of Arendt. O'Neill may be read as extending Arendt's point about the connection of community and political freedom to make explicit that community is also necessary for moral autonomy, That is, she makes the case that there is a social dimension to the critical and impartial nature of moral deliberation in Kant's ethics. Kantian autonomy, O'Neill argues, is "self-discipline" or "self-determination," and is the ground of reason itself, both practical and theoretical: "[Reason] is merely autonomy in thinking and acting, considered in the abstract."[14] But on O'Neill's reconstruction of Kantian autonomy, reason is a social "construction" in process, begun and to be continued by a labor force of "workers," according to a "negative" *plan* (laid out in the "Doctrine of Method") "to refrain from adopting plans that others cannot adopt. Those who are to be fellow workers must at least refrain from basing their action on basic principles that others cannot share" (23). Reason, moral as well as political, must abjure force, power, and polemic as procedures that undermine its very purpose (9). Human autonomy itself is a construction in process, never fully achieved and never defined once and for all; its builders are subject only to the constraint that their own work not constrain its further development. Autonomy may therefore take on a plurality of forms in various contexts and at various times in history.

This is very far removed from the rigid, ahistorical egoism and self-sufficiency traditionally attributed to Kantian accounts. Moreover, by claiming that autonomy is the ability to think of oneself as a member of a community of "workers" who take it upon themselves to further autonomous *action* as well as thought,[15] O'Neill forges a link, not obvious in Arendt, between moral autonomy and the ability to see oneself as a member of a community of agents all working to realize a vision of human political freedom. Being morally autonomous means being able to see oneself as a member of a community that separates itself, at least in thought, from one's de facto community to act as a "task force" for resisting illegitimate authority and for building new forms of legitimate (i.e., noncoercive) authority.[16] On this account moral autonomy requires a form of solidarity, not isolation.

THE AESTHETIC DIMENSION

Both Arendt's account of the social nature of political autonomy and O'Neill's extension of it to include practical reason are extremely important reinterpretations of Kantian autonomy. But both, in my view, should be carried further to take into account what Kant himself eventually took quite seriously, namely, the *aesthetic*, that is, *felt*, dimension of reflective judgment. It is particularly surprising to find this aspect glossed over, if not ignored, in Arendt, who is dealing directly with Kant's account of *aesthetic* reflection in the third *Critique* as the source of his politics. And yet, immediately after her discussion of the community nature of reflective, critical thought she adds a caution:

> I must warn you here of a very common and easy misunderstanding. The trick of critical thinking does not consist in an enormously enlarged empathy through which one can know what actually goes on in the mind of all others. To think, according to Kant's understanding of enlightenment, means *Selbstdenken*, to think for oneself, "which is the maxim of a never-passive reason. To be given to such passivity is called prejudice," and enlightenment is first of all, liberation from prejudice. To accept what goes on in the minds of those whose "standpoint" . . . is not my own would mean passively to accept their thought, that is, to exchange their prejudices for the prejudices proper to my own station. (*Lectures*, 43)

Here Arendt does not want students to be confused into thinking that Kant is advocating the actual adopting of the thoughts of all others as our own. She is certainly correct, but the reason she gives here is not that such an acceptance of other's thoughts would defeat the "anti-authoritarianism" of critical reason, but rather that, because such an adoption rests on a feeling, it would be too "passive." Empathy (*en* + *pathos*, a *feeling*) is passive, presumably the mere "reception" of the very feelings of others, and for this reason is out of place here, she claims. What is really at the heart of the matter for Arendt is a kind of disinterested, distanced *thinking* that eschews passively "feeling with" (sympathy for) others.

In comparing the judgment of beauty (taste) in the third *Critique* to the process of political criticism, she then not surprisingly focuses on the contemplative side of aesthetic experience: the "spectating" subject reflecting upon the beautiful object rather than the feeling of pleasure to which this reflection gives rise and which finds expression in the judgment "This is beautiful." It is Kant's discussion of the possibility of the universal communicability of *thoughts* rather than feelings that interests her, and she is anxious to distinguish communicability from expression ("communication is not expression") (*Lectures*, 70). She spends a good deal of time elucidating Kant's conception of a *sensus communis* as "like an extra mental capacity (*Menschenverstand*) that fits us into a community." It is, she says, the ability to communicate thoughts, and not merely to express needs and emotions (*Lectures*, 70). For Arendt, Kant's "common sense" is to be understood in terms of the three "maxims" of thought that Kant mentions in the section (40) devoted to "Taste as a kind of *sensus communis*" (think for oneself; put oneself in thought in the place of everyone else; think consistently—in agreement with oneself).

However, the maxims, although surely important to Kant, are not strictly part of his analysis of taste. He warns that the "common human understanding" whose principles the maxims serve to elucidate "is not being included here as part of the critique of taste" (CJ AK V 294). Moreover, once having presented them, Kant "resume[s] the thread from which I just digressed" to say

> that taste can be called a *sensus communis* more legitimately than can sound understanding (*Verstand*), and that the aesthetic power of judgment deserves to be called shared sense* more than does the intellectual one, if indeed we wish to use the word "sense" to stand for an effect that mere reflection has upon the mind, even though we then mean by sense the feeling of pleasure. We could even define taste as the ability to judge something that makes our feeling in a given presentation *universally communicable*, without mediation by a concept.
>
> *Taste could be called a *sensus communis aestheticus*, and common understanding a *sensus communis logicus*.

Kant sums up by saying: "Hence taste is our ability to judge *a priori* the communicability of *feelings* that (without mediation by a concept) are connected with a given presentation" (CJ 296; emphasis added).

It is important to look more closely at Kant's views on the nature of judgments of taste than Arendt does. An explicit aim of Kant's "Critique of Aesthetic Judgement" (roughly the first half of the *Critique of Judgement*) is to show that we have the capacity, in addition to the capacity for publicity of thought, for publicity of feeling. This latter capacity (i.e., the *sensus communis aestheticus*) makes possible the universal communicability of certain feelings a priori. That is, since all human beings are sentient and sensuous "earthbound" beings, Kant argues, certain feelings may be expected to result when we reflect upon the world around us in an aesthetic way. If we presuppose no interests in knowing the thing or in its usefulness to us or even in its moral worth in the process of this reflection, the resultant pleasure taken in aesthetic reflection is *shareable* in principle by all. Thus a kind of universality, "universal communicability," is possible for feelings of pleasure. This willingness to grant the existence of such pleasures in universal conditions a priori is a landmark new position for Kant.

Not just any pleasure will do, of course. This pleasure is based on a certain sort of judgment that Kant calls "reflective aesthetic." The "reflection" Kant has in mind here is aesthetic because it involves no application of a particular concept, and hence is not "cognitive." The pleasure itself is central to the judgment. In judging aesthetically, Kant says,

> we do not use understanding to refer the presentation to the object so as to give rise to cognition; rather, we use imagination . . . to refer the presentation to the subject and his feeling of pleasure or displeasure . . . this reference designates nothing whatsoever in the object, but here the subject feels himself, how he is affected by the presentation. (CJ 203)

A judgment of taste is a way of relating to the world that results not in cognitive or moral experience of it, but rather in a special sort of feeling of pleasure (or displeasure). This pleasure is the consciousness of what Kant describes as a "free play" of the imagination with the manifold of representations given in sensation. As a feeling, it is not articulated in concepts or principles, but is nevertheless universal, because based on capacities that all human beings share, and on those alone.[17] Kant argues that the feeling expressed in judgments of taste rests on a general human capacity for feeling pleasure in mere imaginative play with the formal aspects of the objects we perceive. This "play" involves the "attunement of the cognitive powers [imagination and understanding] that is required for cognition in general."[18] The consciousness of this "attunement" is the pleasure felt as a person contemplates beauty.

Kant calls this universal (or "universally communicable") feeling of pleasure "disinterested" because it rests on a kind of relation between the subject and the world that involves no particular concern (cognitive, moral, or even gratificational) on the part of the subject for the existence of the object itself. That is, a pleasure is disinterested (*ein uninteressirtes Wohlgefallen*) when it is the result of reflecting upon an object where "what matters is what I do with this presentation within myself, and not the [respect] in which I depend on the object's existence."

Disinterested pleasure is really the counterpart of the impartiality that Arendt focuses on in her discussion of Kant's maxims of judgment. The difference is that the former is *aesthetic*: whereas impartiality is directed to thinking, disinterest is a property of feeling. A focus on the *aesthetic* character of the judgment of taste reveals the possibility, given Kant's views, that "impartial" or "critical" empathy—"feeling along with" someone else—is possible. Arendt's exclusion of empathy from her interpretation of "enlarged thought" is thus too restrictive. The range of feelings that admit of universal communicability may be limited by the conditions of disinterest, but where these conditions are met, aesthetic publicity, "the publicity of pleasure," is altogether possible, for Kant.

O'Neill, perhaps even more so than Arendt, appears not to be comfortable with aesthetic considerations; she reiterates in her *Constructions of Reason* the strict separation of feeling (desire) and reason that Kant puts forth in the *Foundations*. It seems to me, however, that Kant's later views on the importance of aesthetic feeling could be of some use to her account, for the following reason: O'Neill's reconstruction of Kantian autonomy requires commitment to criticism and to community. But how does one become part of it? To gain employment with the team of workers constructing autonomy one must pledge refusal "to bow under an alien yoke" (58), and this means, for O'Neill, the refusal to act on anything that is not a principle of reason. "What count as the principles of reason cannot hinge on variable and contingent matters, all of which, however intimately human, are alien causes" (58). Alien causes for O'Neill are "animal causes": "desires, drives, inclinations and the like" (72). As with Arendt, the mature and independent builder of autonomy is a "reasoner." For O'Neill, this reasoner acts only on the Categorical

Imperative of autonomy: "Think for yourself!" and the promise to do so is the pledge this reasoner must take in order to work to further human autonomy.

However, O'Neill, like Arendt, does not really address the issue that to take this pledge to think for oneself requires a prior "self" that is to do its own thinking and acting, and the consequent question raised of how that "self" came to be. Arendt mentions the problem only in passing: "But one can be this [self-]legislator only if one is oneself free; whether the same maxim is valid for the bondsman as for the free man is open to question." This of course, is a problem that Kant himself needs to address. Unfortunately he does not do so in any systematic way, although he is aware of some version of this problem in his "Enlightenment" essay, when he notes that certain guardians (*Vormünder*) see to it that any development toward self-determination is portrayed as extremely dangerous to those under their control.[19] But as Victor Seidler points out, it is necessary to ask of Kant (and in this context, also of Arendt and O'Neill) whether "the subordination of our needs and wants, feelings and desires, actually prepar[es] us to take this kind of control over our lives."[20]

Where autonomy is conceived as the ability to refuse to listen to *any* of one's desires, needs, and wants there would appear to be no room for the possibility of autonomy to be gained from listening to and respecting any of one's feelings, even those that might properly be viewed as "common to all." Thus, to borrow Seidler's example, viewing desires and feelings as a source of temptations and deception rather than knowledge, we will not be likely to question a doctor's diagnosis or become involved in understanding it. We are rather more likely to entrust ourselves absolutely to the alien authority of a medical system that systematically undermines autonomy by treating patients as non-agents. Or to take another example, a woman who finds herself in a relationship with a man whose authority over her is established by tradition may find herself feeling used, frustrated, and dissatisfied. Given the complexity and force of social conditioning, however, she may be in no position to articulate this frustration. However, it seems reasonable to see in these feelings at least the beginnings of autonomous thought and the basis for eventual autonomous action on the part of the person experiencing them.[21] But if feelings and desires are "alien" determinations to be abstracted from in order to follow the command "Think for yourself!" the subject's first gropings toward autonomy will be undermined by the "maxim" of that very autonomy that she is attempting to achieve.

Especially on a constructivist reinterpretation of Kant, where autonomy is a project to be ever more finely tuned but never absolutely achieved, issues of development toward and preparation to become autonomous cannot be separated from the construction of principles of autonomy. If autonomy requires adoption of a maxim that ultimately may undermine the possibility of becoming autonomous, it is undermining the heart of its own project. O'Neill cannot allow this, and yet by suggesting that "desires, drives, inclinations and the like" are *always* alien determinations that impede entrance to the community of builders of human freedom, her account of autonomy appears to hinge on precisely the sort of self-defeating maxim she wants to rule out.

Arendt and O'Neill are concerned primarily with analyzing Kant's concept of autonomy as it appears in the fully autonomous agent, which approach is understandable given that it is Kant's own approach in much of his writings on ethics. Thus I am not suggesting that either of them is committed to the view that feelings and emotions play no role whatsoever in the development of autonomous structures in the subject.[22] But neither do they consider the possibility that individual development toward self-determination is itself part of the very meaning of human autonomy, or to use O'Neill's language, that autonomy is a psychological as well as social construction, always in process in the individual as well as in the community.

SOME KANTIAN SUGGESTIONS FOR AN AESTHETIC DIMENSION OF AUTONOMY

Kant himself never *recanted* his views on the negative impact of desires, wants, and needs on morality. Yet his aesthetic theory opened up the possibility of feelings that play a positive role in the development of moral subjectivity, and Kant himself was aware of the implications his new views on aesthetic theory might have for his account of morality. He claimed that beauty could symbolize morality, arguing that there is a strong analogy between the judgment of beauty and moral judgment, part of which was the analogy between the disinterest and impartiality of the two (CJ, sect. 59, 353–54). He entertained the view that aesthetic reflective pleasure may serve as a developmental bridge to morality, helping human beings make the transition to morality more easily (CJ 354), and he even suggests at one point that disinterested pleasure can give rise to certain non-self-centered interests in nature (CJ, sect. 42). Clearly Kant is not relying on the more simplistic separation of feeling and reason suggested in the *Foundations*. In fact, it is precisely a concern for showing the integration of feeling and reason that led him in his aesthetic theory to go beyond describing the conditions under which feelings can be universally communicable (the conditions of "taste") to say something about the importance of aesthetic expression and about the interests to which it gives rise.

An example may be found in his account of the "Ideal of Beauty." Here Kant argues that ideas of reason, (perfect human virtue, for example, which necessarily includes autonomy) may be "made visible, as it were, in bodily expression" through the union of "pure ideas of reason" with "a very strong imagination" not only in the artist but in the receiver, in what he calls the "Ideal" of beauty (CJ, 235, sect. 17). Such judgments are then no longer "mere judgments of taste" he says, but they nevertheless give rise to "correct" ideals that produce a "great interest" in us. An interest, Kant says, is the "liking" (*Wohlgefallen*) that we connect with the thought (representation) of the existence of an object. It is therefore connected with wanting the object; it is "a liking for the existence of an object or action."[23] Putting these together, it follows that the reception of artistic embodiments of moral ideas creates feelings in us, or desires for the existence of that object. Kant does not pursue this, but it is perfectly consistent with all that he says here that aesthetic experiences of this sort could lead one to *feel* the need for the existence of rational "ideas" in oneself such as autonomy.

Similarly, Kant's discussion of "aesthetic ideas" holds out the possibility that feelings may play a positive role in moral development in conjunction with a creative imagination: "an aesthetic idea is a presentation of the imagination . . . that makes us add to a concept the thoughts of much that is ineffable, but *the feeling of which quickens our cognitive powers and connects language, which otherwise would be mere letters, with spirit*" (CJ 314). Kant argues that the gifted artist is capable of producing concrete images in words, sounds, or visual images that create feelings in the receiver that neither the artist nor the receiver (nor anyone else) could ever express conceptually. Nevertheless these feelings are the aesthetic manifestation of moral ideas. One implication of this, although again, Kant does not draw it out, is that it is possible that such feelings may themselves be a kind of moral/aesthetic pleasure in, or even desire for, the existence of such moral ideas as autonomy.

Kant's account of a transformative (*umbildende*) power of the imagination in connection with the expression of aesthetic ideas is also extremely interesting. In the third *Critique*, Kant in effect changes his mind about the extent to which the imagination may be creative,[24] arguing that it has the power to portray a new reality beyond the one that actually exists: "For the imagination ([in its role] as a productive cognitive power) is very mighty when it creates, as it were, another nature out of the material that actual nature gives it. We use it to entertain ourselves when experience strikes us as overly routine. We may even restructure our experience" (CJ 314). This is not to say that imagination actually produces "another nature" but rather that it is capable of expressing, or "making visible" ideas that otherwise are not expressible. Keeping in mind that for Kant, the notion of a perfectly self-determining moral agent is ultimately an idea of reason, and hence not expressible cognitively, it is evident that the imagination may have an important role to play in creating aesthetic images that have an effect on how people feel about themselves and others.

Although Kant did not draw out the social or moral implications of an "empowered" imagination, it is worth pointing out the ways in which such a concept could be an important part of a theory of autonomy that is sensitive to developmental issues. If a social or social constructivist notion of autonomy is to work, it ought to allow for the necessity of certain desires and feelings that first make it possible for dependent persons to sense, if not to articulate, that they *are* dependent, and that they *need* to become self-determining (i.e., autonomous). What is required if this is to occur? "Reason" or "thought," when conceived as completely unconnected with "mere" sensation and feeling, unable to incorporate a feeling or sense of something being wrong, can be of little use. On this model those feelings that conflict with the thoughts and reasoning of others can only be labeled "neurotic," "paranoid," or "irrational." Clearly it is important that persons in dependent situations who have these negative feelings be able to imagine the possibility of a world in which their particular feelings, desires, and fears are not written off as irrational and pathological, and in which they have a hand in making the decisions that affect their lives. The ability to project even only a dim image of themselves as full members of a society that takes their inarticulable feelings seriously and views them as genuine agents is crucial to the process of becoming articulate, and hence autonomous.

So in addition to finding a place for feelings, imaginative projection ought not to be underestimated in any account of the social construction of autonomy. This is clear from the importance of "make-believe" to children's development, wherein whole worlds are invented, worlds within which children imagine themselves operating freely and effectively without adults. It is also clear from the fact that art, music, literature, and drama have always played important roles in movements for social change. The social force of art—its ability to challenge, uplift, and motivate individuals—must be seen in part as a result of its ability to take concrete "worldly" materials and imaginatively transform them into realities that expand our abilities to feel what others feel and to envision alternative situations.

In the preceding I have only begun to follow up on some suggestive aspects of Kant's aesthetic theory in the context of feminist concerns about autonomy and self-determination. Still, I have shown that tracing the implications of what amount to mere "theoretical suggestions" in Kant's aesthetics could be extremely valuable for a developmental theory of moral autonomy. Whatever the merits or demerits of his account of autonomy in the *Foundations* and other ethical writings, in the third *Critique* Kant developed an account of feelings that was far more nuanced than is typically attributed to him. He came to hold that the pleasure we take in contemplating art and beautiful objects is capable of being shared by everyone, thus opening the possibility that there are other aesthetic experiences that may be shareable, namely, any that are based on conditions of experience shared by all. A reconstruction of Kant's aesthetic theory might focus on those feelings, for instance, that are created by frustrated desires for self-determination in the individual, since these may very well be seen as "universal" desires and feelings, tied as they are to necessary conditions of full human moral development.

An autonomous human subjectivity that is understood as at least in part aesthetic—felt and imaginative in addition to critically rational and social—is, I believe, part of Kant's final vision of human subjectivity. Some such account is crucial to a developmental account of autonomy, since such an account contests the view that human feelings and hopes are "alien" to our moral and political selves. Developmental accounts also require a notion of how it is possible for nonautonomous subjects to envision possibilities alternative to the actualities that make them *feel* dependent and incompetent. Kant's complete account of human subjectivity, far from ending with an isolated superhero, attempts through aesthetic considerations to relocate the moral reasoner in the world of feeling and imaginative anticipation. How well he succeeded and whether all the implications of his aesthetics for subjectivity square with all of his moral theory are separate questions. What I have shown here is that the attempt itself is important to feminist conceptions of human freedom, and for this reason the aesthetic dimension of Kantian autonomy ought not to be overlooked.

Notes

Reference to Kant's work in this paper are to the standard Prussian Academy of Sciences edition (1902–) of Kant's collected writings. Quotations from the *Critique of Judgment* are taken from Werner Pluhar's translation (Indianapolis: Hackett, 1987), and references to the *Foundations of the Metaphysics of Morals* from Lewis White Beck's translation (New York: Macmillan, 1990). Both indicate Academy edition pagination in the margins.

1. Cf. Carol Gilligan, *In a Different Voice: Psychological Theory and Women's Development* (Cambridge: Harvard University Press, 1982).

2. L. Kohlberg, *The Philosophy of Moral Development* (New York: Harper and Row, 1981), and *The Psychology of Moral Development* (New York: Harper and Row, 1984).

3. Cf. for instance Kristen Waters, "Women in Kantian Ethics: A Failure at Universality," in *Modern Engenderings*, ed. Bat Ami Bar-On (Albany: State University of New York Press, 1994).

4. Immanuel Kant, "What is Enlightenment?" trans. Lewis White Beck, in *Foundations of the Metaphysics of Morals* (83–90); AK VIII 35–41.

5. Immanuel Kant, *Anthropology from a Pragmatic Point of View*, trans. Mary Gregor (The Hague: Martinus Nijhof, 1974) (124–25); AK VII 257. Kant contrasts patience, a "feminine virtue" with courage, a principled virtue, which, as he says that America Indian males also don't seem able to exhibit it, is apparently a virtue peculiar to European males. In the *Critique of Judgment* (hereafter cited as *CJ*) Kant associates indolence and dissipation with high culture, and he argues in the *Anthropology* that "woman's" purpose is to further culture. See *CJ* AK V 432–33, 121–22, and *Anthropology* (169) 306.

6. *Foundations of the Metaphysics of Morals* AK IV, 446–47, trans. L. W. Beck (New York: Macmillan, 1985). See also Barbara Herman's important article "On the Value of Acting from the Motive of Duty," *Philosophical Review* 90 (1981): 359–82, on this subject before concluding that Kant's ethical views, even in the *Foundations*, are correctly captured by this picture. Also see her most recent book, *The Practice of Moral Judgment* (Cambridge: Harvard University Press, 1993). A good defense of certain notions of autonomy free of "the more extreme Kantian baggage that usually travels with them" may by found in Thomas Hill, "The Importance of Autonomy" in *Autonomy and Self-Respect* New York: Cambridge University Press, 1991).

7. For a succinct refutation of this criticism of Kant's *Foundations*, see Beck's introduction, xxi.

8. See for example, Alison Jaggar, *Feminist Politics and Human Nature* (Totowa, N.J.: Rowman and Allanheld, 1983), esp. 44 and 131, for a critique of autonomy when understood as self-sufficient and isolated individualism.

9. See for instance, Nancy Fraser, *Unruly Practices* (Minneapolis: University of Minnesota Press, 1989), 47, and Rita Felski, *Beyond Feminist Aesthetics: Feminist Literature and Social Change* (Cambridge: Harvard University Press, 1989), 150–53.

10. Hannah Arendt, *Lectures on Kant's Political Philosophy*, ed. and with an interpretive essay by Ronald Beiner (Chicago: University of Chicago Press, 1982), 5.

11. Lewis White Beck, in *Kant: Selections*, ed. L. W. Beck (New York: Macmillan, 1988), bibliographical essay, 478.

12. Ibid., 39. The quote from Kant is from "What is Enlightenment?"

13. Arendt herself notes that "Publicness is already the criterion of rightness in [Kant's] moral philosophy" (49).

14. Onora O'Neill, *Constructions of Reason: Explorations of Kant's Practical Philosophy* (Cambridge: Cambridge University Press, 1989), 64.

15. Ibid., 76. O'Neill uses Kant's terminology when she states that this view "locates freedom and autonomy in the capacity to think of oneself as a member of the "intelligible world." She interprets talk of "worlds" in Kant to be talk of standpoints (59–63).

16. This sounds remarkably like Marilyn Friedman's account of "communities of choice." Friedman is of course referring to actual communities, but this similarity between her revised version of communitarianism and O'Neill's reinterpretation of Kant suggest the intriguing possibility that the twain could meet. See Marilyn Friedman, "Feminism and Modern Friendship: Dislocating the Community," *Ethics* 99, no. 2 (January 1989): 275–90.

17. Cf. *CJ* sect. 9 (216–19).

18. *CJ*, sect. 21, 238–39. This section argues that the "attunement" that is universally communicable therefore justifies the presupposition of a *sensus communis*.

19. "What is Enlightenment?" 35–36.

20. Victor Seidler, "Kant, Respect, Individuality and Dependence," in *Kant's Practical Philosophy Reconsidered*, ed. Yirmiyahu Yovel (Boston: Kluwer Academic Publishers, 1989), 245.

21. On the need to recognize that there are degrees of autonomy, and for a careful characterization of different levels of autonomy, see Diana T. Meyers, "Personal Autonomy and the Paradox of Feminine Socialization," *Journal of Philosophy* 84 no. 11 (November 1987): 619–28.

22. In an essay entitled "Agency and Anthropology in Kant's *Groundwork*," O'Neill suggests that this is a possibility for Kant as he "neither denies nor discusses whether a different, moralized conception of desire might have a more central role in the moral life" (In *Kant's Practical Philosophy Reconsidered*, ed. Yovel, 70.)

23. *CJ* 204, 207. Also see the *Foundations*, 459 n.

24. In the *Critique of Pure Reason*, Kant argued that "to attempt to realize the ideal in an example, that is in the [field of] appearance, as, for instance, to depict the [character of the perfectly] wise man in a novel, is impracticable. There is indeed something absurd, and far from edifying, in such an attempt" and that "the products of the imagination" represented by "painters and physiognomists" are represented as being "incommunicable, shadowy images" (trans. N. Kemp Smith [New York: St. Martins, 1965], A569/B597–A71/B599). Although Kant never ceased to be skeptical about the moral character of artists' intentions, he did change his mind about the communicability of the aesthetic ideas of genius. See Rudolf Makkreel, *Imagination and Interpretation in Kant: The Hermeneutical Import of the Critique of Judgement* (Chicago: University of Chicago Press, 1989) for a study of the development of Kant's notion of imagination.

8

The Concepts of the Sublime and the Beautiful in Kant and Lyotard

Cornelia Klinger

The interest I take in this somewhat remote and seemingly esoteric topic does not result from my occupation with aesthetic theory in general, though indeed aesthetics is one of my major fields of study. I became interested in the categories of the sublime and beautiful not so much for their own sake but because of their place in a broader framework.

I contend that the pairing of the beautiful and sublime is part of a long list of dualisms that form the grid of Western philosophical thought and one of the basic patterns of Western culture in general. The way in which the ideas of the beautiful and sublime are conceived of and how they are contrasted with each other is analogous to the polarizations of form and matter, mind and body, reason and emotion, public and private, having and being, activity and passivity, transcendence and immanence. The common denominator of these and other binary oppositions lies in the dualism of culture and nature. In different ways and perspectives man's relation to nature is at the heart of all of the above mentioned polarities. Within the framework of an almost exclusively male-dominated system of thought this relation to nature has been (and still is) conceived as most problematic.

The dualisms in which traditional Western thought abounds imply the dualism of gender. Or, put the other way around, the great dualisms of the Western philosophical tradition are attributed to what is considered to be the character of the two sexes. Every person socialized in our culture infallibly classifies reason and rationality as male, emotions and sentimentality as female; the gender connotations of activity and passivity are just as evident; we all know that women belong in the private sphere while the public is man's domain, and finally the association of man with culture and woman with nature also finds various direct expressions.

Hence, a feminist critic trying to demonstrate the gender implications, not to say the gender bias, of traditional philosophy is well advised to take a closer look at all of these binary concepts. I agree with Moira Gatens who calls the discovery of the connection between the various polarities of Western thought and the conceptualization of gender difference a decisive step in a feminist approach to philosophy: "the dichotomies which dominate philosophical thinking are not sexually neutral but are deeply implicated in the politics of sexual difference. It is this realization that constitutes the 'quantum leap' in feminist theorizing."[1]

In addition to these general reasons why it is useful to investigate such dual structures in all branches of philosophy, there is also a special reason for turning attention to the form this dualism has taken in aesthetics. It occurs to me that a renewed and intensified interest in the category of the sublime has evolved in aesthetic theory (and related fields) over the past ten or fifteen years. A plethora of publications documents a virtual revival of a concept that had appeared old-fashioned, and beyond any hope for a comeback only a few years before. Even more striking than this reemergence is that it is only *one* term of what used to appear as a binary concept that is now back on stage. It is only the idea of the sublime that suddenly meets with an intensified interest whereas the idea of the beautiful seems to be lost for good. While once the beautiful had been the dominant idea of which the sublime had been a mere variant, a kind of subspecies, it now seems as if the rise of the sublime takes place at the expense and detriment of the beautiful. The category of the beautiful is not only left out of the limelight but obscured by it. The now-common opinion about the beautiful is that it has generated into the commercialism of advertisement and design and therefore, does not deserve any serious consideration in the context of aesthetic theory.[2] The harmonious and harmonizing qualities of the beautiful are perceived as unfit to correspond to the fragmented, frac- tured, alienated, distorted, ugly traits of modern reality.

Now, if the general assumption is valid that there are gender connota- tions implied in the concepts of the sublime and beautiful and in their mutual relation, then what kind of bearing does this new development have against this background? Does the analogy simply end here, or is the one-sided rise of the male-identified category of the sublime a foreshadow or symptom of some mysterious masculine reaction taking place on the backstage of cultural theory while the "Triumph of Femi- nism" is still performed at the theater of society and political theory?

Given these different sorts of questions, we confront a twofold task. First, I shall outline the concepts of the sublime and beautiful in their classical formulation as found in Kant's *Critique of Judgment*. For the question of how the ideas of gender and gender relations are woven into this classical pattern of the sublime and beautiful I shall draw on Kant's contemporary and admirer, the German poet and writer Friedrich Schiller and his interpretation of Kantian concepts. In the second part of my essay, I shall discuss the recent revival of the idea of the sublime by referring to one of its most important promoters, the French philosopher Jean-François Lyotard. As Lyotard himself takes up Kant's theory and gives an interpretation of the *Critique of Judgment*, the two parts of the paper covering the late eighteenth century and the late twentieth century are closely connected.

Compared to some other dualisms (for example, the polarity of form and matter or mind and body), which can be traced back to very ancient roots, the polarization of the sublime and beautiful is relatively young. It is only with the onset of modern times, in the second half of the eighteenth century, that they become an important subject of philosoph- ical discussion. Of course, this is not to say that the ideas of the beautiful and also the sublime were altogether unknown before that time but it is only then that they are developed into cornerstones of an aesthetic theory; it is only in this era that aesthetics evolves as a full-fledged discipline in the canon of philosophy. Especially the concept of the sublime becomes very fashionable. Beginning about midcentury "an almost obsessive interest in and proliferation of material about the sublime"[3] can be observed. Kant or Schiller, who will serve as my examples here, are by no means the only authors who take up this topic: the reflections of Edmund Burke, for example, are much more familiar to an English-speaking public.

It is not a mere historical coincidence that the polarization of the sublime and beautiful and in particular, the rise of the sublime take place at the same moment of Western history when gender relations undergo, not a real revolution, but a considerable reshuffling in the wake of the Enlightenment and as a concomitant of the political and social revolutions that mark the beginning of the modern epoch. The best way to demonstrate the validity of this contention would be to give an analysis of an work Kant published in 1764 (this means almost thirty years earlier than his *Critique of Judgment*, 1790) entitled *Observations on the Feeling of the Beautiful and Sublime.*

The third out of four sections that constitute this work is dedicated to the question "The distinction of the Beautiful and Sublime in the Interrelations of the Two Sexes." It is here that Kant explicitly associates the beautiful with femininity and the sublime with masculinity. Still more interesting is that in this text Kant gives a short outline of the principles of women's education. The question of which role women should play in modern society and how they should be prepared and educated for their function was hotly debated at that time. Kant's ideas are quite close to what Jean-Jacques Rousseau in his famous novel *Emile* has written on the education of Emile's companion Sophie.

Kant differs from Rousseau in translating the normative conceptions of polarized gender roles that the two thinkers share into the language of aesthetics. The gender difference is expressed in aesthetic terms, and vice versa: gender difference is inscribed in aesthetic categories. Kant subsumes woman's essence, her entire being, under the category of the beautiful and thus contrasts her to man who is identified with the idea of the sublime (or with dignity or nobility): "The fair sex has just as much understanding as the male, but it is a *beautiful understanding*, whereas ours should be a *deep understanding*, an expression that signifies identity with the sublime."[4] The way in which the clear statement of equality in the first part of the sentence ("as much understanding as the male") is immediately followed by an assertion of difference between the sexes in the second part is a characteristic feature of Enlightenment thought. With the growing success of modern rationalism and the revolutionary ideas of universal human freedom and equality, the application of the same principles to both sexes grew unavoidable. Nevertheless, only very few thinkers of the age were ready to draw the radical conclusions that ensue from these principles; the majority of Enlightenment philosophers made every endeavor to find new foundations for gender difference in order to legitimate the status quo of gender hierarchy. Though the structure of society and the division of labor between the public and private realms underwent significant changes, the new bourgeois society was still dependent on women's subordinated domestic role. Hence, the tentative efforts to apply the ideas of freedom and equality to women met with fierce resistance.

Not only woman's rational but also her moral capacity is cast in aesthetic terms by Kant: "The virtue of a woman is a beautiful virtue. That of the male sex should be a noble virtue. Women will avoid the wicked not because it is unright, but because it is ugly; and virtuous actions mean to them such as are morally beautiful. Nothing of duty, nothing of compulsion, nothing of obligation! Woman is intolerant of all commands and all morose constraint" (*Observations*, 81). To be exempt from duty and compulsion may seem like a promise of freedom and may therefore have a good ring in our ears, but still there cannot be doubt that woman is thus reduced to a secondary status: "Among moral attributes true virtue alone is sublime. There are . . . good moral qualities that are amiable and beautiful", but "they cannot properly be included within the virtuous disposition" (57). Women's beautiful virtues are discriminated against as "adoptive virtues" (61) in opposition to man's sublime virtues which are "genuine virtue" (61). As woman is exempted from the moral law, she is excluded from the full status of humanity; in Kant's view the true sense of being human is defined by the capacity for moral principles.

I do not want to go into a detailed discussion of Kant's *Observations* but there are questions that deserve to be raised because the answers foreshadow a central point of the discussion of the beautiful and sublime in the *Critique of Judgment*. The question is, Why are beautiful and sublime virtues differentiated from each other? And how does Kant explain the superiority he ascribes to the sublime virtues? I think that we would expect an answer like the following: sublime virtues reach a higher degree or greater amount of the desired moral good, or are a safer and more reliable way to achieve it. Kant, however, affirms the contrary: as beautiful virtues are a natural disposition, almost a kind of instinct that a benevolent providence has placed into the hearts of men, they are a much more common and less defective source of moral behavior and action (*Observations*, 74). So, obviously it is not an argument of moral expediency or utility that justifies the precedence of the sublime virtues over the beautiful. The distinctive and decisive feature lies in Kant's assertion that the sublime virtues are independent of a benevolent providence; they are not given by nature as a kind of instinct but result from human freedom and are an accomplishment of reason.

This is the principle we have to keep in mind; it is a key to understanding what follows. Summarized very simply, it says: all that distinguishes man from nature, makes him independent of and sets him above nature, is of itself noble or sublime and hence ennobles man. This valuation involves a gender hierarchy: the female principle is identified as immersion in nature whereas it is a male prerogative to surmount nature's confines and to attain the autonomous moral law. The gendered implications of the beautiful and sublime that were explicit in Kant's *Observations* will become invisible in the *Critique of Judgment*. But the implicit gendered connotations of immersion in nature versus distance from nature will play an even more important role. It is under this guise that a gender subtext is present in the *Critique*. In Schiller's elaboration on Kant's concept this gender subtext will reemerge to the surface.

Now I turn to Kant's *Critique of Judgment*. I shall not bother you with a lengthy introduction into one of the most important works of modern Western philosophy but shall focus strictly on the notions of the beautiful and sublime. Still, I cannot avoid giving some "technical data," that is, a few of Kant's definitions that may sound strange and complicated because of their terminology.

The beautiful is defined as resulting from a connection between imagination and *understanding*, whereas the sublime follows from a combination of imagination and *reason*. (Just as a reminder: a mutual relation between imagination and understanding or reason is a requisite for human cognition; the distinction between *understanding* as the capacity to form notions and *reason* as the faculty for ideas is the basis of Kant's theory of human cognition as developed in his *Critique of Pure Reason*).

The two faculties, understanding and reason, are not only different in character but also the relations in which they enter with imagination are of completely different kinds. The relation of imagination and understanding is a harmonious one; a feeling of the beautiful arises when our understanding is in harmony with nature, when the form of a natural object is corresponding to our rational capacity and conveys to us the impression of a meaningful whole or totality. In Kant's wording: "in the estimate of the beautiful imagination and *understanding* by their concert generate subjective finality of the mental faculties."[5] The beautiful "is directly attended with a feeling of the furtherance of life, and is thus compatible with charms and a playful imagination."[6]

By contrast, the relation of imagination and reason is based on conflict and therefore is accompanied by a feeling of "displeasure."[7] This displeasure is "arising from the inadequacy of imagination in the aesthetic estimation of magnitude."[8] In accordance with other contemporary theories of the sublime, Kant differentiates between the mathematically and the dynamically sublime; it is either the quantum (numerical magnitude) of a phenomenon or the might of nature that exceeds our imagination: "the feeling of the sublime, may appear . . . in point of form to contravene the ends of our power of judgement, to be ill-adapted to our faculty of presentation, and to be . . . an outrage on the imagination."[9] Conflict, disharmony, struggle, and violence are the predominant features of the sublime and yet, there is also a strange kind of attraction, a "negative pleasure"[10] connected to it.

What is the source of this attractive and pleasing aspect of the sublime? Kant answers: "the inner perception of the inadequacy of every standard of sense to serve for the rational estimation of magnitude is a coming into accord with reason's laws, and a displeasure that makes us alive to the feeling of the supersensible side of our being, according to which it is final, and consequently a pleasure, to find every standard of sensibility falling short of the ideas of reason."[11] In the same process as we painfully experience the incapacity of our imagination we discover or are reminded of our capacity of reason as independent from and superior to the senses and to nature. The "feeling of our possessing a pure and self-sufficient reason"[12] is at the core of the category of the sublime: "a feeling comes home to him [the visitor of Saint Peter's in Rome] of the inadequacy of his imagination for presenting the idea of a whole . . . and in its fruitless efforts to extend this limit [of imagination] recoils upon itself, but in doing so succumbs to an emotional delight."[13] Thus, the delight of reason results from the defeat of imagination. The mind is "incited to abandon sensibility and employ itself upon ideas involving higher finality."[14] The ultimate idea of higher finality is the moral law. The feeling of the sublime that is aroused by some phenomena of external nature (e.g., "the prospect of mountains ascending to heaven, deep ravines and torrents raging there, deep-shadowed solitudes")[15] is nothing but a reflection of man's own sublimity that consists in his independence from nature as a rational, as a moral being: "Sublimity . . . does not reside in any of the things of nature, but only in our own mind, in so far as we may become conscious of our superiority over nature within, and thus also over nature without us (as exerting influence upon us)."[16]

The German poet Friedrich Schiller who has written widely on aesthetic theory has taken up and further developed Kant's concepts of the beautiful and sublime. In Schiller's essay *On the Sublime* some aspects of Kant's theory find an even more accentuated formulation than in Kant's own writing. First of all, Schiller elaborates on a question that was so self-evident for Kant that he did not even put it, namely, why independence from nature is so extremely important and highly valued. Schiller is more outspoken on why man fears nature; through his argumentation it becomes visible how this fear is transformed into a claim to superiority. It is not some strange idiosyncrasy peculiar only to Schiller (or Kant) that finds expression in Schiller's lines but an attitude that underlies much of modern Western thought and determines its specific will to the domination of nature.

Schiller views man as "[s]urrounded by numberless forces, which are all superior to him and hold sway over him."[17] Man undertakes every effort to escape from this threatening situation and, indeed, his intelligence (*Verstand*) enables him to invent "artificial" means to strengthen his position in the struggle against nature, so "that up to a certain point he actually succeeds in reigning physically over everything that is physical" (*On the Sublime*, 136). But still man's efforts inevitably founder at a certain point: that is, he cannot overcome death. Death is the "single point where he [man] is under constraint and bound," yet this one single point is sufficient to turn "his boasted liberty" into nothing (*On the Sublime*, 136). Nevertheless, Schiller holds onto the idea that being human in the full sense is irreconcilable with his succumbing to any exterior force: "he must be man in the full sense of the term, and consequently he must have nothing to endure, . . . contrary to his will. Accordingly, when he can no longer oppose to the physical forces any proportional physical force, only one resource remains to him to avoid suffering any violence." He must "*annihilate* as an *idea* the violence he is obliged to suffer in fact" (*On the Sublime*, 137). Man is capable of doing so, insofar as he is a moral being, and participates in a higher order than that of nature. Schiller is in agreement with Kant that it is the moral law that raises man above the confines of nature and in a way serves as an instrument to dominate nature by other means: "Man is in the hands of nature, but the will of man is in his own hands" (*On the Sublime*, 141).

The aesthetic category of the sublime is "a sensuous means to teach us that we are something more than mere sensuous natures" (*On the Sublime*, 141). The way in which Schiller describes the functioning and the effect of the sublime is quite similar to Kant's standpoint. But Schiller is once again more elaborate than Kant when it comes to justifying the priority the sublime takes over the beautiful:

> In the presence of beauty, reason and sense are in harmony, and it is only on account of this harmony that the beautiful has attraction for us. Consequently, beauty alone could never teach us that it is our destination to act as pure intelligences. . . . In the presence of the sublime, on the contrary, reason and the sensuous are not in harmony, and it is precisely this contradiction between the two which makes the charm of the sublime. . . . Here the physical man and the moral man separate in the most marked manner; for it is exactly in the presence of objects that make us feel at once how limited the former is that the other makes the experience of its force. The very thing that lowers one to the earth is precisely that which raises the other to the infinite. (*On the Sublime*, 141)

The more Schiller lays stress on the opposition between the sublime and the beautiful, the more he elevates the sublime on the one hand and denigrates the beautiful on the other, the closer he draws to the image of femininity in which the negative aspects of the beautiful become condensed. This point is reached at the end of the following passage that I must quote in full:

> the sublime opens to us a road to overstep the limits of the world of sense, in which the feeling of the beautiful would forever

imprison us. It is not little by little (for between absolute dependence and absolute liberty there is no possible transition), it is suddenly and by a shock that the sublime wrenches our spiritual and independent nature away from the net which feeling has spun round us, and which enchains the soul more tightly because of its subtle texture. Whatever may be the extent to which feeling has gained a mastery over men by the latent influence of a softening taste (weichlicher Geschmack), when even it should have succeeded in penetrating into the most secret recesses of moral jurisdiction under the deceptive envelope (Hülle) of spiritual beauty, poisoning the holiness of principle at its source—one single sublime emotion often suffices to break all this tissue of imposture at one blow to give freedom to the fettered elasticity of spiritual nature, to reveal its true destination, and to oblige it to conceive, for one instant at least, the feeling of its liberty (On the Sublime, 143)

At this point the imagery of femininity has grown so dense[18] that Schiller, the poet, the playwright, finds a personification and a plot to summarize the essence of his (and Kant's) concept: "Beauty, under the shape of the divine Calypso, bewitched the virtuous son of Ulysses, and the power of her charms held him long a prisoner in her island. For long he believed he was obeying an immortal divinity, whilst he was only the slave of sense; but suddenly, an impression of the sublime . . . seizes him; he remembers that he is called to a higher destiny—he throws himself into the waves, and is free" (On the Sublime, 143).

This rich passage of Schiller's essay would deserve a much more detailed comment than the limited space of this chapter allows. So I shall not mention the interesting implications of his emphasis on the violent, disruptive, sudden character of the sublime against the background of modern aesthetics that favor shock and cruelty as its main principles—long after Schiller.

Throughout the whole history of Western culture the concept of nature has been oscillating between two extremes: nature is viewed as benign and nurturant, a meaningful whole, an organic order in which man, nature's beloved son, takes the supreme place; equally present, however, is nature as chaotic, constantly threatening man's life and liberty, or rather, an iron cage ensnaring man in a relentless life-

and-death cycle completely inconsiderate of his aims and aspirations, indifferent to his suffering.

It is well known that woman is purported to be closer to nature than man because of her specific bodily functions; moreover, the idea of femininity is conceived in close analogy to the idea of nature and thus shares both of nature's aspects: compared to man who aspires to transcend not only the limits of nature but of any given order (including the rules of society), woman is viewed as benign and harmless, a creature subjected to nature and without a chance or the will to rebel against her condition. She is not defying death because she lacks man's audacious intellect, his creativity, his will to independence and power, his determination not to obey any but self-given, autonomous laws. In the same vein but on another level (i.e., with respect to society), woman is perceived as more conventional than man, complying with and obedient to the rules of any given society. She does not challenge the natural order of things, nor does she challenge the social order. And yet, the dark, wild, and threatening features of nature are attributed to woman as well. However submissive and therefore despised she may be, there is a never-ending suspicion against her, against the seductive power of (her) nature that threatens to entrap man in sensuality and at the same time to subvert his status as a rational being and destroy the order of society: "for every glowing portrait of submissive women enshrined in domesticity, there exists an equally important negative image that embodies the sacrilegious fiendishness."[19]

I conclude my digression on Schiller. He has helped us to shed some light on certain aspects that underlie Kant's theory of the beautiful and sublime in a more concealed manner. Schiller does not depart from Kant's concept of the sublime: it is Kant's idea that he takes up and elaborates. He only articulates what Kant assumes: he explains why man feels challenged and threatened by nature and he restores the explicit identification of nature and immersion in nature with femininity. Now, approaching Lyotard and considering his interpretation of the same Kantian concepts will reveal still other aspects present in Kant's text: while Schiller has elaborated on certain complexities in the concept of nature Lyotard will bring to light the violent features of the experience of the sublime; more than that, he will connect them too with the gender theme. Hence, he will make reappear the third *Critique*'s concealed gender subtext just as Schiller did, but from a different perspective.

Quite similar to Schiller, Lyotard translates Kant's austere philosophical terms into a poetic picture. Lyotard himself calls his account of Kant's theory a *novel* (*un roman*). This novel is so strange and amazing that I cannot help quoting it in almost full length. Lyotard introduces all of Kant's notions in a personified form. The concept of imagination appears as the mother and reason as father who together engender the sublime:

> the father is satisfied, the mother is unhappy. The sublime child is emotionally mixed, ambivalent, comprising pain and satisfaction. This follows from the fact that in terms of the genealogy of the so-called faculties of cognition the parents stem from two different families. She is "judgement," he is "reason." She is an artist, he is a moralist. She reflects, he determines. The moral law (the law of the father, paternal law) makes up its mind and determines the mind to act (determines the spirit of action). Reason wants good children, and requires imagination to bring forth just moral principles. But the mother, the reflective free imagination is only able to deploy forms without any pre-determined rule, without defined or definable aims. . . . The sublime is the child of an unfortunate encounter. Misfortune, because the Idea shows so little willingness to concession, the law, the father is so authoritarian, so unconditional is the respect he demands, that it is impossible (he does not care) to reach at a voluntary consent . . . with imagination. He drives the forms apart, the forms drive themselves apart, they become exuberant in his presence. He fertilizes the virgin devoted to forms disregarding her consent. He does not demand anything but respect for himself, for the law and its realization. He does not need a beautiful nature. The only thing he demands imperatively is a raped, overpowered and exhausted imagination. Giving birth to the sublime, she dies, believes to die. . . . Violence, force is necessarily linked to the sublime, that breaks free and rises. . . . Imagination must be violated for it is from her pain, through her rape that the pleasure to envision or almost envision the law is obtained.[20]

Lyotard concludes his story with the following remark: "You will smile about this childish scenario."[21]

I guess our first impulse would be (at least my first impulse was) to take this smile as an ironic smile. We could assume that Lyotard grossly caricatures Kant's conception in order to bring out the gender connotations. In some sense this is indeed so. But then, we should expect Lyotard to dissociate his own position clearly from Kant's at some point. Actually, I cannot find any trace of such a critical attitude in Lyotard's essay. It may sound paradoxical: although he unmasks and exposes the working of gender, the function of gender symbolism in Kant's theory, Lyotard does nothing to distance himself from it. On the contrary, I contend that Lyotard reinforces and exceeds the sexist traits of the sublime in a fashion and to an extent that not only finds no basis in Kant's writing but is even in open contradiction to Kant's position. There are some elements in Lyotard's reading of Kant that can be explained neither by exaggeration as an instrument of critique nor as an interpretation of Kant's intentions; instead, they must refer to Lyotard's own standpoint.

I see at least two such elements that pertain much more to Lyotard's "L'intérêt du sublime" than to Kant's. First, Lyotard celebrates the sacrifice on the part of the imagination that Kant had simply viewed as inevitable. Let me put it bluntly: Lyotard overtly rejoices in the rape of imagination while Kant views it as a necessary duty in the name and service of the moral law. Kant viewed imagination as overpowered but not as raped; Kant emphasizes duty where Lyotard celebrates pleasure and triumph. Lyotard himself drew my attention to this aspect: he comments on this difference of attitude as he refers to Kant's explicit warning against any "enthusiasm" accompanying the sacrifice that the moral law demands.

Second, and even more important, Lyotard takes the obliteration and reduction of the beautiful to an extreme. Taking up his family story of the faculties of cognition once again, Lyotard relates that imagination, the mother of the sublime, had a love affair with understanding (Verstand) prior to her unfortunate encounter with reason. This previous relationship is described by Lyotard as a perfectly happy one. We could now expect him to identify the beautiful as the child of imagination and understanding analogous to the sublime as resulting from the union of imagination and reason. But this is not the case. By help of yet another metaphor, namely that of fruit and blossom, Lyotard reduces the status of the beautiful: "The beautiful is not the fruit of a contract but only the blossom of a love relationship and, as everything that did not result from an interest, it passes away."[22] Lyotard grants this happy union between imagination and understanding neither legitimacy, nor creativity or permanence, whereas the disastrous relationship of imagination and reason appears suddenly in a surprisingly favorable light. Lyotard expressly calls the sublime "the fruit of a contract"—without one word of explanation how this opinion fits with his own account of a brutal rape. Apart from such immanent contradictions in Lyotard's family story, it is even more unfounded as an interpretation of Kant's theory. Not only does Lyotard's differentiation between blossom and fruit remain without justification in Kant; the marginalization of the beautiful is in open contradiction to the position and weight of the beautiful in Kant's *Critique of Judgement.* Despite Kant's appreciation of the sublime as an important intermediary between sensibility and practical reason (morality), it should not be overlooked that the beautiful is still the predominant aesthetic category.

It is obvious from his writings on art and aesthetics that the interest Lyotard takes in the sublime is not limited to the historical aspect of an interpretation of Kant's *Critique of Judgement.* Therefore, the final part of this chapter will be dedicated to Lyotard's essays on contemporary art and art theory in which the idea of the sublime plays a role (as, for example, in his essay "The Sublime and the Avant-garde" and other essays on the same or related topics). I have already mentioned that Lyotard plays a particularly active part in the recent revival of the sublime in the context of aesthetic theory.

Basically, there are two questions to be raised. First, how is Lyotard's concept of the sublime as pertaining to the context of contemporary art and (art)theory related to his interpretation of the historical concept of the sublime in Kant's *Critique of Judgement?* Second, does the gender symbolism associated with the ideas of the beautiful and sublime that Lyotard's reading of Kant's text helped so much to uncover have any impact on Lyotard's own position in the current debate?

A short answer to both questions. In brief: (1) there are considerable differences between the eighteenth- and the twentieth-century concepts of the sublime; (2) as far as I am familiar with Lyotard's writings on this subject, there is no allusion to gender apart from his account of Kant's theory quoted above.

The longer answer must start with a consideration of the differences between Kant's and Lyotard's perspectives. I see three major dissimilarities. First, when Kant thinks of beautiful or sublime objects or phenomena he thinks of natural objects or phenomena in the first place. The categories of the sublime and beautiful belong to an aesthetic theory of nature and it is only as a second (although very well possible) step that Kant applies them to the arts. With Lyotard it is not just the other way around; rather, the idea of nature has almost completely disappeared, and it is exclusively with respect to avant-garde art and literature that the concept of the sublime is used.

Second, the inadequacy of the imagination in confronting an over-powering impression is at the center of both Kant's and Lyotard's understanding of the sublime. But whereas for Kant this event was a portent of a higher order in which man participated as a rational and moral being, there is no such horizon to Lyotard's intellectual universe. For him the sublime does not represent anything, on the contrary, it is the sign of the "unrepresentable" and it is in the name of what is beyond any given and possible order that the sublime assumes significance. Lyotard's thinking is not only postmetaphysical (i.e., well beyond the idea of a metaphysical worldview) but also postmodern: he has also discarded Kant's concept of an autonomous rational and moral order.

Third, this fading away of a metaphysical worldview has important implications for the situation of the human subject. As the sublime is no longer referring to a meaningful moral universe, the disruptive and disquieting experience of the sublime is not made up for by the comforting certainty that the intimidated subject is citizen of a higher and more perfect world. While in Kant's theory the sublime helped man to become aware of his identity as a rational and moral being, Lyotard, conversely, views the sublime as an ideal instrument for the deconstruction of this very same identity. The sublime becomes a weapon to cut through the treacherous unity of subject-identity. Given these profound differences between Kant's and Lyotard's views, we have to put the same question the other way around and ask whether there is any "family resemblance" at all—without which the use of the same term, the notion of the sublime would be unfounded.

As far as similarities are concerned, it seems that Schiller comes back to mind much more easily than Kant. Lyotard's concept of the sublime shares Schiller's highly pathetic attitude, the heroic gesture of breaking free from the bonds of a surrounding reality. Lyotard agrees with Schiller in emphasizing the violence of this sudden motion, the tearing apart of the texture of reality that is painful for the subject of this action and at the same time inflicts pain on its object, thus oscillating between a self-denying ascetism and cruelty (rape). By the end of the twentieth century the specific masculinism of the sublime that evolved with the rise of the modern subject in the eighteenth century has lost its original ontological and moral framework but the masculinist gesture of breaking away from a given order is retained. Having lost its justification and purpose in the service of a higher aim, it is reduced to a gesture of rigid resistance against any given reality, combined with the intention to cause pain for the pleasure as an aim in itself.

Of course, for Lyotard it is not the realm of nature, as for Kant and Schiller, from which the sublime must help us to break away. Instead it is the realm of the social that has taken this place. It is not the spell of sensuality (or female sexuality) that must be overpowered from a firm rational and moral standpoint; but the conventions of society must be ripped through by aesthetic, artistic innovation.

> The art lover does not experience a simple pleasure, or derive some ethical benefit from his contact with art, but expects an intensification of his conceptual and emotional capacity, an ambivalent enjoyment. Intensity is associated with an ontological dislocation. The art object no longer bends itself to models, but tries to present the fact that there is an unpresentable. . . . The social community no longer recognizes itself in an art object, but ignores them, rejects them as incomprehensible, and only later allows the intellectual avant-garde to preserve them in museums as the traces of offensives that bear witness of the power, and the privation, of the spirit.[23]

Although it is not possible to identify the given reality of modern society with the beautiful order of nature, still the strange double aspect in the motives of man's flight from nature's beauty emerges. On the one hand, the complacent conventionalism of society appears as banal, our smooth everyday ways of thinking, behaving, and perceiving reality appear as contemptible yet harmless. The contempt of the conventional aspects of society resembles the disrespect of benign and harmless nature. In both cases it is the "unmanly" attitude of easy, unquestioned compliance in a given order that is not man-made or self-willed that causes contempt. On the other hand, there is in both cases a threatening element looming in the background. The way in which Lyotard describes the frightening aspect of social life is surprisingly close to the terror

Schiller ascribes to the ensnaring powers of nature. In Lyotard's view the fear of fusion, unification with an all-encompassing whole is transferred to the social sphere and reemerges here as the fear of totalitarianism. Alluding to Hegel, Lyotard warns us that terror is the price we have to pay for the illusion of unity. Lyotard asserts: "The nineteenth and twentieth centuries have given us as much terror as we can take. We have paid a high enough price for the nostalgia of the whole and the one, for the reconciliation of the concept and the sensible. . . . Under the general demand for slackening and for appeasement, we can hear the mutterings of the desire for a return of terror, for the realization of the fantasy to seize reality. The only answer is: let us wage war on totality, let us be witnesses to the unrepresentable; let us activate the differences, and save the honor of the name."[24]

From this brief summary of Lyotard's position it should have become clear that the overt misogynism traditionally associated with the sublime disappears as soon as it is no longer man's relation to nature that is at issue. Yet this does by no means imply that the extreme masculinist outlook disappears as well. On the contrary, from a feminist point of view there is reason enough to object to this pervasive masculinism of modern culture.

As Lyotard holds onto the concept of the sublime he is tied down to a concept of modernity that he actually started out to leave behind. As we could learn from Kant and Schiller, the idea of the sublime paradigmatically embodied the self-image of modern man breaking away from any predetermined order of things. Now Lyotard intends to use this same concept as a symbol of the effort to break away from modernity. But the idea of the sublime is so imbued with the spirit of modernity that it virtually derails Lyotard's intentions. The historical heritage of the concept of the sublime weighs heavily on its contemporary use, leading it into a wrong direction.

Lyotard's intention to deconstruct the petrified modern ego by exposing it to the disturbing experience of sublime aesthetic innovation is belied by the fact that this bold exposure to the "unrepresentable" presupposes, requires, and at the same time constitutes the subject of the heroic avant-garde artist. The figure of the artist embodies the cult of the autonomous, sovereign, creative, and almost godlike modern subject in its ultimate masculine form. To substitute the concept of the moral and political subject with the aesthetic subject is nothing new and no step beyond the framework of modernity; rather it is one of its most characteristic features.

I am not the only critic of Lyotard to state with some surprise that he, who claims to be the spearhead of the postmodern project, affirms a modern notion of art and artist (thus reinstating the modern subject). Lyotard himself has expressly confirmed this observation several times and one of his German disciples positively speaks of a congruence between "hard modernism" and postmodernism.[25] In his article "Postmodernism and the Born-Again Avant-Garde" John Tagg ridicules the clearly masculinist overtones of a postmodernism that turns out to be nothing but "hard modernism":

> Like John Wayne, out of the smoke and dust of postmodernist explosion, we begin to see the familiar chunky outlines of a rough but redeeming modernism. There is the singleness of purpose, the showdown on the frontier of the possible, the fearless interrogation, the high-noon drama on which hangs the fate of social, psychological and epistemological renewal, the restless need for change, now stripped of any illusion of progress, but with its eyes fixed on a horizon which is endlessly different yet somehow always the same. If this is postmodern, it is evidently not a radical break with modernism but a moment of the same structure, opening on the production of ever new modernisms.[26]

From a feminist point of view, it must be our predominant interest to leave behind this kind of modernism/postmodernism and to prevent the production of ever new modernisms of the same brand—a task to be fulfilled without reproducing the futile gesture of heroic rupture. And there is much more at stake than just the question of gender and of justice to women.

The devastating effects of modern man's efforts to transcend the contingency of the human condition by overpowering and dominating nature (and the human beings who are symbolically identified with nature: the savage, the child, the woman) have become only too obvious by the end of this century. The masculinist resistance against nature has proved both destructive and self-destructive. At the same time this masculinist attitude directed against the threat of a totalitarian society has proved to be most ineffective. The existence of an active and lively avant-garde scene in Germany or Russia in the twenties was by far too weak a power to stem the tide of totalitarian catastrophe.

Moreover, from a certain historical distance we must recognize that the sublime gesture of *épater les bourgeois* and the bold defiance of society belong to the realm of a myth of avant-garde art and artists, a far cry from historical reality. Recent research in the history and art history of that period shows that the avant-garde movements and their heroes were much less detached from and opposed to their surrounding social reality than they pretended.[27] As for the German and Italian avant-garde, their distance from fascism has not always been so great and beyond doubt as the fate of the persecuted avant-garde artists suggests.[28] But even if this myth of the avant-garde may have made some sense during the first half of the century, as it corresponded to the self-image of a powerful aesthetic movement, this understanding of art and artist has almost completely faded away today.[29] In other words, Lyotard uncritically reproduces an image of avant-garde art and artist that was never fully valid and is now almost completely irrelevant.

All in all, Lyotard's idea of a sublime avant-gardism is not only a most undesirable but (fortunately) a very unlikely project. The pervasive masculinism of the project of modernity that took shape in Kant's days had been linked to the promise of a new autonomous moral and social order after the decline of the metaphysical worldview. By the end of the twentieth century the hopes and promises of modernity seem to have failed. The masculinist gesture that is retained has lost its measure and aim.

Notes

1. Moira Gatens, *Feminism and Philosophy: Perspectives on Difference and Equality* (Cambridge: Polity Press, 1991), 92.

2. See Christine Preis, "Die Ästhetik des Schönen ist längst unkritisch zum Design verkommen," in *Das Erhabene: Zwischen Grenzerfahrung und Grössenwahn*, ed. Christine Preis (Weinheim: VCH acta humaniora, 1989), 25.

3. Barbara Claire Freeman, "The Rise of the Sublime," typescript, 1.

4. Immanuel Kant, *Observations on the Feeling of the Beautiful and Sublime*, trans. John T. Goldthwait (Berkeley and Los Angeles: University of California Press, 1960), 78.

5. Immanuel Kant, *The Critique of Judgment*, trans. with analytical indexes by James Creed Meredith (Oxford: Clarendon Press, 1928; repr. 1964), 4; hereafter cited as *CJ*. German ed.: *Kritik der Urteilskraft*, in *Kants gesammelte Schriften* (Berlin: Königl. Preussische Akademie der Wissenschaften, 1913), 5:258. Pluhar's translation: "when we judge the beautiful, imagination and *understanding* give rise to a subjective purposiveness of the mental

powers" (Immanuel Kant, *Critique of Judgment, including the First Introduction*, trans. with an introduction by Werner S. Pluhar [Indianapolis: Hackett, 1987]), 115.

6. *CJ*, 91 (244); Pluhar's translation: "carries with it directly a feeling of life's being furthered, and hence is compatible with charms and with an imagination at play" (98).

7. *CJ*, 106 (257); Pluhar's translation, 114.

8. *CJ*, 106 (257); Pluhar's translation: "arises from the imagination's inadequacy, in an aesthetic estimation of magnitude" (114, 115).

9. *CJ*, 91 (245); Pluhar's translation: "a feeling of the sublime, then it may indeed appear, in its form, contrapurposive for our power of judgment, incommensurate with our power of exhibition, and as it were violent to our imagination" (99).

10. *CJ*, 91 (245); Pluhar's translation, 98.

11. *CJ*, 106 (257); Pluhar's translation: "our inner perception that every standard of sensibility is inadequate for an estimation of magnitude by reason is [itself] a harmony with laws of reason, as well as a displeasure that arouses in us the feeling of our supersensible vocation, according to which finding that every standard of sensibility is inadequate to the ideas of reason is purposive and hence pleasurable" (115).

12. *CJ*, 107 (258); Pluhar's translation: "feeling that we have a pure and independent reason" (116).

13. *CJ*, 100 (252); Pluhar's translation: "For he has the feeling that his imagination is inadequate for exhibiting the idea of a whole, [a feeling] in which imagination reaches its maximum, and as it strives to expand that maximum, it sinks back into itself, but consequently comes to feel a liking [that amounts to an] emotion [*rührendes Wohlgefallen*]" (109).

14. *CJ*, 92 (246); Pluhar's translation: "induced to abandon sensibility and occupy itself with ideas containing a higher purposiveness" (99).

15. *CJ*, 121 (269); Pluhar's translation: "any spectator who beholds massive mountains climbing skyward, deep gorges with raging streams in them, wastelands lying in deep shadow" (129).

16. *CJ*, 114 (264); Pluhar's translation: "Hence sublimity is contained not in any thing of nature, but only in our mind, insofar as we can become conscious of our superiority to nature within us, and thereby also to nature outside us (as far as it influences us)" (123).

17. *Works of Friedrich Schiller*, vol. 8, *Aesthetical and Philosophical Essays* (Boston: S. E. Cassino, 1884), 136.

18. This is even more obvious in the German version of the above-quoted passage; the expression "weichlicher Geschmack" (softening taste) is very close to "weiblicher Geschmack" (feminine taste) and the word "Hülle" (envelope, veil) evokes the association of female dress.

19. Klaus Poenicke, *"Nature's Gender: Zur Konstruktionsgeschichte des 'Schönen' und 'Erhabenen,'* " typescript, 12.

20. My translation. See J.-F. Lyotard, "L'intérêt du sublime," in *Du sublime*, by J.-F. Courtine, M. Deguy, E. Escoubas et al. (Paris: Belin, 1988), 167f.: ["Sur l'arbre généalogique dit des 'facultés de l'âme,' la génitrice est une 'sensation,' un état de sentiment de plaisir et de peine, comme le géniteur.] Mais le père est content, la mère malheureuse. L'enfant sublime sera sentimentalement contrarié, contradictoire: douleur et satisfaction. C'est que dans la généalogie de facultés dites 'de connaissance' . . . les géniteurs viennent de deux familles étrangères. Elle est 'faculté de juger,' lui 'raison'. Elle est artiste, il est moraliste. Elle 'réfléchit,' il 'détermine.' La loi morale se détermine, et détermine l'esprit à agir. La raison veut de bons enfants, exige engendrer des maximes morales justes. Mais la mère, l'imagination réfléchissante, libre, ne sait que déployer des formes, sans règle préalable et sans but connu, ni connaissable. . . . Le sublime est l'enfant d'un malheur de rencontre, celle de l'Idée avec la forme. Malheur parce que cette Idée se montre si peut consessive, la loi (le père), si autoritaire, si inconditionelle, l'egard qu'elle exige si exclusif, que ce père n'a que faire de

trouver aucun consentement . . . auprès de l'imagination. Il écarte les formes, ou les formes s'écartent, se démesurent, en sa présence. Il féconde la vierge vouée aux formes sans égard pour sa faveur. Il n'exige d'égard qu'à lui-meme, à la loi, et sa réalisation. Il n'a nul besoin d'une belle nature. Il lui faut impérativement une imagination violée, excédée, épuisée. Elle mourra en enfantant le sublime. Elle croira mourir. . . . La violence, la 'vigueur,' est nécessaire au sublime, il s'arrache, il s'enlève. . . . L'imagination doit etre violentée parce que c'est par sa douleur, par la médiation de son viol que la joie de voir, ou presque voir, la loi s'obtient."

21. "On sourira de ce scénario enfantin," "L'intérêt du sublime," 168.

22. ["Dans sa liaison avec l'entendement, 'avant' de rencontrer la raison il pouvait se faire que cette liberté de 'formes' se trouvat à l'unisson du pouvoir de régler, et qu'il naquit de cette rencontre 'un bonheur' exemplaire. Mais en tout cas, pas d'enfants.] La beauté n'est pas le fruit d'un contrat, elle est la fleur d'un amour, et, comme ce qui n'a pas été concu par intéret, elle passe" (167).

23. J.-F. Lyotard, "The Sublime and the Avant-Garde," in The Lyotard Reader, ed. Andrew Benjamin (Oxford: Blackwell, 1989), 206.

24. J.-F. Lyotard, "Answering the Question: What is Post-Modernism?" in Innovation and Renovation, ed. Ihab Hassan and Sally Hassan (Madison: University of Wisconsin Press, 1983), 341.

25. See Wolfgang Welsch, Unsere postmoderne Moderne (Weinheim: VCH acta humaniora, 1987), 201.

26. John Tagg, "Postmodernism and the Born-Again Avant-Garde," in The Cultural Politics of "Postmodernism," ed. John Tagg (Binghamton: Department of Art and Art History, State University of New York at Binghamton, 1989), 3.

27. See, for example, Kenneth E. Silver, Esprit de corps: The Art of the Parisian Avant-Garde and the First World War, 1914–1925 (Princeton: Princeton University Press, 1989).

28. See, for example, Peter Ulrich Hein, Die Brücke ins Geisterreich: Künstlerische Avant-garde zwischen Kulturkritik und Faschismus (Reinbeck: Rowohlts Enzyklopädie, 1992).

29. See, for example, Diana Crane, The Transformation of the Avant-Garde: The New York Art World, 1940–1985 (Chicago: University of Chicago Press, 1987).

9

Feminist Themes in Unlikely Places: Re-Reading Kant's *Critique of Judgement*

Marcia Moen

> Humanity on the one side indicates the universal feeling of sympathy [empathy], and on the other the faculty of being able to communicate universally our inmost feelings.—Kant, *Critique of Judgement*[1]

INTRODUCTION

Who would think, based on the *Critique of Pure Reason* (C1) and the *Critique of Practical Reason* (C2) alone, that Kant would make the statement I have used as epigraph, locating our humanity in our capacities for empathy and the communication of one's innermost self? It somehow doesn't square, I thought, when I first felt a need to think about this. I was already familiar with feminist critiques of Kant that addressed, for example, his contribution to what Alison Jaggar has called "normative dualism," the idea that the world can be understood in terms of dichotomies in which one member of the pair is valued more highly than the others.[2] Besides objecting to the epistemological dualism that elevates abstract rationality over the life of feeling, feminists have been analyzing problems that result from Kant's atomistic ontology of the person, and giving considerable attention to the poverty of the corresponding moral theory in which the ideal is the autonomous self who recognizes and affirms as universal moral law the idea of perfect impartiality. These difficulties are not theoretical only. Normative dualisms have shaped political thought and policy and have, in diverse and sometimes diffuse ways, worked their way into our ordinary consciousness as ordinary persons—into our concrete, complex social and interpersonal lives.

The *Critique of Judgement* (C3), however, reorients one's thinking about Kant, as it reoriented Kant's own thinking. I shall first locate in a general way several of the conceptions from C3 that readers will recognize as feminist concerns. I shall then focus more sharply or technically on certain concepts that I have chosen to develop in particular. Those concepts are clearly "there" in Kant, if only we look, but I shall occasionally suggest new names for some, to establish connections with more recent theory. At that point I shall move to the bulk of the paper, which is structured in terms of four unlikely themes—unlikely for Kant, that is—that I had found in C3 when I first conceived this essay: loss of the isolated ego or subject, the value of felt connectedness, the significance of embodiment, and the restoration of narrative complexity. I have tried to approach the material in the spirit of a good-faith conversation, an attempt to connect on common ground and explore there some ideas, the better to see just how our own thinking can benefit from what we do find in common, and to pass beyond those barriers on our own road to inquiry that Kant, in particular, has helped to make so heavy, so hard to push away. Re-reading Kant is worth our time, as feminists, for two reasons. First, simply this: we understand ourselves better when we understand our history. The conceptual forces that have shaped the minds of our male predecessors and colleagues have shaped our thinking too, profoundly. Second, a re-reading of Kant suggests particular agenda items we would do well to address. I shall argue for certain changes in our critiques of Kant's epistemology, and for the need to increase our own efforts to revise the ontology of modern philosophy, especially the ontology of the person. Similarly, witnessing what Kant does and does not do with his concept of "hypotyposis" urges upon us the need for a nondyadic, nonreductive semiotic (or cultural theory).

Conceptions of Mutual Concern

First, Kant promoted the insight that knowledge is constructed. This is not yet the idea of social construction of reality; for the most part, Kant thought the "mind" did the constructing, although in C3 where culture is finally examined, his thought opens *in the direction* of social construction. Similarly the concept of a transcendental unity of apperception (TUA) holding all representations of an object together sets the course for what later becomes the accountability and responsibility of the knower (a focus in feminist critique of science, for example). Second, despite his apparent devaluation of feeling and the sensual as sources of moral knowledge, Kant assigns to the faculty of Sensibility an indispensable role, or rather, roles: Sensibility must provide intuitions in C1 or our concepts are empty and cognition fails. But furthermore, Sensibility in the guise of the *sensus communis*, as faculty of holistic sensing, is equally indispensable, for all judgments—cognitive, moral, and reflective alike. In fact the body itself, as locus of *sensus communis* registers all cognition, all representations, and the *Lebensgefühl* or feeling of life (which is how we experience the *sensus communis*) is itself continuously modulated by this registering process. Third, on the basis of those discoveries (especially the *sensus communis* and *Lebensgefühl*) Kant came to recognize the cognitive value of reflective knowledge, the locus of which is not the objective, singular TUA but rather the space of intersubjectivity, where one subject is connected with others in a knowing community, via their mutual connections and transactions with shared objects of thought. With hindsight, an obvious move would have been to the concept of a relational self, like that being developed by feminist thinkers today. But that move was impossible for Kant to make, given his acceptance of the idea of the atomic individual, the essentially separate, desperately autonomous self. Although it is far from providing a relational view of the self, Kant's concept of intersubjectivity *is* adequate to account for the fact that we have, and can cultivate, felt connections, connections both with nonhuman nature and among ourselves, even connections with our future. Fourth, when we choose to cultivate felt connections we are valuing them. One of the most significant accomplishments of C3 is that it inexorably links knowing, as in C1; doing or valuing as in C2; and in C3, feeling. It links the epistemic, the practical or moral, and the aesthetic. Yet ultimately

Kant's position is that priority goes to the practical. In the life of a mindful organism, the sequence runs from felt value that holds one's attention, to inquiry and reflection, and on to judgment and active, interpretive response. Thus, and we can make this points five and six, in C3 Kant comes to affirm the importance of (re)contextualizing the abstract, and begins to articulate the cognitive and creative benefits of the interrogation of holistic feeling, the cultivation of felt knowledge. Indeed C3 reveals the importance in general of including holistic methods and principles among our means of inquiry. Seven, although Kant still operated most definitely within a dyadic problematic, his dyads are not always dichotomies. This does not do him enormous credit perhaps, but in watching what frustrates his work and closes down paths he might have taken, we witness the limitations of theory, even powerful theory, built upon dyadic relations. Those limits, like the related limits imposed on Kant's understanding by his acceptance of an atomistic ontology of the person, are, in my opinion, the theoretical problems that most hinder Kant from carrying even further the inquiry begun in C3, beyond the point where he in fact left off. Hindrances thrown up by his upbringing, character, and temperament are another matter, and for another time.

Summary in Terms of Focus Concepts

As we cross the *Critiques*, Kant's concept of the subject changes, until in C3 we get the subject as what I call a "cultural participant" exercising a "will to interpret."[3] This concept of the subject comes in response to both epistemological and ontological problems implicit in C1 and C2. The epistemological problems are resolved by appealing to the function of feeling in cognition, specifically the role of the *sensus communis*, *Lebensgefühl*, and *Geistesgefühl* (spiritual feeling). The ontological problems are addressed by appealing to our connectedness, as established by our embodiment and our material culture. A person is "more" than is represented by her discrete and aggregate sensory interactions with the world (sensations, intuitions) and more also than is represented by her discursive thoughts and expressions. That "more" resides in the full life of the body and in the material cultures of which the participant subject is a member. It is both social and individual; it is communicable and semiotic (hence social), and at the same time is contingent and a matter of agency (hence individual). We may identify that "more" with what Kant calls the supersensible—which, as it turns out, is also superdiscursive. In its presence within us (i.e., insofar as we instantiate it), I call it the transcendental semiotic function (TSF). The TSF links subject and object through the mediation of semiosis, or as Kant says, hypotyposis. It is the condition of possibility of culture, operating with the same double movement of presenting and explaining, holistically projecting and determinately constructing, that defines the transcendental deduction in C1. With hindsight we can say the TSF does this through the generation and interpretation of symbols—something that Kant realized he had just begun in C3 to explore, and that he thought merited much more exploration. To clarify these conceptions (which run against the grain of much traditional thinking about Kant) we must include in our thinking a holoscopic perspective, which allows for both internal relations among parts of a whole (as in organisms, or in communities), and for contingency. Without internal relations we get the nonsubject of much postmodernist thought. Without contingency we get a deterministic form of dialectic. I submit that neither is any more desirable than the dichotomous dyadic thinking of which Kant and other moderns are often rightly accused. When we include the holoscopic perspective, however, it is only a short extrapolation (or perhaps only a matter of restatement) to a morality of participation, and to a multimodal epistemology that can easily accommodate the conception of knowledge as praxis, a concept insisted on by many feminists. Eventually a relational ontology would follow, but not unless and until the incipient paradigm shift that begins in C3 were to be carried out further.

LOSS OF THE ISOLATED EGO/SUBJECT

Section Introduction: The *Critique of Judgement* recontextualizes the former two *Critiques*, and in that process, significant shifts occur in Kant's conceptions of the self or subject. Corresponding changes occur in Kant's conceptions of time, the context of the self as presented in each *Critique* respectively, and also in his arrangement of epistemological questions regarding the self as knower who understands, affirms, and creates or expresses.

Kant is well known among feminists—and with justification—as champion of rational objectivity as a mode of knowing and of autonomy as ultimate principle of moral being. Yet those concepts of knower and of moral agent are modified in the *Critique of Judgement* where the self becomes a reflective participant in a perceptual world and in a cultural process. In C1, you and I are the *same*, as transcendental unity of apperception (the involuntary spontaneity of the epistemic ego, the point-ego that subtends incipient perceptual consciousness). In C2 we are *identical*, as autonomous moral agents in voluntary conformity to law or principle. In C3, we are *analogous*, as voluntary participants in an aesthetic, cultural process—a process of reflective transactions with purposive objects. We may all feel the purposiveness of such an object, but purposiveness is not a determinate concept and hence, as individuals, the participation in the development of the aesthetic idea that we undertake as we attend to the purposive object will differ from person to person. (Furthermore such transactions with purposive objects, when projected back onto C2, reveal a possible approach to persons as purposive others, others who are neither fully autonomous nor fully determinate in their purposes.)

The transcendental unity of apperception really is *ego*, rather than subject in a richer sense, and from C1 alone we would not see how Kant's transcendental idealism could explain why there are many individuals each with his or her own *Geist* rather than one *Weltgeist*. The transcendental unity of apperception is merely a unifying function. But it is that, a unifying function, not the passive mirror that served Descartes and Hume as metaphor for the mind. It separates itself from its object and grasps them in synthetic representations. Susan Bordo in *Flight to Objectivity*, her study of Descartes and his time, explicates the importance of that first move, the separation of ego from object.[4] The second move, the synthetic, unifying function, marks Kant's rejection of the Cartesian paradigm in favor of the thesis that knowledge is constructed. To be sure, construction here means merely that the mind gathers particulars under its own universal forms, not that a subject situated in history and culture contributes to a "social construction" of knowledge emergent from that situation. Nonetheless, Kant prepared the way, as Bordo, Lorraine Code, and others have acknowledged:

> It is certainly possible to see in Kant's thought, ahistorical as it is, an opening onto the more perspectivist and historicist

understanding of knowledge that begins to develop in the nineteenth and twentieth centuries.[5]

Hence Kant prepares the way for analyses of knowledge as construct and for contextualizing epistemic activity so that the knower, and not just the known, comes under epistemological scrutiny.[6]

And feminist writers have done precisely that: they have brought the epistemic activity of the knower under epistemological scrutiny in various ways. Some, including Evelyn Fox Keller and Alison Jaggar, have made use of sociological studies and psychoanalytic theories (e.g., that of Nancy Chodorow)[7] to problematize the way in which, as Keller puts it, objectivity (as cognitive trait) is linked with autonomy (as affective trait) and masculinity (a gender trait) in the development of scientists in mainstream Western culture at this time.[8] Noting that for Kantians autonomy is also a moral virtue, I would add that indeed it is typical of feminist thinkers to insist on linking the epistemic and the moral.

As instantiating the TUA (transcendental unity of apperception), you and I are effectively the *same*. By contrast, in C2 we are individuals, but we are *identical* in that the particulars of our lives are irrelevant to what duty demands of us. Autonomous reason should, Kant says, be the sole determinant of our actions; appeals to emotion or feelings of another sort are womanly, immature, and morally irrelevant. We may grant, with Genevieve Lloyd, the following, "in fairness to Kant": "His point was not that genuinely moral agents must shed their natural inclinations, desires, and affections, but rather that what is distinctively moral about their actions can . . . be expressed entirely in terms of rational principles."[9] Even with these scruples, however, Lloyd rightly rejects the idea that rational principles are alone morally relevant. Seyla Benhabib, criticizing both Kant and John Rawls for their concept of "the autonomous self, as a being freely choosing his or her own ends in life," says that

this moral and political concept of autonomy slips into a metaphysics according to which it is meaningful to define a self independent of all the ends it may choose and all and any conceptions of the good it may hold. . . . The self is not a thing, a substrate, but the protagonist of a life's tale. The conception

of selves who can be individuated prior to their moral ends
is incoherent.[10]

She points out that such "selves" stand in relations of "definitional
identity" and "cannot be human selves at all." Similarly we have from
Code, "in the Kantian scheme, noumenal selves cannot be sufficiently
individuated for their problems and concerns to be adequately understood."[11] It seems to me, paradoxically, that the Kantian self as agent is
both too little individuated and too individual—too little individuated
because the specificities of the agent's life story are ruled out of the moral
court, and too individual in that once those specificities are gone, the
individual that remains is truly "atomic," so separate and autonomous
that its only relations with others are external relations not touching the
core of the self-atom's being.

Some of the high rationality and fierce autonomy recede when the
Kantian self engages in the process of aesthetic reflective judgment. For
Kant, we "think" far more than we can "know" (C1, B146–47); and in
C3 it is the reflective thinker who, as I have said, enters into transaction
with the purposive object. (This of course refers to the judgment of
beauty; for the sublime and for teleological judgment we must tell a
different story, but that will add to, not nullify what I say here.)

Kant's claim that "beauty is a symbol of morality" (C3 § 59) signals a
special relationship between the moral agent who "risks" (as she or he
must) action and the reflective observer who risks (but could refuse)
beauty. Transactions with a beautiful object involve risk because they
are parallel to transactions with another person, as Kant scholars have
noted. The object acquires status as a limiting case, a nonperson or
nonpersonal form which, if it is to be engaged aesthetically and its
transformative potential elicited, must be approached in such a way as
would not violate its integrity, as one ought to approach a person. At
the same time, if the encounter is truly transactional, then the self will
be changed also, restructured by the transaction—perhaps deepened,
strengthened, or clarified. We may not always *want* to be more clear to
ourselves; hence there is risk, and that basic risk may be an obstacle to
our affirmation of what I shall later call a "will to interpret" and define
as a condition of cultural participation. This element of risk is reflected
in Kant's own language where he speaks of "free conformity to law" as
the mode of interaction between the faculties of Understanding and
Imagination in aesthetic reflection. In both C2 and C3, then, the

subject enters freely into form. Returning to Kant's own language, in both cases we have "free conformity to law" (in C2 the moral law as "form of law" itself, and in C3 the aesthetic "idea"). Further, in both moral reasoning and aesthetic judgment we have a priori principles. There are differences, of course, in the two cases: in C3 the a priori principle is subjective—a capacity of the reflective subject for grasping, not cognitively but yet thoughtfully, those conceptually indeterminate but perceptually compelling forms that Kant calls aesthetic ideas and that cannot be compassed by concepts or language. Furthermore, this form, the aesthetic idea, must be supplied by the faculty of Judgment itself, unlike the case of C2 where the moral law is supplied by the faculty of Reason. (That is why the will in C2 is autonomous, but reflective judgment in C3 is "heautonomous.") *Duty* is the same for all, but whereas we impute to all subjects the feeling of purposiveness in the contemplation of *beauty*, the experience renders us, as individuals, part of a cultural process that includes the open-ended expression of the inexponible. The "subjective universality" of the judgment of taste, on the basis of which we "impute" the judgment to others, is no more identical to the "objective" universality of C2 and C3 than the "objectivity" of the moral law in C2 is to the objectivity of scientific knowledge in C1. The relations in question are relations of analogy, not identity. And although Kant uses the expression "subjective universality" in C3, I would argue that the conception he had in mind might better be expressed as an "empathic generality." Thus there can be real particularity in our individual participation in the cultural process. Yet in principle aesthetic ideas are communicable to all, and in attempting to communicate the feeling that they arouse in us, we are both cultivating empathy and exemplifying[12] what it is to value. Whereas in C2 we are "identical"—in that it is by reference to the determinate moral law that we conclude that others should see the demand of duty exactly as I see it—in C3 on the other hand the judgment of taste is, as Hannah Ginsborg puts it "purely self-referential":

> Thus in judging, I take it that I myself, like any other perceiver of the object, ought to be in the mental state corresponding to my present act of judging. . . .[13]
>   . . . In contrast to the case of cognitive judgment, in which I have in mind some determinate way in which the object ought to be judged . . . , my claim to universal agreement [in aesthetic

judgment] does not specify a concept. Instead, I judge that all others should judge the object as I do, where *the only way of pointing to how the object is to be judged (and thus to the "universal rule" implicit in my judgment) is through the example of my judgment itself.*[14]

Rather than abstract universality, we are dealing with concrete exemplification. Rather than morally identical, abstract agents, we have particular but analogous participants in aesthetic reflection. A corresponding ontology of the person would abandon the "atomic" individual; it might well look like the nondualist model Caroline Whitbeck calls for:

> At the core of the ontology that I am proposing is a self-other relation that is assumed to be a relation between beings who are in some respects analogous, and the scope and limits of that analogy . . . are something to be explored in each case. . . .
>   . . . In place of an ontology characterized by dualist oppositions, . . . the self-others relation generates a multifactorial interactive model of most, if not all, aspects of reality. Because the content of each related term is not defined by opposition to the content of the term with which it is paired, these terms no longer mean what they meant in masculist theory.[15]

Such a model, built on the idea of a relational self—an idea put forward by many feminist thinkers working in epistemology and ethics as well as ontology[16]—could accommodate difference without rejecting entirely the idea of an integrated subject, so long as that subject is conceived as an ongoing process of relatively stable integrations and partial dissolutions.

The road from Kant to Whitbeck is long, but a way is opened in the *Critique of Judgement* that recontextualizes both cognition and morality such that each concept is extended. Changes in the conception of the self, as knower and moral agent, would presumably follow.

As the concept of self changes from ego to agent to participant, time, the ontological context of the self, is conceived differently as well. In C1 the self (ego) has no interiority; it is purely exterior, a point in *abstract* mathematical time—linear, spatialized, Newtonian time, all points exterior to all. Knowing is not a process but an act, determinate and certain.

The *moral* subject, by contrast, is purely interior, the Moral Law given within (as fixed as the Forms of Intuition and the Categories of Understanding). Time is again *abstract*, but rather than linear time, the ontological context of the self in C2 is a moral eternity. Willing, like knowing in C1, is not process, but act, determinate, certain—and in this case, purely interior. The subject has an outer life, but in its acts of moral decision, its being *as moral agent*, it must struggle to exclude the outer and to make decisions on the basis of the inner Moral Law alone.

The self as cultural participant in C3 has both an interior and an exterior; and time is lived, organic time, an ongoing, transactional *process*—intersubjective at its peak of complexity, but transactional even in relation to objects other than persons (e.g., beautiful forms). Here we find ourselves at home in lived, organic time. The pleasure consequent upon the judgment of beauty is felt as a *furtherance of the bodily life process* (as I shall discuss later). Reflection on the sublime also generates a specified process, the "checking and then stronger outflow of the vital forces" (C3, § 23).

Those ontological changes in the being of the self and the ontological nature of its temporal habitat are accompanied by changes in epistemological focus: in C1 we discover our common objectivity, in the Forms of Intuition and Categories of the Understanding. In C2, moral action is based on in*tra*subjective determinations. Ironically it is in our moral experience that we appear to be most atomistic and solipsistic; the "kingdom of ends" seems nearly to be an afterthought. Finally, in C3 the focus is on the in*ter*subjective; and one of the first epistemological commitments to emerge in this context concerns the cognitive value of feeling.

VALUING FELT INTERCONNECTEDNESS

Section Introduction: By the time he was writing C3, Kant recognized that feeling is an essential part of all cognition, including both theoretical and moral knowledge, although an examination of the function of feeling, especially in moral knowledge, raises both epistemological and ontological questions (Kant seems not even to have recognized the latter). The *Critique of Judgement* reconceptualizes the other *Critiques* in such a way as to enable us (like Kant) to see and value our connectedness, a move that resolves some of the epistemological questions and might well, if extended, create the relational ontology for which many feminists have called.

Feeling and Cognition

Kant has rightly been accused of valuing our rational functions over the others, including feeling, and much has been written about his partial acceptance of the dualism that pits reason against feeling and has traditionally bowed to the former.[17] He may talk about feeling in connection with aesthetic judgment, critics say, but at most he deals only with an intellectualized "feeling." It would seem on these grounds that both "interconnectedness" and "felt" refer to something for which Kant had little regard.

Yet, in C3 we are told that our humanity consists in our capacity for sympathy [better: empathy] and our ability to communicate our inner-most feelings. Further, a new faculty is identified: the *sensus communis*, our capacity for sensing holistically (§§ 20 and 40). Kant himself anticipated one difficulty concerning this concept: it is easily confused, he said, with "common understanding." But there is another ambiguity as well. Scholars have taken *sensus communis* to mean "common to all of us," and indeed it does have that meaning. But Kant also asserts that the *sensus communis* is operative in *all* judgment, and this is reflected in the second aspect of the term's ambiguity. Yes, it provides a shared sense of beauty, but it also does more; it is the *subjective principle of all judgment*, and it is holistic (the significance of which I shall discuss later).

Kant draws the term *sensus communis* from the medievals (who draw it from Aristotle, *De Anima*, book 3, chap. 2 4268b10–15). The medievals distinguished (1) *sensus externi*, those with external organs; (2) *sensus interni*, seated in the brain; and (3) the *sensus communis*, the holistic sense that results from uniting the sensations of the separate external senses to form a single, holistic representation.[18] The *sensus communis* tells us that the sweetness and the whiteness are attributes of the same sugar. It constitutes a holistic grasp of the object of our attention, a Gestalt. We might call it "intersensible." Or, since in Kantian terms what we feel in aesthetic judgment is a "harmonious interplay" of our cognitive faculties, particularly Imagination and Understanding, we might say the *sensus communis* is an "interfacultory" principle. I submit that it is this sense or feeling that Joseph Lawrence refers to when saying, in "Logos and Eros," that C3 "refers us to a 'feeling,' an aesthetic dimension which has an intellectual function insofar as it guides the scientific investigation of nature."[19] It is also the "feeling" and the "sense" referred to by Harald Pilot in his essay on the "ethics of experiential thinking" where he says, for example,

1. that there is a perceptually guided activity of thinking which is a kind of non-propositional judging, although it is a necessary condition for gaining knowledge, [and]
2. that just this kind of perceptually guided activity is the grounding condition of that feeling expressed by judgments of taste.[20]

Pilot continues (having distinguished external and internal judgments of taste, the former depending on the latter):

> An internal judgment of taste does not have a proposition as its cognitive content. It is a thinking which results in the presentation of the perceived object within consciousness, Its cognitive content may be understood as an individual sense corresponding to the object of perception which is neatly tied to its object.[21]

Just as the *sensus communis* is a faculty in the exercise of which the organism functions holistically, its objective correlate is holistic also. That correlate is purposiveness, the form of purposiveness (C3 § 11) that is neither a product of individual human will (moral purpose) nor reducible to mechanism and its categories. Kant refers to holistic feeling as a "feeling of life," a *Lebensgefühl* (C3 § 1); and whereas *Gefühl* (feeling) is not *Sens* (sensation), I think it a mistake to say that *Gefühl* represents feeling mentalized rather than really sensed or felt.[22] Pilot makes a similar point about the holistic character of the operation in saying that the judgment of beauty (purposiveness without purpose) depends on two conditions:

1. there is a certain holistic character of the object;
2. there is a certain way of grasping a given manifold of empirical intuition in the free interplay of imagination and understanding. . . . The holistic property of the object corresponds to the way of the grasping. . . . The mode of grasping a beautiful object is an activity fulfilling the principle of the autonomy of judgment.[23]

The "mode of grasping" is also, like its object, holistic, and is a function of the *sensus communis;* furthermore, the judgment is doubly autonomous—heautonomous, as we may recall, in the case of beauty. But again, the *sensus communis* operates in *all* judgment, not just the judgment of taste. Pilot, for example, is talking primarily about the "experiential thinking" that goes into the construction of empirical concepts, as described in the "Critique of Teleological Judgment." He sees this process of "nonpropositional thinking" as a use of analogy in which "aspects" are projected onto objects problematically until a satisfactory intuition of the object has been built—all of which must occur before the intuited object and its concept can be used in propositional thought. Makkreel similarly describes teleological judgment as a project-and-construct process:

> the appeal to analogy . . . means that the organic whole projected is at best an indirect or symbolical presentation of the imagination, not a full or direct intuition. Instead of mechanistically constructing a whole as the sum of all of its parts, reflection projects the whole aesthetically, as it were, on the basis of some of its parts.
>
> . . . The closest we can come to the archetypal or intuitive intellect is to represent the whole of some object as a guideline for the process of forming it from its parts.[24]

Thus it is not only in artistic or mathematical creation[25] that the productive imagination is guided by a holistic feeling; the empirical investigation of nature relies on that same process of felt, experiential thought. The "Teleological Judgment" section of C3 fills out the picture of theory construction in the natural sciences by adding to the a priori principles of C1 the work of empirical investigation where reasonable but not fully determinate judgments of reflection are the mode of living scientific discourse, in both the "social" and the "natural" sciences.

But what happens when the object to be known is another human being, herself a subject; that is, when the cognition in question is self-knowledge or knowledge of another person? What happens when we turn to moral knowledge? This very question raises difficulty when we ask it in reference to Kant. The question is less problematic in the case of self-knowledge than in the other, as Kant could certainly agree that we have a holistic, pre-analytic sense of self, and we are instructed by him to scrutinize our own motives in assessing the moral worth of our actions. But even this seems thin. And it gets worse when we consider knowledge of the other in the moral context. Indeed insofar as Rawls and Kant are like-minded on this, knowledge of the other should be set aside in (determinate) moral judgment. True, one should know whether the other is a rational being (rather than an infant, for example), and one might even grant that leniency in legally imposed punishments is acceptable, but the moral judgment would remain: you must! (or you must not!) Thus even the *relevance* of knowledge of the other (and of enriched self-knowledge) to moral judgment is in doubt. Furthermore, it is hard to see what knowledge of the other could be, how it could be acquired, except by inference. But does not the very existence among us of this question—this puzzlement about what knowledge of another person could possibly be if it is not inferential—show us (as does the "problem of other minds") that something has gone dreadfully wrong, in our theorizing? The problem is ontological. If persons are "atomic"— only externally related, and fully autonomous—then what knowledge of persons is possible except discursive, inferential knowledge? If the boundaries of the self are hard rather than interpenetrating, then our prospects for moral knowledge are grim.

The problem, then, is *also* epistemological. Yet here it is easier to see a resolution within Kant's own problematic. Just as the view of objective knowledge offered in C1 is supplemented and modified in the "Teleological Judgment," so the view of the moral life offered in C2 is supplemented and modified in the "Aesthetic Judgment." We can at the least appeal to the *sensus communis* and the reflective, experiential, nonpropositional thinking, guided by feeling, that goes on in empirical investigations of nature. We can move from theoretical knowledge to moral knowledge via the *sensus communis*—the faculty that Kant "discovered" as a condition of possibility of aesthetic judgment and then realized was the "subjective principle" of all judgment. The linkages among theory, aesthetic judgment, and moral knowledge are reflected in Kant's assertion that beauty is a "symbol" of morality (§ 59). Kant would certainly reject the nineteenth-century idea that beauty and morality are the same. But both moral and aesthetic judgment, as I have indicated, are volitional and evaluative. To say that something is beautiful is to say "there is something of value here." Furthermore, judgments both of morality and of beauty require an integration, an integrity in the psyche of the one who judges. (Kant refers to this as "harmony" among the faculties.) The harsh light of C2 gave us a picture of the moral agent as one devoted to a single, ultimate purpose, the selection of maxims consistent with the moral law of impartiality; the softer (and clearer) light of the "Aesthetic Judgment" illuminates each person as a complex of multiple purposes: some moral, some aesthetic or expressive, some determinate and others in the indeterminate state more accurately described as purposiveness without purpose. At these points of choice—which begin (and may remain) with the nonpropositional choices made possible by the holistic *sensus communis—Lebensgefühl* attains to *Geistesgefühl* (C3 § 54), as it becomes articulate,[26] whether the articulation occurs simply as modulation of feeling (that is, of *Lebensgefühl*) or whether it occurs as discursive articulation. *Now* self-knowledge, and at the same time empathy, is possible. To feel with the other is to grasp the other's purposes, or, when no determinate purpose can be sensed, then to grasp the other's purposiveness, his or her status as author of purposes. It is thus that, in the exercise of the *sensus communis*, subjectivity becomes intersubjectivity. The space of feeling is, after all, the space where intersubjectivity as a phenomenon can be explored experientially: consider the hunch that comes to the scientist discussing a scientific puzzle with her peers, or the urge to share one's appreciation of beauty, or the dawning in consciousness of the likeness of that appreciation to the empathic appreciation of particular others whom one has come to know. (Ted Cohen, for example, has referred to the beautiful object as a limiting case of one-who or that-which is taken as an end, something to which intrinsic (disinterested) worth is granted).[27]

Moral knowledge is possible, and in a richer sense than knowing one's motives. It is possible through the practice of reflective judgment, which includes and respects felt-knowledge. To be sure we have extended the concept of knowledge or cognition here, beyond the strict sense Kant held it to in C1, but it is Kant himself who made the extension. Moral knowledge requires attention to articulate feeling *as* feeling—not feeling as transformed into discursive, propositional knowledge, but rather feeling itself modulated by present, living experience and reflection. (This is not, of course, to deny that our moral reflections must *also* be attentive to fact and to argument.)

In the context of teleological judgment (and concerning especially the question of extrinsic purpose in nature; that is, whether there is an intelligent and moral creator), Makkreel comments: "If the *Critique of*

Judgement can be generally characterized as one that discovers pure feeling to have a transcendental value, then its final contribution in §91 is to show how the feeling of conviction can generate a reflective cognitive assent demonstrating a human consensus."[28] Since the experience of beauty is one kind of experience that has moved people to entertain the question of a creator, it is easy to imagine a person, contemplating beauty, going through a process of reflection with the following phases: from feeling of pleasure to "feeling of conviction" to "cognitive assent" to ———? For the last place, Makkreel suggests "human consensus." While of course he is appealing here not to a Gallup poll but to what he takes to be widely experienced, I would still not want to put it entirely that way. I would suggest, rather, that the last term be "the will to interpret," a term I shall later explain.

Thus feeling is present in all cognition (the *sensus communis* is operative; the modulated *Lebensgefühl* and articulated *Geistesgefühl* are felt). That is, on the basis of a mode of feeling that is at once subjective and possessed of form, comes intersubjectivity, along with both self-knowledge and empathy. Surely we all experience feelings of connection, but whether we value them enough to generate the aspect of volition I call the will to interpret (and to be interpreted) is another question. We cannot assume this last step is easy; that is, without effort, or risk.

Valuing Connection

"[H]umanity on the one side indicates the universal feeling of sympathy [empathy], and on the other the faculty of being able to communicate universally our inmost feelings" (§ 60). These words are poignant when one remembers they are embedded in a theory for which a central organizing image is that of the atomic individual. Even the intersubjective self of C3 is not the relational self called for in much feminist philosophy.[29]

Yet, the intersubjective field as Kant understands it does open onto many dimensions of connection; to begin with, connection with non-human nature. I am not forgetting Kant's wildly exaggerated sense of the moral status of humankind in the natural economy, but at least a small beginning is made in the third *Critique*, on the way toward putting us back into our natural habitat. The holistic sense of purposiveness that draws us into and holds us in contemplation of natural beauty is a feeling of being at home in the world, and a sense that something is of value here. It is a felt connection between us and the rest of the natural universe. In the language of an earlier time, perhaps Plato was right, in *Symposium*, to suggest that if the true and good and beautiful are one, it is beauty that is the most accessible, not to say irresistible. It draws, and holds, our attention. And if involuntary spontaneity (the TUA) is the start of cognition, attention is the beginning of valuation. Sara Ruddick, in her own reflections on "Maternal Thinking"—and drawing on the thought of Simone Weil and Iris Murdoch—makes this point clearly as she develops her concept of "attentive love." Regardless of what one thinks about the appropriateness of the maternal metaphor as a vision of selves-in-relation, one can affirm the cognitive-affective-volitional process that follows from the "identification of the capacity of attention and the virtue of love."[30] Feminists generally and rightly insist on the processive interleaving of the epistemic with the practical-qua-moral, and of these with the practical-qua-effective-action in the material world. Attentiveness (or as we sometimes say, "consciousness") begins that complex process. Donna Wilshire refers to the orientation as a holistic "minding"—as in minding the store, or the baby.[31] Without mindfulness we cannot value; if we look *through* the natural world and see only a commercial resource, never giving it our intransitive attention, we neither know nor value it. But beauty insists. And Kant insists that the pleasure we feel in the transaction between ourselves and the beautiful object is not subsequent to that transaction but rather pleases "in the act" (I would say in the process) of judging. Concerning our connection with nature there are, in addition to Kant's analysis of pleasure taken in the purposiveness-without-purpose of a beautiful object, his ideas of the "technic" of nature (nature appears to be art) and conversely of artistic genius (art as nature, working in or through the genius).

The experience of pleasure taken in the purposiveness of objects in nature anticipates person-to-person connections as well. (Cf. "beauty is a symbol of morality.") The language Kant uses in projecting those connections is that of "imputation" (we impute the judgment to others), "subjective universality," and "exemplary necessity." As I claimed earlier, Kant is running analogies here, not asserting identities. (Similarly, "objective" does not mean in C2 what it means in C1: for Kant the theoretical and moral domains are quite distinct but can be analogically displayed, in analysis, to facilitate comprehension of the total picture of being-human; hence, for example, his use of the same four "Moments" to organize all three *Critiques*, even though he varies their order.) To "impute" the judgment of taste to others is not to hold them morally reprehensible if they do not assent to it. I accord the judgment "exemplary necessity" in that I take the object to be an example of nature's purposiveness without purpose and, correspondingly, take my experience as an example of human response, a response I may expect to be widely shared. And the "subjective universality" of the judgment of beauty is neither merely subjective nor logically universal. It is *inter*subjective, and it is empathically "universal"—a quality better expressed, perhaps, as "empathic generality."

And that is probably as close as Kant will come, given his ontology, to internal rather than external relations among people. The idea of imputing the judgment of beauty to others leads to no full-fledged and thoroughly explicit revision of Kant's moral theory in C3; to so assert would certainly be overstatement. But some of the requisite concepts are provided, and others intimated; and even without a sharp revision of moral theory as presented in C2, C3 provides a *recontextualization* of the moral life, restoring it to its place within our natural and communal environments. Furthermore, reflectively raising the question of the intelligent and moral creation of the world-whole should point the finger by analogy to the intelligence and morality of *our own* contributions to our material worlds. Makkreel finds in C3 a "faith" that is "practical and communal" rather than doctrinal (59).[32] But if we are to use the concept of faith at all, it must be a *prospective* faith—a commitment, a *will to carry on*, to participate in the ongoing interpretation process that is our material culture—and to do so with continual reflection on the intelligence and morality of our contributions. Then we, and our products, stand as concrete examples of the subject/object transactions that have constituted both. Feelings of ungrasping pleasure (Kant's "disinterested" pleasure), the assurance that something is of value (Makkreel's "feeling of conviction")—yes. But with due respect, I hesitate at "cognitive assent," let alone "human consensus." "Assent" is too easy; "consensus," too universal. I shall continue to use "the will to interpret" as the final and open-ended last phase of the sequence. The expression signals a morality of participation: an idea Kant did not sufficiently explicate, but one for which he more than prepared the way by introducing into the discourse, in the way he does, his concept of "hypotyposis" or semiotic activity (which I shall discuss shortly).

SIGNIFICANCE OF THE EGO'S EMBODIMENT

Section Introduction: The concept of the body is another that appears (or works implicitly) differently in the changing contexts of the different *Critiques*. Inclusion of the *sensus communis*, as one guise in which Sensibility operates, shows that Kant's often proclaimed devaluation of feeling and of the body needs rethinking. I shall argue that even the "supersensible" is embodied twice over: in the body of the individual human organism and again in material culture. In some contexts the supersensible is postulated as a substrate of nature; in others it is instantiated in the being of persons and their expressive products. There is indeed an apparent paradox here, in the embodiment of the supersensible, but that is precisely a signal that a paradigm shift is taking place in C3. The concept of a transcendental semiotic function helps to clarify that shift.

The Body and Sensibility

I have pointed to shifts in the concept of the subject and the concept of time as we cross the *Critiques*. The concept of the body changes also. In C1 the body is merely a *physical object* like any other. In C2 it is the *locus of desire*. In C3 the body is *locus of pleasure and judgment*; it participates in the processes of nature as well as in the cultural process.

There is no doubt that Kant devalued the sensory in serious ways. Yet it behooves us to rethink exactly in what ways and to what extent that is true, lest we fail to see ways in which it is not true—fail to recall, for example, that sensing is an integral part even of the method of transcendental deduction in C1,[33] and that it has a dominant role in reflective judgment as that concept is developed in C3.

Robin Schott has argued that for Kant, the only form of sensibility that contributes to cognition is intuition, and that intuition, as our immediate apprehension of an object, excludes feeling (in general), emotion, sensuous pleasure, desire, and especially bodily awareness.[34] This is true in large part, but it leaves out of account Sensibility as *sensus communis* or as operative in *Lebensgefühl*, Kant's treatment of which, unexpectedly, illuminates and reinforces feminist epistemology's insistence on the legitimacy of the holoscopic.[35]

Sensibility as a faculty in C1 both provides sensory data and assigns sensory objects-to-be a position in linear space/time and a place circumscribed by a category of the Understanding. Looking at it from the opposite direction, if Sensibility cannot schematize or "present" a concept by supplying for it an intuition, then the concept cannot count as knowledge[36] and is at best a regulative idea. In tone, Kant's treatment of Sensibility in C1 is neutral: the faculty simply has an essential function in the construction of knowledge. In C2, however, Sensibility, now in the form of the sensual, is devalued, in comparison with practical reason as a source of practical, moral motivation. C3 dismisses charms, but not the experiential transaction with the beautiful object, to which charms are merely adjunct. Appreciation of charms does not establish that the person judging the object aesthetically grasps both its holistic character and the seemingly determinate relations among its parts (i.e., that she sees its "exemplary necessity"). On that issue, charms are beside the point; the point being, in C3, communication, specifically, empathy and the communication of one's feelings.

For Kant, communication requires form,[37] either conceptual form or the forms of material culture. My perceiving the form of purposiveness signals to me that you too will find pleasure in the beautiful object. The material form, whether in nature or in artifact, stands to mediate to you the enthrallment I now feel, should you choose also to give your intransitive attention to it. Nor must we forget that all these particular forms (material and conceptual) are articulated against a background of feeling that is yet partially unformed—as ultimately it must (partially) remain since it is constantly changing, registering each representation that takes shape. But this too, this background, is feeling. Taken as faculty it is the *sensus communis;* taken as bodily experience, it is *Lebensgefühl.* It is present (it instantiates itself) not only in pleasurable contemplation but equally in the feeling that guides teleological reflection while empirical concepts (and, I would add, cultural imperatives) are yet in formation. A processive and relational ontology might do better justice to these experiences, but Kant with his structural and atomistic or meroscopic ontology (taking the perspective of the part-to-part) has nonetheless recognized and articulated them (almost, one is tempted to say, in spite of himself). Such is their importance.

The sense of beauty, then, while it is properly called a "sense," is not sensation; it is a modulation of the holistic *Lebensgefühl* as the perceiver enters into form by engaging in the reflective transaction of attention or contemplation. The experience of beauty, Kant says, is a direct bodily feeling of "the furtherance of life." Similarly, he continues, when we turn to the aesthetic judgment of the sublime we experience a "checking" and a subsequent "stronger outflow" of the "vital forces" (§ 23).

> An *objective relation* can only be thought, but yet, so far as it is subjective according to its conditions, *can be felt* in its effect on the mind; *and, of a relation based on no concept . . . no other consciousness is possible* than that through the sensation of the effect. (§ 9, emphasis added)
>
> *All representations,* sensible or intellectual, are subjectively united to gratification and grief, because they all *affect the feeling of life.* And gratification and grief are *ultimately corporeal* (as Epicurus said), because life without a feeling of bodily organs would be merely consciousness of existence without any feeling of well-being or the reverse, i.e. furthering or checking of the vital powers. *The mind is by itself alone life (the principle of life), and hindrances or furtherances must be sought outside it and yet in the man, hence in union with his body.* (§ 29, emphasis added)
>
> We may . . . readily concede to Epicurus that all *gratification,* even that which is occasioned through concepts excited by aesthetical ideas, is animal, i.e., *bodily sensation. This does not prejudice the spiritual feeling* of respect for moral ideas, which is not gratification at all but rather an esteem for self (for humanity in us), that raises us above the *need* of gratification. (§ 54, emphasis added)

Thus all representations affect our feeling of embodied life. As animal, corporeal beings, we possess (as does my cat) a *Lebensgefühl*. That does not "prejudice" or preclude our having also a *Geistesgefühl* (a feeling that includes but is certainly not exhausted by feelings of respect, although we tend to think of the moral context when we read, in translation, "spiritual feeling"). In *Geistesgefühl, Lebensgefühl* acquires articulation not limited to language but inclusive of our entire material culture. By itself alone, where there is mind there is already life, but not yet a concrete, temporal, human life; for the latter, the "animating principle" must be embodied. *Geistesgefühl* is still *Gefühl*. The body registers all cognition. This is not the same as bodily sensation; the difference is between *Sens* and *Gefühl*.

The Supersensible

The modulation that occurs in *Gefühl* continues during our consort with the "supersensible" as much as with the sensible; it is the former, the supersensible, to which I now turn. The "supersensible" amounts not to an absence of the sensible but to the presence of what sensibility cannot achieve alone. The supersensible is itself embodied, twice so—after all, Sensibility (a faculty) is not the body, and the supersensible is not immaterial.

Knowledge, constructed from the mind's Forms of Intuition and Categories of the Understanding, has strict limits in the first *Critique*: We can properly know or cognize nothing that exceeds them, although we can *think* beyond the parameters of mathematical, homogeneous space and time, and the logistic and mechanistic Categories of the Understanding. We seem scarcely able to stop thinking beyond them; Reason persistently introduces ideas that transgress the limits, and that is the context in which Kant's discussion of the supersensible appears in C1.

Thinking experientially, it is hardly difficult to see that there may well be realities that exceed our sensorium (I don't know what my cat does with her whiskers but I don't think they are only for measuring doorways). Transcendental critique, however, requires that ideas of the infinite, the eternal, or telic relations be referred to an objective correlate; hence we must postulate a supersensible "substrate" of nature, although we cannot determine that idea further in a priori perspective. Such "ideas of reason" as God, freedom, or telic phenomena are restricted to a negative role as regulative principles; thus are the limits of understanding defined. The "Critique of Teleological Judgment," however, reconceptualizes the supersensible as substrate of nature in a positive way, enlarging Kant's previous view of our knowledge of nature by accounting for the *empirical, inductive life* of science.[38] In C3 the supersensible contributes not to an untrustworthy, pretentious dialectic but to a creative process of reflective judgment.

The supersensible presents itself quite differently in our practical, moral lives, where it appears not as substrate at all, but as function. In a word, I participate in the supersensible as I instantiate value through the exercise of moral freedom. And, just as the supersensible appears as substrate in both C1 and in the "Critique of Teleological Judgment," the supersensible as function (from C2) is repeated in the "Critique of Aesthetic Judgment." This is reflected in the idea of beauty as a symbol of morality; that is, the idea that the reflective processes are analogous in the two cases inasmuch as in both cases we have a "free conformity to law."[39] Yet the differences are great: the *Critique of Judgement* extends the ideas of freedom, universality, and especially purpose beyond the guise in which they appear in C2 and the *Metaphysics of Morals*. C3 moves us from the universality of law to that of communicability (§§ 41, 59), from arid "kingdom of ends" to community and culture (§§ 41, 42, 50, 83), from freedom as autonomy to freedom as heautonomy (i.e., creativity [§ v]), and from determinate purpose to purposiveness (§ 11). The determinate fitting of maxim to universal formal law changes to a strong concept of reflective judgment that recontextualizes those moments (far fewer than Kant would have it) of the moral life where we do think in terms of rules or principles. And in those other, non-rule-driven moments of moral reflection, attention to feeling is part of the normal process.

Again, I am not claiming that Kant set out consciously and deliberately to revise his conception of morality so as to place at its heart an imperative to communal and cultural participation, an imperative to interpret and be interpreted. Kant's vision, even his revised vision, could not accommodate that much change. But a solid beginning is there. Reading C3, we witness a paradigm shift in process, leading toward a generative principle that would foreground culture and open-ended purposiveness. I shall return to this later, but first I explore the concept of the supersensible from within the prevalent dyadic paradigm of modern philosophy, centered, in Kant's case, on the subject-object dyad.

In its *objective* reference, the supersensible in C1 is the "substrate" of nature (the frame for the house whose walls are built by empirical investigation and inductive thought). In C2 it is the rational will. And in C3? In C3, and in objective reference, the supersensible presents itself as the function of symbols: indirect presentations of a universal in intuition, as distinct from schemata or archetype/ectype relations. The symbol, the self-instantiating function, merits much thought. Kant said: "This matter has not been sufficiently analyzed hitherto, for it deserves a deeper investigation" (§ 59). This comment comes on the heels of a brief discussion of the fact that when reflecting on an object such as the state, our choice of symbols or metaphors as we develop our understanding is crucial; symbols (as I would put it) are self-instantiating. When cultivated, they generate their own interpretations, including but not exclusively propositional interpretations. Using Kant's own example, the image or intuition of a hand mill generates a particular idea ("universal") of the state. The particular intuition determines how we reflect on the state, what we attend to, and then articulate as a concept of statehood. If we began with the intuition/image/symbol of an organism, that would generate a differently articulated concept of statehood. This procedure is different from what happens in schematism, where the concept (the universal) is given and imagination must "bring an intuition under" it, or in typic where the idea of the moral law is given and thought must look for analogues in nature and in maxims. In the latter two cases (schematism, typic) the universal (concept, idea, law) is given and the particular must be provided by imagination. In the symbolic procedure on the other hand, the particular is given and the universal (e.g., the concept of the state) must be generated. Here we leave behind established concepts and reinvent understanding, with more concern for the reflection process than for certainty. Thus, looked at as object (in a dyadic paradigm), the supersensible is (i) substrate of nature, (ii) the rational will, and (iii) the symbol function.

The supersensible is also in us. In its *subjective* reference the supersensible is in C1 the self-control of the objective investigator who refrains from dialectical speculation of the sort Kant shows us in the Antinomies. In C2 it is the self-control that resists and thereby modifies desire; it is the sense of self whereby one feels a moral directedness. In C3 it appears in several guises: it is that in us which responds to natural beauty and sublimity; it is also what Kant calls "genius" and "spirit," defining genius as the creativity of one who generates and spirit as the capacity of one who communicates "aesthetic ideas"—defined as sensible configurations with more meaning than determinate concepts can ever convey. Similarly, the supersensible is the creativity of the scientific investigator who generates the "rational ideas" that cannot be proved by logical process but are "proofed" or tested in abductive reasoning and theory-construction. As self-control and as creativity (which itself requires self-control) then, the supersensible operates in all our endeavors.

As the text that Kant said would mediate between the theoretical C1 and the practical C2, the *Critique of Judgement* might be called the critique of praxis. It does allow for an integration of nature and culture so that the moral life, involving both, can be transformed from a rule-bound affair of atomic individuals belonging to a "kingdom of ends" into an empathic, communicative, and reasoned thinking/feeling process. Granted, Kant was enough of a modern to employ dyadic conceptions such as objective and subjective, and that makes the comprehension of connectedness difficult. Even though in C3 connectedness, as I have argued, is clearly valued, under the operative ontology in C2 the moral agents who make up the "kingdom of ends" are as external to one another as nineteenth-century atoms. Despite the move to intersubjectivity, heavy residues of that ontology remain unchanged in C3. Yet conceptual changes are occurring in Kant's thinking, and these changes link culture with morality. In the "Critique of Aesthetic Judgement" the issue becomes not nature and freedom but nature and *art*; not nature and autonomy but nature and *heautonomy* (the creativity that projects the universal as well as constructing the particular); and in the "Critique of Teleological Judgement" the issue is not so much natural law and moral law as it is nature's creation and human creativity. Furthermore the real concern is less with the intelligence and morality of a creator god than with the morality and intelligence of *our own* creative endeavors—in which the supersensible in us is operative.[40]

"Supersensible" does not, of course, mean supernatural. And in us, the supersensible is not beyond all modes of bodily feeling; it is merely beyond Sensibility, as the faculty was initially described in C1. Since that faculty is an abstraction, in a very real sense we can say that in C3 we go beyond Sensibility to a full, human, bodily life, beyond the abstract to its concrete source—to the body.

In exceeding the sensible, the supersensible commits other excesses as well. Ontologically, it exceeds the mechanistic. Epistemologically, it exceeds the schematizable and the discursive. In C1, "rational ideas" cannot be presented in intuition, and ipso facto they exceed the discursive also; schematism cannot occur, the imagination cannot run through them, make its *discursis*, to present a coherent object. In C3 however, we find that rational ideas can be presented in intuition *indirectly*. Reflective judgment finds a symbol, reflection upon which projects or generates the "same rule of procedure" (§ 59) as thought turns to the idea symbolized and shapes it according to the symbol-image being employed (cf. the example of the state). Reflection proceeds by analogy, and does not rue the transparency lost by the indirectness of its presentations.

The supersensible in C1 and in those portions of C3 concerned with the epistemic relation of humanity to the world-whole (mainly in the "Critique of Teleological Judgement") appears as *substrate, postulated* either as regulative idea for the heuristic use of determinate judgment or as reasonable but problematical hypothesis for the thought experiments and empirical concept-building of reflective judgment. On the other hand, the supersensible in C2 and those parts of C3 (mainly but not exclusively in the "Critique of Aesthetic Judgement") concerned with our practical involvement in the world appears as a *function, instantiated* in moral action and cultural participation. If Kant were to pursue more thoroughly the emergent paradigm toward which his work clearly tends, it would look like some (not all) semiotic frameworks (namely those that can overcome dualism in a positive way).[41] Hence I call Kant's supersensible in its appearance as function the "transcendental semiotic function" or TSF.

The Transcendental Semiotic Function (TSF)

The transcendental semiotic function or TSF, as I call it, is the supersensible—and superdiscursive—in us, conceived as function. There is more in us, which we sense, than can be discursively represented, more than can be articulated discursively in "linear" propositions. There is also more than can be sewn up and presented in discrete and determinate intuition, more than can be constructed from discrete sensory elements in linear aggregation (which we *can* do, for example, with Humean sensations). This more, sensed or felt holistically as *Lebensgefühl,* is the supersensible in us.

The TSF is a function in the mathematical sense, a relation that links two "fields" (as when we say X is a function of Y, meaning X is related to Y in a determinate way). The fields over which the TSF is applied are the subject field and the object field. These fields are linked by semiosis; or, in Kant's terms, hypotyposis. Subject and object are mediated, brought into epistemic relation, by schemata, analogue-relations, or symbols. Looking at the cognitive process, at one extreme is a definite "point-ego" in mathematical time with a single function: the transcendental unity of apperception (TUA) whereby the subject "constitutes" its object. At the other extreme is a multiple set of open-ended processes in organic time whereby our material culture as object constitutes us (with our active cooperation; Kant is not giving us or even tending toward social construction unmitigated). Putting this all another way, the field over which the TSF as function operates is experience as constituted by subject-object transactions. Semiosis—reflection, discourse, visual imagery, visceral felt-formations, and so forth—mediates our human subjectivity and the object-world in which we live.

As I have stated, Kant represents the supersensible not only processively, as function, but also structurally, as substrate—a rationally inferred analogue of what we experience as substance. Suppose we consider how the supersensible appears as we move from *Critique* to *Critique* in sequence. (I shall use "A" for Aesthetic and "T" for Teleological.) In C1 the supersensible is *substrate*; in C2, *function*; in C3A, *function*; and in C3T, *substrate*. So the supersensible is both substrate and function, but the supersensible as function ultimately takes priority, for it is via the TSF as function that the substrates are postulated: the TSF is the supersensible as generative source of creative and productive activity. It surpasses the schematic-discursive aspects of our being and experience: we are both more concrete and more collective or connected than they alone would reveal.

As rational beings, we posit a substrate for the a priori; as sensing, feeling beings we posit a substrate for empirical experience. In the first case the positing occurs *by inference*. In the second, we posit the substrate *feelingly*—we sense its presence as an object-field corresponding to the *Lebensgefühl*, the holistic feeling stratum that goes on registering every representation of every component of what eventually comes to be the concept that does the job[42]—a process of attending both inwardly and outwardly after the manner of Barbara McClintock and her corn.[43]

Why I use "semiotic" and "function" to name the TSF should now be plain. As for "transcendental," there are several reasons. First, Kant's transcendental philosophy overall was conceived as an inquiry into the "conditions of possibility" of knowledge; and just as the TUA (transcendental unity of apperception) is a condition of possibility of objects appearing to a subject, so the TSF is a condition of possibility of interpretation; that is, of culture, conceived broadly so that it includes both science and morality among its parts or modalities. Furthermore, the singularity of the TUA (recall that it is not even individual; you and I are the same as instantiations thereof) is matched by the inherent sociality of the TSF (semiosis being inherently social). Or better, the singularity of the TUA is *recontextualized* by the sociality of the TSF. The social thus returns to the singular as its context. In addition, I take "transcendental" from Kant's "transcendental deduction," defined as a justification[44] that *explains and presents in one*, in contrast to a metaphysical deduction that presents a "what" without asking the transcendental question, the "how"—How is this knowledge possible? (C1, A12–13, B40, A56–57, B159, etc.). If we ask the "how" question, then we see a particular "what" as an instance of a function. Like a transcendental deduction, the symbolic or semiotic process is *self-instantiating*—the form is projected or presented, and then explains or constructs itself (via its experiences, not in an idealist sense) by carving out its internal articulations—or, to use a more semiotic terminology, it generates its interpretations.

Thus the TSF, the function that explains-and-presents, postulates-and-instantiates, here concomitantly *postulates* the supersensible *as substrate* and *instantiates* it *as value*. This is what makes it necessary for Kant to talk not just about law but about the form of law; not just about purposiveness but the form of purposiveness; conversely this is what requires him not to simply use the system of logic (as form) to structure the Table of Categories but to justify that use—in other words, requires him to "deduce" his deduction. Ultimately the entire "Critical" Kantian philosophy stands as this justification. Consideration of the imperative to explain-and-present concomitantly renders somewhat less cogent, I think, claims that Kant has *simply* excluded the material, the sensuous, or embodiment from his account of theory construction, practical reason, and even to an extent aesthetic judgment (as in his claim that purposiveness, not charms, is the base of the judgment). Kant's bleak view of sensuality as rich erotic experience (even in Audre Lorde's sense of "erotic")[45] may have been motivated by his pietist religious background and his Prussian sternness; but the distinction of form and embodiment was driven by the transcendental imperative to explain and present concomitantly, and by his concern with communicability and the assumption that form is required for communication—an assumption I think is necessitated by the idea of persons as atomic individuals. I mean these comments not as an apologia for Kant but simply as a reminder of the complexity of the situation. (And I am mindful of the need to ask what motivated that imperative, those concerns, and that assumption.)

RECAPITULATION

Thus far I have said that the epistemological mode investigated in C3 is intersubjectivity; that the time of C3 is lived, organic time; and that the subject is conceived as a voluntary and creative participant in the cultural process.

I have pointed out that in C3 our humanity is defined as our capacity for empathy and communication; that the condition of possibility of this capacity is the existence of a holistic *sensus communis* that senses such qualities as purposiveness in its objects; and that this process of sensing, empathy, and communication is felt in the subject as a *Lebensgefühl* and (sometimes) *Geistesgefühl.*

I have said that in C3 the body functions as a locus of feeling (e.g., the *Lebensgefühl*) and thereby as a locus of judgment, since many judgments are and should be based on feeling. I have shown that according to C3 the subject, enabled by the supersensible in which she participates, is both responsive (to the beautiful and sublime) and creative (in science as well as art). The supersensible is also superdiscursive, and is itself embodied twice over: in the bodily life of the human individual and in material culture. It is present in the individual as a generative transcendental semiotic function that can be focused in its activity by a will to interpret.

In this way, insights reconceptualized in C3 transform universality from law to communicability; freedom from autonomy to creativity; purpose to an open-ended purposiveness. These transformations, together with the concept of symbolism, allow Kant to transform his vision of our common life from one of rules and external relations to one of culture and community. It is that to which I now turn.

RESTORATION OF NARRATIVE COMPLEXITY

Section Introduction: Today, "narrative" has come to represent concreteness, particularity, and connection—concrete connectedness in real, lived time. It is reflective judgment that finds and builds concepts and other forms the "universality" of which is prospective, carried forward in organic time and in material culture, without closure. In C3 the perspective is that of a *Welt als Schöpfung* (world as creation) rather than *Natur als System* (nature as system), and much changes when we engage the world from that new perspective. We see room for narrative, a richer narrative than the story of the moral agent abstracted from life. In addition, science and moral thinking can be reconceived here in terms of purposiveness; and when this is done the result is more in line with feminist views. This in turn reveals the need both for what I will call a "will to interpret" and for a nondyadic problematic.

The supersensible, superdiscursive is instantiated in use as the TSF. It generates symbols as sources and products of reflection. *The task of reflective judgment is to fill out a life.* Here we take no direction from an a priori; we freely seek (construct) a "universal" (an aesthetic or rational idea) to make sense of those aspects of our lives and thought that fall outside the clean lines of mechanistic principle and moral law. Kant rejected the "dogmatic" metaphysics of his predecessors, and seems to have been unaware that he was himself constructing a "speculative metaphysics" in Whitehead's sense: not saying what is, but exploring how we can make sense of things. But reflective judgment, under Kant's analysis, does just that.

The mechanistic and legalistic have closure; the products of reflective judgment do not. In reflective judgment the epistemic and moral subject becomes the creative subject. Symbolic expressions (indirect presentations of ideas) are indeed constrained by the epistemic and existential fields within which they operate. Nonetheless they are quite freely developed and retain the indeterminacy that is so fecund, the openness that provokes our entry into the interpretation process, challenges us to the will to interpret. The "universal" we seek, the idea we pursue, is of a kind to be always and ultimately indeterminate—its universality a *prospective* universality, conditioned by our acts of valuation, praxis, interpretation. In exceeding the sensible (meaning here the objects of the faculty of Sensibility as conceived in C1) and the discursive, reflection *recontextualizes* what was abstracted, reduced, in C1 and C2. The epistemic object as symbol is prospectively the site of multiple meanings; therefore the subject in reflection and communication *must* abstract, *but* we need not abstract just the linear, just the discursive,[46] nor just the "sensible," the sensory object of the faculty of Sensibility, which object is a reduction of the richer phenomena of Gefühl.

The transcendental semiotic function (TSF), as condition of possibility of interpretation, is ipso facto a *condition of possibility of the restoration of narrative complexity* to the abstract accounts of human thought and being we have in C1 and C2, for the complexity comes from context and concreteness.

Keeping in mind that the supersensible (in its occurrence as TSF) is neither unembodied nor immaterial, let us revisit *Lebensgefühl* and *Geistesgefühl*. The *Lebensgefühl* exceeds Sensibility, and does so *because it resides in the body*. Similarly the *Geistesgefühl* exceeds discursive, propositional thought, and does so *because it resides in semiotic systems, in the materiality of culture*.

To speak of culture is to speak of purpose, which Kant defines as a relation of idea to existence. The concept of *purpose* pervades all of Kant's *Critiques* and is overtly a major theme of C3, and indeed his most explicit discussion of *culture* occurs also in C3, mainly in the "Critique of Teleological Judgement" where the matter is divided into consideration of intrinsic purpose and extrinsic purpose (although there is the discussion of nature and art in the "Critique of Aesthetic Judgement"). The discussion of intrinsic purpose addresses the question of organisms as "natural purposes"; the section on extrinsic purpose concerns the possibility of a purposive relation between humanity and nonhuman nature, where questions arise such as these: Is nature there for our use? Is it purposive for our understanding? If so, does it have an intelligent and moral creator? And in answering those questions, Kant clearly employs a conception of cognition that extends well beyond what "cognition" meant in C1. I have argued that in C3 it includes felt knowledge and holistic knowledge, not only the schematic and discursive cognition of C1; similarly, Makkreel points to symbolic, interpretive knowledge:

> The postulate of a moral, intelligent cause of the world . . . becomes the object of a *Fürwahrhalten* that Kant is now willing to call a mode of *Erkenntnis*. He speaks of *symbolische Erkenntnis* of God. . . . Kant transforms his conception of *Fürwahrhalten* from its original first *Critique* meaning of a hypothetical holding something to be true to its final meaning of a cognitive assent rooted in a reflective feeling of conviction.[47]

In fact it is only C1 that excludes purpose from cognition, from that which can be known; it is not, after all, among the Categories of the Understanding. And yet, even in C1 purposiveness is present; *it has already operated*, for it has been assumed in the very setting up of the Table of Categories; Kant has assumed that the "Moments" or parameters of logical judgments, as determined by the logic of the day (quantity, quality, relation, and modality) are relevant parameters for ascertaining the Categories of the Understanding. That is why a transcendental "deduction" was needed. Indeed one might say that the task of the entire Critical philosophy is to collect on that gamble. Thus in recontextualizing C1 by placing it in the larger context offered by reflective judgment, we are actually *retrieving* a relation (purpose) already projected.

In C2, of course, purpose is present as the relation or trajectory of idea to existence where the idea is determined by the rational, moral will. The perspective of C3, in turn, is the perspective of *Welt als Schöpfung*, rather than *Natur als System*, and from that perspective (one more compatible with feminist views though certainly not "there" yet) both science and morality are *parts* of culture. Revisioning *science* would run something as follows: On the "objective" side of the story, we can say that nature's creative forces have produced a world from which mechanism's abstractions are drawn and shaped into determinate laws. On the "subjective" side we can now see that the knowledge expressed in "laws of nature" has been shaped already by reflective judgment (setting up the Categories). The question then becomes, does our logic, from which the Moments are derived, in fact apply to the real? Is it purposive for articulating the real? Is it "fitted" to the task?[48] The concerns of C3 regarding purpose thus make us aware once again of the limits of science (Kant tells us there will never be a Newton for a blade of grass (§§ 75, 78)) but they also provide a new understanding of the power of science, by allowing for an account of its inductive, analogical, and empirical elements. And they place science solidly in a context of purposiveness and purposes. To be sure, the fact that Kant was concerned with the purposiveness of logic for articulating the real, with organisms as natural purposes, and with the general relation between humanity and nonhuman nature does not mean he was ready to challenge the purposes of science and scientists as feminists are now doing, by challenging the choice of research projects, their methodologies, their funding, or the interpretation of their results. But at least the stage is set, the context located.

We need to rethink the *moral* life also, from this new perspective. Just as the idea of *Welt als Schöpfung* brings together *nature* and culture, so also it brings together our cultural and our *moral* being. I am author of my acts; and after rejecting the idea that the value of life lies *simply* in our enjoyments, Kant writes, "There remains then nothing but the value which we ourselves give our life, through what we cannot only do but do purposively" (§ 84, p. 284). We create value by our choices. Once value has been created, we may rightfully be encouraged to enjoy it, but the value has been created by our actions and therein lies the exhilaration Kant feels in contemplating our moral being, our self-creation and value-creation. The purpose of morality is, after all, to produce a coherent life. But surely Kant would have seen that the hard part about moral decision-making as he had construed it in C2 lies in the typic, the process of formulating a maxim and judging whether it is a sufficient analogue of the Moral Law. Reflective judgment carries this out. Alternatively, this issue of choosing a maxim can be formulated in terms of purposiveness: the task is to judge whether a maxim is purposive for the ends of the Moral Law. Is the maxim I construct fitted for the task? Does it have the form of moral law? Does it contribute to the purposiveness of a coherent moral life? Just as questioning science in terms of its purposes and purposiveness makes an opening, still very small, for feminist critique, such an account of the *reflective* rather than the legalistic moral life opens toward feminist thinking.

The link between beauty and morality can also be reformulated in terms of the interrogation and expression of a felt purposiveness. Contemplating beauty with its purposiveness makes us want to sustain the contemplative state; similarly the purposiveness of a maxim (and the action it prescribes) for the construction of a coherent life signals us to sustain that maxim as guide to action. (And the moral feeling of respect is a felt confirmation of the purposiveness of our actions.)

Pervasive throughout the *Critiques*, then, the ideas of purpose and purposiveness provide a central organizing image for our lives and thought, suggesting a cultural imperative, we might say, that the practical/moral should be the center of our lives, a commitment urged upon us also, and often, by feminist thinkers.[49] But doing that requires voluntary assent: *a will to interpret, to contribute* to the cultural process. And if we *are* to participate not just by interpreting but also by *being interpreted,* hearing what others make us out to be, then those who are dominant must agree to be interpreted by others including the subordinated—must face the subordinate classes' interpretations of them. Without mutual interpretation there are two risks, both of which can imperil communities. One risk is that socially subordinate groups *lose the will to interpret*, to participate, having given up on the process. The other risk is that those who are socially dominant lose or *refuse the will to be interpreted*, thereby cutting themselves off from *intelligent* participation that recognizes our interdependency and understands the mutually constitutive relations between individual and society, and among different social groups. White Anglo women, for example, especially those who are educated and work in professions, are familiar with both dangers, since they belong in both categories: still subordinate in relation to men but socially dominant, by virtue of social arrangements, in relation to working-class women or to racial or ethnic minorities.[50]

It is through that cultural process of mutual interpretation, if at all, Kant suggests, that we may attain a "highest good" (e.g., § 83). Makkreel cites Kant's 1791 essay "On the Failure of All Attempted Theodicies," saying:

> Kant rejects traditional theodicy as a "sophistical" or "*doctrinale Auslegung*" . . . and argues for a new kind of moral theodicy that provides an "*authentische Interpretation*" (VIII, 264). Traditional or doctrinal theodicies used regulative ideas of theoretical reason to make pseudo-determinant judgments about history. . . . Kant's authentic interpretation will use regulative ideas of practical reason merely to guide our reflective judgments about what we can make of ourselves in history.[51]

If there were a highest good, it would reside in interpreting and being interpreted. But we can settle, I think, on using the will to interpret and be interpreted to attain goods of a more ordinary kind.

Knowledge residing in symbols and their interpretation is ipso facto social, and indeed the will to interpret is a *social* imperative, but it is an *individual* imperative as well. Meaning may reside in the social, but will, given Kant's ontology at least, resides in the individual. And while, in interpretation, the individual and the social are mutually constitutive, note that for Kant, the dialectic here is without closure; it remains indeterminate, *given the richness of symbolic thought and expression*. We may "hope" for the adequacy of our formulations to the ideas in question and for the assent of others to them, but the contingencies always remain, the outcomes dependent on our wills. While the structure of Kant's explicit paradigm is certainly dyadic, it is not altogether dichotomous, especially in C3. It is not only with regard to individual and society that we see this; we find it again with respect to the sensible and the supersensible, which do not form a dichotomous opposition but rather a relation of abstraction to context. And if it seems a paradox to say the sensible is abstract and the supersensible is rich, concrete, and contextual, we must remember that Kant's "Sensibility" as mental faculty—like Hume's "sensations," or twentieth-century "sense data"—is abstract indeed, a massive abstraction from life as experienced, reflected upon, and known in the extended sense of "knowledge" or "cognition" with which Kant is working by the end of the "Critique of Teleological Judgement."

But a truly nondyadic paradigm does not come clear and unambiguous for a century, and then not in the structuralist and semiotic theories of Continental Western thought that are among Kant's constructivist inheritors. One appeal that would be helpful, I think, would be to the triadic semiotics and triadic ontology of C. S. Peirce, who once said he had been "suckled at the breast of Kant." The advantages of a triadic paradigm are several. It represents a degree of complexity sufficient to accommodate a semiotic, nonreductive ontology of the person and a correspondingly complex epistemology. It also rejects all claims to ultimacy or single explanatory principles (including any that might be made by its own champions). In its positive constructions it generates instances of itself that work as anchors (not foundations) for stable formations that, though stable, are not fixed and may eventually resolve themselves into the stream of semiotic reflection and understanding, to be replaced or carried forward by other forms. Of course, Peirce's solution is neither a magical solution nor the only one possible. But we do need a theory, a vision, that fulfills the transcendental imperative to present-and-explain in one, a principle or method both stabilizing and genera-tive, both structural and processive—or else we need to accept the postmodern imperative of radical, immanent, and ultimate incommensu-rability.

One of the differences between a genuinely nondyadic paradigm and the postmodernist view is that the latter is meroscopic, taking the perspective of part-to-part (and assuming hierarchical relations even as it deconstructs *some* or other such relation), Feminists have sometimes found such deconstruction useful.[52] But at the same time, feminists, while they do employ meroscopic analyses, find themselves often resorting to the imagery of a *web*, as an alternative to images of hierarchy (one part set above the other with which its relations are external). This reflects, I think, the insight that holistic concepts or *holoscopic* principles (those that take the perspective of the whole) are required to articulate some sorts of complex phenomena without reducing them to the point of falsification by denying or masking their complexity. Organisms, for example, are more than a sum of mechanical parts, as Kant saw ("no Newton for a blade of grass"). Many feminists would argue, as I would, that human communities are also of this nature; that is why Kant's "kingdom of ends" from C2 seems so peculiar as a vision of community, which is surely more than a congregation of individuals. We need to be able to account for wholes in which the parts are not merely in external relation (e.g., mechanism) but rather are internally related, so that each is partially constituted by its relation to the others. Reductive abstraction can be useful but we must remember what it is, so that we do not, for example, regard the world of science (atoms, muons) as the real world.

Holoscopic principles should be among our alternatives in epistemology as well as ontology. In Kant we see such principles in his idea of a transcendental deduction as one that presents-and-explains, in one. I have adopted/adapted Makkreel's notion of projecting and constructing, mapping it in effect onto Kant's present-and-explain. The whole (whole concept, principle, image) is projected, but with its parts and their relations yet indeterminate; then the inner articulation occurs as precise concepts are constructed. The whole is sensed and projected; then intellect sets in, as concept construction (and eventually theory construction) is carried out. Wilshire's account of the mythic mode of thought with its holoscopic "minding" of things can serve as an example,[53] and Barbara McClintock's work in genetics is another case of holistically attending to and "minding"; that is to say, a sensing for patterns in the phenomena one is trying to comprehend.

One danger of holism, however, is as I have said that it become a dialectical determinism, where the future is built into the past as are the coming frames in a cinematic film. This is where the element of indeterminacy, contingency becomes important. For Kant, both autonomy and heautonomy result in genuine contingency: the contingency of moral will and also of the broader will to interpret. The future is not built into the past. What comes to be—and what comes to be known—depends on our own wills as well as on the material contingencies of natural conditions and cultural circumstance. Knowledge is praxis, and by the time we get to the recontextualizing in C3 of what had been abstracted in C1 and C2, the Kantian text is ripe for the conclusion, asserted often by feminists, that the active life is as essential a part of knowledge-building as the intellectual or the intuitive.[54] The present is heavy with the past (not the future), and the future is always an arm's length away. For Kant, then, *both* meroscopic, discursive knowledge and holistic intelligence are required to make sense of the world that is, and the world we want to be.

Kant's concept of hypotyposis—an incipient semiotics—incorporates holism on another level, also, in terms of social theory. Once again, as symbol users we are both concrete and collective, in our being both as individuals and as members of communities, inscribed in our respective material cultures. But the *development* of the semiotic perspective had not yet occurred, and when it did, it was stormy, with many contending factions, from structuralism to classical pragmatism to postmodernism. And that is a field of contention that feminists inherit.

In sum, holistic concepts and holoscopic principles are needed because they combat excessive abstraction and reductionism; they allow for internal and mutually constitutive relations among parts of a whole; and they therefore lend themselves to the idea of relational selves, as well as to the idea of holistically attending and projecting a holistic conception that is "true" to what is felt but is then modified as its parts and particulars are gradually constructed. Holistic modes of being and knowing are opaque to thought that is unrelentingly discursive or meroscopic (proceeding part to external part)—hence human experience is opaque thereto. Human experience is replete with mutually constitutive relations, and with contingencies. Reformulating an earlier point: if we forget the mutually constitutive relations, we go to an extreme of postmodernist thought; if we forget the contingencies, we go to a deterministic, bipolar dialectic. The irony is that even the postmodernist champions of "narrative" do not provide a reading or analysis adequate to narrative—to the concreteness, particularity, and connectedness which the term has come to represent. Indeed one might say that Kant's transcendental imperative (as I have called it) to present and explain in one, is *more* adequate to that complexity. Our lives are themselves the presenting, and provide concreteness. The stories we tell in articulating the living are the explaining, and they provide the particularity of each teller. The living and the telling *become* (never *are*) one insofar as the particular one-telling becomes part of the process in which we interpret and are interpreted; that is, insofar as her particular narrative and my particular narrative are connected in *our* story, a story in which there will be limited continuities and islands of coherence despite the fact that a hope of unlimited continuities and complete coherence would certainly *not* be one of those "*rational* hopes" Kant would allow us. To this extent the postmodernists are surely correct.

CONCLUSION

Kant's discoveries in the writing of C3 reinforce, albeit in a sometimes subterranean way, the importance of the process perspective, the importance of context, and the need to include the holoscopic. In a more developed way, with his notion of intersubjectivity, Kant anticipates the relational self—although his ontology will not let him actually make that move; and with his idea that knowledge is constructed, he anticipates a time when knowers are held responsible and accountable for the conceptions they author and the methods they use to arrive at them. An incipient semiotic is another of his legacies.

In a still stronger and more detailed way, re-reading the *Critique of Judgement* leads me to three conclusions concerning directions in which it would be well for feminists to move. First, the ontological question needs to be addressed again, especially the ontology of the person. Without that, our epistemological critique will be inadequate. We do not need a "foundation" in the traditional sense of some incontrovertible underlying principle; but we do, I think, need an anchor, something that provides local stability according to the waters in which we find ourselves when we address a particular problem (i.e., according to context). Seeing the limitations imposed on Kant by his atomistic ontology suggests that the concept of a relational self, which many feminists have called for, is indeed a move in the right direction, and more than worth carrying further. Second, we need to rethink our critiques of Kant's dualism. For example, we must look not only at *Sens* versus reason, but also at the reductive *Sens* versus its contextual *sensus communis* and *Lebensgefühl*. For Kant, when Reason goes beyond discursive understanding of experienced phenomena, it is *not inevitably* engaging in the illegitimate dialectic of C1; it may also be engaging in the very different activity of contextualizing that to which our strictly discursive understanding would limit us if it were our only mode of thought. Similarly *feeling (qua Lebensgefühl)* goes beyond meroscopic elements (sensations, discrete intuitions); the meroscopic and discrete are contextualized by holistic sensing. We will miss important abstraction-to-context relations such as these if we fail to examine the place of holistic concepts and holoscopic principles in Kant's thought. When we *do* include the holistic, we see that Kant's conceptions may be dyadic, but they are not always dichotomous. The relation between the sensible and the supersensible is another dyad that is not a dichotomy as we might think, but is rather an abstraction-to-context relation. Third, sometimes even nondichotomous dyads create aporias. By looking at those junctures where Kant is stymied by his problematic because it is dyadic (even if not dichotomous), we can see the need for a semiotic and specifically, a semiotic that is nondyadic, and nonreductive.[55] If we could accomplish that, we could construct a pluralism that would restrain *unrestricted* forms of relativism and at the same time would clearly reject all claims of singularity and absolute validity or truth. Such a move might illuminate, for example, the place of postmodernist feminism among other current feminist positions.

The plea I have made for (i) the urgency of ontology, (ii) caution in epistemology, and (iii) invention in semiotics might be restated in the following way: with his idea of intersubjectivity, Kant set the direction for a relational self, and with his concept of hypotyposis he set the direction for a nonreductive semiotic. Both are directions in which feminists have been moving, quite beyond what Kant was able to do—but not far enough. The task is still ours.

Notes

1. § 60; citations consisting of section numbers alone will refer to Kant's *Critique of Judgement.*

2. Alison Jaggar, "Human Biology in Feminist Theory: Sexual Equality Reconsidered," in *Beyond Domination: New Perspectives on Women and Philosophy,* ed. Carol C. Gould (Totowa, N.J.: Rowman and Allanheld, 1983), 23.

3. This language is from Josiah Royce, *The Problem of Christianity* (Chicago: University of Chicago Press, 1968).

4. Susan R. Bordo, *The Flight to Objectivity: Essays on Cartesianism and Culture,* SUNY

Series in Philosophy, ed. Robert C. Neville (Albany: State University of New York Press, 1987).

5. Ibid., 47.

6. Lorraine Code, *What Can She Know? Feminist Theory and the Construction of Knowledge* (Ithaca: Cornell University Press, 1991), 114.

7. Nancy Chodorow, *The Reproduction of Motherhood: Psychoanalysis and the Sociology of Gender* (Berkeley and Los Angeles: University of California Press, 1978).

8. Evelyn Fox Keller, "Feminism and Science," in *Feminist Theory: A Critique of Ideology*, ed. Michelle Z. Rosaldo, Nannerl O. Keohane, and Barbara C. Gelpi (Chicago: University of Chicago Press, 1982), 119.

9. Genevieve Lloyd, *The Man of Reason: "Male" and "Female" in Western Philosophy* (Minneapolis: University of Minnesota Press, 1984), 69.

10. Seyla Benhabib, "The Generalized and the Concrete Other: the Kohlberg-Gilligan Controversy and Moral Theory," in *Women and Moral Theory*, ed. Eva Feder Kittay and Diana T. Myers (Totowa, N.J.: Rowman and Littlefield, 1987).

11. Code, *What Can She Know?* 125.

12. There is a double exemplification going on. In its "modality" the judgment of taste attributes an "exemplary necessity" to the object, while at the same time in the act of judgment the subject exemplifies the act of valuation.

13. Hannah Ginsborg, "On the Key to Kant's Critique of Taste," *Pacific Philosophical Quarterly* 72, no. 4 (December 1991): 290–313.

14. Ibid., 306, emphasis added.

15. Caroline Whitbeck, "A Different Reality: Feminist Ontology," in *Beyond Domination*, 75–76.

16. In addition to Whitbeck, see Code on the compatibility of autonomy and interdependency; Chodorow for a psychoanalytic account of the differences in the psychosexual development of girls and boys; Marilyn Friedman, "The Social Self and the Partiality Debates," in *Feminist Ethics*, ed. Claudia Card (Lawrence: University Press of Kansas, 1991) for an evaluation of how social distance affects partiality in moral thinking; Carol Gilligan, *In a Different Voice* (Cambridge: Harvard University Press, 1982), for an influential discussion of relationship as a factor in the self-definitions of women; Evelyn Fox Keller, *Reflections on Gender and Science* (New Haven: Yale University Press, 1985) for an application of Chodorow et al. to the development of scientists; and Sarah Ruddick, "Maternal Thinking," in *Feminist Studies* 6, no. 2 (Summer 1980) for a discussion of maternal relationship in particular.

17. See Bordo, *Flight*; Sandra Harding, "Why Has the Sex/Gender System Become Visible Only Now?" in *Discovering Reality: Feminist Perspectives on Epistemology, Metaphysics, Methodology, and the Philosophy of Science*, ed. Sandra Harding and Merrill B. Hintikka (Dordrecht: D. Reidel, 1983) and *The Science Question in Feminism* (Ithaca: Cornell University Press 1986); Alison Jaggar, "Love and Knowledge: Emotion in Feminist Epistemology," in *Women, Knowledge, and Reality: Explorations in Feminist Philosophy*, ed. Ann Garry and Marilyn Pearsall (Boston: Unwin Hyman, 1989); Keller, "Feminism"; and Genevieve Lloyd, *The Man of Reason*, among many others.

18. Richard McKeon, ed., *Selections from Medieval Philosophers*, vol. 2 (New York: Scribner, 1930), 494.

19. Joseph Lawrence, "Logos and Eros: The Underlying Tension in Kant's Third Critique," *Idealist Studies* 22, no. 2 (May 1992): 130–43, 136.

20. Harald Pilot, "Kant's Theory of the Autonomy of Reflective Judgment as an Ethics of Experimental Thinking." *Nous* 24, no. 1 (March 1990): 111–35, 112.

21. Ibid., 128.

22. *Sens* receives discrete elements; *Gefühl* is holistic. Furthermore, Kant knew Aristotle's

254   Aesthetics

work well, and I see Kant's view of the self as closer to Aristotle's than to those of Descartes or Hume, for example.

23. Pilot, "Kant's Theory," 131.

24. Rudolf Makkreel, "Regulative and Reflective Uses of Purposiveness in Kant." *S J Phil* 30, suppl. (1991): 49–63, 56–57.

25. Donald W. Crawford, "Kant's Theory of Creative Imagination," in *Essays in Kant's Aesthetics,* ed. Ted Cohen and Paul Guyer (Chicago: University of Chicago Press, 1982).

26. Compare Richard Aquila's account ("Unity of Organism, Unity of Thought, and the Unity of the *Critique of Judgement,*" *S J Phil* [1991]: 139–220) of the movement from pre-articulated to conceptually articulated wholes.

27. Ted Cohen, "Why Beauty is a Symbol of Morality," in *Essays in Kant's Aesthetics,* ed. Ted Cohen and Paul Guyer (Chicago: University of Chicago Press, 1982), 235.

28. Makkreel, "Regulative," 59.

29. In addition to the writers cited in note 15, see Sarah Lucia Hoagland, "Some Thoughts about 'Caring,' " in *Feminist Ethics,* and Joan C. Tronto, "Women and Caring: What Can Feminists Learn about Morality from Caring?" in *Gender/Body/Knowledge,* ed. Alison M. Jaggar and Susan R. Bordo (New Brunswick: Rutgers University Press, 1989) for further ethical analysis of how different types of relatedness affect the moral context and which, if any, could appropriately stand as paradigmatic of moral relationship (with particular focus on the suitability of the mother-child relationship).

30. Ruddick, "Maternal Thinking," 347.

31. Donna Wilshire, "The Uses of Myth, Image, and the Female Body in Re-Visioning Knowledge," in *Gender/Body/Knowledge,* 98.

32. Makkreel, "Regulative," 49–53, 59.

33. The presenting or projecting that constitutes one fork of the deduction (by definition a concomitant presentation and explanation) is first sustained feelingly, prior to and during the construction or explanation which the entire critical philosophy constitutes. I shall develop this idea shortly in the text.

34. Robin M. Schott, "Kant's Treatment of Sensibility," in *New Essays on Kant,* ed. Bernard den Ouden and Marcia Moen (New York: Peter Lang, 1987).

35. See Evelyn Fox Keller, *Reflections,* for a discussion of Barbara McClintock's manner of working, as an example of attending nonreductively to complex wholes. Ruddick's concept of "attentive love" is another holistic attention, and in this is similar to what Wilshire calls "minding" as an attentiveness to large and holistic patterns.

36. It is, strictly speaking, not even a concept, but Kant does not always distinguish between concepts and ideas.

37. It must be so, given the atomic individual, for then communication by direct interpenetration is ruled out. Putting it another way, an epistemology built on dyadic relations of universal to instance will never make communication short of amazing, not to say magical.

38. See John H. Zammito, *The Genesis of Kant's Critique of Judgement* (Chicago: University of Chicago Press, 1992).

39. In moral thinking "free conformity" refers to the autonomy of the moral agent in conforming to the Categorical Imperative. Concerning aesthetic judgment the expression refers to the "free play" (e.g., § 9) of the faculties of Imagination and Understanding, where the Imagination configures sensations thereby generating forms although unconstrained by the conceptual forms of Understanding.

40. See, for example, the idea that in genius nature "gives the rule to art," § 46.

41. I am thinking here primarily of C. S. Peirce's semiotics, based on the positive concept of a "triadic relation" that cannot be reduced to combinations of dyadic relations. By contrast Saussure's semiology retains a dyadic conception of the sign (signifier-signified) and thereby must bracket out the diachronic process of signification and interpretation. This dyadic

conception spread along with the structuralist movement, and on into poststructuralist and postmodernist thinking, where there is almost a formula of positing a dichotomy and then "deconstructing" it, revealing its inadequacies, all of which could be done in a positive way if we had begun with conceptions adequate to the complexities of higher-order relations.

42. See Pilot's concept of "experiential deliberation" employing a "non-propositional kind of judgment" in the gradual construction of empiricial concepts—especially his discussion in his part 3, § 2, on the role of analogy in that process.

43. Keller, *Reflections*, 158–76.

44. Kant knew well Ciceronian rhetoric, in which the "deductive" question is the question of justification.

45. Audre Lorde, *Sister Outsider* (Trumansburg, N.Y.: Crossing Press, 1984) uses "erotic" to refer to the creative energy, psychic and emotional, that "colors" and "heightens and sensitizes" *all* experience (57) and provides the stamina needed to pursue changes in the world.

46. Particularly forceful in exploring "nonlinear" thought and expression are the so-called French feminists such as Luce Irigaray, *This Sex Which Is Not One*, trans. Catherine Porter and Carolyn Burke (Ithaca: Cornell University Press, 1985). Helpful discussions of her work in this direction include Andrea Nye, "The Voice of the Serpent: French Feminism and Philosophy of Language," in *Women, Knowledge, and Reality*, and Nancy Fraser and Sandra Lee Bartky, ed., *Revaluing French Feminism: Critical Essays on Difference, Agency, and Culture* (Bloomington: Indiana University Press, 1992). See also Wilshire on the difference between "linearity" on the one hand and, on the other hand, the process of "minding," the attentiveness of which makes possible the perception of large and holistic patterns.

47. Makkreel, "Regulative," 59.

48. Cf. the ecofeminist contention that current policy concerning the natural world omits critical elements of the reality, such as our ecological needs.

49. This is so pervasive a commitment among feminists, expressed in one way or another, that it nearly goes without saying. However, in reference to authors I have cited or shall cite, see Lorraine Code, *What Can She Know?* and *Epistemic Responsibility* (Hanover: University Press of New England, 1987); Jaggar, "Feminist Ethics"; Lorde, *Sister*; and Maria C. Lugones and Elizabeth V. Spelman, "Have We Got a Theory for You! Feminist Theory, Cultural Imperialism and the Demand for 'The Woman's Voice,' " in *Women and Values: Readings in Recent Feminist Philosophy*, ed. Marilyn Pearsall, 2d ed. (Belmont: Wadsworth, 1993). Also see Jane Flax, "Women Do Theory," in *Women and Values*.

50. See, for example, Lugones and Spelman, "Have We Got a Theory for You!" Good collections of similar material include Gloria Anzaldua, ed., *Making Face, Making Soul—Haciendo Caras: Creative and Critical Perspectives by Women of Color* (San Francisco: Aunt Lute Foundation Books, 1990); Cherríe Moraga and Gloria Anzaldua, eds., *This Bridge Called My Back: Writings by Radical Women of Color*, 2d ed. (Watertown, Mass.: Persephone, 1981); Marianne Hirsch and Evelyn Fox Keller, eds., *Conflicts in Feminism* (New York: Routledge, 1990); Gloria T. Hull, Patricia Bell Scott, and Barbara Smith, eds., *All the Women are White, All the Blacks are Men, But Some of Us are Brave: Black Women's Studies* (Old Westbury, N.Y.: Feminist Press, 1982); as well as bell hooks, *Feminist Theory: From Margin to Center* (Boston: South End Press, 1984) and others of hooks's many books.

51. Makkreel, "Regulative," 61.

52. For the controversy over feminism and postmodernism, see Linda J. Nicholson, ed., *Feminism/Postmodernism* (New York: Routledge, 1990).

53. Wilshire, "Uses of Myth," 98.

54. See note 22.

55. See, for example, Peirce's triadic semiotics and his "Thirdness" as an ontological principle, especially in "The Architecture of Theories" (6.7–34) and the other four articles published in *Monist* beginning in 1891.

10

Sensus Communis and Violence: A Feminist Reading of Kant's Critique of Judgement[1]

Kim Hall

Many philosophers who have written about Immanuel Kant's work have cited the French Revolution as one important influence. For example, in his introduction to the *Critique of Judgement* Werner S. Pluhar notes, "Although Kant was greatly interested in the rest of the world (he greeted the French Revolution with enthusiasm and listened to and read with eagerness the accounts of other people's journeys), he himself never traveled outside East Prussia."[2] While the French Revolution was certainly important for Kant's thinking, I consider here an influence that has been eclipsed in much of the commentary on Kant's work: the context of colonial expansion. In particular, I argue that the narratives of discovery and conquest written by Christopher Columbus and Hernán Cortés are significant for Kant's thinking in the third *Critique*.

My reading of Kant's third *Critique* is informed by work in feminist and postcolonial theories, which explore the intersections of gender, race, class, and sexuality in their analyses of oppression. In particular, my reading of Kant's *Critique of Judgement* will focus on some of the examples he employs in his discussion of beautiful objects. Reflection on Kant's examples can illuminate the attitudes about gender and race that inform his analysis of the beautiful. In addressing these issues I argue that *sensus communis*, the condition necessary for judgments of the beautiful, is founded upon violence.

Intrinsic to an understanding of Kant's thought in the *Critique of Judgement* is an understanding of *sensus communis*—its composition and its workings in the judgment of the beautiful. In the third *Critique sensus communis* is the moment of judgment that opens the way in which human beings, insofar as we are moral beings, belong together in community. This "belonging together," this finding oneself a member of community, is what one learns in contemplating the beautiful. To the extent that judgment for Kant constitutes a moment in which human beings belong together in community, *sensus communis* is the defining moment of judgment.

In the third *Critique*, *sensus communis* shapes the universal communicability of the beautiful. It is a demand, a contract dictated by our very humanity. Kant writes, "[W]e judge someone refined if he has the inclination and the skill to communicate his pleasure to others, and if he is not satisfied with an object unless he can feel his liking for it in community with others. Moreover, a concern for universal communication is something that everyone expects and demands from everyone else, on the basis, as it were, of an original contract dictated by our very humanity" (*CJ* 164). The terms of the contract are both explicit and implied. The explicit terms of the contract include the idea that one is necessarily a part of the community of judging subjects in the contemplation of the beautiful, even when one is utterly alone. Implied but equally vital is the violence at the heart of moral community. The nature of this violence is the subject of the present discussion. What is the beautiful such that it is the mark of violence in Kant's *Critique of Judgement*? When considered in the context of the voyages of Columbus and Cortés the violence informing judgments of the beautiful in the third *Critique* becomes clearer.

At first, it may seem strange to read the third *Critique* in the context of Columbus and Cortés. After all, Columbus wrote in the fifteenth century, Cortés wrote in the sixteenth century, and Kant wrote at the end of the eighteenth century. In addition, while both Columbus and Cortés were unquestionably directly involved in the use of physical force to conquer the indigenous populations of the Caribbean and Mexico, Kant never traveled more than a few miles outside of his native Königsberg. How, then, is it possible to consider similarities among Kant, Cortés, and Columbus?

Consider again Pluhar's remark that Kant eagerly read accounts of other people's journeys even though he never traveled himself. Kant, who was "greatly interested in the rest of the world,"[3] was undoubtedly familiar with the narratives of colonization written by Columbus and Cortés. Indeed, the importance of their voyages and their grip on the imaginations of Europeans cannot be overestimated. Columbus's 1493 letter was rapidly translated and widespread throughout Europe. In fact, less than a month after Columbus finished the letter in which he describes his "discoveries, it was published in Barcelona and widely circulated."[4] Stannard notes, "At least seventeen different translated editions appeared throughout Europe within five years following Columbus' return from that first voyage" (*AH* 64). Thus, given his interest in other people's travels, it is highly likely that Kant was also familiar with the contents of Columbus's letter in the eighteenth century. Columbus's influence on Kant is also evident in Kant's use of examples in the *Critique of Judgement*, particularly in his discussion of the Caribs. Kant can be compared to Cortés and Columbus insofar as the examples of indigenous populations and women in his text justify and legitimate colonial expansion and the subordination of women.

In *Orientalism* Edward Said writes that "nearly every nineteenth-century writer (and the same is true enough of writers in earlier periods) was well aware of the fact of empire."[5] For Said, intellectual activities such as history, philosophy, and literature played just as significant a role in the genocide that characterized colonialism as actual invasions and killing. These writings justified colonialist expansion and the violence that went with it through their beliefs in the supremacy of the West in areas of aesthetics, morality, political organization, religious belief, and so forth. If Said is correct, his observation would also apply to Immanuel Kant. While Kant was writing "after" Columbus and Cortés, he was writing "before" the colonial expansions of the nineteenth century that were influenced by the industrial revolution.

Before proceeding to a more detailed reading of Kant's examples in the third *Critique* it would be useful to clarify what I mean by violence in my analysis of *sensus communis*. It is not difficult to argue that the genocide that accompanied the so-called voyages of discovery was violent. Columbus, who was eager to obtain all of the wealth of the lands he "discovered," cut off the hands of Indians who did not give him the required amount of gold.[6] Killing indigenous peoples was a sport for the soldiers, and it was not unusual for infants to be taken from their mothers and smashed against the rocks (AH 71). Four years after Columbus's arrival the indigenous population fell "from eight million to four and five million," and in 1508 (twelve years after Columbus's arrival) the indigenous population was "down to less than a hundred thousand" (AH 74–75). Cortés's troops learned a lot about invasion and conquest from Columbus's experiences, and his invasions were no less marked by sadistic killing of indigenous populations (AH 76).

In my exploration of similarities among Kant, Columbus, and Cortés I am not claiming that Kant's analysis in the third *Critique* is identical to these voyages and narratives of conquest. There are indeed many differences. For example, Kant never physically participated in a voyage of discovery and colonization. Thus, I am not suggesting that the violence of Kant's text is identical to the physical violence directed at indigenous populations by European conquerors. Rather, I wish to make an ideological connection among the three. When representations of indigenous peoples (male and female) and white European and Euro-American women on the page reinforce racist and sexist ideology, the violence directed toward indigenous men and women and white European and Euro-American women is rationalized and legitimated by those representations. Kant's, Columbus's, and Cortés's texts are violent to the extent that the ideology informing their texts justifies patriarchal and colonial authority as well as the use of violence when that authority is threatened.

In his *American Holocaust*, David Stannard asks, "Did those Europeans and early American white colonists treat Indians and Africans as they did at least in part because of a racist ideology that long had been in place—or was Euro-American racism in the Americas a later development, even a product of white *versus* Indian and white *versus* black conflict? In short, which came first, the carrying out of terrible and systematic damage to others or the ideology of degradation?" (AH 269). Stannard's point is that it is hard to make a clear distinction between racist acts and racist ideologies that pave the way for the acceptability of those acts. The violence at the heart of *sensus communis* in Kant's *Critique of Judgement* is the violence of a racist and sexist ideology that justifies and reinforces Western European patriarchal hegemony. This ideology is what links Kant, Columbus, and Cortés, and reading Kant in the context of colonial expansion can provide further insight into Kant's thought, particularly for feminist philosophers who are concerned with the intersections of gender and race.

According to Kant, to say that something is beautiful is to have the right to expect agreement from everyone else. To do otherwise is to use the term "beautiful" incorrectly. If one cannot demand of everyone else that she or he agree in a judgment of the beautiful, what is experienced is not beautiful and, in Kant's mind at least, whether or not the person who claimed to be experiencing the beautiful has any taste at all is cast into question. For Kant, such a misuse of judgment is a mark of bad taste and the mark of a bad soul:

> For he must not call it *beautiful* if [he means] only [that] he *likes* it. Many things may be charming and agreeable to him; no one cares about that. But if he proclaims something to be beautiful, then he requires the same liking from others; he then judges not just for himself but for everyone. . . . That is why he says; The *thing* is beautiful, and does not count on other people to agree with his judgment of liking on the ground that he has repeatedly found them agreeing with him; rather, he *demands* that they agree. He reproaches them if they judge differently, and denies that they have taste, which he nevertheless demands of them, as something they ought to have. (CJ 55–56)

According to Kant, to say that every person has her or his own peculiar taste is the same as saying that there is no such thing as taste at all (CJ 56). In other words, in matters of taste there ought to be universal assent. But what is the nature of the demand for universal communicability in Kant's third *Critique*? What is it about the beautiful that demands a universal liking, a universal pleasure? What is the standard of beauty at work in the *Critique of Judgement*?

In the third *Critique* the universal communicability of the beautiful is possible to the extent that the beautiful is a symbol of the moral. Judgments of the beautiful teach us something about the way in which one belongs in community and about morality. For Kant, there is a connection between the beautiful and the moral, and this connection is the basis behind his assertion that the ideal of the beautiful is found solely in the human figure: "[W]e must still distinguish the ideal of the beautiful, which for reasons already stated must be expected solely in the human figure. Now the idea in this figure consists in the expression of the moral; apart from the moral the object would not be liked universally and moreover positively" (CJ 83). It is in this sense that the beautiful person is the moral person. For Kant, it is *man*[7] who admits of an ideal of beauty, who admits of a certain perfection (CJ 81).

Because the beautiful is the symbol of the moral, it can lay claim to everyone's assent. One can assess the values of other people and demand universal agreement in the contemplation of the beautiful because everyone, according to Kant, has a similar maxim in *his* power of judgment. As Kant himself puts it, "Now I maintain that the beautiful is the symbol of the morally good; and only because we refer the beautiful to the morally good (we all do so naturally and require all others also to do so, as a duty) does our liking for it include a claim to everyone else's assent, while the mind is also conscious of being ennobled, by this [reference], above other people too on the basis of [their having] a similar maxim in their power of judgment" (CJ 228). Judgment of the beautiful is inextricably related to a sense of duty and, in that regard, it is the moral vocation and destiny of human beings. This destiny for which humans work is *sensus communis*, a moral community. In the *Critique of Judgement* Kant frequently refers to this essential relationship between the beautiful and the moral and justifies the demand of universal communicability as "man's natural propensity to sociability" (CJ 62).

Sensus communis, the belonging together of human beings in moral community, is the moral vocation of human beings, and it is the necessary foundation of judgments of the beautiful. Kant has this in mind when he writes, "[M]an is the ultimate purpose of creation here on earth, because he is the only being on earth who can form a concept of purposes and use his reason to turn an aggregate of purposively structured things into a system of purposes" (CJ 314). In other words, things in nature are ultimately there for *man* because, as a moral being, *man* is the ideal of beauty and perfection. Final purposes, according to Kant, cannot be found in nature, therefore, *man* because he contains *his* final purposes within *himself*, is the "lord of nature" (CJ 318).

Kant's claims here resemble the declarations of both Columbus and Cortés that they were the rightful lords of the lands they conquered in the name of Spain. Columbus saw himself and consequently "civilized" Europe as the beacon of morality and law for the people he conquered in the name of Spain. On 16 December 1492 Columbus writes, "And they are so fitted to be ruled and to be set to work, to cultivate the land and to do all else that may be necessary, and you may build towns and teach them to go clothed and adopt our customs."[8] Both Columbus and Cortés saw Europe (in their case, Spain) as the rightful lord of the Caribbean and Mexico, the "New World."

The idea of *man's* superiority over nature, which is expressed in Kant's claim that *man* is the rightful lord of nature, is a part of the foundation of the ideal of unlimited progress, an ideal that was inherent to colonial expansion. Both Cortés's and Columbus's letters described in great detail the amount of beauty and wealth that they found, and both expressed their belief that their "discoveries" would enhance the wealth and glory of Spain. In addition, the idea of *man's* superiority over nature has implications for women, who have been considered closer to nature in the history of Western thought.[9] To the extent that women have been so considered, the assertion that *man* is the rightful lord of nature can be interpreted as an assertion of *man's* authority over women. However, in order to consider the applicability of this interpretation to Kant's work, it is necessary to consider Kant's discussion of women in the third *Critique*.

SENSUS COMMUNIS AND WOMEN

While Kant is clear that the nature of the beautiful is not about objects insofar as the object's existence is of no importance, reflection on his examples of beautiful objects in the third *Critique* (especially when the objects discussed are women and "primitive" people and customs) reveals much about the ideas of race and gender that inform Kant's analysis of the beautiful.

Throughout the third *Critique* Kant discusses women's figures, clothing, habits, and so forth, and women's bodies are often presented in the text as examples of beautiful objects about which the community of judging subjects would agree. Consider Kant's remark that "if we say, e.g. that is a beautiful woman, we do in fact think nothing other than that nature offers us in the woman's figure a beautiful presentation of the purposes [inherent] in the female build" (CJ 179–80). Who is the "we" who judges a woman's figure and clothing? To the extent that women appear in Kant's text as objects of judgment, women are absent from the community of judging subjects. Judgments of the beautiful require an awareness of the moral law within oneself and the ability to apprehend it. *Sensus communis* is also necessary for judgments of the beautiful. To say that an object is beautiful is to say that the object is beautiful for everyone, and one feels the need to communicate one's pleasure with others.

Kant's essay "Of the Distinction of the Beautiful and the Sublime in the Interrelations of the Two Sexes" raises questions about the place of women in the community of judging subjects. In this essay, Kant discusses the differences between men and women, especially in relation to how men should speak to women and how women should be educated. In all cases, it is clear that men should not discuss any "serious" matters with women. Rather, women should concern themselves with such matters that would make them pleasant hostesses at parties or the "pleasant object[s] of a well-mannered conversation."[10] In addition, Kant declares that women are not to be told things that would require rigorous thinking on their part.

Kant's assertions about the appropriate behavior and education of women become all the more relevant for the present discussion given Kant's definition of humanity in the third *Critique* as that which is both the universal *feeling of sympathy* and the ability to engage universally in very intimate conversation (CJ 231). When these two qualities are combined they constitute the sociability that befits humanity and distinguishes human beings from animals (CJ 231). The fact that women are not to be told anything that would require serious thinking and that men should speak to women in very limited ways (e.g., as objects of well-mannered conversation) raises questions about whether or not women are considered by Kant to be a part of humanity in the way that European men are a part of humanity (e.g., as participants in conversation about serious matters). In order for judgments of the beautiful to be "pure" according to Kant, they must transcend the particularity of the object and, as such, judgments of the beautiful require a certain rigor in contemplation. Women are a part of humanity, but their "proper" role for Kant is passive objects, not active participants.

For Kant, women are objects to be admired in a way similar to any work of art. However, women do not possess the rational capacities necessary for participating in conversations about intellectual matters. And to the extent that this is so it would be difficult for women to possess the capacities for pure aesthetic judgment. I do not mean to suggest that Kant did not believe that European women were human. My point is that the place of women in Kant's *Critique of Judgement* is as objects and as helpmates to men.

Kant's claim that women possess a beautiful rather than a deep understanding[11] provides further evidence for his belief that women are inferior. Because a woman's understanding is only beautiful, she "will learn no geometry; of the principle of sufficient reason or the monads she will know only so much as is needed to perceive the salt in a satire which the insipid grubs of our sex have censured. The fair can leave Descartes his vortices to whirl forever without troubling themselves about them."[12] Kant further asserts that "[t]he content of women's great science, rather is humankind, and among humanity, men."[13] Here, Kant defines the place of women in human community as that of helpmates to men and as reproducers of human beings. Given his belief in women's inferiority, it is doubtful that Kant thought that women were capable of apprehending that which is universal in aesthetics and morality.

In addition to indicating that women are deficient judging subjects, the context of Kant's discussion of women in the third *Critique* indicates that "women" in his text refers to European women of a privileged class. Kant refers to the Caribs and the Iroquois in some of his examples in the third *Critique;* however, Carib and Iroquois women are absent from his discussion. While European women occupy a secondary place in the community of judging subjects in the third *Critique,* Carib and Iroquois women have no place. One wonders if Kant thought that Carib and Iroquois women were not "real" women. In her book, *Ain't I a Woman: Black Women and Feminism* bell hooks discusses the devaluation of black womanhood that was an intimate part of the mentality of white men who owned slaves. While white women were placed on pedestals as models of true womanhood, enslaved black women were denied the status of "real" women.[14]

For Columbus and Cortés, Indian men and women were treated more like exotic animals rather than fellow human beings. In his journal Columbus writes frequently about capturing men and women and taking them back to Spain as examples of his "discoveries." According to David Stannard, "The treatment of Indian women is particularly revealing, in light of the Catholic *machismo* ideology of the Spanish that celebrated the purity of their own women" (AH 84). During his second voyage Columbus "gave" an Indian woman to an Italian nobleman, Michele de Cuneo, for his "enjoyment." Cuneo describes his rape of the Indian woman "given" to him by Columbus and her initial resistance of him. In the end, Cuneo declares that "she seemed to have been brought up in a school of harlots" (AH 84). According to Stannard, Cuneo's description is the first known document of a sexual encounter between a European man and an Indian woman, and it set the tone for future myths of Indian women in European (and Euro-American) imaginations (AH 84).

One could argue that, in terms of their attitudes toward Indian women, comparisons among Columbus, Cortés, and Kant are unfounded. After all, Kant was not shaped by the "Catholic" *machismo* that characterized Columbus's and Cortés's attitudes toward Indian women. On the other hand, Kant's descriptions of the "fair" sex do not pertain to the lived experiences of Indian women. Kant's descriptions of dinner parties where women make pleasing hostesses is a world of "civilized" society. It is a world far removed from his description of the more "primitive" world of the Caribs and the Iroquois in the third *Critique*. Kant's admiration of "the fair" coexists with his erasure of Indian women. For Columbus and Cortés the "purity" of Spanish women is defended while Indian women are raped, captured, killed, and despised. For all three, the essential being of women is defined by men in order to ensure and justify men's social and political dominance. In narratives of conquest dominance of the colonizers is marked by the access that the male colonizer has to colonized women, and the atrocities of colonialism are committed in the name of protecting white European and Euro-American women.

KANT'S COLONIAL DISCOURSE

While European women are examples of beautiful objects in the third *Critique*, women are by no means the ideal of beauty. The idea of beauty in the third *Critique* is found in the figure of the warrior. For Kant, the warrior is the most esteemed of all citizens:

> For what is it that is an object of the highest admiration even to the savage? It is a person who is not terrified, not afraid, and

hence does not yield to danger but promptly sets to work with vigor and full deliberation. Even in a fully civilized society there remains this superior esteem for the warrior, except that we demand more of him: that he also demonstrate all the virtues of peace—gentleness, sympathy, and even appropriate care for his own person—precisely because they reveal to us that his mind cannot be subdued by danger. Hence, no matter how much people may dispute, when they compare the statesman with the general, as to which one deserves the superior respect, an aesthetic judgment declines in favor of the general. (CJ 121–22)

In this passage, the "savage" is opposed to the warrior. The warrior, whose "civility" is marked by "good" manners and a neat appearance, is claimed by Kant to be held in high regard even by the "savage." With these pronouncements Kant echoes and reinforces a myth that is all too familiar in justifications of colonial interventions: the myth that colonization is a "civilizing mission." Kant's warrior is the epitome of the civilized man, a man who brings law, morality, and science to the "savage" and is respected by the "savage" for improving the world he has conquered. The presence of works of art and philosophy is usually cited as "evidence" of "civilization," and indigenous works of art and philosophies have been devalued by defenders of the superiority of Western civilization who assert that the indigenous peoples of the Americas and the people of Africa, the Middle East, and Asia have "not yet produced, will never produce, an Einstein, a Stravinsky, a Gershwin,"[15] and (one could also add) a Shakespeare, a Kant. The savage in Kant's text praises the warrior because the warrior, who has conquered his land and people brings "civilization" to "primitive" peoples.

Columbus and Cortés also believed that they brought civilization to the indigenous populations that they "discovered." From the moment Cortés arrived in Mexico, the many tribes of indigenous people were immediately labeled by Cortés as the enemy, foreigners in their own land. Mexico, a land in which many different cultures had flourished for thousands of years separate from European influence, was a land that Cortés claimed to have discovered, as if it had been previously uninhabited. Cortés took many liberties such as naming the land "New Spain," as if it had no name of its own. In his letter Cortés wrote of his amazement that the "barbarians" lived in harmony and order far away from any knowledge of God and isolated from "civilized" nations.[16] Immediately, Cortés began claiming all of the wealth of the land as the property of Spain, as "Your Majesty's gold and jewels."[17] Like Columbus, Cortés believed that it was his moral vocation to conquer, "pacify," and "civilize" the Indians.

When colonization is legitimated as a "civilizing mission" the violence that is an inherent part of colonization is obscured. Kant, Columbus, and Cortés remain silent about the violence of genocide in their celebration of the superiority of the colonizer who "civilizes" the "sav-ages." Kant is complicit in the creation of a climate of acceptability for European imperialism through his descriptions of indigenous populations as "primitive" and as entering Civilization and History only when they came into contact with Europe.[18] Many Western intellectuals, politicians, and military officials justified and distorted colonial invasion by declaring it "for the good" of the colonized.

In the third *Critique* Kant's descriptions of Carib and Iroquois peoples provide further evidence for Kant's belief that indigenous peoples are not "civilized." For example, Kant writes, "Initially, it is true, only charms thus become important in society and become connected with great interest, e.g., the dyes people use to paint themselves (roucou among the Caribs and cinnabar among the Iroquois), or the flowers, sea shells, beautifully colored feathers, but eventually also beautiful forms (as in canoes, clothes, etc) that involve no gratification whatsoever, i.e., no liking or enjoyment. But in the end, when civilization has reached its peak it makes this communication almost the principal activity of refined inclination, and sensations are valued only to the extent that they are universally communicable" (*CJ* 164). In this passage Kant reinforces the colonial myth that Indians are "savage," "uncivilized." Civilization has not yet reached its peak in worlds of feathers, body paint, and canoes. Presumably, contact with civilization would only come with European influence and authority. Kant's descrip-tions in this passage also indicate his familiarity with narratives of contact with Carib and Iroquois peoples. Because the word "Carib" was first brought to the attention of Europeans by Columbus, it seems likely that Columbus was one of Kant's influences in his descriptions of Carib people.

It is important to note that Kant's use of the word "Carib" in the passage quoted earlier is itself laden with a colonial political agenda. The literature concerning the Carib originated in the fifteenth century with Columbus's voyage of conquest, and "Carib" first becomes associated with the eating of human flesh in his letters and journal.[19] Columbus writes, "Thus, I have found no monsters, nor report of any, except of an island which is *Carib*, which is the second to the entrance to the Indies, which is inhabited by a people who are regarded in all the islands as very ferocious, [and] who eat human flesh."[20] As a result of Columbus's description, Carib became a word associated in the European imagination with all things evil and savage, the opposite of "civilization."[21]

It is interesting to reflect on the place of Kant's warrior, who is the most respected of all citizens, in relation to the place of the Carib in the text. Columbus described Caribs as warriors who ate human flesh, and Columbus's description of the Carib continued to be associated with the opposite of European civilization from the fifteenth through the nineteenth centuries.[22] The Carib in Kant's *Critique of Judgement* is a warrior; however, he would not be the warrior who is the most esteemed of all citizens. Kant's warrior is represented in contrast to the "savage." The "savage" may praise the warrior, but the "savage" cannot be the respected general. Kant's general is courageous but also gentle and peaceful. In his description of the Caribs, whose art is not art produced at the peak of civilization, Kant reinforces the colonialist mythology that indigenous peoples are "primitive" (the opposite of civilized) and provides a ground for the justification of genocide of the Caribs as a part of a civilizing mission.

BEYOND *SENSUS COMMUNIS*

While Kant, Columbus, and Cortés deny the existence of any "civilized" society apart from their own, the existence of Pre-Columbian art and Aztec poetry attests to the existence of civilizations that were already developed before contact with Europe. The Aztecs left a legacy of poems. Some of these poems bear witness to European attempts to obliterate their culture:

> We mourned for ourselves, our lot.
> Broken spears lie in the by-ways,
> we have torn our hair out by the roots.

Palaces stand roofless, blood-red walls.
Maggots swarm the square and huts.
Our city walls are stained with shattered brains.

Water flows red, as if someone had dyed it,
and if we drink
it tastes of sulphur.

In grief we beat our fists
against the walls of our mud houses,
a net of holes our only heritage . . .[23]

The violence voiced in this poem exposes the lie that colonialism was a "civilizing mission." In terms of the present concern with Kant's third *Critique* the violence described in the poem also reveals the unlikelihood that the colonial warrior would have been praised and respected by colonized peoples. Kant's warrior is a part of the colonialist myth that the colonizer is benign, that the colonizer has only the "best" interests of the colonized peoples at heart, and that colonization of indigenous populations is necessary in order to civilize "primitive" peoples.

There are numerous references to "primitive people," "barbarians," and "savages" in the third *Critique*. Kant's reinforcement and ultimate legitimization of patriarchal European superiority through the use of examples of "primitive others" establishes a connection to Cortés and Columbus. All three are bound by views of race and gender that shape the framework of their ideas, and to the extent that all three promote an image of non-European indigenous peoples as "backward" and "savage," all three perpetuate the myth of the superiority of Western European man.

Through exploring the ideologies of race and gender that shape Kant's construction of *sensus communis* and judgments of the beautiful, I have revealed how these ideologies rationalize European patriarchal dominance in Europe and the Americas. In undertaking this project I have considered the implications of Said's remarks that no European scholar in the nineteenth century and earlier was writing in ignorance of colonialism.[24] When read in this light, Kant's writing in the *Critique of Judgement* can be compared with the narratives of Cortés and Columbus in ways that reveal the political commitments of Kant's text. It is the justification of colonization and the subordination of women informing Kant's third *Critique* that shape the violence at the heart of *sensus communis*.

Notes

1. I thank Robin Schott for her many helpful suggestions. Her careful reading of earlier drafts has made this a much better essay. Of course, I take responsibility for any mistakes that remain.

2. See Werner S. Pluhar, "Translator's Introduction," in *Critique of Judgement*, by Immanuel Kant, trans. Werner S. Pluhar (Indianapolis: Hackett, 1987), xxx; hereafter cited as *CJ*.

3. Pluhar, "Translator's Introduction," xxx.

4. See David E. Stannard, *American Holocaust: Columbus and the Conquest of the New World* (New York: Oxford University Press, 1992), 64; hereafter cited as *AH*.

5. Edward Said, *Orientalism* (New York: Vintage Books, 1978), 14.

6. Stannard, *AH* 71. See also Ward Churchill, *Indians Are Us? Culture and Genocide in Native North America* (Monroe, Maine: Common Courage Press, 1994), 31.

7. I have chosen to maintain Kant's use of the masculine "generic" for human beings here due to my belief that Kant was writing for and about men. Kant's establishment of *man* as the ideal of beauty announces a problematic that haunts the rest of the third *Critique*.

8. Christopher Columbus, *The Journal of Christopher Columbus*, trans. Cecil Jane (London: Anthony Blond, 1968).

9. Many ecofeminists have analyzed the connections between women and nature. For further discussion of this issue see Greta Gaard, *Ecofeminism: Women, Animals, Nature* (Philadelphia: Temple University Press, 1993) and Susan Griffin, *Woman and Nature: The Roaring Inside Her* (New York: Harper and Row, 1978).

10. Immanuel Kant, "Of the Distinction of the Beautiful and the Sublime in the Interrelations of the Two Sexes," in *Philosophy of Woman: An Anthology of Classic and Current Concepts*, 2d ed., ed. Mary Briody Mahowald (Indianapolis: Hackett, 1983), 197.

11. Kant, "Of the Distinction of the Beautiful and the Sublime," 194.

12. Ibid., 194–95.

13. Ibid., 195.

14. bell hooks, *Ain't I a Woman: Black Women and Feminism* (Boston: South End Press, 1981).

15. Aimé Césaire, *Discourse on Colonialism*, trans. Joan Pinkham (New York: Monthly Review Press, 1972), 30.

16. Hernán Cortés, *Letters from Mexico*, trans. and ed. Anthony Pagden (New Haven: Yale University Press, 1986), 108.

17. Ibid., 137.

18. See Immanuel Kant, "Idea for a Universal History with Cosmopolitan Intent," in *Perpetual Peace and Other Essays*, trans. Ted Humphrey (Indianapolis: Hackett, 1983), 32. Here, Kant writes in a note, "For if one begins with Greek History—the one through which all other more ancient or contemporary histories have been preserved or at least authenticated; if one follows the influence of the Greeks on the formation and malformation of the body politic of the Roman People, who engulfed the Greek nation, and the influence of the Romans on the Barbarians, who in their turn destroyed the Romans, up to our own time; and if, as episodes, one adds to this the national histories of other peoples, inasmuch as knowledge of them has bit by bit come to us from these enlightened nations; one will discover

a course of improvement conforming to rules in the constitutions of the nations on our continent (which will in all likelihood eventually give laws to all others)."

19. See *Wild Majesty: Encounters with Caribs from Columbus to the Present Day*, ed. Peter Hulme and Neil L. Whitehead (Oxford: Clarendon Press, 1992), 3.

20. Ibid., 15.

21. Ibid., 4.

22. Roberto Fernández Retamar, *Caliban and Other Essays*, trans. Edward Baker (Minneapolis: University of Minnesota Press, 1989), 9.

23. See *Flower and Song: Poems of the Aztec Peoples*, trans. Edward Kissam and Michael Schmidt (London: Avid Press Poetry, 1977), 111–12.

24. Said, *Orientalism*, 14.

Part IV

Political Philosophy

11

Kant's Patriarchal Order

Hannelore Schröder
Translated by Rita Gircour

Before I start my discussion of Kant's *Metaphysische Anfangsgründe der Rechtslehre* I would like to introduce a few reflections by Theodor Gottlieb von Hippel (1741–96), to show the enormous differences in the theories of these contemporaries. Von Hippel was mayor of Königsberg and belonged to the same social circle as Kant did and even to his circle of friends. Yet in terms of their ideas on justice, law, and ethics they have little in common. Von Hippel is no metaphysician; he is a lawyer. The bases of his argumentation are his observations of reality and his sense of justice, not a priori definitions. He seeks to depict "life" in his writings, not ideas. In contrast to the canonized *Rechtsphilosophen* Kant, Fichte, and Hegel, he argues in favor of human and civil rights for women and is a unique representative of truly radical egalitarian politics.

Equally in contrast to the three "great thinkers" who continue to unconsciously reproduce the theological and philosophical dogmas or, as apologists, consciously defend them, the work of von Hippel is not known in mainstream academic circles. The three are ideologists of difference; von Hippel is a theorist of equality, the only feminist German man of his time, who should be known as an exceptionally unprejudiced and broadminded critic of law and political philosophy.

In 1792 von Hippel published his *Über die bürgerliche Verbesserung der Weiber*, a title inspired by the much debated work by Ch. C. W. von Dohm, *Über die bürgerliche Verbesserung der Juden* (1781). Thereby he turns "the woman's question" into a political issue just like "the Jewish question." "In our days there are so many recommendations for the improvement of the civil rights for Jews; should a real people of God (the other sex) deserve any less care?"[1]

The exclusion of all women from the so-called human rights of the French Revolution of 1789 was ample reason for von Hippel to criticize this political scandal resolutely and often ironically. However, being a high-ranking civil servant he had to publish this work anonymously as he attacked the king of Prussia, civil servants, and in general "the men of God's Graces"—and as the advocacy of human rights for women was seen as ridiculous and totally absurd.

CRITICISM OF POLITICAL IRRATIONALITY

"I believed one should take evil by its roots, and not leave out the role of the State. France, where everything is equal now, has left our sex unaffected. Unforgivable! How can a nation that exists *par et pour* the fair sex ignore that sex in this equality for all that is so highly praised the world over?" (*Ü* 13). "In this time where human rights are preached from the roof tops . . . men say a clear *no* to women." And: "The new French Constitution deserves my repeated reproach because it allowed a whole half of the Nation to be forgotten. . . . All Men have equal rights. All the French, men and women, should be free and citizens. All proposals for *dégradation civique*, which proclaims certain men unworthy of the honour of being a French citizen as a punishment for crime, have not been extended to the other sex. This sex must therefore be cursed: 'Your Fatherland has found you guilty of an infamous act' (*Ü* 121), the crime of being born female." He pointed out that one woman clearly expressed her anger. She addressed the national assembly stating: "that there is no word in the Constitution about women, although the mothers should be citizens of the state . . . Sadly I am commemorating her today" (Ü 123). Von Hippel was clearly referring to "The Declaration of Human and Civil Rights for Women" by Olympe de Gouges (1791).[2] Likewise, he calls "for the destruction of the Gallant Bastilles, the domestic cages and the civil dungeons that hold the fair sex captive" and he recommends "improvement of the civil rights for women," claiming that human and civil rights for women will lead to a new form of government that "will be beneficial for both hemispheres of the human race" (Ü 17–18).

Against Pseudo-Enlightenment

"Reason . . . that is crucial; never can the state take it upon itself to repress it. And how can it be a robber of freedom while its main task is to further that which is the basis for its existence? When the Estates [classes] can only be represented by their own peers then how can one exclude women from those public services that deal with legislation and enforcement of the legal system?" (Ü 124). In other words, how can one exclude women from the right to vote, the legislative and judicial powers at the time when the burghers in Prussia and elsewhere demand the right to represent themselves? Hippel states: "Can it be denied that every Codex of Law can only be based on the principle of natural equality?" He goes even further: "the other sex has a right to demand from the state that it provides justice for them." And: "Is it just, reasonable, advisable and just human that our entire sex is being elevated to an Estate and seen as the centre and reason for existence of the other sex?" (Ü 129–30). This is a clear attack on Rousseau and on the French Republic and their ideology and policies that elevate men to a privileged estate over all women.

"This Roman legal principle: that one has to measure the other by the same standards with which one measures oneself, seems to have lost its power here completely" (Ü 14). The *Do ut des* principle doesn't apply when the "I" is male and the "You" female.

Might is Not Right

Civil servants serve one "single state circus" and not the "common good": "Truly the Gentlemen thus occupied do not serve the state, but the state serves them." And: "The law of the most reasonable is, in their somewhat loose but unmistakable translation, the law of the strongest: and who would dare to deny that power, as long as it is at the helm, is reasonable?" (*Ü* 126–27). "Society presupposes equality among those who are joined in it, which is what the creator of mankind has aimed at." And: "In all societies in which women participate one sees a sort of decency spreading: and would this not also be the case for states . . . when women have access?" (*Ü* 21).

Today, more than two centuries later, "unsere deutsche Herren Männer" to use Von Hippel's term, are still fighting the democratic participation of women in parliament, government, the legal system, and other public services. This political fact points to the continuity of undemocratic, patriarchal *Realpolitik* as well as Von Hippel's *Real* utopian anticipation.

Against the Dualist Anthropological Ideology

Von Hippel poses the question: "Are there any other differences between men and women other than the sexual organs?" (*Ü*, chap. 2, 23f.), putting into question the dominant theological and philosophical dualisms that justify the exclusion of women because God and Nature have decreed it so.

God wants equality

Von Hippel rejects the theological dogmas and replaces them by his own egalitarian interpretation of Genesis: As people, Adam and Eve were born equal: "Neither one raised the other, neither one got the idea to place themselves over the other and claim paternal rights. . . . If one would wish to credit one partner in this first human couple on the basis of the oldest document, then Eve would receive the apple of discord—since Adam's fall was caused by her, because it was through her that he let himself be talked into the use, the application, the breakthrough of reason. . . . She broke the chain of instinct that held back reason. Reason should be called Eve in memory of her. . . . That is how it was with the first revolution, and this is how it should be in any subsequent one that deserves to be called one" (Ü 23–24). Von Hippel interprets Genesis as "an image of human liberation and in the origin of state of society." Women are thus born free and equal. "It is only in a far later time when it is said that your will must be subjected to your husband's will and he should be your master!" (Ü 25). This would certainly count as heresy, and this original and courageous exegesis would certainly have meant a trial for heresy and dismissal from his position as mayor had the name of the author become known.

Nature wants equality

According to Von Hippel "In the anatomy of the two human sexes nature does not seem to have had the intention to either establish a distinct difference between the two, or to favour one at the expense of the other. . . . Differences other than those of the sexual organs have so far been eluding the knife of the anatomist." Moreover: "In reaching that great goal of nature, where humans are making the divine image of the creator [human procreation] the female sex makes a decidedly more substantial contribution than the male sex, both in terms of substance and form. In order to prepare very wisely in this respect, would nature have wanted to build women weakly and incomplete?" And: "Would the all powerful Nature have left its representative, the Mother, weak for bringing not only the weak persons of her own sex into the world but also the strong ones of our sex?" (Ü 26–27). Von Hippel does not take the twisted sophistries of the *Weiberfeinde*, or woman haters, seriously "because straightforward argumentation comes down in favor of women!" "Lebensart, Sitten und Kleidung" are responsible for the differences in physical power, not nature (Ü 32). Furthermore he asks: "Are there sex differences among the souls? Are there souls that are exclusively fit to live in female bodies? And who is the courageous Argonaut who sailed this unknown sea? . . . Which methods did we embark upon? Did we select them so well that correct results could be expected from them? . . . Can we risk a system according to which such a decisive segregation line can be drawn with certainty for the entire half of the human race?" (Ü 36–37). Or are men acting "like His Infallibility on the other side or the Alps?" (Ü 38). "It is superiority of mind, greater powers of judgment . . . and other positive characteristics that men ascribe to themselves at the expense of the female sex as their firstborn right. They own this whole Earth . . . God given—as the noble lords!" (*Ü* 38). And that is precisely what the nobility had always claimed for itself, and what the revolution fought. He accuses his own sex of "lacking the moral strength and intelligence that you wish to deny the other sex out of pure envy" (*Ü* 248).

Von Hippel reserves some sarcasm for the beard, "this masculine, and in fact rather inconvenient sign of honour" leads men to "the correct conclusion that a lack thereof must mean that Nature has denied them the disposition for mental capacities and has therefore relegated them to a far lesser class of human beings. . . . What a glorious role for a beard to play . . . what a decent argument" (*Ü* 39). About education he asks: "Can the capacities (of women and girls) develop . . . when no caring hand grooms them? When everything in fact conspires to suppress and when possible eliminate them?" And: "Would we prefer to blame nature for the production of defects to save our system?" Such is the system "of royal preferential treatment for men" (*Ü* 40–41) at the expense of human rights for women.

The arbitrary nature concept of the *Naturrechtler*

Von Hippel launches some very serious accusations at the philosophers of natural law and the politicians: "the basis for all claims is taken from nature, a *Urkunde*, that has this in common with all other such major documents that in it everyone will find what they are looking for. Any history, any fact, will have to endure that it will be bent to fit us, and even the most truthful man will put a little of himself into every history and every fact, so that everything touched by man will contain something of him . . . a whole school of collectors of variations and commentators contributed their sense and nonsense to every *Urkunde* up until such time as an *Authentika* appears" that "decides on the value or lack of value of the difference between human beings" (*Ü* 36–37). Von Hippel is clearly taking aim at the antifeminists and anti-Semites when he writes: "Pseudo-enlightened men and pseudo-intellectuals" should stay away from designing a "naturally determined social ranking system." "The problems of our days are constitutional, are based on nonfacts and wishy-washy pseudo-rationality" (*Ü* 44). Then, apart from their manipulations and inconsistencies, there is also the partiality, about which Von Hippel has this to say: "the last people to be psychological judges are we, because we are so much a party" (*Ü* 248). And: "Man, being his own sculptor, can make either a god or an animal out of the piece of marble that nature gave him, as he wishes. . . . The only claim that I wish to make is that when nature started creating the human race it left most of it to us ourselves" (*Ü* 15). Where prejudice fights against reason, the latter perishes, "man changes without improving. A foolproof mark of all feeble-minded men, from the throne to the last clerk's stool." The state, however, "has the obligation to treat those who nature created equal according to equality and justice and return them their rights and with it their personal liberty and independence, civil rewards and civil honour; If the cabinets, courts, lecture halls, counters and ateliers were opened to women, according to the wishes of nature and according to what a civil society should wish, . . . then the welfare of the state and happiness would establish itself everywhere . . . and humanity would make a major step toward its great destination" (*Ü* 207–8).

Against Patriarchal Marriage

"Thank God there have always been women who feel that the state of humiliation is too big a test . . . and who do not bemoan their femininity but rather the arbitrary way their sex is treated by our sex" (*Ü* 18). Von Hippel uses the terms "slavery" and "the iron pressure of despotism," which take from women their sense of freedom and choke the very thought of the rights taken from them. "As prosecutor and judge in one and the same person," men have placed a yoke on "the other half of human creation" where women are not granted rights but only have recourse to the "Gnadenweg" where by the grace of men they are granted only so much as long as "she doesn't infringe on his royal rights and doesn't destroy his crown" (*Ü* 38). "Why shouldn't women be persons?" (under the law, and not even be granted rights under private law.) "A wife who is under the legal rule of the lord and master spouse and is a slave subjected to the power of someone else . . . only has grace to depend on." He argues that a contractually based, equal relationship should be put in place of this patriarchal marriage of master and slave. "Long ago people have unlearned that marriage is an equal partnership, that the power in marriage rests with both spouses side by side" (*Ü* 101). "To do someone a favor by taking away justice from them means to trample a law of nature . . . to sell the firstborn human right for a meal of lentils" or "to sabotage rights with presents" (Ü 103–4).

So the devastating opinion of the lawyer von Hippel is that in a so-called constitutional state human rights are violated. He asks himself, in the face of so much irrationality: "Since there can be no other gods among the people than the men of God's grace . . . : How can the human race be advised and helped when men continue so one-sided?" (Ü 14). And finally he writes for like-minded people: "Let us look forward to the day of liberation for the fair sex, when people endowed with equal rights will no longer be thwarted and when, what is so obviously equal, will no longer be distinguished on such arbitrary grounds (Ü 15).

These few quotes from his 275-page publication show what sensible insight into the problems in the relationship between men and women was possible in Germany at the time. The self-proclaimed enlightened contemporaries look like the biblical patriarchs hanging on to their beliefs and superstitions, in comparison to his ethics and legal philosophy of equality.

Kant's *Rechtslehre:* The Self-Destruction of the Categorical Imperative[3]

The *Rechtslehre* is the first part of the *Metaphysik der Sitten* (1797). As most other natural law philosophies, securing the economic and political interests of the burgher is at the heart of it. These interests go in two directions: up against the nobility, and down against all women. The right, or privilege, of the burgher is paramount with regard to ownership of goods and human beings.

In the *Rechtslehre* Kant discusses having and acquiring something: "Das Privatrecht von äusseren Mein und Dein überhaupt."[4] In this he defines a General Principle of external acquisition, divided into

1. "Vom Sachenrecht" [*Sachen* are things; *Recht* can be rights or law]
2. "Vom persönlichen Recht" [in which he discusses various kinds of contracts, but not the marital contract]
3. "Von dem auf dingliche Art persönlichem Recht"

It is under this curious third division, completely invented by Kant, that he deals with marital, parental and *Hausherren* (which I shall translate as "patriarchal") rights. What is curious about this is the combination of *dingliche Art* (of a thinglike quality) with *persönliches Recht* (individual or personal rights). I shall concentrate on this third division because the relationship between men and women is discussed here.

In 1798 Kant published some "Explanatory Remarks" in response to a critic. This critic had claimed that "the right of citizens to possess other persons as if they were things and to treat them as things" was contradictory and against reason. Kant is not persuaded and dogmatically insists on his point in his chapter "Justification of the Notion of an Individual Right of a Thinglike Quality."[5]

Dualistic anthropological ideology

Kant determined the existence of "two human races"[6]: man and beings. Kant distinguishes for these two "races" three relationships (apart from the relationship of man to God, which I will not discuss here). He does so in his "Enteilung nach dem subjektiven Verhältnis der Verpflichtenden and Verpflichteten" (R 33). Anyone expecting these relations to include all people equally in a rational civil rights philosophy—published, after all, eight years after the French Revolution—will be disappointed. Kant distinguishes three categories:

1. The legal relation of man and beings having both rights and duties ("Adest, Denn das ist ein Verhältnis von Menschen zu Menschen").
2. The legal relation of man and beings having no rights only duties ("Vacat. Denn das wären Menschen ohne Persönlichkeit [Leibeigene, Sklaven"). Note: They are *Res* not *Persona* as is shown in Kant's own explanatory reference to serfs and slaves].
3. The legal relation to beings having no rights or duties ("Vacat. Denn das sind vernunftlose Wesen, die weder uns verbinden, noch welchen wir können verbunden werden").

The question is, which beings without reason who cannot be actively or passively under legal obligation are referred to here? Animals, perhaps, but what else? Kant does not make clear in this part of the publication where he places the relationship between men and women. However, throughout the publication and in his other work Kant makes very clear statements on women, whom he does not subsume in his notion of man, which leads him to the conclusion (specified below) that women are not persons and therefore do not have (equal) rights and duties.

He lines up three old patriarchal dogmas, citing God, Nature, and custom.

God wants complete inequality

Kant refers to the biblical "He shall be your Lord and Master [the man gives the orders; the woman has to obey them]"; this is what marital law states and that is how it should stay. The men have legal privileges, the women are deprived of rights, and this, to him, is not in contradiction with "der natürlichen Gleichheit eines Menschenpaares," or natural equality of a couple (R 96).

Nature wants complete inequality

Natural equality of women and men is certainly not Kant's anthropological principle. All women are by nature inferior and therefore "naturaliter und civiliter Unmündige" (unmündig, meaning one not legally considered adults) (R 131). All men on the other hand are superior in nature and therefore "civiliter mündig." They are born as Herren sui iuris and moreover as Herren, that is, lords and masters over women. Kant feels that male privileges are justified by "die natürliche Überlegenheit des Vermögens des Mannes über das weibliche" (R 96) (the natural superiority of the capacities of men over those of women). It is from this ahistorical, dualistic view and not from an egalitarian view on humanity that Kant constructs "ein natürliches Erlaubnisgesetz" (R 93) that allows men legally to take the lord and master privileges over women who are granted no rights.

The customary law has always been unequal

Kant incorporates in his "natürliche Gesetzeslehre" that which "doch immer stillschweigend, immer im Gebrauch gewesen ist" or, that what has always tacitly been the custom (R 186). But is it reasonable to keep things a certain way just because they have always been that way? And is that in itself a good reason for keeping things that way? How enlightened his argumentation!

With these three axioms Kant destroys the basis for his own self-proclaimed universal, egalitarian *Rechts- und Sittenlehre*. On the one hand he destroys it for all women. On the other hand he destroys it for the (male) citizens, as the (male) nobility could legitimize its privileges with exactly the same dogmas that Kant has just declared legitimate, and use it to debunk the equality claims of citizens as illegitimate.

These irrational, yet for Kant self-evident premises, serve him as a basis for the legitimation of two quite different relations. First, relations of "Mensch zu Mensch," which must be translated here as male to male, where contractual relations are based on freedom, equality, and reciprocity, through which only males are persons and citizens. Second, relations between these patriarchal citizens and their subjected women (noncitizens). The men are at the same time lord and master over reified female human beings *(verdinglichte Menschen)* where legal relations are based on total lack of freedom and lack of rights securing the injustice of male dominance imposed on women whom God and Nature wish to see, once and for all, as nonpersons and noncitizens. (Note: "reified" here is not used in a Marxist sense).

Basic Contradictions and Apology

Kant wishes to integrate this actual antagonism in his system, equal rights among men as well as unequal rights between men and women; as a consequence his *Rechtslehre* is a hodgepodge of contradictions, inconsistencies, paradoxes, and ambiguous definitions. The basic contradictions are these:

Maxim: General contractual relations: all *Menschen* (men) in a civil society settle their property interests on the basis of binding rights and duties (freedom, equality, and reciprocity) in contracts, which a constitutional state upholds and enforces. This maxim is universal.

Negation: The maxim above is not universal; namely, the relationship between men and women is not contractual but is one of privilege and dominance, governed by laws made by patriarchs excluding all female participation in the lawmaking process. These are the

Ehe-, Familien-, und Hausherrenrecht (laws on marriage, family, and patriarchs). Contracts between men and women are against the law (*gesetzeswidrig,* to use Kant's word).

Apology: In quite blatant contradiction to the claims made for negation, Kant claims that the type of marriage he advocates is nevertheless at the same time a contractual relationship anyway, although according to his own criteria, legitimate and legal relationships among persons must be based on equality. So either marital law has a contract at the heart of it, or patriarchal privilege supposedly means equal rights between a master and the oppresed.

How Does Kant Argue these Basic Contradictions?

General contractual relationships

Following Rousseau's "Man is born equal" from the *Social Contract,* Kant states that members of the "bürgerliche Gesellschaft" (civil society) are born free. As he puts it: "Freiheit . . . ist dieses einzige, ursprüngliche, jedem Menschen, kraft seiner Menschheit zustehende Recht." (Freedom is the unique, original right granted to every person on the basis of his humanity.)

As Kant also claims that freedom exists insofar as it can coexist with other people's freedom, and that freedom means not having to be subjected to the arbitrary rule of both persons/parties/partners. He literally says: "Die angeborene Gleichheit, d.i. die Unabhängigkeit, nicht von Anderen verbunden zu werden, als wozu man sie wechselseitig auch verbinden kann; mithin die Qualität des Menschen sein eigener Herr (sui iuris) zu sein, imgleichen die eines unbescholtenen Menschen . . . weil er keinem Unrecht getan hat" (R 47). (The inborn equality, that is, the independence not to be entered into an obligation by others unless the obligation can be mutual; that is, the quality of a human being to be his own master [sui juris], just like that of a noncriminal person because he has not committed a crime.)

So these are his criteria for persons, partners in a contract, and burghers. But one must be male and not a criminal in order to claim one's humanity and right to freedom. Kant adopts the sui juris construction, specific to patriarchal legal practice: one is master over oneself, and thus has the right to autonomy, that is, having the right to own oneself.

The whole female population has thus been eliminated from Kant's notion of humanity and from his definition of members of society or population. These are arbitrary, ideological definitions in which he defines one part of humanity as the whole, and eliminates the other part from the definition. What Kant does is, to define women as *Wesen* (beings) without human quality, and to disqualify them from their inborn humanity: they are objects owned by men/*Herren*. He turns male persons and citizens into the legal owners and users of these (human) things.

Herren-privilege instead of contract

Women as the legal property of *Hausherren*

The "auf dingliche Art persönliche Recht" is a special right, namely a privilege to the *Hausherren* (patriarchs). As Kant puts it, it "ist das des Besitzes eines äusseren Gegenstandes als einer Sache und des Gebrauches desselben als einer Person" (R 92f.). (It is that of the ownership of an external thing, as a thing [*res*] and the use of it in the same way as a person.)

So this is the legal double status of women as object and yet as person, which is completely illogical and self-contradictory: when a person is a *Gegenstand* (another word for thing), the legal *Sache* of an owner, one would imagine that the owner would use such a person as a thing, which destroys the human status of the (human) thing. It is not possible to be both a person and a thing under the law as the two are mutually exclusive in Kant's own definition of person (someone who isn't subjected to the arbitrary rule of others). Now a *Sache* is, according to Kant's own words: "aber zum blossen Werkzeuge de Willkür eines Anderen gemacht . . . und gehört zum Eigentum (*dominium*) eines Anderen, der daher nicht bloss sein Herr (*herus*), sondern auch sein Eigentümer (*dominus*) ist, der ihn als eine Sache . . . und nach Belieben . . . brauchen, und über seine Kräfte verfügen kann. Durch einen Vertrag kann sich niemand zu einer solchen Abhängigkeit verbinden, dadurch er aufhört, eine Person zu sein; denn nur als Person kann er einen Vertrag machen" (R 153). ([A *Sache* is someone made] into a mere tool of the arbitrary rule of another . . . belonging to the property of that other who is therefore not only his master but also his owner who can use him as a thing and who can use his strength . . . as it pleases him. Nobody can engage in this form of dependence by contracts because he ceases to be a person by it, and only as a person can he enter into a contract.) So what Kant himself is saying here is that being a *Sache* or property destroys one's status as a person. Should one wish to argue consistently, then the conclusion would be a woman's status as a person is destroyed when Kant makes women and girls the property of the *Hausherren* (patriarchs).

In the quotation above Kant describes serfs as *Sachen*. They lost their status as persons because they have committed a crime and they can even be sold (R 101). Women have no person status because they are born female, which is crime enough to obtain the status of nonperson, of born serfs. The only exception Kant makes for wives and daughters is that they cannot be sold, but other than that they are in every respect the property and objects for use by the *Hausherren*. This "special right" of not being subject to sale, is for Kant already a limitation to the *Sachen* status of women and a sign of a minimum of *Person* status: their sole special "individual right" consists of not being subject to sale. What a tribute to their humanity!

So if they are not 100 percent things, to what percentage are they persons? Two percent? They are the property for life of either the father or the husband; they just cannot be sold to a third party. This is sheer mockery of human rights for women. In this context Kant perverts his own set of notions of person, freedom, equality, and all of the other basic philosophical legal concepts into their opposite! Just think, if what he does here is legal, then any member of the nobility can legally use the person of Kant himself as his property, with reference to the fact that his "individual right" consists of the fact that he cannot be sold.

Legalizing the robbery of women by protecting the property of *Hausherren*/Burghers

Kant's own definition of *Sachenrecht* is: "the real definition should be as follows: the right to a *Sache* is a right to the private use of that *Sache*" from which it follows that "I can exclude every other owner from the private use of the *Sache*" (R 69). This means that it is not legal for another *Herr* to use a human *Sache*, since that is a violation of the legal owner's rights, which cannot be allowed in Kant's civil society. From a woman's perspective, however, it means first and foremost that they are robbed of their most essential human rights, the rights to be or to become persons, that is, citizens, autonomous, free and equal.

However, this is not how Kant sees it. He does not see the above as a fundamental violation of the human rights of women, because he doesn't see them as human beings, but as things. Nor is the negation by patriarchs of women's most fundamental of human rights, namely, the right to be a person in one's own right, a legal, philosophical, or ethical problem for Kant. Following the written and unwritten laws, and double standards of his time, Kant rigorously represents the interests of his sex in Prussia by stating that it is legitimate for female *Untermenschen* to be excluded from human rights a priori and that it should stay so. To Kant this is not in contradiction with his self-proclaimed universal Natural Law, or with his ethical and legal Categorical Imperative. He does not recognize that he is sabotaging his own claim that his maxims are universal. Maxims where half the cases or more are exceptions to the rule are not maxims.

Patriarchal marriage and family law and law governing domestics

In the relationship between men and women Kant renders the egalitarian form, the contract, inoperative and puts a "natural *Hausherrenrecht*" in its place. This, according to Kant is "the most personal right," which allows men to legally acquire women. The German word for "acquire" is *erwerben*, which I shall discuss below, and this privilege allows the *Erwerbung* of three *Gegenstände* (things): "Der Mann erwirbt ein Weib" (the man acquires a wife) using the marital law—as well as children and domestics (*R* 93). As a consequence wives are not persons, since they are property. As such there is only one person, namely the owner/*Herr*, which Kant misleadingly calls couple, family, or parents, as if the wives shared in any way in the male *Herren* status. Yet Kant himself states that only men are "Herren über das Hauswesen" (masters of the house) or "die häusliche Gesellschaft" which is an unequal relationship "of one who gives the orders and one that obeys them" (*R* 100). This definition implicitly follows the old patriarchal common law construct: "the husband and wife are one person in law; That is, the very being or legal existence of the woman is suspended during marriage, or at least is incorporated . . . into that of the husband."[7] Kant nevertheless speaks of "couple" or "parents"; the patriarch is husband and wife, father and mother, in one and the same person.

Relevant here are Kant's own definitions of *Erwerbung*. "Ich erwerbe etwas, wenn ich mache (*efficio*), dass etwas mein werde." (I acquire something when I make that that something become mine.) And: "Das Prinzip der äusseren Erwerbung ist nun: Was ich (nach dem Gesetz der äusseren Freiheit) in meine Gewalt bringe, und wovon ich als Objekt meiner Willkür Gebrauch zu machen ich (nach dem Postulat der praktischen Vernunft) das Vermögen habe: was ich (gemäss der Idee eines möglichen vereinten Willens) will, es solle mein sein, das ist mein" (R 67). (The acquisition principle is thus that what I [according to the law of freedom] bring into my sphere of power, and of which I have the competence of turning it into the object of my arbitrary rule [in accordance with the postulate of practical reason] and what I wish to be mine [in accordance with the idea of a possibly common will] is mine.) The "common will" may be read as the will in accordance with the will of other male owners. So only the will of men in this acquisition of property is relevant; the female-born objects of ownership have no will.

Objects of acquisition are such things as land, the labor and services of others, or "the other person himself" (R 68). In this way the male population has the monopoly to acquire and use all goods and moreover the entire female population. In Kant's own words: this *Erwerbungsart* (manner of acquisition) is "ein dinglich-persönliches Recht (*ius realiter personale*) des Besitzers . . . einer anderen Person als eine Sache" (R 68) (the right to own another person as if it were a thing). So the *Sache* is the object of arbitrary rule of its owner, legally brought into the sphere of his power, and can be used any way the owner sees fit. Only the property owners are persons, their (human) property is *Sache*, nonperson. Wives (and grown daughters) have no property of their own, meaning they do not own their bodies, their children, their labor, their wages, their inheritance, their dowry or presents, and so forth. Everything is the property of the *Hausherren*, and this ownership can be legally enforced. Fathers acquire children in much the same way as the slave owners acquired the children of their slaves. The mothers have duties but no rights, not even to their children. Kant has proclaimed "a fatherly right to give orders" (R 99) and a father has the right to have runaway children caught and brought back (like lost animals, no less) as a consequence of his *ius in re* (R 185); or, as Kant puts it "Kinder als einem Stück des Hauses [piece of the furniture] . . . wenn sie entlaufen sind, . . . als Sachen (verlaufene Haustiere) (sich zu) bemächtigen."

When boys grow up they escape "their dependence thus far," become *mündig* and their own masters *(sui iuris)*. When grown daughters stay at home they do so as "domestics of the *Hausherren*" (R 186) and as his property. He can bring them back with force (R 186), "wenn es (Gesinde) ihm entläuft, kann er es durch einseitige Willkür in seine Gewalt zurück bringen." Wives are no better off with their status than children and servants.

To his critics Kant defends himself by claiming that these things are "all means to my end," and that this reification happens "ohne Abbruch an ihrer Persönlichkeit" (R 184); that is, not at the expense of their personality! His end turns out to be the "Bewirkung . . . des Interesses" furthering interest, the "Erhaltung des Hauswesens" that is, the property of the *Hausherren* and citizens. So robbing the entire female population of their rights with robbery as its main goal is the true face of Kant's *Rechts- und Sittenlehre*, the postulate of his practical reason. Reason is the dark irrationality of "appalling backwardness" (T. W Adorno).

One only has to compare his ideology with *The Declaration of Human and Civil Rights for Women* by Olympe de Gouges, written in 1791, to see how reactionary Kant is in comparison to some of his contemporaries. These property laws and lack of rights for women really existed in Prussia at the time and, according to Kant, that is how things should stay. The servant of the state is affirming the status quo as *vernünftig*. The relations between men and women in general must follow the laws prescribing the property-marriage. Contracts between men and women as free persons, instead of marriage law, are condemned by Kant as illegitimate, morally objectionable, and therefore illegal. Such contracts are *ad libitum*, not for life and can be dissolved. The mutual agreement on rights and duties laid down in contracts is not at all *ad libitum*, but make the parties liable to uphold them. It is only because the state refuses to consider these contracts as valid and refuses legal protection that they become *ad libitum*.

Thus, dictates of patriarchal marriage law can be circumvented by partners laying down their own conditions in a contract. Kant won't have any of that! Such contracts may be planned for life, and be terminated only under certain conditions, as is the case with other types of contracts. What Kant does not want is the possibility of termination. Divorce is unthinkable. Indeed, he is almost papal in his condemnation of free and equal contracts between men and women: *Schandverträge (pactum turpe)*, pacts of shame are against the law, since intercourse outside marriage is qualified as "sich entmenschen" (to dehumanize oneself) (R 185). This is one of the many illogical statements made by Kant, since by his own definition the partners in a contract stay persons and human at that, whereas the most fundamental form of dehumanization takes place in the type of marriage Kant advocates.

What Kant finds particularly gruesome is to apply his own theory on contracts to the relationship between men and women. Death and destruction are brought in. Such contracts are beastly, cannibalistic, and deadly since women die in childbirth. As if his marriage offers them better protection! The men will die of exhaustion due to the sexual demands made by women. In Kant's own words: "aufgezehrt von Erschöpfungen . . . von öfteren Ansprüchen des Weibes an das Geschlechtsvermögen des Mannes" (R 185). This is a deep superstition that Kant may have borrowed from *Hexenhammer*[8] a none-too-enlightened publication. If Kant preaches enlightenment at all, which supposedly liberates people from superstition, then he seems to have failed rather miserably here.

Because Kant declares all free contracts as *pactum turpe* (R 185), against the law, all resulting children are illegitimate and their mother's shame, pariahs without rights, "eingeschlichen (wie verbotenen Ware)," sneaked in like forbidden goods. This is true legal and moral terror. He calls the relationships themselves "concubinage" and classifies them with prostitution as if a contract between a man and a woman can only be "die Verdingung einer Person zum einmaligen Genuss (pactum fornicationes)" (R 95); or, turning a person into an object for brief pleasure, a fornication pact. To him in any case, "ein Kontrakt der Verdingung . . . eines Gliedmasses zum Gebrauch eines Anderen, mithin . . . einer Person, die sich selbst als Sache der Willkür des Anderen hingeben würde" (R 95–96) (a contract to rent out a sexual organ for use by another, that is, a person who turns herself into a thing of arbitrariness of the other). But women are subjected to the use of others—that is, to the caprice of the masters—and become things precisely in the legal marriages Kant suggests. Kant only seems able to understand women as objects of men's caprice. Is that out of stupidity or maliciousness? "The desire a man has for a woman is not directed toward her because she is a human being, but because she is a woman; that she is a human being is of no concern to the man."[9] This vulgar and cynical disdain for women does not befit a Great Philosopher.

At any rate, he thoroughly discredits the idea of contracts in those instances where it should apply to women. In contracts women would claim some rights, set limits to the degree to which they could be robbed of their rights. This would jeopardize and undermine the total protection of the ownership rights. Kant will not allow *Eigentum* and *Herrschaft* to become less secure; therefore, he won't allow such contracts. They are not protected by law; they are legally null and void, whereas marriage is legal and legally enforceable.

Herren privilege (marriage): Contract between equals?

In blatant contradiction to his marriage law, which ensures dominance and secures property, but which does not allow marriage on a contract basis, Kant uses the words "Ehe-Vertrag" and "Gemeinschaft freier Wesen" (yes, marriage contract and unity of free beings) and calls this "ein Verhältnis der Gleichheit des Besitzes, sowohl der Personen, die einander wechselseitig besitzen, als auch der Glücksgüter" (R 94–95) (a relationship of equality of ownership, both of the persons who mutually own each other and of the earthly belongings).

Although the relationships bewteen men and women can only be regulated by law *(lege)* in what comes down to a dictate of the law since women are excluded from the legislative process, and although Kant explicitly condemns free contracts as illegal and shameful, Kant repeatedly uses the term marriage contract apologetically for patriarchal marriage: for instance, in his definition "a contract between two persons of the opposite sex with mutual rights and duties" (R 96), which he contradicts already in the next sentence by saying that such a relationship does not come about *pacto* (by contract) but only *lege* (through law) (R 97), not based on equal rights and duties.

Is a man's acquisition of a woman as a thing, discussed above, at the same time the acquisition of the man by the woman, given this "mutual ownership"? And how can we have persons who mutually own each other when the wife is not a person, and as such cannot own her master?

Kant adds that the married couple has "wechselseitigen Gebrauch ihrer Geschlechtseigenschaften" or the mutual use of each other's sexual characteristics (R 97). And this while women have to serve their *Herren* as the dehumanized things owned by them for their "einseitigen sexuellen Gebrauch," one-sided sexual use, discussed above. Do women as property have the same rights as the property owners? Do they own their *Herren* as the *Herren* own them? Is the property of the *Herren* also their property? Do serfs own their masters?

Kant says (R 195) that two equals cannot be subordinate vis-à-vis one another or else we have a contradiction. However, when Kant deals with women, he stacks one contradiction on top of the other. His talk of the "wechselseitiger Gebrauch ihrer Geschlechtseigenschaften" or the mutual use of each other's sexual characteristics is not only scandalous because he wishes to regulate this use by law, but also because there is no mutuality to be found in his concept of marriage. The law is that men have the "right" to use women for any purpose, including sex.

So Kant gets entangled in a chaos of self-contradictions. Claims he makes in one sentence are contradicted in the next; marriage is and is not a contract. Kant protects the privileges of the patriarchs yet claims marriage is a contract between equal partners, where a relationship based on privilege and lack of rights is supposed to be equal. Women are both things and persons. Men are both the owners of women and yet their equal partners.

Because Kant particularly seeks to protect the "one-sided arbitrariness" that is the legal privilege of men to subject women to their rule, he defends patriarchal marriage. Oppression by contract is illegal, as he states so clearly himself: "ein Vertrag aber, durch den ein Teil zum Vorteil des Anderen auf seine ganze Freiheit verzichten tut, mithin aufhört eine Person zu sein, folglich auch keine Pflicht hat, einen Vertrag zu halten, sondern nur Gewalt anerkennt, [ist] in sich selbst widersprechend, d.i. null und nichtig" (R 101), declaring null and void contracts in which one of the parties is forced to give up his freedom and personhood.

In the appendix (Anhang) Kant justifies his idea of "auf dingliche Art persönliches Recht" once more and rather pointedly: "Es ist das Recht des Menschen, eine Person ausser sich als das Seine zu haben" or, the right of a man to have another person as his. He then goes on to explain "das Seine" saying that there is a big difference betwen the expressions "this is my father" and "this is my wife" where the father is not property, but the wife is. To quote Kant: "Ich sage hier auch nicht: eine Person als die meinige . . . sondern 'als das Meine' . . . zu haben. Denn ich kann sagen: 'dieser ist mein Vater' das heisst lediglich 'ich habe einen Vater.' Aber ich kann nicht sagen: 'ich habe ihn als das Meine.' Sage ich aber: 'mein Weib,' so bedeutet dieses ein besondres, nämlich rechtliches, Verhältnis des Besitzers zu einem Gegenstande (wenn es auch eine Person wäre), als Sache. Besitz (physischer) aber ist die Bedingung der Möglichkeit der Handhabung (manipulatio) eines Dinges als einer Sache." And further, "Das Seine bedeutet: das Seine des Niessbrauchs (ius utendi, frutendi) unmittelbar von dieser Person, gleich als von einer

Sache . . . als Mittel zu meinen Zwecken, Gebrauch zu machen" (R 183–84). (I do not say here: a person as mine . . . but to have her as my property. Because I can say: "this is my father," which only means "I have a father." But I cannot say "I have him as my property." But when I say "my wife" then it means a special, legal relationship between a legal owner and his object (even if this object is a person), as a *res*. Possession (physically) is the condition of the possibility of maintaining (*manipulatio*) of a thing as a *res*. . . . His own means: his for his own ususfruct (*ius utendi, frutendi*), to make use directly of this person, in the same way as of a thing . . . as a means to my end.)

Kant is thus a crude apologist for his marital pseudo-contract, reiterating all the things mentioned above, legal ownership and use for own purpose in the appendix.

The ideology of marital "contract," used by contract theorists defending in fact the patriarchal marriage (laws) and with it the exclusion of women from the constitutional state, has been used apologetically from the Enlightenment to today. This mislabeling has been strongly criticized as early as 1825 by William Thompson and Anna Wheeler:

> Each man yokes a woman to his establishment, and calls it a contract. Audacious falsehood! A contract! Where are any of the attributes of contracts, of equal and just contracts, to be found in this transaction? A contract implies the voluntary assent of both contracting parties. Can even both parties . . . by agreement alter the terms, as to indissolubility and inequality, of this pretended contract? Can any individual man divest himself . . . of his power of despotic control? . . . Have women been consulted as to the terms of this pretended contract? A contract, all of whose enjoyments . . . are on one side, while all of its pains and privations are on the other side; to the other, unqualified obedience, and enjoyments meted out or withheld at the caprice of the ruling and enjoying party. Such a contract, as the owners of slaves—the law of the stronger imposed on the weaker, in contempt of the interest of the weaker. As little as slaves had to do . . . in the enacting of the slave-codes, have women in any part of the world had to do with the partial codes of selfishness and ignorance, which every where dispose of their right . . . in favour of those who made the regulation; particularly that most

unequal and debasing code, absurdly called the contract of marriage.[10]

CONCLUSION

Elsewhere Kant says that "animals are there merely as a means to an end. That end is man."[11] Since he defines women as means to the ends of men he classifies women as natural serfs or animals. Such beings have no end of their own. So he reduces half of the human population as means to the ends of his sex. This is taking his categorical imperative *ad absurdum*, canceling it himself. His *Rechts- und Sittenlehre* is null and void, falling with the untenable premise that women are not human beings.

I end with one of von Hippel's devastating criticisms of the likes of Kant. "When a writer does not recognise his great mission . . . of protecting human beings from evident injustice, then he deserves to be oppressed himself. When he can justify turning one sex into the born despots of the other, then he is only capable of aping the mores of common men and parrotting the upper classes like a drunk: he should just abolish claims to rational judgement" (*Ü* 252).

Notes

1. Theodor Gottlieb von Hippel, *Über die bürgerliche Verbesserung der Weiber* (Berlin, 1792; repr., Frankfurt, 1977), 20–21; hereafter cited as *Ü*.

2. Hannelore Schröder, "The Declaration of Human and Civil Rights for Women (Paris, 1791) by Olympe de Gouges," *History of European Ideas* 11 (1989): 263–72.

3. "Act only on that maxim whereby thou canst at the same time will that it should become universal law."

4. I. Kant, *Metaphysische Anfangsgründe der Rechtslehre*, ed. Bernd Ludwig (Hamburg, 1986), 51; hereafter cited as *R*.

5. Ibid., 183f.

6. I. Kant, *Gesammelte Schriften* (Berlin, 1902–83), 2: 228.

7. William Blackstone, *Laws of England*. 4th ed. (1899).

8. Jacob Sprenger, *Malleus Maleficarum* (Cologne, 1488). According to this canonical treatise on witchcraft, a succubus devil (witch, woman, prostitute) draws the semen from men.

9. Morris Stockhammer, *Kant Dictionary* (New York, 1972), s.v. "sex."

10. William Thompson and Anna Wheeler, *Appeal of One Half the Human Race, Women, Against the Pretensions of the Other Half, Men, to Retain Them in Political, and Thence in Civil and Domestic Slavery* (London, 1825; repr., London, 1983), 54–65.

11. Stockhammer, *Kant Dictionary*, s.v. "animal."

12

How Can Individualists Share Responsibility?

Annette C. Baier

Those of us who find methodological individualism a limiting and ultimately stultifying assumption in social philosophy, yet who are grateful for the freedom of thought and speech that encourages us to voice our discontents with this and other orthodoxies of the liberal tradition, have no difficulty in making room in our more communitarian social philosophy for the value of independence of thought, the virtue of sturdy individualism. Any intelligent society will provide for its own vigorous but peaceable criticism, for a supply of unorthodox views to keep its own orthodoxies honest. So the liberal communitarian will see there to be a collective responsibility to nurture independence of thought in the members of society, a collective responsibility to nurture in individuals a sense of their individual duty to avoid mindless conformism.

Just as the methodological individualist can and usually does recognize some duty to associate, so the social constructionist in ethics and political philosophy can recognize a shared public duty to encourage individual persons to think their own thoughts, have their own reactions. Anyone who treasures her own freedom of thought and speech will want to protect it, and to encourage in others those independent thoughts whose expression requires its presence.

Kant, writing about the social virtues, says "It is a duty to oneself as well as to others not to isolate oneself, but to use one's moral perfections in social intercourse. While making oneself the fixed center of one's principles, one ought to regard this circle drawn around one as also forming an all-inclusive circle of those who are citizens of the world."[1] Good citizenship, at least for propertied males, will be part of moral virtue for the principled Kantian with virtuous cosmopolitan sentiments. Clearly Kant did not mean "cosmopolitan" to exclude "patriotic." Just as each principled person will not isolate himself from his fellow citizens, in a state where the rule of law, administered by just magistrates, harmonizes with the rule of the self-legislated moral law, so each principled nation will not isolate itself, but will have not merely respect for, but social ties to, other nations living under their own rule of law. It is to be a sort of Leibnizian harmony of moral monads, organizing themselves into associations that enhance and preserve rather than threaten the individual sphere and freedom of each. The tightest possible association between persons will be by lifelong contract within marriage (a form that Kant avoided), or friendship tied by vows of friendship; the next, the quasi-contractual tie of fellow citizens under a common magistrate and a common law; the loosest but not least important tie, that of cosmopolitan sentiment linking all mutually respectful autonomous persons in practices of "affability, sociability, courtesy, hospitality, and gentleness (in disagreeing without quarreling)" (MM 474). (Presumably these cosmopolitan sentiments are to be largely reserved for those who are citizens of nations with whom our own nation is not currently at war, as Kant takes perpetual peace to be more an idea or ideal of practical reason than a realistic expectation.) The moral law, as Kant understands, basically requires each rational person to respect other rational persons, where "respect" is quite compatible with nonassociation, indeed, is seen to be threatened by too close an association. (Kant in the Lectures on Ethics, reportedly said that even to our best friends we should not reveal ourselves in our natural state as we ourselves know it, as this would be "loathsome" and would put mutual respect at risk.)[2] The perfect duties that this law recognizes, forbidding acts showing disrespect for another person's rights, are to be enforced by public law, while duties to have the morally obligatory ends of one's own moral perfection and the happiness of others, so cultivating the motives that will ensure dutiful action, are left to the enforcement of private conscience,[3] assisted by the expressed moral judgments of fellow persons.

This is one picture, a very individualist one, of the relationship of an individual person and her moral responsibility to more-encompassing spheres of action and responsibility, in particular to the nation-state and the so-called family of nation-states. The individual person is to be a "fixed center" of her principles, but is to take it as an individual duty to avoid isolation. At one revealing place early on in the *Metaphysics of Morals*, Kant endorses Ulpian's three principles of right, *Honeste vive*, *neminem laede*, and *sui cuique tribue* (Live honestly, harm no one, to each his own) and his gloss on the latter two runs this way: "Do not wrong anyone, even if, to avoid doing so, you should have to stop associating with others and shun all society. (If you cannot help associating with others), enter into a society with them in which each can keep what is his."[4] Citizenship, indeed any interaction with others, is to be entered into only if one need not break one's version of the moral law to do so, only if one can do so without wronging oneself or others. Just how one possibly could "shun all society" is unclear, and it may be that Kant took it to be only a theoretical option. What is of interest for my purposes in this essay is his considering social cooperation and group membership not to be of primary moral importance. They are presented as something that we can indeed make morally tolerable, but that involve some moral risks that would be avoided in solitude.

This is only one strain in Kant's thought, and it is in some tension with the version of the Categorical Imperative that tells us to act as members of a realm of ends. A one-member realm would be a limit case of a realm, and if one exiled oneself to some small island and lived alone, then, however one acted, it would be a bit strained to call that acting as a member of a realm, from whose other members one had rightly exiled oneself, for fear of wronging them or oneself. It will be a very loose social union, if it unites the solitary occupants of some such archipelago only by the mutual agreement to leave one another alone. Kant's "realm of ends" is usually construed, both by him and his commentators, as some sort of republic in which the res publicae are more extensive than a collective willingness to leave each other undisturbed. At the very least there will be the "public goods" of courts of justice, and penal institutions. Yet problems remain about how each person's sphere or circle are to fit into any larger all-inclusive circle, how the autonomy of each is to be reconciled with the lack of any right of resistance against tyranny, and with the status of passive citizenship with which all women, servants, and unpropertied persons, are supposed to content themselves.[5] The metaphor of circles or spheres combining to make larger circles or spheres requires either a Nozickian notion of a "space" around each individual sphere, or the Cartesian and Spinozist concept of a "twisted circle," if the individual small circles are to fit snugly into a supercircle. But Kant's demotion of more than half of human persons into second-class personhood is actually more like the remedy that Descartes took when hypothesizing the shape of the particles or separately moving parts of his plenum universe. Some particles are now spherical, he supposed, while others have had to keep less regular shapes in order to fit into the interstices between the heavenly spherical bodies.[6] This Cartesian physics, where the movement of the more perfect spherical bodies required the adjustive movement of smaller, more flexible, and less heavenly bodies, seems to have been taken over by Kant into his moral metaphysics, where the moral place and allotted space of servants and women is adapted to allow free movement for the autonomous male circles or spheres.

This republic of republics, the United States of America, whose "more perfect union" its Constitution seeks to further, is one in which Kant's moral philosophy receives very respectful attention from its currently more influential social philosophers. It is also a republic that was found by one early observer, Alexis de Tocqueville, to have a national characteristic for which he coined the word "individualism": a peculiarly American trait of exhibiting not some admirable trait of sturdy self-reliance, determination to think for oneself, resistance to blind social conformity, but rather a complex of tendencies that he took to show both "deficiencies of the mind and perversity of the heart."[7] What exactly did he mean? And do those contemporary theorists of American democracy, such as John Rawls, who look to Kant for help in articulating the basic moral principles underlying our public norms, look to a theorist whose own thought displays the sort of elitist or at least selective individualism that de Tocqueville generously found to derive from "erroneous judgment, more than from depraved feelings"? (I say elitist, for the individualism that de Tocqueville found in America was found in its white males, not in blacks or in married women.) I suggest that we should answer yes to this question, while also acknowledging that de Tocqueville's criticisms are also part of our heritage here, so that our political ideals and our ideas about collective responsibility are in a state of unsatisfactory tension. I shall do little to resolve the tension, but shall restrict myself to describing it and recommending that we need to be more critical of the Kantian strand in our intellectual heritage.

The noun "individual" is a relative latecomer in the English language, not occurring until the seventeenth century. The earlier adjectival form has the sense of "indivisible." Individualism, as de Tocqueville defines it (and as its coiner, he cannot be defining it wrongly) is not so much a determination to be one unified self, not to divide oneself up into plural personae, as a disposition of "each member of a community to sever himself from the mass of his fellow creatures and to draw apart with his family and friends" (DA 2:118). The OED gives as its first sense of "individualism" the sense that de Tocqueville gives it, then moves to more recent senses: "self-centred feeling or conduct as a principle, a mode of life in which the individual pursues his own ends or follows his own ideas, free and independent individual action or thought, egoism." Here we have included both the near-egotism that de Tocqueville intends the word to convey, plus the independence of thought and action that gives us our concept of sturdy individualism as a virtue.

Egotism, de Tocqueville thinks, originates in blind instinct, but he finds individualism to be more reflective, a product of judgment, even if erroneous judgment. "Egotism blights the germ of all virtue; individualism, at first, only saps the virtues of public life; but in the long run it attacks and destroys all others, and is at last absorbed in downright egotism. Egotism is a vice as old as the world, which does not belong to one form of society more than to another: individualism is of democratic origin" (DA 2:118). He contrasts the close but limited ties binding people together in aristocracies, with democracies, where "the bond of human affection is extended, but relaxed." American ties are theoretically to all fellow Americans, but in fact "the interest of man is confined to those in close propinquity to himself." And even that interest has narrow bounds: "not only does democracy make every man forget his ancestors, but it hides his descendents, and separates his contemporaries from him; it throws him back for ever on himself alone, and threatens in the end to confine him entirely within the solitude of his own heart."

What prevents this threatened solipsism, on de Tocqueville's analysis, is voluntary association of individualists, with the press as communicative vehicle. White male Americans struck this aristocratic French observer as constantly ready to form a new association, be it to provide entertainment, to enforce temperance, or to send missionaries to the antipodes. He writes, "The first time I heard in the United States that a hundred thousand men had bound themselves publicly to abstain from spiritous liquors it appeared to me more like a joke than a serious engagement" (DA 2:132). He saw, however, it was no joke, but a manifestation of a special need in democracies, an "artificial" creation of mutual ties, through voluntary association of like-minded people. "In democratic countries the science of association is the mother of science; the progress of all the rest depends on the progress it has made" (DA 2:133). So voluntary association compensates for individualism, and the press facilitates communication between far-flung individuals united in various common causes, including political causes.

So where is the deficiency of the mind, and perversity of the heart? Why should this "individualism," when combined with an eagerness for voluntary association and the cultivation of a free press, lead to egotism and to the sapping of the virtues of public life? Why should it lead to a forgetting of ancestors, and an ignoring of the interests of our descendants? Among the voluntary associations eventually formed will be the Daughters of the American Revolution, and various organizations formed to protect parks, wilderness areas, and other goods, for our descendants. What public virtues are threatened by replacing inherited ties with voluntary loyalties, by replacing fixed rank with equality of opportunity for advancement, deferential with independent thinking, especially once slavery is abolished, and once women get the vote? Public life will surely be different in a democratic republic, peopled by geographically and socially mobile individualists, than in a republic where the domiciles and ranks of persons are more fixed, where association is less voluntary and more hierarchical, but why should it not have its own virtues? And in particular, why should democratic individualists lose the memory of what they owe their ancestors who forged the democracy, or be less concerned than others to preserve what they value for their descendants?

If recent historians of this nation such as Gordon S. Wood[8] are right, some of the framers of the U.S. Constitution were themselves appalled at what it seemed, by the end of their lives, that they had wrought. They had intended to institute a republic that would foster the traditional republican virtues of public service in the gentry, and appreciative docility in the lower classes, leaving traditional hierarchical ties between master and slave or servant (not to mention man and woman), largely untouched. Wood, in *The Radicalism of the American Revolution*, quotes Thomas Jefferson's lament in 1825, "All, all dead, and ourselves left alone amid a new generation whom we know not, and who knows not us." Instead of the classical republican virtues, the new republic was spawning the new commercial and capitalist virtues of individual market enterprise, conspicuous consumption in the working class as well among their "betters," a radical egalitarianism that threatened traditional class structure, and all too little public spiritedness. So within one generation there was that "forgetting of ancestors," or at least of their aspirations, that de Tocqueville found striking.

Rather than look only at de Tocqueville's own answers to these questions, which plausibly enough point to the risks of leaving the protection of public values to voluntary support for them, support that may wax and wane, and to the dangers of majority despotism and the fickleness of the mass of voters, I shall return to Kant, and to the version of republicanism that he erected on his individualist foundations. As I have indicated, I do this because of the recent appeal to Kant by John Rawls, one of the ablest and most influential defenders of this republic's liberal tradition, and because of the general enthusiasm among moral, social, and political philosophers for Kant's views,[9] or at least for those of them that are most familiar, through the regular teaching of Kant's *Groundwork of the Metaphysics of Morals*, along with the sparse attention given to his *Doctrine of Right* (only recently available in unabridged translation).[10] If Rawls sees Kant, rather than Mill, Locke, Hume, or Burke, as giving us a moral and social philosophy that best articulates the basic principles of this nation's scheme of cooperation, then we more detached observers (since I speak as a U.S. resident who is not a U.S. but a New Zealand citizen, and who did not imbibe the ideology of American democracy with my mother's milk, nor with my school lessons in history and social studies) presumably may without irrelevance turn there, to understand what relationship there is, and is believed to be, between individual autonomous persons and the life that they live together under one constitution and one set of laws, and between individual and collective responsibility.[11] I shall ignore the complication brought in by the fact that this nation is a federal union of states, so that we all live under both state and federal law, since this by no means unimportant aspect of American political life is not one that Rawls has emphasized, nor one whose relationship to individualism de Tocqueville had views about.[12] Kant's remarks about federations of republics, in *Perpetual Peace*,[13] while they build on his earlier views about cooperation between fellow citizens within a republic, do not have much to say about the way that such federation affects or is affected by the sort of autonomy that belongs to individual citizens, nor about the way the individual responsibility of persons for their own choices somehow sums, in a democratic republic, to the states' and the nation's responsibility for its choices (say, the choice to fight the Gulf war, and to inflict the massive casualties that the Iraqi people suffered in that war, or to return the Haitian refugees to Haiti, or to cut down Oregon's forests to supply timber, or to fail to get aid to the starving in East Africa, or to have no women candidates for the presidency). That is the issue that my title promises, and that I now begin to approach.

It is very easy for a citizen in a large nation like this one to wash her hands of any responsibility for any decision taken by any public officials. Especially when one deplores a particular decision, one's inclination is to say that "*they* should not have done that," where they are some decision-makers, and we, the critics of it, see ourselves as blameless, not because the pressure we brought to bear on the official decision-makers failed to change their mind, but simply because we did nothing except observe and deplore. It was not our decision, we think, and so whatever the harm done by it, it was none of our doing. The dirty hands belong always to the politicians, not to those who let them be elected and who passively contribute to the maintenance of the institutions that give them their particular share of power. We may deplore the fact that a particular judge gets appointed for the rest of his life to the Supreme Court, when many people think him demonstrably unfit, and wonder about the fitness of those who had the power to appoint. There will be ephemeral outbursts of indignation, a flurry of witty cartoons and popular jokes, but few of us tend to feel "*we* have done something dubious, something our children and grandchildren may curse us for." We think: "*they* did something dubious." We share responsibility by dividing it in such a way that we can always pass the buck to the politicians for the really important decisions that affect many people's lives for many decades. It is conveniently passed along to those with a taste for the exercise of power, those willing or keen to take public office. The ordinary citizen can tell herself that her share of responsibility is the very modest one of casting an informed and thoughtful vote in the election of representatives, and perhaps writing an occasional letter to a congresswoman, or even going to the lengths of participating in some peaceful protest march. Beyond that, the responsibility rests with elected legislators, with the president and his appointed assistant executives, and with appointees to the Supreme Court. The fourth estate, the press, may be seen as having the special public responsibility of keeping others well informed, and of supplying a range of opinions in the commentary that is provided. Each person's public responsibility, even that of president and of Supreme Court judges, will be circumscribed.

Kant took the hallmark of republicanism to be a clear separation of powers. "Republicanism is that political principle whereby the executive power (the government) is separate from the legislative power."[14] Kant a few paragraphs before had said that "a *republican constitution* is founded on three principles: firstly, the principle of the *freedom* of all members of society (as men); secondly the principle of the *dependence* of everyone on a single legislature (as subjects); and thirdly the principle of legal *equality* for everyone (as citizens)." Lest we be misled, we should quickly note that the equality in question "is perfectly consistent with the utmost inequality of possessions" (*PP* 75) and with the need of wives to obey husbands, and that qualifications for active citizenship are "of course being an adult male" (*PP* 78). It seemed to Kant a matter of course that women should be merely passive citizens, as he saw no real chance that they (we) might become economically independent, so in a position to have and express a will of our own, and so be fit to vote, let alone to stand for office. "All women," he writes, and "in general anyone whose preservation in existence depends not on his management of his own business but on arrangements made by another (except the state) lack civil personality, and their existence is, as it were, only inherence" (*MM*, pt. 1, § 46). (One might think professors also might be seen to share this nonsubstantiality, depending as they do for their livelihood on some college to hire them, so allowing themselves to be mere underlings or *Handlanger*. Kant says that private tutors fall into this category, but not schoolteachers, so presumably professors in state universities count as "independent" in Kant's sense, but those in private universities may be in a dubious position.

We should note that de Tocqueville's views on the proper position of women are no improvement on Kant's. He writes that "I have frequently been surprised, and almost frightened, at the singular address and happy boldness with which young women in America contrive to manage their thoughts and their language . . . amidst the independence of early youth an American woman is always mistress of herself" (DA 2:238). Not for them the "virgin bloom" and "innocent and ingenuous grace" of young Frenchwomen of the period, which de Tocqueville clearly preferred, as promising more "affectionate wives and agreeable companions to man" than did the typical young American woman, with her "masculine strength of understanding and manly energy," her "confidence in her own strength of character," and "the free vigour of her will." But how was such understanding and free will exercised? In renouncing her independence in the bonds of matrimony. Here de Tocqueville waxes near rhapsodic. Americans, he writes "admit that as nature has appointed such wide differences between the physical and the moral constitution of man and woman, her manifest destiny was to give distinct employment to their various faculties . . . the Americans have applied to the sexes the great principle of political economy which governs the manufactures of our age, by carefully dividing the duties of man from those of woman, in order that the great work of society be the better carried on. In no country has such constant care been taken as in America to trace two clearly distinct lines of action for the two sexes" (DA 2:252). He praises American women for attaching "a sort of pride to the voluntary surrender of their will," and making it their boast "to bend themselves to the yoke, not to shake it off" (DA 2:253). In a peroration to his chapter on this enlightened American understanding of the relation of the sexes, he writes, "As for myself, I do not hesitate to avow that, although the women of the United States are confined within the narrow circle of domestic life, and their situation is in some respects one of extreme dependence, I have now here seen women occupying a loftier position; and if I were asked . . . to what the singular prosperity and growing strength of that [American] people ought to be attributed, I should reply—to the superiority of their women" (DA 2:255). This lofty superior position of voluntary female bondage was of course one not destined to last, but there are still plenty of Tocquevillians who deplore the less "efficient" current division of labor that the emancipation of women has brought. What de Tocqueville called "the clamour for the rights of women" is still seen to tend to bring what he termed a "trampling on her holiest duties" (*DA* 2:253). For this redrawing of the lines of male and female responsibility, within the family and within society, women have been those most responsible. Their "clamour" may have been inadvertently aided and abetted by the demand for their labor in factories during the First World War, as well as patronized by a few male writers like John Stuart Mill (who in his introduction to Reeve's translation of de Tocqueville chooses not to comment on this glorification of women's lofty destiny of domestic servitude, perhaps because he was not in very great disagreement with it). Responsibility for the redrawing of male and female social roles soon became a shared one, as it took men to pass the Nineteenth Amendment, giving women the vote and the right to stand for office. And the responsibility for the non-nomination of any woman for president, and for the male club atmosphere of Senate committees (such as the Judiciary Committee that we all saw in a memorable televised action in the Thomas hearings) is also a shared one, shared by both female and male descendants of those superior self-sacrificial women whom de Tocqueville praised, and of their enlightened menfolk, who, like Kant, claimed one version of autonomy for themselves, and showed their respect for women by their confident expectation that they would take pride in voluntarily renouncing any aspirations to autonomy, in order to become more satisfactory helpmeets to men.

Kant writes that the inequality existing between substantial propertied males, with the right to vote, and the rest of their more "passive" and dependent fellow citizens, who lack civil personality, "is in no way opposed to their freedom and equality as men (*als Menschen*), who together make up a people," and that the laws enacted by the active members of the state must not be contrary to "the natural laws of freedom and of the equality of everyone in the people according to this freedom, namely that anyone can work his way up from this passive condition to an active one" (*MM*, pt. 1, § 46). But Mary Gregor may not have mistranslated in rendering *Menschen* as "men,"[15] as Kant elsewhere (in the *Anthropology*) makes it quite clear that he does not expect women to "work their way up" to civil personality.[16] Individual private tutors may advance to becoming schoolteachers, male professors in private universities to positions in state universities, but women seemed to Kant naturally doomed to be under the control and protection of men.[17] Nor is the inequality between active citizen and ruler seen as incompatible with the autonomy of each active citizen. Kant takes care to "prevent a republican constitution from being confused with a democratic one," and sees direct democracy as "necessarily a despotism," in that "it establishes an executive power through which all the citizens make decisions about (and indeed against) the single individual without his consent. . . . This means that the general will is in contradiction with itself, and thus also with freedom" (PP 100–101). Only by representative government can this contradiction be avoided, and even then, Kant writes, "the smaller the number of ruling persons in a state, and the greater their powers of representation, the more the constitution will approximate to its republican potentiality" (PP 101). So Frederick II of Prussia might be taken to represent and serve his people. As ruler, he was separate from the body of active citizens who theoretically constituted the legislature, and had theoretically made a social contract giving their ruler his authority, retaining for themselves no shred of any right of rebellion against perceived abuses of such power. "The reason a people has a duty to put up with even what is held to be an unreasonable abuse of supreme authority is that its resistance to the highest legislation can never be regarded as other than contrary to law . . . for a people to be authorized to resist, there would have to be a public law permitting it to resist, and that is, the highest legislation would have to contain a provision that it is not the highest, and that makes the people, as subject, by one and the same judgment sovereign over him to whom it is subject. This is self-contradictory" (MM 131). This argument of Kant's depends on the assumption that the supreme legislative authority is not in fact the people, but is some sovereign power who theoretically unifies and acts for the people (that is, for the active citizens among them). "The legislative authority can belong only to the united will of the people" (MM, pt. 1, § 46, p. 125). But this union into one will is interpreted to mean general tacit consent to some de facto sovereign, and "a people should not inquire with any practical aim in view into the origin of the supreme authority to which it is subject" (MM 129). The claim that there would be incoherence in a supreme law that contained a provision making it subject to some other will repeats, in a logicized version, the earlier claim of Hume's, in his essay "Of Passive Obedience," that no viable constitution can contain the explicit permission to overthrow it. But Hume, unlike Kant, distinguishes the legally recognized entitlement to rebel (which would be a self-destructive measure for any constitution to contain) from the moral liberty to resist tyrants. Since morality for him is not seen as a set of laws, he is not under the same pressure as Kant seems to be to fit positive law neatly into a so-called moral law. He can coherently say that there can be no recognized right to rebel, but there are conditions in which it is not wrong to rebel. It is best not to try to spell those conditions out too precisely, Hume says, as that would give the impression that we *were* issuing a conditional right to rebel. In any case the conditions cannot be so precisely determined in a generalized context-neutral manner.[18] Kant's apparent endorsement not merely of a legal but of a moral prohibition of rebellion depends upon the status of the rebelling people as *subjects*, not as sovereign. Their legislative role has been entrusted to a unifier of their wills, to their sovereign ruler, whom they are now obliged to obey. This seems to reduce the actual meaning of autonomy, even for those with civil personality, to something far short of giving to themselves the laws they are expected to obey. They are to obey the powers that be, and to give to the old claim that "all authority is from God" this sense: "the presently existing legislative authority ought to be obeyed, whatever its origin" (MM 130). If supreme authorities are perceived to be abusing their power, imposing unjust taxes, or going to war against the interest of their subjects, subjects can organize to present their complaints, but not resist.[19]

This may seem an odd version of republicanism, and of the moral ideals behind it, to be taken as the model for a representative democratic republic such as this one, which began in a revolution. The notion of equality seems to be degraded by Kant into equality before a law enacted by some de facto sovereign legislative body, and some de facto ruler, to whose authority some mythical consent has been given by a mythical vote of all the propertied males, whose property and male privileges (including disciplining their wives) are taken to be protected by this law. Autonomy is degraded from lawmaking power into the right to complain against laws seen to be unjust. It is particularly degraded for servants and women, who are required to submit not just to the law and the magistrate, but also to other human masters. But even for those deemed to have civil personality it seems an empty sham, if there is no guarantee of a voice in the actual election of lawmakers, let alone of voice in determining the content of the laws. Can this be a variant of the republican ideal that inspired the founding fathers of this nation? So what exactly was and is that ideal?

Gordon Wood, in his article "Classical Republicanism and the American Revolution" quotes from a letter written by John Adams in 1807, that he has never understood what republicanism is, and thought no man ever did or will. He concluded that republicanism "may signify any thing, every thing, or nothing."[20] Wood himself finds that the Roman republican ideals of Cicero, Virgil, Sallust, and Tacitus had a great appeal for eighteenth-century social philosophers, for Hume, for Montaigne, for Jefferson. The appeal lay both in the republican alternative to absolute monarchy, the preference for what Hume called "mixed" constitutions, and also in the civic humanist ideals of individual character, emphasizing as they did those of public service, sociability, and the ambition to civilize any remaining "barbarians." Wood quotes from Addison's play *Cato:*

> The Roman soul is bent on Higher views:
> To civilize the rude unpolish'd world,
> And lay it under the restraint of laws;
> To make Man mild, and sociable to Man;
> To cultivate the wild licentious savage—
> With wisdom, discipline, and the liberal arts;
> Th' embellishments of life: virtues like these
> Make human nature shine, reform the soul,
> And break our fierce barbarians into men.

This civic humanist ideal of civilized gentlemen spreading gentility and the rule of their law to licentious savages, whom they felt free to displace and dominate in their civilizing colonial ventures, is seen by Wood to come soon into conflict with the less aristocratic and rather rougher ideals of an increasingly egalitarian frontier and commercial society, of an increasingly "entrepreneurial-minded and bumptious American people," whose tie to one another was to be seen by de Tocqueville not as classical virtue but as "Interest," and an interlocking of private and of public interest. Yet the republican ideal did not vanish, and has not vanished.

We get an interesting variant of it in Ronald Dworkin's concept of the "personification" and the "integrity" of a political community. It is of particular interest for my purposes here because Dworkin links these ideas to a concept of the collective responsibility of such a community. Taking the case of corporate responsibility as an example, he argues that we can and do hold corporations responsible for, say, defective products, even in cases where no individual can be blamed for failing in his or her special responsibilities within the corporation. We treat the corporation or other community as a moral entity, even while allowing that "the community has no independent metaphysical existence, that it is itself a creature of the practices of thought and language in which it figures."[21] This "deep personification" affects the practices of thought and language, in particular of responsibility-allocating language, that will be used. Even in bids for exoneration from responsibility for such scandals as Watergate, Dworkin notes that the bumper stickers that appeared read not, "Don't blame me; I voted against Nixon," but "Don't blame me, I'm from Massachusetts," where the innocence claimed was not that of a powerless voter, but of a proud member of a relatively innocent alternative and smaller community. We sometimes spontaneously take on a share in the collective responsibility of a group we belong to, even a very large and not very unified group. One rather ghastly example of this is given by Kant. Writing about appropriate forms of punishment for crimes such as murder and treason, he endorses the death penalty, but not the drawing, quartering, and exposing of the criminal's corpse, as, Kant writes, "that could make the humanity of the person suffering it into something abominable" (MM, pt. 1, 142). (Not, notice, the humanity of those who do such things, but of those to whom they may be done—it is public decency that is seen to be offended by them.) In a similar vein Kant notes, in the *Lectures on Ethics*, that women who were found guilty of poisoning their husbands were in England burned at the stake, rather than hanged and exposed on a gibbet, as both a more decent and an appropriately fearsome public death for those guilty of "insidious underhand conduct . . . far viler than violence." The English punishment is apparently endorsed by Kant, "for, if such conduct spread, no man would be safe from his wife."[22] (Kant seems to assume that every wife will have nonmoral motive for such a master-destroying act, and indeed by his account of the rights of husbands they surely did. How convenient that the *jus talionis* supplies an appropriately fearsome penalty that at the same time does not offend too much against public decency. The veil of flames is to protect the public from unseemly visions of female depravity.) Kant takes it that we may identify, *qua* human beings, with the publicly shamed and dishonored criminal, and he also sees the people to have at least a residual responsibility to see to it that murderers are duly executed, so we may also identify with the executioner's deed, and share responsibility for it (MM, pt. 1, § 49). These will be cases of the sort that Dworkin cites, of our reacting as involved members of some group, even when our direct responsibility (for the crime or for its punishment) may be most minimal.

Dworkin applies his idea of deep personification, and of group integrity, to political association, to co-citizenship. He writes, "Once we accept that officials act in the name of a community of which we are all members, bearing a responsibility we therefore share, then this reinforces and sustains the character of collective guilt, our sense that we must feel shame as well as outrage when they act unjustly" (LE 175). Part of the appeal of the personification idea to him is that it helps us to make sense of the weight given, in legal decision-making, to very general principles such as "equal protection," enshrined in the Constitution. We do not simply change our laws to fit them to current perceptions of morality or of justice; we strive to show that the changes are licensed or demanded by something already in our legal tradition. We strive for an "integrity" that is cross-generational. So changes on matters such as slavery and the rights of women are seen as changes demanded by something in the spirit of the laws we already had, however strained it may be to make that claim. Communities have principles, ideals of justice, that may, at a given time, be only imperfectly encoded in their laws and constitution. The procedure for amendment of the U.S. Constitution itself implicitly allows for this contrast between the content of the law, and the principles expressed in that content. Dworkin sees commitment to integrity as a political virtue to rule out arbitrary differences of treatment, and to safeguard us from legislation motivated only by political compromise. And he sees a particular version of political community to cohere best with the recognition of integrity as a political virtue. This is what he calls the "model of principle," which understands people to be "members of a political community only when they accept that their fates are linked in the following strong way: they accept that they are governed by principles, not just by rules hammered out in political compromise" (LE 211). Politics then becomes "a theater of debate about which principles the community should adopt as a system" (LE 211), while also recognizing that each member's rights and duties "arise from the historical fact that his community has adopted that scheme, which is then special to it, not the assumption that he would have chosen it were the choice entirely his. In short, each accepts political integrity as a distinct political ideal" (LE 211). The choice has been made, by the founding fathers, and integrity demands that current citizens respect their choice, and fit their own reforms into the rhetoric inherited from their tradition.

Such founders (as were parents) were "fathers," and Dworkin has apparently no time for currently fashionable he/she's, in his text. It is a male citizen whose version of the ideal of integrity he gives, and one of the cases he instances to show how the ideal of integrity works is that of fathers' authority over daughters, in such matters as marriage. Since Dworkin wants to treat a political community as an association, then the structure of other nonvoluntary or not fully voluntary associations like the family is of natural interest to him. Taking the actual historical fact of a culture that believes that equality of concern for men and women requires "paternalistic protection for women in all aspects of family life," Dworkin supposes that a proper appreciation of the responsibilities of family membership would lead even someone who regards such paternalism as unjust to hold that "a daughter who marries against her father's wishes has something to regret. She owes him at least an accounting, and perhaps an apology" (LE 205).

This would seem to leave female citizens of this nation with a tremendous amount of apologizing to be done to the paternalistic culture whose laws and legislature[23] they are slowly changing. Integrity as an identification with the faith of our fathers may be a lot easier for white men than for blacks and women, the way Dworkin presents it. For there is no denying the sexism and the racism[24] present in this tradition, just as there is no denying the sexism in Kant's much-admired version of autonomy, and which turns out on closer inspection to be a monopoly of a few representative propertied males. Those who are latecomers to civil personality, to the right to liberty and political participation, will tend to see the discontinuity more than the continuity in amendments like the Fifteenth and Nineteenth.

Still, even passive citizenship had its responsibilities, and those of us who accept Dworkin's plea for use of the concept of cross-generational shared responsibility, and who are women, will take some responsibility for the long toleration of our own domination, and relegation to the category of passive subjects. All adult daughters who trusted fathers to look after their interests, all wives who trusted husbands to vote for them, or to represent them in legislative assemblies, bear the responsibility for their foolish entrustings, just as much as the trusted are accountable for their abuses of their trust. We allocate individual responsibility by our trusting and our acceptance of trust, but the responsibility for the allocation rests on both trusters and trusted,[25] as well as on those distrustful lookers-on who deplore the way discretionary powers are being distributed to individuals and to agencies, yet do nothing to stop it, or to try to reform the system. We share the responsibility for the way we allow responsibility to be individually divvied out, and so we cannot escape some of the blame, when that individual responsibility is badly exercised.

Divvying out responsibility—"you see to the luggage while I pay the cab driver"—is one way to share tasks that we both want done, and normally such forward-looking division of responsibility will be accompanied by a similar allocation of backward-looking responsibility.[26] So if something goes wrong—I let myself be cheated by not counting the change the cab driver gives me, you abandon one piece of luggage since your bad back makes carrying all of it at once too painful for you, and that piece disappears—we may each take the blame for our separate failures to get our separate agreed tasks done competently. But if we both knew about your bad back and my tendency to overtrustingness, then should we divvy up the blame in this way? Who is responsible for the bad task allocation? Both of us, equally? Or me more, because I was proposer, you a mere accepter of my proposal? Insofar as financial loss is involved, we will have to come to some agreement about how it is to be shared, and it is certainly not obvious that I should accept the mere ten dollar loss on the cab fare, while you fork out several hundred dollars to cover the cost of replacing the missing case and its contents. And if your bad back is injured by the initial attempt to cope with all the luggage, it will be arguably unfair to make you bear the larger financial loss as well as the pain—not because you were mere accepter of a plan that I suggested, but rather because we were in this together, both faulty for acting on a bad voluntarily entered-into cooperative scheme.

The intended point of this example is to illustrate that there is always a question not just of responsibility for discharging one's accepted task in an acceptable manner, but of accepting the task in the first place, of going along with the scheme that allotted one this particular task. In the example I have there was no coercion to complicate the matter; where the task allocator possesses significant threat advantage over the other parties, so that their agreement to the proposed division of labor is not a free agreement, then of course the proposer of the plan bears a special responsibility, especially when his proposal includes provisions to see to it that he keeps the upper hand. But even then, the other parties bear some responsibility for going along with the bad cooperative scheme. Women who let men keep the role of initiator and decision-maker, despite their proven abuse of the powers that role allocation gave them, were not merely victims of the oppressive scheme, but co-conspirators, even when their agreement to their own role of meek helpmeet was not entirely unforced. Just as, if you knew of my unreliability as handler of the purse, you could and should have risked my anger by stepping in to say, "No, better if I do the paying and you take the luggage," so women might have been better advised to risk the ire of the master-sex by disputing their right to rule. As I, if I knew of your bad back, should not have proposed that you carry the luggage, so men, if they believed that women were indeed more "ductile" than men, should for that very reason not have encouraged them to take on roles that carried the risk of disempowerment, roles that might have long-term ill-effects on their moral spines. The responsibility for the continuation of schemes of cooperation that progressively disable some of the coopera-tors, and progressively concentrate coercive power in the hands and voices of others, is almost always shared, and never easy to divide without remainder into individual portions. Nor, where past evils are concerned, is there any particular point in trying to allocate individual blame, unless what we are doing is trying to recompense living victims of a bad scheme by taking from the living victimizers. When our main goal is to change the cooperative scheme for the better, we may adopt affirmative action measures toward those who as a class were disabled by the old bad scheme, and may even engage in some temporary "reverse discrimination" in order to get the scheme effectively changed. But we should see such measures as attempts to end dangerous concentrations of power, attempts to empower those who were disempowered by the old scheme, not as attempts to do individual justice, to give to each what that one deserves. If we, oppressors and oppressed, accept a joint responsibility for the bad old scheme, then we need not look at the disempowerment of the old masters as their "penalty," nor at the new advantages of the formerly disadvantaged class as something that each one of them "deserves," as compensation for earlier mistreatment. For individual persons in that class may have avoided suffering the usual disadvantages: some women were not oppressed, some men were not op-pressors.

If we insist on clinging to the idea that moral responsibility must divide without remainder into the bit that is mine and not yours, and the other bits that belong exclusively to other specific individuals, then not only will we limit the sorts of shared action we engage in; we will drastically limit our ability to reform our inherited schemes of cooperation for the better. We will bog down in endless disputes about just who should get what portion of the blame for past evils, about just who deserves what compensatory advantages now. Kant in the *Metaphysics of Morals* writes that ownership is a concept correlative with that of a noumenal self—a property right is *possessio noumenon* (MM, pt. 1, § 5). Kant is speaking here of rights to external things, and like John Locke he believes that such things, particularly land, were originally possessed in common (*communio fundi originaria*), private ownership being consequent upon a general will to allow individual claims by occupation. What Kant believes with respect to which tasks are a given person's own tasks, and whether originally there was a common task, from which private tasks were divided out by general agreement, is less clear. Rawls, who invokes the idea of a common fund of human talents,[27] may be adapting not just a Lockean but a Kantian concept of common fund of at least some crucial components of human life, human work, and human responsibility. (Did Kant believe that there was a common fund of reason, from which your reason and mine derive? Can a Kantian take a social view of reason? Did Kant believe that the respect-worthy humanity in each person is a derivate of some species-being that commands respect? The answer is not clear.) But it is in any case hard to see how essentially *individual* responsibility for action can be geared to essentially *collective* rights to goods, and to essentially shared responsibility for the "general will" that divvies out the individual tasks and goods that particular persons get as their individual allotments. If the noumenal self is an individualist, he will insist on dividing up what was common, blurring the traces of the act of division, and disowning responsibility for this crucial action, as well as for maintaining what it brought about.

The Kantian form of individualism that has been and is still being appropriated in the American tradition has two fatal and connected flaws. It has no account of really shared responsibility, but only for pooled or passed-along individual autonomy and responsibility. Its version of the way the realm of ends legislates for itself, far from providing the basis for a democratic society, in fact degenerates, in Kant's own version of it, into lawgiving by some elite, accompanied by willing subjection of the rest. And when we look in Kant's writings and in most of the tradition that honors him to see just how this legislating elite is to be constituted, we find there the fairly undisguised "integrity" of a patriarchal and sexist tradition. If we are to avoid the deficiencies of the mind and the perversity of the heart this Kantian tradition incorporates, then it is time that we stopped paying deferential lip service to Immanuel Kant, or indeed to any other preachers of the piety that consists in reverence to the faith of our patriarchal fathers.[28] If we do turn to Continental Europe for our social theorists, we should turn not just to the Prussian who glorified individualism, but to the Frenchman who criticized it, and to those who rejected the sexism of which both of them were guilty. We must mine our multifarious traditions for worthier versions of equality, of mutual respect, and of how responsibility is to be shared than the versions that we find in Kant. If we cannot find them in any of our inherited traditions, we should be willing to be called revolutionaries. In the American tradition, that label is surely not dishonorable.[29]

Notes

1. Immanuel Kant, *Metaphysics of Morals*, trans. Mary Gregor (New York: Cambridge University Press, 1991), 474 (appendix to part 2, *The Doctrine of Virtue* § 48); hereafter cited as MM.

2. See *Lectures on Ethics*, trans. Louis Infield (New York: Harper Torchbooks, 1963), 206–7.

3. I have discussed Kant's version of the enforcement of morality in "Moralism and Cruelty: Reflections on Hume and Kant," *Ethics* 103, no. 3 (1993): 436–57.

4. MM, pt. 1, *The Doctrine of Right*, 62.

5. See MM, pt. 1, general remark following § 49, pp. 129-33.

6. René Descartes, *Principles of Philosophy*, pt. 3, § 52.

7. Alexis de Tocqueville, *Democracy in America*, trans. Henry Reeve, in two volumes with a critical appraisal of each volume by John Stuart Mill (New York: Schocken Books, 1967), 2:118; hereafter cited as DA.

8. Gordon S. Wood, *The Radicalism of the American Revolution* (New York: Knopf, 1992).

9. Even those who have fairly fundamental disagreements with Kant, such as David Gauthier, seem to feel obliged to offer "subversive reinterpretations," and to appropriate the Kantian terminology, as if to give a borrowed authority to their own views; see "The Unity of Reason: A Subversive Reinterpretation of Kant," in *Moral Dealing*, by David Gauthier (Ithaca: Cornell University Press, 1990), 110–26.

10. The Library of Liberal Arts translation by John Ladd, *The Metaphysical Elements of Justice* (Indianapolis: Bobbs Merrill, 1965), which was all we had before Mary Gregor's translation, omitted large sections of Kant's text.

11. I have argued for the moral centrality of the concept of responsibility, over that of individual rights, in "Claims, Rights, Responsibilities," in *Prospects for a Common Morality*, ed. Gene Outka and J. P. Reeder Jr. (Princeton: Princeton University Press, 1993).

12. He does of course discuss at length the advantages and disadvantages of a union or federation of republics, and marvels at the "surprising facility" of the plain American citizen in distinguishing the jurisdictions of state and federal law; see *DA* 1: chap. 8; quotation from p. 185.

13. Immanuel Kant, *Perpetual Peace*, in *Kant's Political Writings*, trans. H. B. Nisbet, ed. Hans Reiss (New York: Cambridge University Press, 1970); hereafter cited as *PP*.

14. *PP*, second section, first article, 101.

15. See her remark on the translation of that term in her "Note on the Text," xii, of MM.

16. In *"What is Enlightenment?"* (1784) he might charitably be read as including "the fair sex" in the class of those who might take "the step to maturity," but the *Anthropology* and the *Metaphysics of Morals* do not take this possibility seriously. For a different and more charitable reading of the passages I have been citing, see Christine Korsgaard, "Creating the Realm of Ends: Reciprocity and Responsibility in Personal Relations," in *Philosophical Perspectives*, vol. 6, *Ethics*, ed. James Tomberlin (Atascadero, Calif.: Ridgeview, 1992).

17. "Only if placed in positions of authority over others should we point out to them their defects. Thus a husband is entitled to teach and correct his wife"; Kant, *Lectures on Ethics*, 232.

18. See Richard H. Dees, "Hume and the Contexts of Politics," *Journal of the History of Philosophy* 30, no. 2 (April 1992): 219–42, for a helpful discussion of Hume's position.

19. For a different more liberal reading of Kant, see Christine Korsgaard, "Taking the Law into Our Own Hands: Kant on the Right to Revolution," unpublished manuscript.

20. Quoted by Gordon S. Wood, "Classical Republicanism and the American Revolution," *Chicago-Kent Law Review* 66, no. 1 (1990): 14.

21. Ronald Dworkin, *Law's Empire* (Cambridge: Belknap Press of Harvard University Press, 1986), 171; hereafter cited as *LE*.

22. *Lectures on Ethics*, 232.

23. I am thinking of the activity of organizations such as EMILY ("Early Money Is Like Yeast") and WISH ("Women In Senate and House").

24. For documentation see, for example, Andrew Hacker, *Two Nations: Black and White, Separate, Hostile, Unequal* (New York: Scribner, 1992).

25. I have explored the ethics of trust and distrust in my Tanner Lectures, in *Tanner Lectures on Human Values*, vol. 13 (Salt Lake City: University of Utah Press, 1992).

26. See Kurt Baier, "Moral and Legal Responsibility," in *Medical Innovation and Bad Outcomes: Legal, Social, and Ethical Responses*, ed. Mark Siegler, Stephen Toulmin, Frank E. Zimring, and Kenneth F. Schaffner (Ann Arbor, Mich.: Health Administration Press, 1987), 101–30, for a discussion of forward-looking, or "task" responsibility, to backward-looking responsibility.

27. See John Rawls, *A Theory of Justice* (Cambridge: Belknap Press of Harvard University Press, 1971), 100ff.

28. I do not of course deny that many who saw and see themselves as Kantians or neo-Kantians have had a welcome liberalizing influence on political and social developments. The idea of equal respect for all persons continues to be a liberating and inspiring one.

29. This paper derives from a talk given at Yale University in April 1992. I have benefited from the critical comments given on that occasion by David Schmidtz, and also by other members of the Yale audience. My colleagues Nicholas Rescher and Steven Engstrom also offered helpful criticisms.

13

The Gender of Enlightenment

Robin May Schott

Enlightenment is one of the most debated themes of contemporary intellectual discourse. The eighteenth-century claim that progress is possible through the use of reason and the advancement and spread of knowledge is summed up in Kant's dictum, "Have courage to use your own reason!"[1] This view has been reiterated and updated by contemporary defenders of Enlightenment such as Jürgen Habermas. In Habermas's view, the Enlightenment tradition is the only possible source of rational judgment in the face of the irrationality, prejudice, blind obedience to authority, and violence that characterized the darkest days of German history under Hitler. It is only through Enlightenment that developing rational criteria for the critique of domination and for the possibility of emancipation is possible.[2]

Criticism of Enlightenment commitments have abounded in many diverse quarters. Earlier members of the Frankfurt school of social theory, such as Horkheimer and Adorno, argued that enlightenment represents Western culture's attempt to dominate sensuous existence by means of a controlling rationality that finds its fullest expression in the historical period of the eighteenth century. Far from ensuring the progress of reason and emancipation, enlightenment reason, epitomized in the historical period of the Enlightenment, has resulted in the return of the repressed, in the eruption of barbarism in twentieth-century Germany.[3] Recent writers such as Berel Lang have reiterated the thesis that links the philosophical project of the Enlightenment. In Lang's view, the Enlightenment's claims for universal truths and its extreme notions of the individual, autonomous, ahistorical self contribute directly to genocide.[4] In his view, the Enlightenment's insistence on the universality of rational judgment makes it unable to deal with any claims of particularism, and any judgments influenced by historical factors. The obvious exclusion of women, servants, and Jews from the call to Enlightenment coexisted with its principle of tolerance.[5] Ultimately, according to Lang, the inability of Enlightenment rationality to provide controls for determining the status of groups excluded from its domain leads to the possibility of unbounded destruction of these groups.[6]

Criticism of the project of the Enlightenment from postmodernist quarters has been just as intense. Writers such as Lyotard, Derrida, and Foucault, loosely grouped by others (though not by themselves) under the umbrella of postmodernism, have attacked the hegemony of Enlightenment rationality, its claim to grasp universal truth, and the concomitant rejection of any form of historicity or particularism. Enlightenment, it might be said, disenfranchises not only other possible interpretations, but the groups that initiate these interpretations. It thus readily can be wielded as an instrument of power in the service of its own vision of scientific truth.[7]

Feminist theorists have a particularly embattled relation to the question of Enlightenment. Some feminists argue that the Enlightenment tradition of individual reason, progress, and freedom, is a precondition for the discourse of women's liberation, and for the political gains that women have won. Even feminists who have a qualified relation to the Enlightenment (i.e., who argue that its fulfillment would bring the historical task of self-scrutiny), suggest that women have not yet had their Enlightenment.[8] On this view, even though women have been viewed by Enlightenment thinkers as not fully rational, and even though women have been severely restricted in their educational opportunities (prerequisite for achieving the free use of reason), nonetheless one should demand that the Enlightenment be completed by incorporating previously excluded groups. It is appealing for many to use the Enlightenment tools of rationality and objectivity to argue the case for women's emancipation.[9]

On the other hand, many feminist theorists argue that the fundamental commitments of the Enlightenment are antithetical to feminist politics and theory, and that feminists must throw their caps in the ring with postmodern critics. Not only have Enlightenment thinkers excluded women from the province of autonomy, but feminist notions of self, knowledge, and truth, are contradictory to fundamental Enlightenment commitments.[10] Feminists, like postmodernists, are skeptical of all transcendental, transhistorical claims for truth, and argue that "universality" is itself a reflection of the experience of the dominant social group. On this view, feminists are committed to showing that reason is not divorced from "merely contingent" existence, that the self is embedded in social relations, that the self is embodied, and is thus historically specific and partial. Jane Flax writes, "What Kant's self calls its 'own' reason and the methods by which reason's contents become present or self-evident, are no freer from empirical contingency than is the so-called phenomenal self."[11] Moreover, feminists argue that this desire to detach the self from contingency and embodiment is itself an effect of particular gender relations, itself an expression of the flight of masculinity from the temporal, embodied, uncertain realm of phenomenal existence.

Before evaluating the claims laid on the present by the philosophical project emerging from the Enlightenment, and in particular its implications for feminism, I shall make some brief historical comments about the situation of women during the Age of Enlightenment. Although this discussion is best left to historians, it is an important context for understanding Kant's discussion of Enlightenment. I shall then discuss Kant's notion of self-imposed tutelage and emancipation in his essay, "What is Enlightenment?" and repose the questions of autonomy and heteronomy from a feminist perspective.

Historians are divided about the historical implications of the Enlightenment for women. It was certainly not a period of unambivalent progress for women. The most positive reading of this period is that the Enlightenment legitimized safeguards in theory that were not secured in practice for nearly another century.[12] Considering the Age of Enlightenment in France, Claire Moses argues that the eighteenth century ended in repression. The uniform legal system enshrined the Rousseauesque concept of the difference of women from men. The Civil Code recognized the rights of all citizens, but excluded women from citizenship. Therefore, women's status worsened in relation to men's status. Moreover, some women's status worsened absolutely. Whereas earlier some noblewomen could escape the full harshness of patriarchal laws, these opportunities were now erased.[13] Moses argues that the eighteenth-century views of women were contradictory, providing both encouragement for the emergence of feminism, and the weapons to gun it down. For example, the Civil Code served as a rallying point for women, in enshrining the Rousseauesque concept of the difference between women and men, in which women remained subordinate to men. Not only did it incite feminist protest because it discriminated against women, but in proclaiming the political significance of sex, it intensified women's sense of sex identification.[14]

The Enlightenment's theoretical legitimization of the rights to organize, lecture publicly, and publish freely, were not secured for women in France until 1879. In the years that followed, women won the right to secondary education, the gradual opening of the university to women, the right to practice "public" professions (newspaper publishing, medicine, law). In 1907, women were granted equal authority with the father over children and the right to control their own earnings, but women in France had to wait until 1944 to gain the right to vote.[15]

In terms of women's education in the Age of Enlightenment, it is clear that women's literacy in France lagged far behind men's.[16] The feminist political activist Olympe de Gouges dictated all her works to a secretary because she was unable to write. And the four youngest daughters of Louis XV, after several years at the convent, were still illiterate. Despite deficiencies in formal instruction, many women were able to complete their education independently.[17] Women's education in France varied significantly depending on their class and region. Upper-class girls and daughters of the bourgeoisie received their early education at home, and later were sent to a convent until they were to be married. Although there are idealized descriptions of life in convents, a more realistic picture includes harrowing practices such as girls being punished by being sent to pray alone in the vaults where nuns were buried.[18] The social function of the convents was most important;

reading, writing, and catechism occupied a distant second place. Other "safe" subjects included the lives of the saints, needlework, and sewing, whereas novels, mythology, physical or natural sciences, ancient philosophy, and even history except in its most elementary form remained taboo.[19] Girls from impoverished families depended on charity schools for education, which provided training in manual skills and crafts. Although progress in the education of women in France was achieved in the eighteenth century (the level of literacy improved; the need for organized public education was recognized), women's exclusion from formal higher education and participation in the professions during this period continued to hamper their achievements.

Women were also excluded from university education in Germany as well (including Königsberg University where Kant studied and taught) during the Age of Enlightenment.[20] And although universities were not exactly a hotbed of cultural innovation during the eighteenth century,[21] universities remained the locus for philosophical and scientific work in Germany during this century.[22] Women's exclusion from university life was considered so natural that only the most recent scholars of German education make note of it. By 1914, women constituted 7 percent of the student body in Prussia—a dramatic increase in their enrollment since 1900.[23] Women's absence from the academies ensured their exclusion from training for medicine, law, and government positions in Germany until the late nineteenth and twentieth centuries.[24]

It is in this historical context that Kant's views of women is situated. Far from challenging women's exclusion from education on egalitarian grounds, Kant mocks women's attempts at serious philosophical and scientific work. Kant asserts that women's character, in contrast to man's, is wholly defined by natural needs. Woman's lack of self-determination, in his view, is intrinsic to her nature. He writes, "Nature was concerned about the preservation of the embryo and implanted fear into the woman's character, a fear of physical injury and a timidity towards similar dangers. On the basis of this weakness, the woman legitimately asks for masculine protection."[25] Because of their natural fear and timidity, Kant views women as unsuited for scholarly work. He mockingly describes the scholarly women who "use their books somewhat like a watch, that is, they wear the watch so it can be noticed that they have one, although it is usually broken or does not show the correct time."[26] Kant's remarks on women in the *Anthropology* echo his sentiments in *Observations on the Feeling of the Beautiful and the Sublime*. In that early work, Kant notes, "A woman who has a head full of Greek, like Mme. Dacier, or carries on fundamental controversies about mechanics, like the Marquise du Châtelet, might as well even have a beard, for perhaps that would express more obviously the mien of profundity for which she strives."[27] In Kant's view, women's philosophy is "not to reason, but to sense." And he adds, "I hardly believe that the fair sex is capable of principles."[28] No wonder that under these conditions the woman "makes no secret in wishing that she might rather be a man, so that she could give larger and freer latitude to her inclinations; no man, however, would want to be a woman."[29]

In providing the Marquise du Châtelet with a beard, Kant suggests that there is a contradiction between women and scholarship that is rooted in a natural condition, not a social one. Some biographical remarks about the Marquise du Châtelet help in evaluating Kant's views. By the time of her death in 1749, Emilie du Châtelet was a well-known scholar, and not only in French intellectual circles; she had been elected to the Bologna Academy of Sciences. She had published on the metaphysics of natural science, on the nature of fire and heat, and on the nature of force. In addition, she had completed a translation of Newton's *Principia Mathematica*, and had anonymously co-authored with Voltaire a popularization of Newtonian physics.

Despite her scientific vocation, Emilie du Châtelet was hampered throughout her life by her inability to obtain the systematic learning provided to boys, to be educated in an institutional context as opposed to a private tutoring situation, and to travel freely and work undisturbed by household obligations. Thus, she was hindered in carrying out anything like a long-term research program.[30] Because her intellectual training was limited to her relationship with a small set of famous figures (e.g., Voltaire), it was difficult for her to take the step from tutelage to independence. Her responsibilities for family, household, friends, and social duties made it impossible for her to lead the life of a full-time scientist. She was able to achieve as much as she did by functioning on four or five hours of sleep a night. When necessary, she survived on even less, dipping her arms in ice water in order to stay awake.[31]

Although the discipline required for the Marquise du Châtelet to accomplish scientific work matches Kant's own stern discipline in life, it is clear that Kant had little sympathy for the frustrations of intelligent women like her. His views are further illustrated by his correspondence with Maria von Herbert, an intelligent young aristocratic woman who had studied Kant's writings together with a male friend. In a letter to Kant dated January 1793, Maria von Herbert writes to Kant of her own personal despair and frustration with her life. "Even when I am not frustrated by any external circumstances and have nothing to do all day, I'm tormented by a boredom that makes my life unbearable."[32] Although Kant had responded to an earlier letter of Maria's that discussed her moral failings, he failed to respond to this letter. Instead, he sent it on to another young lady as an example of "mental derangement" that occurs when young ladies succumb to "the errors of a sublimated fantasy."[33] He failed to consider the possibility that this young woman's despair may have arisen in part from external circumstances that smothered her urge to do something in the world. In my view, the lives of these two women provide counterexamples to Kant's view concerning the inverse relationship between civil freedom and freedom of mind. The restrictions placed on these women's lives did not encourage the flourishing of their intellectual development, but rather furthered the very form of intellectual tutelage that Kant ostensibly deplored.

It is important to bear in mind concrete historical features when evaluating the philosophical work of the period. Social practices are not "outside" the sphere of culture in which philosophy operates. Rather, philosophy can be viewed as a reflective appropriation of cultural and historical traditions.[34] Therefore, in turning to Kant's essay, "What is Enlightenment?" new perspectives are disclosed if one asks: What could this conception of Enlightenment have meant to women of the period? And how would women's experiences have challenged Kant's formulations?

Kant has only one reference to women in particular in this short essay. He writes, "the step to competence is held to be very dangerous by the far greater portion of mankind (and by the entire fair sex)."[35] His general indifference to differentiating the possibilities of Enlightenment for men and for women appears to arise from his view that the subject of Enlightenment (humanity) that is called upon to free itself from self-imposed tutelage is a universal one. He never qualifies his claim by saying it is for masters and not their servants, men and not women, Christians and not Jews. Therefore, any reference to particular kinds of groups or classes of individuals in society seems out of place. Enlightenment, in Kant's view, is summed up in the motto, "Have courage to use your own reason!"[36] Where this courage comes from, what conflicts within individuals' lives it encounters, what factors interfere with its realization—none of these are Kant's concerns. Rather, Kant's project is to address Enlightenment as a demand for the individual to use reason; and reason, as Kant's critical writings attest to, is viewed as a universal, ahistorical faculty.[37]

And yet for the contemporary reader, the question of inclusion and exclusion of particular groups in the domain of enlightened thought becomes pressing. As the critics of Enlightenment mentioned above have argued, the universal subject of enlightened thought had particular unacknowledged qualifications. As already noted, Kant claims that all women are afraid of Enlightenment (Kant did *not* turn his attention to how this fear might be counteracted). Similarly, it is difficult to see how Kant might include servants or domestics in his call for Enlightenment, since these latter are, in Kant's view, a legal possession of the master. In his letter to C. G. Schutz dated 10 July 1797, Kant writes of this relationship as follows: "The right to use a man for domestic purposes is analogous to a right to an object, for which the servant is not free to terminate his connections with the household and he may therefore be caught and returned by force."[38] In Kant's claim that the servant "belongs" to the master like an object, it is difficult to see how there would be any domain left to the servant in which reason could be exercised freely. Historically, women of all classes and men of the servant class could not share equally with bourgeois men in the "public" exercise of reason, which Kant defines as the "use which a person makes of it as a scholar before the reading public."[39]

Similarly, Kant's discussion of self-incurred tutelage is not formulated with reference to women's experience. Kant begins his essay with the claim that "Enlightenment is man's release from his self-incurred tutelage. Tutelage is man's inability to make use of his understanding without direction from another. Self-incurred is this tutelage when its cause lies not in lack of reason but in lack of resolution and courage to use it without direction from another."[40] In this context, it is helpful to recall the little we know about the lives of women like Emilie du Châtelet and Maria von Herbert. These women did apparently experience their education as being a form of tutelage. Emilie du Châtelet's self-doubt, self-deprecation, and tendency to choose safe, "dependent" research projects such as translation, criticism, and commentary may have been a result of her personal indebtedness to friends such as Voltaire who were already famous, that made it difficult for her to take the step from pupil to colleague, from tutelage to independence.[41] And one can imagine from Kant's response to Maria von Herbert's letters that for him, the only conceivable relation a woman could have to philosophy is to be tutored by a mentor. In his letter to Elizabeth Motherby, Kant notes that Maria refers to his writings "that she read and are difficult to understand without an explanation."[42] The implication is, with a proper explanation, Maria may have been saved from the reefs of her "sublimated fantasy."

Thus, the extent to which these women's tutelage was self-imposed arose from their very desire to gain knowledge and to resist being defined by what is "pleasant and pointless."[43] But their difficulties in escaping this tutelage cannot be explained by "laziness and cowardice" (the reasons Kant gives for mankind's tutelage).[44] Nor is it likely that they were "fond" of this state.[45] Rather, this state of tutelage seems to be a result of social forces and restrictions stronger than these individuals' power to change them.[46]

Just as Kant's discussion of tutelage does not explain obstacles to Enlightenment faced by "humanity," but at best explains the obstacles faced by certain groups of people (e.g., middle-class men with education and civil office who could become, for example, military officers and clergymen), so too Kant's conception of enlightened reason has to be understood as a particular historical construction. For Kant, rationality is possible only on the basis of excluding emotion. He does invoke "courage" in the use of reason, just as elsewhere he invokes "respect" for the moral law. But only the kind of feeling that is "self-wrought by a rational concept" and is not rooted in inclination or fear can be praiseworthy.[47] Concerning emotion in general, Kant expresses only disdain. In the *Anthropology from a Pragmatic Point of View*, he writes, "To be subject to emotions and passions is probably always an illness of mind because both emotion and passion, exclude the sovereignty of reason."[48] Similarly, "passion, on the other hand, no man wishes for himself. Who wants to have himself put in chains when he can be free?"[49] Since emotion and passion threaten the sovereignty of reason, they must be excluded from ordinary consciousness.

Kant's attempt to exclude emotion from rationality is premised on the assumption that his rational posture is itself wholly nonemotional. Yet the emotional currents of Kantian rationality are clearly expressed in his personal correspondence. Maria von Herbert wrote to Kant during a personal crisis, in which she had revealed to a friend that she had formerly loved another man, and this friend now treated her with coldness. Kant responds to Maria in didactic manner. Although Kant acknowledges that in men there is a limit on candor (in some men more than in others) that interferes with the ideal of friendship, he distinguishes this lack of candor from lack of sincerity, from dishonesty in expressing one's thoughts.[50] Kant adjudicates Maria of being guilty of this latter sin, and for rightly feeling the pains of conscience: "For conscience must focus on every transgression, like a judge who does not dispose of the documents, when a crime has been sentenced, but records them in the archives in order to sharpen the judgement of justice in new cases of a similar or even dissimilar offense that may appear before him."[51] Kant admits that he is answering her in the form of sermon: "instruction, penalty, and solace, of which I beg you to devote yourself somewhat more to the first two."[52]

In this letter, Kant epitomizes the ascetic priest described by Nietzsche: the inventor of bad conscience, the upholder of self-punishment, the antagonist to the fulfillment of sensual pleasures. Nietzsche writes in the Genealogy of Morals, "Every suffering sheep says to himself, 'I suffer; it must be somebody's fault.' But his shepherd, the ascetic priest, says to him, 'You are quite right, my sheep, somebody must be at fault here, but that somebody is yourself. You alone are to blame—you alone are to blame for yourself.' "[53]

Kant's response to Maria gives support to the view that his moral philosophy is an existential choice, a manner of living "with our eyes fixed on abstract, impartial principles,"[54] and not merely a position to be held in debates about rational principles. Kant's philosophy is paradigmatic of what contemporary critics call the perspective of impartial reason. As Iris Young writes, "Impartial reason must judge from a point of view outside the particular perspectives of persons involved in interaction, able to totalize these perspectives into a whole or general will. This is the point of view of a solitary transcendent God."[55] But this perspective is built on the assumption that the impartial self is a disembodied, disembedded self. As Seyla Benhabib notes in reference to the impartial self in the theories of Rawls and Kohlberg, "this is a strange world: it is one in which individuals are grown up before they have been born; in which boys are men before they have been children; a world where neither mother, nor sister, nor wife exist."[56] It is a self that abstracts from concrete individuality and identity, and thus ultimately makes the concept of the other as different from oneself incoherent.[57]

One may object that an argument proving Kant's exclusion of emotion from morality does not argue for the role of emotions in ethics. This objection exemplifies the commitments of the Kantian paradigm, to which much contemporary academic discourse is heir. My claim, however, is that this rational detachment is already an emotional posture with consequences for human relations (witness Kant's letter to Maria von Herbert and his refusal to respond to her subsequent letters). But the failure to acknowledge the emotional content of detached impartiality precludes the possibility of evaluating how we are to use emotions, which emotions are positive, and which are negative. As Iris Young notes in reference to the exclusion of desire, affectivity, and need from deontological reason, "Since all desiring is equally suspect, we have no way of distinguishing which desires are good and which bad, which will expand the person's capacities and relations with others, and which stunt the person and foster violence. In being excluded from understanding, all desiring, feeling, and needs become unconscious, but certainly do not thereby cease to motivate action and behavior."[58] Nietzsche notes in the *Genealogy of Morals*, that human beings have the capacity of oblivion, by which "what we experience and digest psychologically does not . . . emerge into consciousness. . . . The role of this active oblivion is that of a concierge: to shut temporarily the doors and windows of consciousness; to protect us from the noise and agitation with which our lower organs work for or against one another; to introduce a little quiet into our consciousness so as to make room for the nobler functions and functionaries of our organism which do the governing and planning. This concierge maintains order and etiquette in the household of the psyche."[59] But as Nietzsche, and following him Freud, Horkheimer, and Adorno have argued, this edifice remains harnessed to the noise and agitation of the psyche. In refusing to acknowledge the existence of nonrational motivations, one forfeits the possibility of self-understanding.

Much contemporary debate in moral theory revolves around the paradigm of autonomy that Kant articulated. Autonomy in Kant's view is the moral equivalent of the Enlightenment motto "Have courage to use your own reason!" In the *Foundations of the Metaphysics of Morals* Kant defines the principle of autonomy in which man is "subject only to his own, yet universal legislation, and that he is only bound to act in accordance with his own will, which is, however, designed by nature to be a will giving universal laws."[60] Just as enlightened reason must exclude the influence of emotions, so moral behavior "wholly excludes the influence of inclination" such as sympathy and sensual love.[61] Only then can rational judgments be universalizable and detachable from the concrete context in which they are made.

Many feminists have vociferously criticized this model of autonomy because of its presumption of detachment, universality, and disembeddedness. Writers such as Carol Gilligan, and those following in her wake, advocate the legitimacy of an alternative to this Kantian model of autonomy, which they call the care perspective. The care perspective, evident in many women's responses to moral dilemmas, emphasizes the individual's connectedness with others. In this perspective, individuals make moral choices by concretely assessing who will be hurt and who will be helped by particular decisions.[62]

The viability of a care perspective has been heatedly debated both within feminist and nonfeminist circles. Feminists such as Claudia Card criticize this conception on the grounds that it presumes traditional gender dualism, itself the product of patriarchal history. They argue that the care perspective advocates traditional feminine virtues, which may be survival strategies for women in forced relationships of dependencies, but are hardly an emancipated vision for the future. On the other hand, many feminists defend this posture as an alternative conception of moral autonomy, as a form of responsibility reasoning motivated by persons' sense of their own concrete identity while still acknowledging human connectedness.[63] Others, like Benhabib, seek to integrate Kantian moral autonomy with care, a position that "allows us to recognize the dignity of the generalized other through an acknowledgement of the moral identity of the concrete other."[64]

The attention given to the debate about impartiality versus care in both academic and popular journals attests to the historical nerve it has touched. To some extent, interest in this debate has been sparked by the problematizing of gender identity in contemporary culture. But the debate's significance is also connected to a paradigm shift in contemporary intellectual discourse—across fields such as psychology, moral philosophy, and literary analysis—a shift that challenges the notion that there is an individual, subjective identity that exists as a deep self, a unified whole, an isolated ego. Challenging the Kantian conception of the subject is certainly not unique to the present debate: it finds historical antecedents in Hegel's concept of reciprocal recognition and in Marx's concept of the fundamentally social character of human identity. But the question of intersubjectivity has achieved a certain historical urgency today, in light of the crisis of the philosophy of the subject.

The phrase "care perspective" may in fact be a misnomer for the analysis of human interrelatedness. "Care" seems too thin, mild, and one-dimensional to account for the dynamics of human connectedness. As experience of intimacy teaches, relations may include feelings of love and anger and resentment simultaneously. Relatedness might express the possible depth of harmony between two individuals, as well as the cruelty that individuals can exercise against each other; and these different dynamics can coexist within the same relationships. Therefore, "care" cannot be taken as descriptive of the range of emotions involved in human connectedness. Moreover, the care perspective cannot be formulated by the normative principle "Be compassionate" or "Take responsibility."[65] The care perspective is committed to concrete, individual decision-making as opposed to abstract, universal rules, which cannot help in deciding between conflicts of responsibilities.

I suggest instead that the radical potential within "care" theories, which go beyond what many of these theorists themselves argue, is to challenge the primacy of the category of autonomy that has prevailed since Kant. In discussing the Kantian subject, Lucien Goldmann once wrote, "That it could never pass from the *I* to the *we*, that in spite of Kant's genius it always remained within the framework of bourgeois individualist thought, these are the ultimate limits of Kant's thought."[66] In our times we may need to perform another conceptual revolution, as Kant did with previous philosophers and as Marx did with Hegel: to reverse the moral weight given to autonomy and heteronomy, and to argue for a concept of moral and political theory that is premised on the heteronomy, the interdependence of individuals.[67] Individuals who have close friends, lovers, children, or parents, do need to make decisions on the basis of what is best for the "we" of which they form a part. Why shouldn't this acknowledgment of relations be a starting point for moral philosophy, as opposed to beginning with the model of the individual as cut off from intimacy, that Kant personified in his own life, and that has become the paradigm of moral philosophy? The health and happiness of these collectivities depend, of course, on balancing as best as possible the conflicting needs of individuals involved in these relationships. From this perspective, heteronomy includes respect for individuals' integrity and desire to make their own decisions; but individual priorities cannot be absolute. Moreover, these groups do change: children grow up, partners separate, individuals die, interests and needs change with personal development. However, to privilege the autonomy of the individual as the primary factor in moral thinking makes human sepa-rateness and detachment morally normative.

A number of objections may be raised to these suggestions. For example, one might argue that even recognizing the primacy of heteron-omy in the moral domain does not undercut the need for a Kantian principle of rational autonomy in the political domain, in order to protect individuals' rights against violent encroachment. A principle that validates the group per se over the individual might pose an even greater danger of exclusion, harassment, and violence than has occurred under the inheritance of the Enlightenment. If radical right, homopho-bic, anti-abortion advocates achieved their "we" as the primary political agenda, imagine what would happen to individual women, lesbian and gay activists, AIDS research and support groups.

A number of responses to this objection are in order. First of all, it is important to point out the discrepancy between Kant's moral theory and a political recognition of equal rights. For example, in the *Metaphysical Elements of Justice,* Kant argues "that one ought to obey the legislative authority that now exists, regardless of its origin" and adds that there can be "no legitimate resistance of the people to the legislative chief of the state."[68] Because Kant viewed legislative authority as grounded in the lawgiving form of the will, the particular laws in society are viewed as morally binding. Thus, Kant's moral theory offers no political protection for, say, women, servants, or Jews, who might have been discriminated against in existing law. As Iris Young argues, in modern normative political theory and practice, impartiality in the public realm is attained by the exclusion of those linked to particular interests, needs, and concrete identities. The notion of the impartial public domain assumes a "homogeneity of citizens. . . . It excludes from the public those individuals and groups that do not fit the model of the rational citizen who can transcend body and sentiment."[69]

If one were interested in developing the political implications of moral heteronomy, I think it would be fruitful to look at examples such as the Scandinavian welfare states, which have a basic commitment to provid-ing fundamental conditions of human dignity, including money, hous-ing, health care, to all the members of the community.[70] One might also consider the political party for women in Iceland, a path the National Organization for Women is seeking to pursue. These political parties seek recognition for a particular group in society. Political conflicts between different groups obviously entail negotiation and compromise, in order to achieve a "rational consensus." But such a consensus can never be achieved, nor be considered fully rational, if it is cut off from concrete identities, needs, interests, and emotions of the individuals within these groups.

How then does one assess the significance of Kant's essay, "What is Enlightenment?" for the contemporary world? With many of the critics of the Enlightenment, I challenge its fundamental conception of rationality, autonomy, and freedom. This philosophical position has been the hallmark of a historical period in Western European and American society characterized by imperialism, the hegemony of dominant groups over other groups excluded from wealth, political power, and often basic human respect. And yet it would be naive to think that we can free ourselves of this heritage merely by intellectual critique. Even in reacting against Enlightenment assumptions, postmodern and feminist critics are determined by these assumptions, often using the very tools they seek to reject. We may be heir to a tradition that constrains our ability to think the unthought, but nonetheless we must respond to the demand to create a new future, shaped by the contributions of women and Third World people, whose history is the underside of Enlightenment tolerance. We must find a way of living the practical contradiction between the past from which we seek to free ourselves and the future that we desire to create.

Notes

1. Immanuel Kant, "What is Enlightenment?" in *Kant on History*, ed. Lewis White Beck (New York: Macmillan, 1963), 3.

2. Habermas argues for "the way back" to Enlightenment, in contrast to Horkheimer's and Adorno's efforts to show its self-destruction; see *The Philosophical Discourses of Modernity*, trans. Frederick Lawrence (Cambridge: MIT Press, 1987), 128.

3. See Max Horkheimer and Theodor Adorno, *The Dialectic of Enlightenment*, trans. John Cumming (New York: Herder and Herder, 1972), xi. I shall rely on context to distinguish the historical period of Enlightenment from Enlightenment as a project of modernity that emerged from this period but continues to lay claims on the present.

4. Berel Lang, *Act and Idea in the Nazi Genocide* (Chicago: University of Chicago Press, 1990), 179ff.

5. I shall discuss Kant's lack of egalitarianism regarding women and servants below. Lang also notes that few figures in the Enlightenment extended their tolerance to Jews. Kant did not view Judaism as having the status of a true religion, but considered it rather a cult based

on external rituals, and therefore removed from the moral domain. Voltaire repeated many of the conventional slurs from the past (e.g., his reference to Jews as "the most contemptible of all nations . . . robbers, seditious"), and clearly considered the Jews to be themselves intolerant (by maintaining their separateness), thereby exempting them from the privilege of being tolerated by others (Lang, *Act and Idea,* 185).

6. Lang, *Act and Idea,* 188.

7. In Foucault's essay, "Kant on Enlightenment and Revolution," trans. Colin Gordon, *Economy and Society* 15, no. 1 (1986): 88–96, he argues that Kant develops an "ontology of the present" in "What is Enlightenment?" that should be distinguished from the "analytic of truth" that Kant develops in his critical philosophy. However, Foucault's critique of Kant does extend to this "analytic of truth."

8. See Christine de Stefano, "Dilemmas of Difference," in *Feminism/Postmodernism,* ed. Linda J. Nicholson (New York: Routledge, 1990), 75. De Stefano's suggestion that postmodernism may be a theory whose time has come for men, but not for women, implies that women still need to carry out the Enlightenment tasks of developing a centered self, and a coherent system of truth.

9. See Jane Flax's discussion of this position in "Postmodernism and Gender Relations," in *Feminism/Postmodernism,* 42.

10. Ibid. Flax writes, "The way(s) to feminist future(s) cannot lie in reviving or appropriating Enlightenment concepts of the person or knowledge."

11. Ibid., 43.

12. Claire G. Moses, "The Legacy of the Eighteenth Century: A Look at the Future," in *French Women and the Age of Enlightenment,* ed. Samia I. Spencer (Bloomington: Indiana University Press, 1984), 413.

13. Ibid., 409–10.

14. Ibid. In terms of the view from Germany, one should note Kant's enthusiasm for the French Revolution and the political constitution that emerged from it. See Foucault, "Kant on Enlightenment and Revolution," 94.

15. Moses, "Legacy," 413–14.

16. For example, between 1719 and 1730, a teacher in the Vosges region asked thirty-six couples to sign the marriage register. Although twenty-three men would write their names, thirty-two of the women were unable to write a cross, much less to write their names. Jean Larnac, *Histoire de la littérature féminine en France* (Paris: Kra, 1929), 132; cited in Samia I. Spencer, "Women and Education," in her *French Women and the Age of Enlightenment,* 95.

17. Spencer, "Women and Education," 83–84.

18. Ibid., 86.

19. Ibid., 84.

20. Some few aristocratic women in Prussia, such as Dorothea von Schlozer, were able to acquire a university education in the eighteenth century. However, they were also frustrated by their inability to use their education. But university education did not open up for women more generally until the twentieth century. As in France, the professions of medicine, teaching, and law began to open up gradually to women in the 1880s and 1890s; see James C. Albisetti, "Women and the Professions in Imperial Germany," in *German Women in the Eighteenth and Nineteenth Centuries,* ed. Ruth-Ellen B. Joeres and Mary Jo Maynes (Bloomington: Indiana University Press), 96.

21. James Schmidt's phrase in correspondence with me.

22. Wolff, Kant, Fichte, Schelling, Hegel, and Schleiermacher were all university professors. By contrast, in England scholars such as Darwin, Spencer, Mill, Bentham, Ricardo, Hume, Locke, Hobbes, and Bacon were not connected with university life. See Paulsen, *The German Universities and University Study,* trans. Frank Thilly and William W. Elwant (New York: Scribner, 1906), 4–5.

23. Charles E. McClelland, *State, Society, and University in Germany, 1700–1914* (Cambridge: Cambridge University Press, 1980), 250.

24. The difficulty for women to gain access to education and cultural authority remains an issue today. Michele Le Doeuff notes that although creative areas in philosophy today do not lie in the area of academic work, it is still cruel to note that since 1974, the number of women who pass selective examinations for teaching jobs has been very small; see her "Women and Philosophy," in *French Feminist Thought*, ed. Toril Moi (Oxford: Basil Blackwell, 1987), 200–201. She explains this phenomenon in part by differences between men's and women's philosophical writing: "Men treat the text familiarly and knock it about happily; women treat it with a politeness for which girls' education has its share of responsibility. If the timidity and the desire to flatter are not too strong, this form of reading can, I think, produce great successes, a distanced kind of reading which enables one to see what is implicit in the text or to pick out the 'gaps' in theorization. The question is whether it is because this kind of reading is not highly valued that the women fail, or whether it is not highly valued just because it is evidently feminine. I prefer the second hypothesis, and would add that the feminine is excluded because it is associated with the idea of lack of authority" (205).

25. Kant, *Anthropology from a Pragmatic Point of View*, trans. Victor Lyle Dowdell (Carbondale: Southern Illinois University Press, 1978), 219.

26. Ibid., 221.

27. Kant, *Observations on the Feeling of the Beautiful and Sublime*, trans. John T. Goldthwait (Berkeley and Los Angeles: University of California Press, 1960), sect. 3, p. 78.

28. Ibid., 132–33.

29. *Anthropology*, 222.

30. Linda Gardiner, "Women in Science," in *French Women and the Age of Enlightenment*, 184ff.

31. Ibid., 189.

32. Immanuel Kant, *Philosophical Correspondence, 1759–99*, ed. and trans. Arnulf Zweig (Chicago: University of Chicago Press, 1967), 201.

33. Letter to Elisabeth Motherby, 11 February 1793, in *Philosophical Correspondence*, 204.

34. Hans-Georg Gadamer, *Philosophical Hermeneutics*, ed. and trans. David E. Linge (Berkeley and Los Angeles: University of California Press, 1976), 28.

35. "What is Enlightenment?" in *Kant on History*, ed. Lewis White Beck, trans. Lewis White Beck, Robert E. Anchor, and Emil L. Fackenheim (New York: Macmillan, 1963), 3.

36. Ibid.

37. See my *Cognition and Eros: A Critique of the Kantian Paradigm* (Boston: Beacon, 1988; pbk., University Park: Pennsylvania State University Press, 1993) for a discussion of Kant's conception of rationality. In particular, see chap. 9.

38. *Philosophical Correspondence*, 236.

39. "What is Enlightenment?" 5. Although Kant did not express particular interest in extending Enlightenment ideas to women, a few of his contemporaries did—notably Theodor Gottlieb von Hippel. Hippel called for improving women's education and in giving women opportunities for meaningful activity. See Ruth P. Dawson, " 'And This Shield Is Called Self-Reliance': Emerging Feminist Consciousness in the Late Eighteenth Century" (in *German Women in the Eighteenth and Nineteenth Centuries*), 158; see also Chapter 11, this volume.

There were many women writers of the eighteenth and nineteenth centuries who have been "unjustly forgotten." However, these women had to struggle against enormous social forces that prescribed women's "proper" role in the home and family. Women writers were not taken seriously. They appeared in the shadows of men, often writing pseudonymously or anonymously in order to get published. Moreover, they faced a certain "vacuum of experience" because of their exclusion from education, government, military office, and business. Patricia

Herminghouse, "Women and the Literary Enterprise in Nineteenth-Century Germany," in *German Women in the Eighteenth and Nineteenth Centuries*, 79–90.

40. "What is Enlightenment?" 3.

41. Gardiner, "Women in Science," 187.

42. *Philosophical Correspondence*, 204.

43. Maria's letter to Kant, January 1793, *Philosophical Correspondence*, 201.

44. "What is Enlightenment?" 3.

45. Ibid., 4.

46. Maria von Herbert did commit suicide, nine years after her last letter to Kant (*Philosophical Correspondence*, 26).

47. Kant, *Foundations of the Metaphysics of Morals*, trans. Lewis White Beck (Indianapolis: Bobbs-Merrill, 1959), 17.

48. *Anthropology*, para. 73, p. 155.

49. Ibid., para. 74, p. 157.

50. *Philosophical Correspondence*, 188–89.

51. Ibid., 189–90.

52. Ibid.

53. Friedrich Nietzsche, *The Genealogy of Morals* in *The Birth of Tragedy and the Genealogy of Morals*, trans. Francis Golffing (New York: Doubleday, 1956), 264.

54. Thomas E. Hill Jr. "The Importance of Autonomy," in *Women and Moral Theory*, ed. Eva Feder Kittay and Diana T. Meyers (Totowa, N.J.: Rowman and Littlefield, 1987), 132. Although Hill is seeking to defend a view of Kantian autonomy as part of a debate about moral principles, not a way of living life, he acknowledges that Kant conflated the two, and thus seems to undercut his own thesis.

55. Iris Young, "Impartiality and the Civic Public: Some Implications of Feminist Critiques of Moral and Political Theory," in her *Throwing Like a Girl and Other Essays in Feminist Philosophy and Social Theory* (Bloomington: Indiana University Press, 1990), 96.

56. Seyla Benhabib, "The Generalized and the Concrete Other: The Kohlberg-Gilligan Controversy and Moral Theory," in *Women and Moral Theory*, 162.

57. Benhabib notes that "Rawls recapitulates a basic problem with the Kantian conception of the self, namely, that noumenal selves cannot be *individuated*. If all that belongs to them as embodied affective, suffering creatures, their memory and history, their ties and relations to others, are to be subsumed under the phenomenal realm, then what we are left with is an empty mask that is everyone and no one" (166).

58. Young, "Impartiality and the Civic Public," 98.

59. Nietzsche, *Genealogy of Morals*, 189.

60. *Foundations*, 51.

61. Ibid., 17.

62. Carol Gilligan, *In a Different Voice: Psychological Theory and Women's Development* (Cambridge: Harvard University Press, 1982). See also articles debating Gilligan's work in *Women and Moral Theory*.

63. Diana T. Meyers, "The Socialized Individual and Individual Autonomy; An Intersection between Philosophy and Psychology," in *Women and Moral Theory*, 139, 152.

64. Benhabib, "Generalized and the Concrete Other," 169.

65. Thomas Hill suggests that these rules are what attentiveness to a "caring" solution implies; "The Importance of Autonomy," 132.

66. Lucien Goldmann, *Immanuel Kant*, trans. Robert Black (London: New Left Books, 1971), 170.

67. The meaning of heteronomy has also to be redefined. In Kant's view, heteronomy refers to everything outside of the universal legislation of reason. All of these other factors

were subsumed under the concept of nature (*Foundations*, 51). Kant's concept of heteronomy provides no tools for analyzing and distinguishing the nature of one's own emotions, the influence of other persons, nor the impact of physical constraints on an individual. Therefore, he has no means of acknowledging the possibility of mutuality between persons, other than a shared abstract respect for the moral law.

68. Immanuel Kant, *The Metaphysical Elements of Justice*, trans. John Ladd (Indianapolis: Bobbs-Merrill, 1959), 85–86.

69. Young, "Impartiality and the Civic Public," 98, 100.

70. Unfortunately, the commitments of the social welfare state in Scandinavia are now in jeopardy: witness recent significant cutbacks in social services in both Denmark and Sweden.

Part V

Philosophy of Nature and
Human Nature

14

Kant, the Law, and Desire

Monique David-Ménard
Translated by Leslie Lykes de Galbert

MAN OF HUMAN RIGHTS

The moral vision of the world based upon the confrontation of the materiality of our acts with a Categorical Imperative that defines man as universally subject to both moral and juridical law, seems—at the end of the twentieth century—to be an unrivaled rampart against human violence and national and international conflicts. It seems that there has been a return to Kantian ethics and to the philosophy of Human Rights, despite philosophical critiques that appeared to have proved that these were abstract and therefore illusory. Hegel demonstrated the logic of this abstraction, which is inevitably and constantly falsified because it ignores the veritable content of the human act; Nietzsche called attention to the traces of cruelty found in Kant's Categorical Imperative; and more recently, Lacan drew a parallel between Sade and Kant by showing that the formalism of the imperative to *jouissance*, in the same way as the moral imperative, is backed up by the universality prescribed by the politico-juridical conception of man. In these debates, Kantian philosophers or believers in a philosophy of Human Rights, always bring out the reductive and ridiculous aspects of attempts to strike down a moral conception of man; they note the danger of defining man as supposedly concrete by virtue of class conflict, arguing that man is no less abstract, no less unreal than the universal man of Human Rights. But those who criticize the formalism of moral philosophy strike back, saying that it is urgent to renounce a conception of universal reason that shelters and suppresses all of the powers of evil; such reason ignores its own fundamental violence. This debate takes the shape of a conflict of antinomies in which each side believes it is destroying the other, while in fact, each returns in kind: in the end, the score ends up being zero, or, one-to-one.

Changing Objects

We need perhaps to change our perspective somewhat in order to understand the milieu in which defenders and adversaries of a universal concept of man are working. In 1764, prior to the development of his ethics, Kant remarked that one-half of humanity ignores relatedness to the law, that women have no sense of the sublime leading to stable principles regarding the human act, that when women act morally, it is never out of respect for the law. He added that whenever a woman is moral, it is because she finds morality attractive: this type of reasoning can only repel moral humans, even if it fascinates them. "Virtue, for a woman, is a beautiful virtue. For the masculine sex, it must be a noble virtue. A woman avoids evil not because it is unjust, but because it is unattractive, and because, for her, virtuous acts mean those which are morally beautiful. For woman, nothing comes out of duty, nothing from necessity, nothing from guilt. A woman is rebellious toward any commandment, any obligation that would annoy her. A woman acts only when it pleases her to do so; the true art here is to make pleasing to her only that which is good. It is difficult for me to believe that the beautiful sex is capable of principles."[1] What is given here is clear: if morality is empirically rare in both men and women, this apparent equivalence must not mask a radical difference. What constitutes men is the confrontation between the maxim of his actions and the Categorical Imperative running through and across all sensible interests. Would this eventual sacrificing of the pathological to serve an exigency of pure form make sense only for men? If what we have here is for us a pleasantry, it could be that this wit spells out a truth that later philosophers— including Kant—seem to have forgotten. ·

Let us return to Kant's idea—which is a masculine fantasy when faced with the feminine—that if women ignore moral obligation, it is because they only appreciate that which is beautiful, and re-read the first part of his affirmation: morality is an affair of men. Indeed, it is an interesting construction, but one founded within a structure of masculine desire. To understand it, one must bear in mind what Freud called the substitutability of the objects of sexual drives. It will be helpful to compare the different forms of this substitutability in men and in women, and then we shall be able to come back to the question, which founds the concept of universal man, of the equivalence of subjects before the law.

Clinical psychoanalysis and the experience of being in love have shown that women have a different relationship to Supreme Good and to guilt than do men; this is because, for women, the eminently variable nature of drive-objects has a different destiny within Freud's substitutability. A woman, or one who identifies with women, does not change her object of desire in the same manner as does a man, or one who identifies with men. Let us be clear about this difference: as Freud noted, the variability of drive-objects, which may change as often as one likes, applies both to men and to women. But the oneness of this general formula covers different subliminatory and drive processes in each sex. Moreover, Freud suggests that there is a multiplicity of possible functions of the drive-object and, thereby, diverse modes of substitution are possible from one object to the next:

> The object (*Objekt*) of an instinct is the thing in regard to which or through which the instinct is able to achieve its aim. It is what is most variable about an instinct and is not originally connected with it, but becomes assigned to it only in consequence of being peculiarly fitted to make satisfaction possible. The object is not necessarily something extraneous: it may

equally well be a part of the subject's own body. It may be changed any number of times in the course of the vicissitudes which the instinct undergoes during its existence; and highly important parts are played by this displacement of instinct. It may happen that the same object serves for the satisfaction of several instincts simultaneously, a phenomenon which Adler (1908) has called a "confluence" of instincts (*Triebverschränkung*). A particularly close attachment of the instinct to its object is distinguished by the term "fixation." This frequently occurs at very early periods of the development of an instinct and puts an end to its mobility through its intense opposition to detachment.[2]

This text has often been commented upon and has even been misinterpreted, for example, by Lacan when he replaced the idea that the object may change as often as one likes, by the very different idea that the object is of no importance.[3] This misinterpretation leads Lacan to a perverse model of drive satisfaction, that is, to his article "Kant avec Sade." More precisely, his reading of Freud's text leads Lacan to a new text in which his idea is that the pervert realizes best of all the drive's circuit by circling an object that is itself indifferent. It is worth noting here that the Kantian human, man of the sublime and of morality, who aligns the pathological with the constancy of principles governing acts, resembles Sade's human being in that the variability of drive-objects is interpreted by both as a matter of indifference: for Sade, it is an indifference with relation to the exclusivity of the interests of *jouissance*; for Kant, it is indifference out of respect for moral law, which declares all sensible interests nonrelevant with regard to the imperative. We may further note that the variability of the object interpreted as indifference or indifferentiation also brings to mind Don Juan who renders women indifferent, one after another, to prevent their taking the form of an Elvira or a phantom who might interrogate him on the subject of his *jouissance*.

But the theme of the variability of drive-objects according to Freud opens many other doors: the last sentence of the above quote is terribly subtle. Freud writes that the early fixation of a drive to an object blocks the mobility of the drive by a resistance to its *Lösung*. This term designates both the dissolution of the early fixation to an exclusive object, and the fulfillment of the drive through an experience of pleasure that momentarily releases drive tension. We have represented here two aspects of the same fixation: the inability to abandon certain objects, and the inability to find objects that would allow pleasure, because they are substitutes. The idea we wish to retain here is that the possibility of finding pleasure is connected to the possibility of renouncing certain objects without this separation necessarily creating an indifferentiation among the objects.

Guilt in the Feminine: A Nightmare

Let us take a psychoanalytic example: on the verge of having to give up the love of a man drifting away from her and whom she loves, and on the day before she is to meet with him, a woman has the following dream: she is standing in line with her daughter; there is a heavy atmosphere which she describes as "going to the slaughterhouse." She leaves this place for a moment to go and do some errands in a lively part of town, taking a beautiful automobile in which to go there; then, she realizes that she is no longer with her daughter and that, being doomed, she should not have left her alone and that in doing so, she is depriving herself of spending these last moments with her daughter; she then wakens, horrified by this nightmare, and has the same feeling the Jews had during the war, knowing that they were to die.

Numerous associations are made during the analytic hour: her friend had recently told her that he wanted to come and visit her daughter; also, her daughter had recently criticized her for going out too often in the evenings. The beautiful automobile reminded her of recent proposals of another man who *has* a beautiful car, as opposed to the man for whom she longs. Further, awaiting death reminds her of accusations sometimes made against the Jews for having remained passive in the face of death, and this reminds her of a sentence in which her friend described himself as passive with women, one day when he was speaking of his relationship with another woman, someone for whom he may well leave this woman, which is the cause of the anxious expectation.

While listening to this dream, one cannot say that this woman ignores guilt, as the nightmare plays out a sort of desperate attempt by her to take on a man's "fault." Guilt is actually played out doubly in this nightmare: at the deepest level, the feeling that going to a rendezvous is like going to the slaughterhouse evokes for this woman the humiliating experience of the Jews in their situation, scenes that often figure as significant dream material. There is no possibility here of subjectification; that is to say, no action is representable psychically by which a human being could become the cause of a violent act and so could feel guilty for having taken responsibility; thus one can share this responsibility with other humans who, by the very repression of this shared violence, are elevated to the universality of subjects of moral law (*Totem and Taboo*, 1913). Indeed, it is in this manner that, in masculine sexuality, guilt and the rapport of acts to moral law are constructed.

It does not work this way for this woman and subjectification follows other paths. In the context of the suffering caused by her current difficulties, the theme of impending death with the accusation of passivity being made against the Jews, is the admission of a sort of radical shame to exist; this shame may be compared to the sign of refusal to have existed, made by Sygne de Coûfontaine, a character in Claudel's *L'Otage*, a sign that Lacan wrote of more recently in his Seminar on the Transference.[4] But in this woman's nightmare, there is no refusal of life being addressed to anyone; there is only the definitive figuration of a doomed hope.

Definitive? Not exactly, for in this nightmare, there is another incidence of guilt that invents a subjective construction whose effect is to limit the brutal feeling of unhappiness: in this dream, the patient tells herself that she is guilty of neglecting her daughter in the face of death, and, in her daughter's opinion, of being too preoccupied by her own relationships with men. On the one hand, guilt here no longer refers uniquely to being; on the other hand, the allusion to errands and her daughter's reproach make way for the replacement of a man with no car by a different one who has a beautiful car. At the heart of this passive waiting for an imposed death, there appears a more negotiable guilt. The reproaches call forth something different from awaiting a death in which she would even be separated from her daughter. The substitution of a man *with* a car for one *without* a car makes way for a secondary, eroticized guilt. In this dream, as is generally the case, eroticism—or drive—circumscribes the anxiety surrounding threatened identity; we understand rather clearly how drive evolves by limiting the death instinct through repetition, which involves displacement. Eroticism transforms and sublimates the death drive, without exactly repressing it; that is, without taking recourse to the imaginary scenario of fault and of castration; this type of scenario creates humans who are defined by a correlation between the "depreciation" of suffering experienced and the universalization of guilt, as Freud says in *Totem and Taboo*.

Kant was doubtless wrong in saying that women ignore guilt, but he was not wrong in sensing that they experience guilt differently from men: by a deprivation of themselves whose only recourse is reverting to situations in which they typically expect the worst. Their guilt is massive, and is not tied to the figuration of a desire to kill (by which the distinction between oneself and the other, between love and hate, would be abolished, as is often the case in men's dreams involving guilt); women's guilt knows no peace through a construction in which the phallus could represent what must be lost to lighten the weight of a fault.

The nightmare itself gives shape to the awaited experience of a dispossession that bears on the dreamer's being; it profiles the fear of an amorous parting by making it fatal. Women have a certain capacity to live and experience situations without recourse, not even recourse to a law prohibiting something; the threat's only limit is in its aggravated representation. And so, the erotic scenario is woven into the very fabric of the suffering that unravels existence: it is the smile that allows the dreamer to emerge from her nightmare and that transforms the guilt; substituting the man who has a beautiful car for the one who is leaving is an invention that allows an exit from the nightmare at the very heart of the anxiety being figured. Substitution here does not create an equivalence between the objects of desire; it does not relegate them to the same insignificance before a law tying the subject down to ideal principles that, by their very constancy, would guarantee the indifference of the objects to be renounced. No, our dreamer invents a substitution that opposes two objects by way of the attribute "car"; this comparison allows for a hierarchy between the two levels of anxiety, and it allows a smile within the nightmare. I have called this "sublimation" rather than "repression." When repression sets in, identification with an ideal "depreciates" drive-objects; they become serialized, and may be substituted indifferently in the very context of the law that is redefining the subject. There is, no doubt, a correlation between the relegation of objects and the effect of subjectification referred to by Lacan when he says that a subject is that one who represents one signifier to another signifier. One object is worth the same as another, one signifier equals another; it is only the place they occupy that allows the subject to exist in the eclipse that joins them together. The opposition between the beautiful car and the man without a car has a different function. The beautiful car is making fun of an abolition that may not be taken here as the eclipse of the subject: when there is abolition, the subject is absent; when a subject emerges, he emerges by way of making fun of the abolition and this is not an eclipse. The beautiful car is not a sign in the sense Lacan gives to "sign" when he says that it represents something for someone;[5] nor is it exactly a signifier, for the reason given above. Rather, it is the figuration of another possible presence that, by its existence, makes the absence bearable. A man with a beautiful car in the place of a man who abandons is a remedy in the dream; it does not launch an indefinite series of objects, precisely because this symbol signifies a possible presence, and an absence that has become representable. One other object is sufficient to eroticize anxiety, it is not necessary to repeat the substitution indefinitely, and the need to change objects does not imply a depreciation of the object in general: the dream speaks of the "desertion" of which the object is capable, and by means of the playful mode of opposition, it invents a possible recourse through the beautiful car. It is enough that the operation allows an escape from the nightmare; this outlet is not "forgetting," for the material that accomplishes the escape retains its reference to the object that lacks; it is in this sense that there is neither relegation of the object, nor repression of the most fundamental anxiety, but rather a transformation. May one say that women are not subjects? Let us say rather that they become subjects differently from men; women become subjects by way of a specific modality of playfully sublimating that which, in their desires, causes suffering and guilt.

KANT, GUILT, AND ITS LOGIC

This prologue allows a different approach to understanding the ethics of the Categorical Imperative and of transgression: different, that is, by making it a destiny of the drive that has its raison d'être but that may in no case be taken as an unconditional norm for truth. Indeed, certain affirmations of Kantian ethics are presented as rationally evident, and yet they become obscure once it has been shown that other vicissitudes of guilt, besides ethics, are real and therefore possible, that is, conceivable.

Beginning in 1763, date of the *Attempt to Introduce the Concept of*

Negative Magnitudes into Philosophy, and through all later texts defining the rapport of our acts to the universality of a law that judges their maxim, Kant's concept of guilt is double: the experience of guilt is first and foremost the experience of being surprised by an imperative that founds our moral consciousness and in the face of which we always fall short. Second, the guilt makes all human beings equal before the law. In the first point, the logic of the real conflict *(realer Widerstreit)*[6] presupposes the opposition of two forces, both of which are effective: in opposition to our consciousness of being determined by law is the consciousness that our sensible interests resist the Categorical Imperative of morality. Throughout his oeuvre, Kant's formulas evolve, confirming his thoughts in this direction. In the *Groundwork of the Metaphysic of Morals* (1785) and in the *Critique of Practical Reason* (1788), he defines the autonomy of will, and respect as negative feeling; that is, a fact of reason that "destroys the presumption" of the sensible, which rejects that which it requests. This rejection is the very effect of the paradoxical presence of the categorical in sensible existence, which Kant still calls pathological. In later texts such as *Religion within the Limits of Reason Alone* (1793), the very idea of a radical but not innate evil places the propensity to evil in opposition to our prior inscription in the order of the law. An innate evil will, that is, one that would destroy law, is declared manifestly unthinkable; in other words, radical evil must be attributed to the use of will that goes against the very foundation of this will; Kant recalls that the logic of the real conflict is the logical operator of this rapport to the law, which, "for us humans," always includes the consciousness of infringement. Here we have the first view of guilt that, according to Kant, founds human beings as such: being surprised by an unconditional obligation that defines our acts and with respect to which we are always at fault.

THE RAPPORT BETWEEN SERIALIZED UNIVERSALS AND THE CATEGORICAL

But, for Kant, rapport to the law also has another side: the relegation of the pathological, or, of sensible existence—as it each time affects us in a specific manner—is the anthropological condition that transforms all intended acts and their contents, into a pretext for using the logical test of universalization of the maxim: even if, in their materiality, our acts are different and specific, the fact of their being able to be put to the test of the universalization of their maxim transforms them into mere matter for the formalism of the law; it also transforms the moral subject into a human bound to the law, irrespective of his desires. One person is equivalent to another: it is this that defines the subject of morality and of law; that is to say, it is the universality of the person that is supposedly the rational expression of being surprised by the categorical law that relegates the pathological in us. When we say that all humans are subject to the law, it no longer means that the law will ever surprise my sensible being; but rather, that whatever my actions, their only value lies in their confrontation with an imperative of universality that makes them all equivalent before the law. The universalization of the maxim of our acts as a test of their morality, produces the experience of being at fault with regard to the Categorical Imperative; this imperative stands in relative indifference to the contents of our acts with regard to the universality of which they are capable through will. So, sometimes guilt is the presence of the categorical within the conditioned; at other times it is the occasion of a redefinition of desire as will, as long as our desires are the simple occasion of defining a universal. A sensible inclination is then a case where a principle is defined, and this is quite different from the experience of being at fault with regard to a transcendent and founding agent. The categorical is the surprise of being faced with the law; universality is the formal test by which our acts acquire common measure and by which subjects become equivalent or even identical with regard to the law: "act so that the maxims of your will may be in perfect harmony with a universal system of laws." It is perfectly clear that to be at fault with regard to a founding imperative is, rationally, a distinct notion from the formal operation by which acts and subjects become equivalent by means of universalization. Yet, when we read Kant, we combine these two separate aspects of morality; we act as if they were one and the same, and we no longer question them. The "for all humans" seems to be the natural explanation of fault with regard to an absolute imperative. There is here an unexplained relation between the categorical aspect of the imperative and the serial universality of the law. But logically, the categorical aspect of the imperative has nothing to do with a serialized universality of acts and subjects of the law. Each of these ideas is clear, and they are distinct and must be distinguished.

So then, what is it that creates the illusory proof of their identity if not the fact that the common point between these two sides of morality is the depreciation of the sensible? A categorical commandment only resembles the test of the universalization of the maxim of our acts if we see them both as a systematic exclusion of the pathological: the categorical is the experience of the rupture produced in us by the brutal appearance of a commandment that founds us; the universal is the indifferentiation of cases and subjects that is produced by submitting our acts to a test of formal logic. The categorical and the universal may only become identical if they have been founded by the relegation of the pathological.

THE ETHICS OF THE UNIVERSAL: TRUTH OF A CONCEPT OR TRUTH OF A FANTASY?

In the aforementioned nightmare, a categorical imperative became apparent: a man must be given up, even if it means "going to the slaughterhouse"; but there is no universalizing factor that makes this necessary renouncement a case of something holding true for all humans. The substitution of one object for another is a way to invent, in the dream, a possibility to accept a separation that has been imposed. One might say that the imperative here is not the same as the Kantian Categorical Imperative, that it is a conditional imperative; and yet, insofar as it demands a renouncement unconditionally, the two have the same status. The difference between the moral imperative and the necessity of realizing a separation consists in the fact that the latter is in no way founded upon the transcendental: the separation presents itself as brute necessity, tied to the departure of a beloved, whose departure must be coped with at the risk of madness and hallucination of his presence; this does not correspond to the juridical aspect of the Categorical Imperative, which defines, in principle, a range of obligation superior to any and all necessities of fact; this aspect of the imperative speaks of a rapport to the law that founds our humanness in such a way, that the effect of suffering produced by the presence of the law would be merely a consequence of what Kant calls autonomy; autonomy would then be belonging to a juridical order that breaks, once and for all, with submission to the pathological. Yet, such a break made once and for all, is exactly what my patient's dream refuses. An unconditionally imposed renouncement does not give way to the idealization of a principle in whose name it is imposed. It is by retaining a trait of the first object (no car) and transferring it onto the second (the other man has a beautiful car) that the substitution avoids idealization of the principle that imposes the renouncement. The renouncement must take place without the fact of love being split from the right to autonomy, which would deny it or relegate it to the ranks of pathological love. And so, there is no serializing of objects in this dream: objects are only presented as equivalent when they are depreciated with regard to a law opposing facts with the law. In our nightmare, on the contrary, the dreamer passes from one object to another by forging an imaginary transition and a difference. She takes the men one by one, one could say, in paraphrasing Don Juan's formula; but here, the arithmetic of desire has an entirely different meaning than for the masculine hero; it is a question of going from one singularity to another while signifying a loss, but the loss is lightened through the humor of a substitution. The fact that our desires are not all-powerful, and that this surprises us as does a nightmare, is called "castration" by psychoanalysts; there is naturally no connection between this castration and a formalization of existence that would allow one to decide a priori what must be renounced for our life to remain tied to principles that would exclude disagreeable surprises.

So, Kant's remark about the amorality of women may be developed by stating that for women, when the claims of the pathological (that is, our desires) must be limited, it is a process in which no law comes to discredit the facts; in other words, there is no idealization of a principle that imposes a renouncement, even if the renouncement is necessary. Now we may ask ourselves if the rupture between fact and a law that judges it, is not in itself a construction; an interesting one indeed, in that it would allow a certain renouncement called autonomy, but one relative, in its "truth," to certain organizations of desire that need to render the objects of desire interchangeable before the renouncement of an object may take place. Then it becomes the truth of a fantasy, perpetually tied to the type of transformation of drives it allows, and not the truth of a concept. Indeed, the categorical imperative does make sense intellectually for women as for men, but it is always accompanied by the effect of a distancing it imposes on our sensible faculty of desiring. Thus, the following question arises: Does the expression of its power of obligation in terms of the universalization of its points of application depend on the fact that only in certain organizations of desire, the law is understood as imposing the relegation of the pathological to a "blow by blow," while appearing as the "once and for all" of the separation between the imperative and the empirical desires being blocked out?

If it is true, as Lacan has suggested, that there is a common ground between Kant and Sade, it is not from the point of view of this typical correlation between, on the one hand, a law that is categorical by way of relegating the sensible, once and for all, and thereby establishing the law, and on the other hand, the repetition of this experience of "blow by blow"; that is, by universally disregarding desires in oneself and in others?

Whether one reads Sade's *Philosophie dans le Boudoir*, Molière's *Don Juan*, or Kant's *Critique of Practical Reason*, it is indeed striking to notice the correlation between the indefinite serializing of the objects of desire, and the sacrificing of all of these objects for the sake of an ideal posed as absolute. This ideal varies in the three cases: for Sade, it is a libertine's pleasure whose only claim is his affirmation which justifies that everything be sacrificed to him, all of the partner's pleasure or any attachment which the subject may feel. For Don Juan, as Monique Schneider recently wrote[7] it is the celebration of unnumbered conquests in the "blow by blow" style, accompanied by a phrase diminishing *jouissance* just when a "beautiful face" orders the exile of the whole series: "As soon as a beautiful face asks it of me, if I had ten thousand, I would give them all for the present one" (act 1, scene 2). Lastly, for Kant, we already know that the "Fact of Reason," by introducing us to the order of rational will, blocks out all of our desires and relegates them to the realm of pleasures and displeasures that are incapable of any a priori determination; they therefore fade into indistinction as their only moral quality is their possibility of serving as material for a noncontradictory law in a possible, human world.

One may argue whether or not, in each of these cases, the term "sacrifice" accurately describes the position of the categorical in relation to the serialized universality of the terms it exiles. This point must be carefully studied, for it is most probably here that we may distinguish Kant's rigor, Don Juan's challenge and Sade's impassiveness. But we must note that these three solutions are argued by the same logic—that of the universal and of the categorical—that presides over the establishment of a Supreme Good. Does this mean that women, or those humans who identify with women, act without reference to the philosopher's Supreme Good, albeit, as Kant's, a pure one?

Notes

1. E. Kant, *Observation sur le sentiment du beau et du sublime* (Paris: Garnier-Flammarion, 1990), 126.

2. S. Freud, *The Standard Edition of the Complete Psychological Works of Sigmund Freud*, translated from the German under the general editorship of James Strachey, in collaboration with Anna Freud, assisted by Alix Strachey and Alan Tyson. 24 vols. (London: Hogarth, 1955–74): 14:212.

3. J. Lacan, *The Four Fundamental Concepts of Psychoanalysis*, trans. Alan Sheridan (New York: Norton Paperback, 1981), 128. On this topic see also Monique David-Ménard, *Hysteria from Freud to Lacan: Body and Language in Psychoanalysis* (Ithaca: Cornell University Press, 1989), 192–93.

4. J. Lacan, *Le Séminaire; livre VIII, Le transfert* (Paris, Seuil, 1991), 326–27.

5. J. Lacan, *The Four Fundamental Concepts*, 157.

6. M. David-Ménard, *La Folie dans la raison pure: Kant, lecteur de Swedenborg* (Paris, 1990), chaps. 1 and 5.

7. M. Schneider, *Don Juan et le procès de la séduction* (Paris: Aubier, 1994), 124–25.

15

The Economy of Respect: Kant and Respect for Women

Sarah Kofman
Translated by Nicola Fisher

Nec femina, amissa pedicitia, alia abnuerit. (When a woman has lost her modesty, she will have nothing more to refuse; Tacitus, *Annals* IV, 3). Quoted by Rousseau in *Emile* with the following commentary: "Did ever an author better understand the human heart in the two sexes than the one who said that?"

To respect women: is this simply to obey the categorical imperative which requires respect with regard to the other as moral personage? Are women solely and simply special cases, models or examples of the moral law which they present and make visible, acquiring by that same law, as all moral persons do, an unalienable dignity which puts them above all price? It is, in effect, as moral personage that man (in general) possesses dignity, that is to say an interior and absolute value which forces man to respect (moral) man in his own person and in that of others, beyond all considerations of social rank, age, or sex, and permits him to contend with all other rational creatures in terms of an original equality. Kant moreover distinguishes respect as a *comparative sentiment* and respect as a *moral sentiment*.[1] The first arises when we compare our personal value with that of another, as, he tells us, in the sentiment "which a child, by simple habit, bears toward his parents, a pupil with respect to his master, or an inferior in general toward a superior." The second implies the restriction of the esteem which we bear for ourselves by the taking into consideration the human dignity of another person. As a moral sentiment, respect is the effect of a maxim by which each is obliged to remain within limits—in his place—so as not to deprive the other of any value to which his humanity gives him the right. While as a comparative sentiment respect implies a measurable and appreciable distance between men, which can go as far as an estimation that one man is susceptible of being a means for the other who is judged superior, and of being treated as somehow a simple commodity having a certain price, as a moral sentiment respect implies not so much the absence of distance as an incommensurable distance, requiring that no man be reduced to playing the role of simple means for the ends of another, nor a fortiori be constrained into so abnegating himself as to become a slave to the ends of another.

This is why, after having distinguished these two kinds of respect, Kant so to speak lets drop comparative respect: it cannot and should not be classed among the first metaphysical principles of the doctrine of virtue "which consider only the pure principles of reason," while "the different forms of respect which should be observed with respect to the other according to the difference in qualities or contingent relations among men, that is to say age, sex, birth, strength or weakness, even social position and nobility, are grounded in part on arbitrary institutions."[2] These different contingent forms of respect should not therefore be the object of a detailed account in the *Doctrine of Virtue*. All the same, Kant does return to them in the paragraph which follows in order, paradoxically, to erase in some way the distinction introduced between the comparative and the moral sentiment of respect, for this time both kinds are described as simple applications of the principle of virtue to particular cases of experience, implying particular rules "modified according to the difference between subjects."[3] They would be only "a schematism for setting forth pure principles of duty." These special cases—which seem to restore respect as comparative sentiment—"would not represent new kinds of ethical obligation (for there is only one, that of virtue in general) but only forms of application, consequently they should not be developed as sections of the Ethics and members of the division of a system (which must follow a priori from a concept of reason) but merely added on to it." It is only in the complete exposition of the system that these "special cases" should be examined in more detail.

Are these special cases of experience really a "schematization of the pure principle of duty"? Can they, as such, all be put on the same level? The respect of one sex for the other, in particular that of men for women: is this not a more special case, supposing it to be a simple "case of application" which must, on this basis, be relegated to some addendum or appendix and, in the name of moral rigorism or critical rigor, be reserved for the exposition of the complete system? What if this "special case" were not an example among others, but a model, a very prefiguration of moral respect? Would it not then come to stain by its empirical impurity the purity, if not the principle, then at least of the motivation of the moral, the purity, that is, of respect for the moral law? And if, in the name of the law which commands respect, for example, that of one sex for the other, it were a question of something quite other than a moral relation of one man (in general) to another man (in general), if the question were, in the name of respect, that of holding women in respect—at a certain respectful distance—would morality not serve as a cover for an operation of a completely different order, an operation of mastery?

Apotrope, umbrella, would respect not always permit the realization of a certain economy, the gaining of *respite* (one knows that *respect* and *respite* are both derived from *respicere*)?

THE PRELIMINARY RESPECT OR THE PREMIUM OF NONSEDUCTION

If one refers to the *Anthropology*—addendum or appendix to the *Doctrine of Virtue?*—the description which Kant therein gives of the relation between the sexes is not one of moral relations wherein each respects the other as representative of the sublimity of the moral law; it is rather one of warlike relations in which each struggles for domination, this last being defined as the using of another for a private end, the motivation of which is the fear of being dominated.[4] In this war it is the so-called weaker sex which has the upper hand—just because of its weakness; men are thereby disarmed, constrained to respect as well as to a whole series of compensations: the right of women to respect seems from the beginning to be a right acquired by their weakness, a measure of protection granted to the weak by the strong.

As always there arises a downright reversal: the weakness of women and all the traits which characterize them[5] are so many levers for controlling men and using them at their will. If women cannot dominate by force, they dominate by indirect means, by the obliqueness of ruse, the art women have to use men for their own ends. Thanks to their charms, to the love they inspire, women enchain their victims and master them through their particular abilities. Two traits, says Kant, quoting Pope (but he could as well have quoted Rousseau, and perhaps he quoted the one to hide what he owed to the other, to the author of *Emile*, which he knew well), characterize the feminine sex: the tendency to dominate and the tendency to please, mainly in public (these are such that the second trait can be assimilated to the first: in trying to please, a woman wishes always to get the upper hand over an eventual rival). The tendency of women is to dominate, but at the same time that of men is to be dominated. This double tendency explains in the last analysis the particular nature of the respect the masculine sex has for the feminine: it cannot be simply reduced to a right accorded to the weak by the strong: it is the will to dominate that drives the arrogance of women, the desire to avert all importunity on the part of man: women require, *in the very name of their sex*, consideration, even if they don't deserve it; that is what respect is. To the woman this permits the eventual economy of virtue and to the two sexes a sexual economy, a certain respite: the woman refuses, the man demands. When woman concedes, it is a favor, and if an inversion were to occur, that would degrade, even in masculine eyes, the value of her sex. The woman must appear cold, not respond too easily to the demand, under pain of her own dishonor. In brief, that which goes to make up the value of her sex and renders woman as such respectable is, for an entire tradition, her reserve, her modesty: "woman must be sought after, so it is required by the attitude of reserve necessary to her sex." Because of her modesty, woman protects herself and protects man; she avoids being demeaned, being for the other sex solely a means of satisfaction. At the same time that she satisfied her will to dominate in educating man to chastity, she educates him to morality; by preventing him from giving himself up to sensuality, "this vice which results from the love of the flesh,"[6] by saving him from the risk of shamelessness, that repugnant vice whereby man makes "use of his person in such a way as to demean himself below the level of the beasts," for he thus gives way entirely to animal inclination, reduces himself to a simple orgiastic object *(objet de jouissance)*, woman prevents man from becoming an object of disgust to himself: from changing himself into a thing against nature, no longer deserving of respect; in brief, from defiling himself and, in his own person, from defiling the whole of humanity.

This transgression of morality which violates duty to oneself at the highest level brings forth such repugnance, says Kant, that it is even held as immoral to call such a vice by its name, as if to name it were to expose it to every eye in all its horror, as if it were openly to display the union of the sexes or, at least, the sex of the woman, laid bare, without discretion, of all disguise, that which can never be looked upon as such without provoking disgust. That which cannot therefore be named without disguise, clearly without risk of defilement.

> Everything happens as if in a general way man feels the shame of being capable of making use of his person in such a way as to demean himself below the level of the beasts, to such an extent that the carnal union of the two sexes in marriage, which is permitted (it is in itself obviously purely animal), demands and requires great care in order to disguise it whenever it must be discussed in civilized society.[7]

Defilement, disgust: a simple transgression of the duties of man to himself, if it does justify a moral condemnation, does not justify such violence in the terms in which it is made. Kant himself remarks that no other transgression of duty to oneself, suicide for example, provokes the same repugnance. Is this not to acknowledge that this vice which is born of the union between the sexes, sensuality or shamelessness, does not only give rise to disgust and moral defilement? If feminine modesty renders woman respectable and prevents man from becoming disgusted with himself, permits him to remain a moral person, it also prevents man from having a completely different disgust: disgust for the sex of woman, to which the full and entire satisfaction of man's inclinations inevitably leads him: feminine modesty permits man to remain man, to remain virile, without succumbing to instability.[8]

The ardor which the sexual drive arouses must therefore be inhibited, curbed by the restrictive conditions which are imposed by both practical

reason (the respect for oneself and others as moral persons) and pragmatic reason (calculation of interest within the sexual economy which
modesty imposes, the respect of women: let man hold them in respect,
at a distance, let woman hold her sex in safekeeping from the importuni-
ties of man and dominate him thereby).[9]

These restrictive conditions are found best realized in marriage, toward
which one should not be skeptical, says Kant, since it is through
marriage that "woman becomes free" although also "man loses his liberty
therein."[10] This is perhaps why in The *Conflict of Faculties* celibacy
figures among the fundamental principles of dietetics for whoever desires
to assure himself of a long and happy life, since "it would be difficult to
prove that those who have reached a great age have been married for
most of the time."

In this economy of respect, there are therefore no benefits without
loss, and these are not of the same nature for the two sexes.

On the one hand, thanks to respect, in spite of her weakness, like a
queen, woman dominates. But at the same time she, who represents
feeling, does not govern. It is man, the minister, who governs through
his understanding:

> The behavior of the husband must show that the well-being of
> his wife is closest to his heart. But he shall be like a minister to
> a king who, mindful of his pleasure, organizes a fête. He begins
> by explaining to him all the deference he owes him, but that, for
> example, there is no money in the coffers, in such a fashion that
> this all-powerful master does what he wants on condition that his
> minister suggests his will.[11]

On the other hand, all that characterizes the feminine sex, its
weakness as well as its mastery—more or less illusory—are, for Kant, to
be situated in a more general economy of nature, and to be thought in
terms of its design: through the device of the war between the sexes for
domination, and hence through the device of what Kant calls human
folly, nature directs the education of man toward morality. Such is the
final goal. From this point of view, respect for women would be in a way
a preliminary respect, a premium on nonseduction being required to lead
to the final respect, moral respect, which it prefigures and recommends.
Respect for women, in this sense, would be the law of laws, a law sacred
among all, the condition sine qua non of the existence of the moral law,

or at least of apprenticeship for submission to it. If woman ought not to provoke disgust, it is because she "constitutes herself as an object of taste for everyone," because she educates in terms of taste, decorum, fine language, disguise, disguise of sex and of language; moral apprenticeship passes through that of decency, of which the corollary is the passage from vulgar parlance to the delicacy of expression which throws a veil over everything "repugnant," the object of disgust and defilement. Woman's veil—the prohibition of her sex—leads, could one say, to the veil or mask of words, to substitution in language, to the opening of the infinite chain of supplements, to a supplementary erasing all "correct" meaning—that is, improper, always already defiled.

In the *Conjectures on the Origins of Human History* Kant insists on the importance of decency (of which the figleaf in the Bible is a symbol) as fundamental to the formation of man as a moral creature, decisive in giving a new orientation to the form of thought, more important "than the whole interminable series of subsequent cultural developments." Decency, defined as the "propensity to provoke in another consideration toward ourselves by means of our good manners" (masking what could incite contempt), the real foundation of all true sociability, is also the first *sign* of the morality of man, of his capacity to respect the other: if "preliminary" respect is a "humble beginning," it nevertheless marks a new era since it prefigures moral respect; it is the index, not of arbitrary conventions, but of the rational nature of man, just as the *refusal* of woman which screens the sexual object from the senses is a "cunning artifice" educating man to reason and at the same time showing it: "the fact of rendering a feeling stronger and more lasting by withdrawing its object from the senses denotes already a certain conscious supremacy of reason over feeling." By refusal, modesty, decency, man is led from purely animal excitations toward ideal excitations, and little by little from animal desire to love and morality. And this passage, just as later in Bachofen and Freud, is also described as separation from the mother, from the maternal breast of nature which man, through his imagination, represents to himself by hindsight as paradise.[12]

Man's education toward reason and morality leads therefore to an emancipation with respect to mother nature, to women, and to feelings, and yet all education necessarily passes through them. Man cannot do without such a passage. Nature's ruse is to use women and their characteristics to arrive at an end to their reign in favor of that of man, all while leaving them the illusion of continuing to rule.[13]

It is, in effect, nature which, fearing for the survival of the species, is supposed to have implanted in woman's nature fear for bodily harm and timidity before physical dangers, weakness which authorizes her to ask men for protection. Moreover, wishing to inspire in men the refined sentiments which bring about culture, those of sociability and decorum, nature would have given the feminine sex ease of speech and expression, the claim to receive from men a welcome of gentleness and politeness, thus according her mastery over men for moral ends. Men would find themselves "through their own generosity enchained without being aware of it by a child and led in this way, if not to morality, at least to that which clothes it, to that decorum of manners which serves it as a preliminary and an introduction."[14] The order of nature, by the tendency of human folly—by the tendency of women—prefigures in this way the moral order, respect for women announces and prepares for respect for man.

If the final goal of nature is moral, if her concern is the safekeeping of Humanity, if in this respect she seems not to privilege either of the two sexes, it remains nonetheless that in this general economy woman seems certainly the loser, because she does not hide, in the last analysis, her wish to be a man (to be able to give more room and more freedom to the play of her feelings), while in return no man wishes to be a woman.[15] This rejection of femininity by both sexes leaves room for the suspicion that the benefits of this whole "natural" enterprise, this economy of respect, are essentially masculine, that behind the goals of nature lie concealed the goals of man (Vir). Behind the proclaimed respect for women, it is indeed very much a question of holding women in awe, and this because they represent a double risk: (1) that of letting oneself fall into sensuality, that is to say the abuse of the sexual faculty, and therefore an excessive spending which could lead to death—whence celibacy as the fundamental dietetic rule; (2) that of allowing the triumph of feeling over reason in oneself, the triumph of the "feminine" over the "masculine": risk of emasculation through loss of reason, risk of forgetting the sublimity of human nature, and that of being reduced to a natural object, to animal nature, and becoming an object of horror and disgust: horribile visu.

The risk of femininity is thus, on the one hand, the risk of death, and, on the other hand, that risk, which respect protects one against, of no longer remaining within human limits, of losing dignity as man, of losing virility, by returning in a regressive way to the breast of mother nature.

THE DOUBLE FASCINATION

And yet this return to the maternal breast is nostalgically called return to paradise by man.[16] That is to say, the violent terms which Kant makes use of, those of defilement, repugnance, horror, and disgust, serve perhaps as a countercathexis to a violent desire to return to the maternal breast. These terms, in their violence, would serve to camouflage this desire just as they would be its sign. Repugnance, horror, would be the simple reverse of an unconscious fascination for women (for the mother), which in Kantian language, refined and civilized, expresses itself in the most modest expression of inclination for feeling, for self-love, inclination for evil. This last, inherent in a finite and fallen creature, is defined by the spontaneous preference for feeling at the expense of the law, by the impossibility of having a holy will. Respect as moral sentiment is the other side of our unworthiness, which we disregard as such, fascinated as we are by our feelings. Thus respect is a negative sentiment. In opposition to love, which attracts, it implies a repulsion, the distancing of that which fascinates; or better it implies quasi-simultaneous attraction and repulsion: that the object which fascinates and seduces is found concealed and at the same time discovered. The *Critique of Judgment*, in bringing up the sentiment of the sublime which always implies respect, describes it as an emotion comparable to a shock in which repulsion and attraction rapidly alternate, both having as origin the same object.[17] Respect—*respectus*—is a new way of looking, *looking behind*. It follows the fascinated look, equivalent to contact at a distance, bound to an impossibility of not seeing, to an immediate proximity which, as Blanchot says,[18] "absorbs you in an immobile movement and a depth without profundity," leaves you disarmed, losing mind or senses as well as the possibility of making sense; which would put you in jeopardy of being crushed, confounded if you did not oppose this look precisely with that other look, respect. The latter gives you respite, permits you to hold yourself apart, keep your distance, to introduce a decision that separates in order to avoid contact and confusion, returns to you your *mobility*— this is respect also as *motivation (mobile)*. Respect distances the horror which is provoked by that depth without profundity, it stops the petrifying and immobilizing movement: it has an apotropaic function.

Respect for the moral law still has traces of the original fascination. It is described as frightening,[19] and the moral law itself seems to be another "object of fascination" which is substituted for the fascination exercised by feeling—by the maternal breast?—by that which in Kant always returns to the "feminine," to a feminine face, even if this is precisely not a face, but rather a faceless depth, without a gaze, perhaps only a voice. The moral law, by its power and majesty, at first disregarded because of the original fascination, because of the "inclination for evil," counterbalances the power and majesty of that feminine "face." This also, in its sublimity and transcendence, is for the imagination "like an abyss in which it dreads its own loss."[20] In the *Critique of Practical Reason*, Kant describes the law as a holy and "solemn majesty" before which men recoil in their unworthiness. They do everything to get rid of this "frightening respect." They try to hold in respect the respect which so severely shows them their own unworthiness, from fear of feeling themselves disarmed, confounded, crushed, humiliated. Such is their presumption. But because they have only an *inclination* for evil, a fragile will which is neither perverse nor diabolical, respect can become a practical sentiment, the moral law a motivation, to mobilize and no longer immobilize them. In this case a veritable conversion is brought about: men can no longer be satiated in the contemplation of the majesty of the law, which crushes them only inasmuch as they are presumptuous but which raises them all the more as they recognize its holiness and sublimity and, correlatively, the fragility of their own nature; but also their own sublimity as rational beings.

Everything takes place then as if the respect for women, preliminary to moral respect, and the inhibitory rules which it introduces in order to curb and defer desires, has as corollary a cleavage of the original fascinating figure whence results a double image: that of sensuality, charged with all evil, a repugnant and disgusting image; that of the holy law, sublime, inheritor of the power and majesty of the original fascinating figure.

SUBLIME AND SUBLIMATION

Should one, and could one say, taking it from there, that the figure of the law and of its sublimity is a "grandiose sublimation" of the figure of the mother? Freud could no doubt effect such a reading, genetic or genealogical, of the moral law, or rather of its figuration, Freud who shows how the respect for the mother which is ordained by the prohibition of incest is at the origin of the cleavage of the maternal figure into a double figure, that of the prostitute, demeaned sexual object with which man can satisfy his sensuality, the perverse constituents of sexuality—to yield oneself to sensual pleasure and to defile oneself—and that figure, sublime and eminently respectable, raised on a pedestal of holiness, the immaculate and untouchable Virgin.[21]

Such a question seems legitimate to the extent to which the moral law implies a preliminary apprenticeship, passing through respect for women; and if we admit that the first woman all men should respect is "the mother," if the condition of the possibility of moral respect is the prohibition of incest, one may ask oneself if respect does not still keep something of its empirical origin even if, sentiment a priori, it could not, for Kant, be so derived.

Kant himself insists on the fact that the word "respect" (Achtung) given to the specific sentiment which determines the a priori relation of man to the moral law envisaged as motivator is certainly the word which fits, that it corresponds to the common experience of respect and the usage of language which is criticized by Schopenhauer, according to whom the Kantian conception of respect essentially depends on a "Judaic" relation of submission to the law. The word respect would have as its object the dissimulation of the theological origin of Kantian morality and the "Jewish stench" which issues from it.[22] Common experience of respect of which the representation of the law under the figure of a "solemn majesty," fascinating and frightening, is the witness. More generally the personification of the law, or even its *aestheticization* sends one back, incontestably, to the common experience of respect, and notably to "preliminary" respect for women, for the mother.

Now Kant considers that aestheticization, if it is an aesthetic artifice (Maschinerie), could still have a moral sense, and that the aesthetics of morals, without being part of the metaphysics of morals, is a subjective representation of it.[23] But again it must be understood just what he means by the aestheticization of the law; it is not to be confounded with a delimitation and a precise determination which would serve as a measure; the law, because it is sublime, is without common measure, "absolutely great under all relations," beyond all comparison, and it could not have an appropriate measure outside of itself because by comparison with it everything else is small.[24] The personification of the law in a figure must precisely figure its incommensurability, its unfigurability, in the sense in which no determinate figure could be adequate to it; that is to say that the figure of the law could not be reduced to the figure of the mother, unless this itself were to figure unfigurability, that is to say sublimity. There is nothing to figure "aesthetically" but the sublime or the unfigurable. In the *Critique of Judgment*, sect. 49, Kant defines the aesthetic idea as a "representation of the imagination which gives much to be thought, without, however, any determinate thought, that is to say any concept being adequate to it; no language could completely express it nor render it intelligible." The aesthetic idea suggests with respect to a concept many inexpressible things of which the sentiment animates the faculties of knowledge, inspiring a soul to the letter of language. This is why the passage from the book of Jewish law[25] which forbids the representation of God would be the most sublime of all, because it forbids the representation of the infinite divinity in any sensible or finite form, which could come to limit and delimit it, and leaves room for the infinite movement of the imagination, indeed to enthusiasm, dangerous only when it is abused. The same applies to the representation of the moral law. It must be forbidden. To believe that, deprived of all that recommends it to the senses, it would find nothing more than a cold lifeless approbation, as if by itself it was incapable of impulsive force or emotion, is to be needlessly concerned. On the contrary: when the senses no longer see anything before them and when only the idea of morality remains, it would rather be "necessary to moderate the transports of an imagination without limits in order not to let it swell into enthusiasm than to call in the help . . . of images or some puerile appearance" which would come to arbitrarily impose limits on the power of extension of the faculties of the soul. Kant said this in "On a Recently Assumed Aristocratic Tone in Philosophy"; it is the empirical representation of the law which castrates and paralyzes reason, emasculates it by taking away its (virile) power of impulsive force. This from the subjective point of view is called respect. Respect prevents the emasculation of reason by setting in motion the transcendental imagination. As motive force it is the equivalent of a schema, because it permits the passage from simple knowledge of the law to its effectuation, the making of the law in general into a singular maxim—in short, that one should be truly mobilized by the law thanks to the setting in motion of the transcendental imagination. More than an a priori sentiment, respect, in this sense, would be an aesthetic idea.

In a footnote to paragraph 49 of the *Critique of Judgment*, Kant writes,

"Perhaps no one has ever said anything more sublime or expressed a thought in a more sublime manner than in that inscription on the temple of Isis (mother nature): I am all that which is, has been and will be, and no mortal has ever lifted my veil."

This inscription, reproduced in a vignette of Segner, was destined, says Kant, to fill with sacred trembling and solemn trepidation him who would begin the study of physics, that is to say introduce himself into the temple of mother nature. Rather than the content it is the form of the expression which is sublime, because it sets the imagination in motion infinitely, promises the discovery of infinitely many mysteries without revealing any, presents the study of physics as an infinite task, interminable because always already prohibited. It is impossible to completely dis-cover mother nature, she is inexhaustible, impenetrable, Behind one veil, there will always be another veil.

Kant therefore forbids the (empirical) representation but not the *aestheticization* of the moral law which, by the infinite movement of the imagination which it provokes, is adequate to the sublimity of the law.

All the same "On a Recently Assumed Aristocratic Tone in Philosophy"[26] seems to contradict these analyses from the *Critique of Judgment*: there Kant sets himself against the aestheticization of the moral law, against, to be precise, its personification in the form of the veiled goddess Isis. This time he puts the accent on the risks and abuses of such an aestheticization. He demands, as he takes on those he calls mystagogues, that the law should not be personified as a beautiful and sensible form, so as to prevent men from being seduced by it, seduced by its voice as if by the pathological voice of a siren, on pain of becoming deaf to the voice of the law of reason. One must avoid the fascination of a sensible and finite voice in order to hear what must be substituted for it, "a ringing voice" which demands resistance to passion, to feeling, a sublime voice which promises nothing in return. But to speak of the voice of the law is to continue to personify it, appealing to a sensible metaphor at the very moment when what is demanded is a turning away from fascination exercised by the senses, and the exclusion of all empirical representation as unacceptable and pathological. There would be therefore a good and a bad personification: one which arrests and paralyzes, another which mobilizes. The inscription on the temple of Isis, by the infinite character of what it evokes, by its grandeur, "I am all that which is, has been and will be," makes Isis herself pronounce the prohibition of her finite representation; it is sublime because it prevents anyone from lifting the veil of Isis, that is to say from giving her an exact and determinate figure. If one fully understands the inscription it becomes permissible to personify the moral law in the figure of Isis because it would be that of the unfigurable. If in "On a Recently Assumed Aristocratic Tone" Kant nevertheless refuses such a personification, it is because a veiled Isis might give mortals a desire to raise this veil, and to master what is not to be mastered, "like those mighty men who claim to have seized this goddess by the train of her veils and thereby made themselves masters." In other words, such a figuration may always run the risk of *fixing* the figure of Isis, into that, for example, of the goddess who murdered Osiris, who recovered every morsel of him except the penis, into that of a phallic castrating mother, taking an analogy for reality, confounding a sensible representation which gives life to an idea with that same idea. And thus losing oneself "in an exalted and mystic vision" in straying from the bounds of the principles of pure reason.

In order to avoid these risks of mastery Kant requires, and this is the minimal condition of a good personification, that an aestheticization be moral and not pathological; in other words, that the personification should come after the idea of the moral law and not before it: "The aesthetic state (affection of internal sense) is either a pathological sentiment or a moral sentiment. The first is the sentiment which precedes the representation of the law; the second can only be its consequence."[27]

> The veiled goddess before whom one way or another we kneel, that is the moral law in us in its invulnerable majesty. Certainly we perceive its voice and even understand very well its commandments, but in listening we doubt whether it comes from man and if it originates in the all-powerfulness of his own reason or if it emanates from some other being whose nature is unknown to him and which speaks to him through his own reason. In the end we would do better perhaps to dispense entirely with this inquiry, since it is simply speculative, and what it is incumbent upon us to do remains the same, whether one founds it on the one or the other principle. The only difference is that the didactic method of bringing the moral law in us under distinct concepts according to a logical method, is alone *properly philosophical*, while the method which consists in personifying that law and making of the reason which commands morally a veiled Isis (as long as we

do not attribute to it other properties than those which the first method discovers) in an *aesthetic* manner of representing [*Vorstellungsart*] exactly the same object, a manner in which it is certainly permitted to trust provided one has already started by reducing the principles to their pure state, to give life to this idea by means of a sensible representation [*Darstellung*], although this is only by analogy, not however without always running some risk of giving in an exalted vision that which is the death of all philosophy.[28]

Kant would not thus admit the moral law to be a grandiose sublimation of the figure of the mother. To believe this is to confound that which comes after which that which comes before, personification and a priori moral principles.

All the same, if the moral law is not derived from experience, does not find its principles there, apprenticeship to morality and respect certainly begin there. Because there is a childhood of the individual and a childhood of peoples, moral respect certainly "begins" with respect for women, for mothers, a necessary "preliminary" for reaching "terminal" moral respect, and education to morality grows from that of religious myths; that is to say, from the personification of the moral law. Chronologically, the "personification" always comes first, before the knowledge of a priori moral principles, and thus indeed risks the contamination of all subsequent "representation" of the moral law. This contamination is present in Kant's own work, in spite of the rigor of the critical enterprise whose goal is precisely to purify the law of all empirical and pathological contamination, and this in order to avoid the paralysis and castration of reason, its emasculation: the metaphors are well and truly Kant's own. The word for "respect," if it is truly the one that fits this double sentiment which humiliates me at the same time that it elevates me, is like a "trace" of that first relation between an infant and that solemn and frightening majesty his mother is to him, the phallic mother figured by Isis, personification of the law.

That the figure of Isis should have been chosen as an analogical representation of the law permits inversely a better comprehension of what it is to respect women: to respect them is to hold them in awe at a distance, in order not to be tempted to lift their veil or master them, an act culpable because of the prohibition of incest, but above all dangerous and doubly dangerous. The lifting of the veil would risk confounding man, crushing him, paralyzing him, *and* depriving woman, the mother, of all her phallic dignity, emasculating her. To put women/mothers on high, to respect them, is to avoid seeing that they have no penis, "that they have nothing to hide."[29] The economy realized by respect is that of the agony of castration, communicated with a gesture of fetishism.

Likewise, to unmask the law would perhaps be to become aware that its authority does not emanate purely and simply from its a priori character, that the a priori is always already contaminated by the a posteriori, the masculine by the feminine, that there is no moral purity any more than there is a *phallic stage*—a stage which would only be masculine and not yet feminine—phantasm of all children, dream of all philosophy.

Respect—for women as for the moral law—is therefore to be seen in connection with that panic reaction which Freud speaks of in *Fetishism*, analogous to that which takes hold when throne and altar are in danger. Respect is the economy of this panic; bound to the anguish of castration, it avoids the death of the human species—and that of philosophy which has always identified the logos with the phallus.

This economy of death requires therefore the rejection in oneself and beyond oneself of femininity, from fear of being in one way or another contaminated by it and perishing from it. Respect for women is always the glorious, moral obverse of the "misogyny" of men.

But this distancing of women does not happen without loss: that of sensual pleasure; and with it, that which Freud calls the necessary unhappiness of the sexual life of man who, not familiarized with the representation of incest with the mother or the sister, cannot fully satisfy his sexual desires, notably in their perverse constituents. Except by going to find "the" whore, sexual object demeaned enough not to evoke the mother: whore who would not be a moral person worthy of respect, above all value and price, but who belongs in the mercantile circuit of exchange, is not to be respected but appraised: in brief, a simple means for the ends of man. In this case, the respect men have for their wives in marriage, if it is a necessary preliminary to their morality, is also that of their immorality toward other women not worthy of the name of Mankind.

Yet the Kantian morality denies sensual pleasure as well, be this at the price of neurosis[30] and misery, except perhaps for those capable of procuring themselves substitute satisfactions by the route of sublimation. This was no doubt the case with Kant who, in spite of the theoretical importance accorded to marriage, managed to remain celibate. And died at a great age.[31]

Notes

1. Immanuel Kant, *The Metaphysical Principles of Virtue* (Indianapolis: Bobbs-Merrill, 1964), pt. 2, sect. 25.
2. Ibid., sect. 44.
3. Ibid., sect. 45.
4. See *The Anthropology* ("The Mania of Domination").
5. Ibid. ("The Character of Sex").
6. Kant, *Metaphysical Principles of Virtue*, pt. 1, sect. 7 ("On Self-Defilement by Sensual Pleasure").
7. Ibid.
8. See *Conjectures on the Origin of Human History*: "Man found . . . that sexual excitation, which in animals is founded on a passing and for the most part periodic impulse, was susceptible in himself of being prolonged or even increased by the effects of the imagination which makes its action felt in a greater measure no doubt, but also in a manner more lasting and uniform, as the object of the excitation is removed from the senses; which avoids the satiety that the satisfaction of a purely animal desire would bring." See also *The Anthropology* ("Pragmatic Consequences").
9. See also *The Metaphysical Principles of Virtue*, sect. 46, where tenderness and virtue are submitted to principles and fixed rules, which prevent too great a familiarity and give as limits to reciprocal love the requirements of respect on pain of being constantly menaced by such interruption as that which takes place among men without education. "When a woman shows her love too forcefully, does she not lose by doing so something of the respect of the other, and respect once corrupted is irremediably lost internally, even if the exterior marks which belong to it (the ceremonial) resume their time-honored way?"
10. *The Anthropology* ("Pragmatic Consequences").
11. Ibid.
12. "Progress is . . . bound up with the emancipation which exiled man from nature's maternal bosom. . . . In the future the difficulties of life will wrest from him more than once the wish for a paradise, his imaginary creation, where he would be able, in an undisturbed indolence and perpetual peace, to pass his existence in dreaming and frolic. Yet between man and the imaginary abode of delights stands inexorable reason which irresistibly impels him to develop his faculties and does not permit his return to the state of natural simplicity whence it brought him. . . . This departure of man from paradise which reason represents as the first abode of the species was only the transition of a purely animal creature from natural simplicity to humanity, from the leading strings of instinct to the government of reason, in a word, from the guardianship of nature to the state of freedom."
13. Sarah Kofman, "Ça Cloche," in *Les Fins de l'homme* (Paris: Galilée, 1981).
14. *The Anthropology*.
15. Ibid. ("Extended Remarks").
16. See note 12.
17. Cf. sect. 27.
18. Cf. Maurice Blanchot, *L'Espace littéraire* (Paris: Gallimard, 1968), 25.
19. Cf. *Critique of Practical Reason*.
20. *Critique of Judgment*, sect. 27.

21. See "On the Most General Forms of Humiliation in Love Life," in *La Vie sexuelle*.

22. "The word *respect* is found where one would expect the word *submission*. Thus in the note (p. 16 R. 20) one reads: '*Respect* simply signifies the subordination of my will in deference to a law. The direct determination produced by the law, accompanied by conscience, is called *respect*.' In what language? What is described to us there is called submission in good German. Yet the word respect would not have been so unfittingly used in the place of the word submission without some reason, there is some intention behind it, and this intention is evidently the following: it is to conceal the origin of the imperative form and the notion of duty, and how they are born from theological morals" *(Foundations of the Metaphysics of Morals)*.

23. See *Metaphysical Principles of Virtue*.

24. See *Critique of Judgment*, sect. 25.

25. Cf. the long *General Remark Concerning the Explanation of Reflective Aesthetic Judgments*.

26. On this text, see the analysis of Jacques Derrida in *Les Fins de l'homme*.

27. *Metaphysical Principles of Virtue*, introduction.

28. *On a Recently Assumed Aristocratic Tone in Philosophy*.

29. See Freud, for example, *New Introductory Lectures*, on feminine sexuality. Also Sarah Kofman, *L'Enigme de la femme* (Paris: Galilée, 1980).

30. See Ferenczi, *Transfer and Introjection*: "I have been able to demonstrate that many cases of impotence of a psychic origin were conditioned by a fearful respect toward women, corresponding to the resistance sometimes opposed to the incestuous object choice (mother or sister) then to an extension of this mode of defence to all women. The passionate pleasure which a certain painter exhibited in the contemplation of things and his consequent choice of career, must have compensated him for all the usual prohibitions of childhood." This text is quoted by Michael Thevoz in *L'Académisme et ses fantasmes* (Paris: Minuit, 1980). The academic painter Gleyhe is a privileged example of those men for whom the consecration of woman, her placement at a respectful distance, her petrifying idealization, is the reversal of their misogyny.

31. This text was given in a first version in the seminar of Jacques Derrida at the E.N.S. rue d'Ulm concerning respect in the works of Kant. It is an extract from a longer work, *Le Respect des femmes* (Paris: Galilée, 1982).

16

Rethinking Kant from the Perspective of Ecofeminism

Holly L. Wilson

Ecofeminism makes the nature-woman connection central to its critique of patriarchy.[1] In patriarchal thought women are identified with nature and thus the fate of nature becomes relevant to how women fare in patriarchal society. When our view of nature and human nature becomes the central question of feminism, rather than gender alone, we achieve a different standpoint from which to theorize patriarchy and from which we can suggest a solution to overcoming patriarchy. Ecofeminists require a new feminist theory in order to make nature a feminist issue. Most ecofeminists articulate the content of this position as a critique of normative dualism (Karen J. Warren, Vandana Shiva, Val Plumwood, Ynestra King, among others).[2] Karen J. Warren calls this new theoretical position transformative feminism and she defines to a great extent, though not completely, what must belong to transformative feminism.[3] For Warren, ecofeminism is a critique of normative dualisms, that sanction domination by privileging one binary term over the opposing one, specifically, culture over nature. Other ecofeminists, like Vandana Shiva, Maria Mies, and Stephanie Lahar, argue that ecofeminism is a theory that is intimately connected to practice. This is not inconsistent with Warren's position, although she has not put it in this way. I take the position that ecofeminism has three basic suppositions: (1) there is a connection between women and nature; (2) transformational feminism is the theoretical position of ecofeminism;[4] (3) transformational feminism is a critique of normative dualisms. From this perspective different feminist issues emerge and hence also the possibility of reevaluating Kant from this perspective.

In "Feminism and Ecology: Making Connections," Karen J. Warren argues that the standard versions of feminism do not make the connection between nature and women an issue; hence none of them can give us the theoretical position that ecofeminism needs. She suggests that we develop a transformative feminism that would include the important insights of the leading versions of feminism (such as the radical feminist assertion of the social construction of gender), while making room for the ecological perspective as well.[5] When we make nature a feminist issue, then the kind of questions we ask when we view Kant from a feminist perspective will be different. An ecofeminist will want to know how Kant relates women to nature, what his theory of nature and human nature is, and if Kant is a normative dualist.

These are not the kinds of issues that the standard versions of feminism have been addressing; as a result the current criticism of Kant may not be justified. Liberal feminism criticizes Kant for not having advocated women's rights;[6] Marxist feminism rejects any account of the human being that is merely rational;[7] radical feminism, in its different forms, is critical of Kant for associating women with reproduction;[8] postmodern feminism rejects the enlightenment subject-object dichotomy furthered by Kant;[9] and socialist feminism criticizes Kant for isolating the rational subject from community and nature.[10] The questions that ecofeminism poses, on the other hand, open us to positions in Kant that may represent aspects of Western tradition that can be appropriated by feminism for transformational purposes. His views on nature and human nature may be compatible with ecofeminist claims about how we must view nature and human nature if we are to take both women and ecosystems seriously.

Kant did not, however, address the issue of environmental ethics as we know it. Nor did Kant ever, to my knowledge, speak of the domination of nature, although he did speak often of the human tendency to dominate one another, and he considered it appropriate that we view nature in such a way that we may also use nature to further a purpose within ourselves, although that purpose cannot be happiness, but only culture.[11] Ecofeminism is concerned about the domination of nature and women, but it is not individual domination or use of nature, but collective domination, that is at issue. So the question is, How is it possible to dominate nature?

Steven Vogel has recently posed such a question, and has concluded that "we cannot violate nature, because we are natural beings";[12] he appeals to Kant's concepts of enlightenment and autonomy to embolden our scientific efforts toward intervention, change, and use of nature.[13] From a feminist perspective, however, the fallacy of this point of view is obvious: if we cannot violate nature because we are natural, then men cannot violate women, because men are also natural. Vogel sets up a normative dualism between human beings as active interveners and nature as passive and inert ("nature has no interest in preventing us" or "nature doesn't care") and then justifies any kind of intervention or change so long as it furthers our "autonomous reason" and our "enlightenment." When such a view of nature is extended to women, then it justifies all kinds of violations, sexual harassment, rape, pornography, and so forth, because "she has no interest in preventing us" and "she doesn't care." It is little wonder that radical feminists have argued so vehemently against Kant. However, we must see that Kant is being used to justify a position without regard to what he really said or meant. For example, Vogel understands autonomy to be something that can be cultivated. For Kant, however, autonomy is not at all something natural and cannot be cultivated. Autonomy is freedom from natural law, and also freedom to legislate the moral law. Michael Zimmerman captures Kant's intention better in his response to Vogel, when he writes, "Autonomy requires us to become integrated with the rest of the natural world, to learn to respect nature, the female, and our own bodies."[14] Autonomy, for Zimmerman and Kant, is the basis of obligation and responsibility. Enlightenment, for Kant, is not freedom from nature.

Enlightenment is freedom from tutelage, that is, freedom from the artificial instruction we receive from other people. Tutelage is perpetuated in pedantry and dogmatism, and this type of domination is collective insofar as Kant identified the schools as the culprits of pedantry and dogmatism.[15] Kant opposes this artificial education, which embondages us, to the natural education we receive from nature, which frees us for our greatest self-esteem. It is impossible to use Kant to justify the kind of position Vogel wants to justify. It is important then to understand Kant, in order to refute such positions, that perpetuate normative dualisms. The relation between nature and domination, and human autonomy and enlightenment is complicated enough to require this entire essay to untangle them.

Ecofeminism and Transformational Feminism

Ecofeminism, in order to be a feminist theory, must make the connection between nature and women explicit. There have been various excellent attempts to do so (Evelyn Fox Keller, Carolyn Merchant, Susan Griffin).[16] These positions are critical of the identification of women and nature. Karen J. Warren, Maria Mies, Ynestra King, and Vandana Shiva, on the other hand, affirm the connection between women and nature, finding it results in a positive position for women.[17] They argue that women are initiating environmental movements, women are naturally more in touch with nature, and women are more involved with maintaining bioregional diversity.[18] Making the women-nature connection explicit, hence, is not a simple matter. On the one hand, Keller, Merchant, and Griffin are criticizing the traditional views of nature as objects and as mechanistic. Warren does not object to the view of nature as object, but argues with Cheney that nature may be viewed this way as long as we limit the claim to truth as perspectival; that is, we acknowledge that the view is dependent on epistemological criteria ("phenomena of interest, the specific measurements taken, and the techniques used to analyze the data").[19] Shiva objects to the mechanical paradigm that views nature as inert and passive *and* as having no value apart from human acting and production of goods. For her, our view of nature is unacceptable if it is viewed as having value only through human culture.[20]

Both Warren and Shiva are, despite their differences, objecting to the same thing. They object to normative dualism. Normative dualism in the received view of nature concludes that nature is inferior to culture. One of the weaknesses in the account of the woman-nature connection that does not make normative dualism the issue is that it tends to perpetuate class and race bias when it assumes that all women have been associated with nature in similar ways, regardless of their class and race differences. Women have been associated with nature in different ways as well: whether one is a white woman or a person of color, or a "colonized" woman, or a "native" woman, a "barbaric" woman, or a "primitive" woman. For instance, upper-class white women seem to be associated with nature as emotions;[21] whereas black women have been associated with nature through their sexuality (as Mammies or "sexually aggressive wet nurse").[22] The only position then that truly universalizes the connection between women and nature, while acknowledging the diverse ways women have been associated with nature, is the one that Warren, Plumwood, and Shiva have developed, which links the critique of patriarchy to normative dualism. It is true that modern science has portrayed nature as passive, inert, and as a collection of mere objects to be manipulated, and women are connected to nature in various ways. The main point is that when nature is viewed this way, and women are identified with nature in the various ways they are, then dominating women is justified. Nature is passive and inferior, women are natural, hence women are passive and inferior; since nature is inferior, it is permissible to use nature for all our arbitrary purposes, hence it is permissible to use women for arbitrary purposes. In their critique of traditional conceptions of nature, Warren and Shiva are less concerned about *how* we view nature than *that* we view nature as inferior to and opposed to culture, because this view allows us to deem women inferior to men.[23] Hence they are opposed to the normative dualistic thinking that justifies dominating practices and strategies.

Normative dualistic thinking, according to Warren, is at the root of all the "isms" of domination, and it is her project to undermine the dualistic and hierarchical way in which we construct nature in opposition to culture. Any feminism that ignores nature in its account of patriarchy is incomplete. And Warren is right, not merely because it is impossible to explain women's oppression apart from their connection to nature, but also because it will be impossible to transform society unless we rid ourselves of all binary oppositions that privilege one member over the other. If white women get the same rights as white men, but racism remains intact, white women become the oppressors. If people of color in this country are given the same rights, but nature is still viewed as inferior then the door is still open to isolating another group of people due to some natural difference and justifying oppression through some allusion to their more natural, primitive, or uncivilized nature.

Warren is arguing for transformational feminism when she makes normative dualistic thinking the focus of her critique of patriarchy. Transformational feminism, as bell hooks presents it, takes as its first premise that all the "isms" of oppression (racism, sexism, classism, naturism, ableism, and so forth) are interconnected, and normative, hierarchical, and dualistic thinking (whites are superior to blacks, men to women, upper classes to lower classes, culture to nature, and able-bodied to disabled) continues to make the oppression of women possible.[24]

In order to overcome normative dualistic thinking, Warren and Shiva believe that we must rethink our relation to nonhuman nature; as Shiva puts it, we need "a new cosmology and a new anthropology which recognizes that life in nature (which includes human beings) is maintained by means of cooperation, and mutual care and love."[25] Dualistic thinking separates human beings from the ecological community; a nondualistic thinking requires that we view human nature as intrinsically connected to nature. It is this element of transformational feminism that sets it apart from the postmodern critique of normative dualism. Warren and Shiva are suggesting a new way of viewing nature as organic, regenerative, and as a co-partner. Ecofeminist transformational feminism attempts to rethink nature such that dualisms do not arise in the first place. Theory, in other words, must be connected with practice.

Transformational feminism calls for a new theory of nature that is organic and in which human beings are viewed as integrated and interdependent members of nature, and this theory must be conducive to action that is environmentally sound. Vandana Shiva has given evidence for a way of viewing nature that is environmentally sound in that it preserves the biodiversity of ecosystems, maintains the sustainability of natural resources, and maintains the sustainability of livelihoods. In "Women's Indigenous Knowledge and Biodiversity Conservation," Shiva argues that in rural India, women's work is diverse; it intersects and interconnects the sectors of production that capitalist-patriarchy creates, and yet their work is hard to quantify.[26] Still, it is precisely women's integrative work and knowledge that preserves biodiversity, and in their context, "survival and sustainability of livelihoods is ultimately connected to the conservation and sustainable use of biological resources in all their diversity."[27] Women, then, are integrated into the invisible ecological energy flow among sectors of dairy management, breeding, farming, and forestry.[28]

For Shiva, women are connected to nature because they are the primary actors in sustaining biodiversity and hence the sustainability of livelihoods. They are also connected to nature because they are actively organizing politically against the reductionist tendency that "subjugates and dispossesses them of their full productivity, power, and potential."[29] Shiva provides a model for the common ground of women's liberation; it is "to be found in the activities of those women who have become the victims of the development process and who struggle to conserve their subsistence base."[30] Women are epistemologically privileged because they are "nearer to the perspective than men and nearer than urban middle-class women."[31] Nonetheless, Shiva also concedes that all women and men are affected in some way by the destructions of the industrial system; hence anyone could in principle have access to the survival and subsistence perspective. Normative-dualisms and patriarchal-capitalist strategies have functioned in various ways to discount indigenous women's knowledge and skills, and it does the same for urbanites as well. In Shiva's account, colonialism and new colonialism created by debt and the free market are the collective culprits of domination. These collective concepts provide a new model for domination and oppression. Domination, in my terminology, can be defined in terms of theoretical colonization. Theoretical colonization invades the seed and the human mind and removes the self-regenerative power of the seed and the self-regenerative and self-provisioning resource of self-esteem from those engaged in self-provisioning activities.

Ecofeminism, then, can provide a new model of feminism based on an understanding of how human beings can be integrated in life-sustaining ways with nature as bio-regional ecosystems. Central to this model is a view of nature as regenerative and as having a kind of organization and balance independent of human production. Nature, in bio-regional ecosystems has its own kind of intrinsic value, apart from market value.

The process of overcoming normative dualism, for Shiva, involves acknowledging the work of women as valuable because it is sustaining.

Val Plumwood, in an extensive discussion of normative dualism and of the traps we can fall into when trying to overcome it, concludes that we must distinguish between the content and value of women's lives in order to overcome normative dualism. She writes,

> traditional femininity was devalued and backgrounded but was also the expression of a range of tasks, values and interests, concerns, areas of life and social orientations of real value and importance; they cannot just be dismissed, because of this denial, as powerlessness. We can reject women's powerlessness without also rejecting the entire content of women's lives and roles and the areas of culture which have been assigned low status.[32]

This means that we have to begin viewing where women have and have had power and contributed value in the ways they are and have been doing so. Overcoming normative dualism means readjusting our evaluation of the worth of women's work, and acknowledging the power that women have and have had.

Kant takes seriously the powers women had in traditional marriage, and the value that women contributed toward furthering civilization, but he does not extend those powers or that value beyond the household. His theory of the connection between women and nature, may well be objectionable from a radical feminist and a liberal feminist perspective; however, it does connect women to nature in a positive way. In addition, Kant argues for a theoretical view of nature and human nature as organic and purposive. He justifies this view epistemologically and hence sanctions it as a type of knowing, although it is not constitutive of nature. The real justification for such knowledge is that it allows us to have a theoretical view of nature that is at the same time enabling of action. I shall argue that Kant explicitly connects women to nature in a positive sense: he uses the purposive view of nature to understand human nature as belonging in regional areas, and he is not a normative dualist.

KANT'S VIEW ON WOMEN AND NATURE

Kant's views on women and nature can be found in his *Anthropology from a Pragmatic Point of View*. There Kant argues that women are distinguished from men, not by "what we make our end," or by a principle that depends on our choice, but rather by the principle of the "conjectural ends of nature."[33] The ends of nature that distinguish women from men are "1) the preservation of the species, 2) the cultivation of society and its refinement by woman."[34] Women propagate and preserve the species and with nature fear for the preservation and propagation of the species. Women also naturally rule men through their more refined feelings of "modesty and eloquence in speech and expression" and their shrewdness for "claiming gentle and courteous treatment by the male."[35] Women differ from men not only sexually (reproduction), but also in terms of gender traits (modesty, eloquence, and shrewdness). Kant claims that both of these differences are natural and not arbitrary (or based on our choice). The question quickly arises as to how a gender trait can be natural, as gender traits are socially constructed.

To interpret this passage we must first recognize that it occurs within the *Anthropology*, and hence it is from a pragmatic point of view. A pragmatic point of view is not a physiological point of view; "physiological knowledge of man investigates what nature makes of him: pragmatic, what man as a free agent makes, or can and should make, of himself."[36] The pragmatic point of view of nature is one that theorizes nature in such a way that human beings can make something of themselves in free agency. In other words, nature is so understood that free action can be actualized in nature. If we understand nature as a totality of objects and as fully determined by efficient causality it is impossible to conceive of how human beings can actualize free action. As Kant argues in the Transcendental Dialectic of the *Critique of Pure Reason*, freedom and nature are two separate realms that do not intersect.[37] In the introduction to the *Critique of Judgement*, Kant argues that the immense gulf between the concept of nature and the concept of freedom that allows no transition is unacceptable for reason, as reason "is to have an influence on" the sensible realm. Hence, Kant continues, "it must be possible to think of nature as being such that the lawfulness in its form will harmonize with at least the possibility of [achieving] the purposes that we are to achieve in nature according to the laws of freedom."[38] Kant then proposes reflective teleological judgment of purposiveness as a theoretical view of nature that allows us to view nature in such a way that our free action is thus enabled.

The pragmatic point of view, then, is that theoretical view of nature that views nature as purposive in order to enable our action. From a pragmatic point of view women are different from men because nature has provisioned different purposes for sex and gender distinction. Nature could have made us a species that reproduced without sexual difference. But nature does nothing in vain. If there is difference, then that difference is purposive for something else. First of all, Kant views nature as having ends and means for achieving those ends. Nature has its own type of organization. This point is relevant for overcoming the normative dualism that views nature as inferior to culture because nature is passive and inert and culture is based on human action. For Kant, nature as purposive, or as "providence," is not passive and inert. Second, nature has provisioned the education and refinement of human beings. So nature is also the teacher of the human species, as Carolyn Merchant has suggested.[39]

When Kant asserts that we can expect the education of human species from nature as providence, he is assuming that nature in the whole is so organized and interconnected that there is a purposive development foreseeable for the human species. It is in this interconnected whole that Kant understands natural sexual and gender difference. Women not only reproduce the human species, they also fear for the preservation of the human species. This position does not appear to be inconsistent with some positions in feminism. When Nel Noddings argues that women root their conception of evil in the mother model of caring, she means that evil is what arouses fears in mothers. A mother fears pain, helplessness, and separation for her children.[40] In other words, mothers fear for the preservation of their children and care for the necessary means for their preservation and well-being.

Now if women take as their primary end the preservation of the human species, then they will also naturally care about the means necessary for that preservation; as Kant argues with respect to the hypothetical imperative, it is irrational to will the end, but not the necessary means for that end.[41] Unlike other species, Kant maintains, the human species has to be educated to its destiny; hence the necessary means for the preservation of the human species includes education.[42] A human being "can be and needs to be educated, as much by instruction as by training (discipline)."[43] Kant has a lot to say about the education of children, youths, and adults.[44] In every case, his account concerns the appropriate instruction for each stage of natural development. For example, Kant believes that children, as opposed to teenagers, should not be required to submit to the rules of duty, but should rather be "guided by mere instinct," so that they learn sociability in their state of "natural joyousness."[45] Kant distinguishes, hence, between natural and artificial (instructional) education.[46] Human beings educate each other artificially, and nature educates the human species naturally. It is this natural education, that is neither socially constructed nor merely natural (if that means unconscious), that Kant has in mind when he characterizes women as naturally having the gender traits of modesty, eloquence, and shrewdness. These gender traits arise out of the conscious interaction between females and males and their respective natural tendencies and purposes.

Males are not entrusted with wombs by nature, but are provided with "greater strength than the woman in order to bring them together into the most intimate physical union, which, insofar as they are still *rational* beings too, it orders to the end most important to it, the preservation of the species."[47] Males too "on the physical side," have an "impulse to preserve [their] species as an animal species."[48] Males contribute to the preservation of the species by uniting with a woman. Since females, too, are rational beings, and not just animals, the intimate physical union is ordered toward the primary natural end of reproduction, which entails the necessity of also preserving the necessary means for educating the developing human being that is reproduced. Human beings are educated to skills that will provide them with the means for subsisting livelihoods. Kant calls these types of skills technical, and they are the types of skills that are necessary for a man "to preserve his wife and children" in civil society where males and females enter into domestic unions.[49] Human beings enter into stable social unions because they also have social inclinations toward one another, and this capacity is "theirs (as rational animals)."[50] Hence, both females and males have sexual reproductive impulses and social impulses to maintain and preserve their union, because as rational animals a stable union is conducive to the preservation and education of new human beings.

The difference between women and men consists in the greater tendency toward fear of physical harm and timidity on the part of women, and the greater tendency toward physical force and strength on the part of men. Women, according to Kant, meet the male's tendencies, as she consciously experiences them, not with physical force, but rather with shrewdness, modesty, and eloquence. Shrewdness or prudence, modesty, and eloquence are all powers rational beings have because they have not only a natural technical predisposition, but also a natural pragmatic predisposition to sociability.

The pragmatic predisposition is the "predisposition to become civilized by culture, especially the cultivation of social qualities, and his natural tendency in social relations to leave the crude state of mere private force and to become a well-bred (if not yet moral) being destined for concord."[51] Women tend to develop the skills of prudence associated with the pragmatic predisposition more readily because they cannot rely on physical force to meet the male tendencies toward physical force. Readiness to use physical force and fear of physical harm are not compatible inclinations. Hence, women have a greater natural tendency toward developing the refined qualities that make for civilization, for civilization is directly contrary to the use of physical force and disharmony. In this sense, women naturally rule men, and are superior to them in their ability to master male inclinations.[52]

As we will see, natural extrinsic purposiveness is about the way one organism uses another for their own purposes. Prudence, as part of the natural pragmatic predisposition is precisely the skill one has for "using other men for [one's] purposes."[53] A woman, according to Kant, does not use others by trying to dominate them directly through force that arouses opposition because of unjust means; rather she uses others indirectly "by the love she inspires."[54] Women are not free from the desire to dominate men, "but they do not use the same means to achieve this purpose as men. Instead of superior strength (which is what the word dominate means here), they use charm, which implies a desire on man's part to be dominated."[55] The natural inclination "toward what is advantageous to us is common to all men, and so too is the inclination to dominate insofar as we can," but men tend to dominate by means of force and women by means of prudence, which if done rightly is not domination at all, but is rather persuasion through eloquence of speech.[56]

Kant attempts to give an account of gender difference that is linked to biological differences and arises out of those biological differences. His account is not meant to establish an efficient causal connection between biology and social destiny. It is an account based on final causality of purposes. It is an account of natural inclinations and tendencies, not natural instincts, and natural predispositions, not natural social traits. His account is thoroughly informed by purposiveness and the teleological judgment that links ends with necessary means.[57] Teleological judgment of purposiveness gives Kant the basis for the claim that women are connected to nature in the sense that women have the greater inclination to fear for the preservation of the species, and, in conscious response to male tendencies, women have a greater tendency toward developing nondominating strategies.

I have not commented on Kant's views on marriage in the civil society, but it seems to me that Kant is not prescribing roles for women; rather, he is describing the roles and powers women actually did have in his society. We may want to reproach him for not having advocated more civil rights for women, but we cannot reproach him for not having accorded women recognition for the civil right they did have, namely, the civil right to marriage. Kant does not portray women as weak, helpless, powerless, or inert. In contrast, it is the fool who believes women are weak and jeers at them.[58] Kant is a philosopher who recognizes the power that women had and the value that they contributed. If we are to overcome normative dualism, according to Val Plumwood, we must recognize the powers women have had even in traditional femininity, even if we choose to exercise those powers no longer.

KANT AND NORMATIVE DUALISM

Kant's critical philosophy has been objected to by feminists because it presents nature as a totality of objects, because the human mind is the lawgiver of passive nature, and because the understanding actively determines the passive manifold of intuition. In this interpretation of Kant, the mind appears to be superior to the body, and human beings appear to be superior to animals. This picture of Kant, however, does not take into account his view of nature and human nature. It is true that Kant offers a theory of nature as a totality of objects in the *Critique of Pure Reason*, but it is not true that he believed that it was a superior view of nature to the one he offers in his *Critique of Teleological Judgement*. Kant explicitly offers an alternative theory of nature that views nature not as a totality of objects, but rather as an interconnected system of purposes, in which the distinction between organic and inorganic nature is central, and where human beings, as organic beings, are viewed as co-members of the system of nature.

Organic beings can be judged through intrinsic purposiveness. Kant defines the principle of natural intrinsic purposiveness: "an organized product of nature is one in which everything is a purpose and reciprocally also a means."[59] This principle excludes any consideration of the inner parts of the living organism as "gratuitous, purposeless, or to be attributed to a blind natural mechanism."[60] We judge the living organic whole in terms of its organization, and that is with respect to how the parts serve reciprocally as means and ends for each other (heartbeats move blood, blood uses the heart to distribute itself). The tree, for example, is both cause and effect of itself in three senses: (1) "a tree generates another tree"; "a tree produces itself"; (2) "a tree also produces itself as an *individual*" in growth; (3) "a tree also produces itself inasmuch as there is a mutual dependence between the preservation of one part and that other others."[61] These three types of production mean that there is integrity within the species, integrity within the individual, and integrity within the parts of the whole organism. The species reproduces itself, maintains itself, and regenerates itself. Organic nature is capable of self-reproduction, self-maintenance, and self-regeneration. The concept of intrinsic purposiveness, however, is not sufficient for establishing the concept of an ecosystem. Organic wholes are given in intuition or sensibly; the whole of the ecosystem and the whole of nature are not given in intuition or sensibly, and thus they are supersensible.

Hence, in order to have the concept of an ecosystem, we have to move to the concept of extrinsic purposiveness, which defines the extrinsic relation between things and beings. Kant defines extrinsic purposiveness as "a purposiveness where one thing of nature serves another as a means to a purpose."[62] In extrinsic purposiveness we can, Kant claims, judge the purpose of things, like air, water, earth as purposive for living organic beings, but we cannot judge organic beings to be purposive for inorganic beings; this is so because inorganic things do not exhibit intrinsic purposiveness. All living beings exhibit intrinsic purposiveness and may be considered ends-in-themselves, insofar as the purpose of the parts are for the production, maintenance, and regeneration of the whole.

However, within extrinsic purposiveness organic beings may be considered either as ends for some other process, or as means for some other end. Within extrinsic purposiveness, the human species has no greater claim than any other living species other than the fact that human beings are the "only being on earth who can form a concept of purposes."[63] We could just as well, Kant suggests, agree with Chevalier Linné, that

> the herbivores are there to moderate the opulent growth in the plant kingdom, which would otherwise choke many species of plants; the predators are there to limit the voracity of the herbivores; finally, man is there to hunt the predators in order to diminish their numbers and so establish a certain equilibrium between the productive and the destructive forces of nature. On this alternative, though man might in a certain respect have the dignity of being a purpose, in a different respect he would hold only the rank of a means.[64]

From the point of view of extrinsic purposiveness, human beings as living organisms are not superior to other living organisms. Human beings are a type of animal, but even animals are not superior to plants. Judgment of objective extrinsic purposiveness permits the conclusion that the human being is the end for plant life, just as it allows the opposite that human life is merely the means to plant life. The ecosystem concept of the interconnected relationship between species is based on the concept of extrinsic purposiveness. In such a judgment, the human species cannot be judged to be superior to any other species. We can conclude then that there is no possibility within judgment of natural purposiveness for concluding that the human species is superior to other species, or is superior to nature. Normative dualism, if it resides in Kant, cannot be located here.

Descartes's mind-body dualism accords superiority to the mind over emotions and the body; as animals have no minds or consciousness, they are inferior to human beings. Kant, too, is criticized for privileging the mind over the body, and human beings over animals. Yet, when we view Kant's moral theory as a whole, including his theory of the purposive system of nature in which free moral action is to be actualized, the dualisms of mind/body and human being/animal do not emerge as clear-cut dichotomies, and certainly not as normative dualisms.

In the *Anthropology*, Kant criticizes Descartes for trying to understand the mind separate from the body, since such an effort results in theoretical speculation that is a "sheer waste of time." He argues that if we ponder natural causes—for example, the possible natural causes behind the power of memory—we can speculate to and fro (as Descartes did) about traces, remaining in the brain, of impressions left by sensations we have experienced. But since we do not know the cerebral nerves and fibers or understand how to use them for our purposes, we still have to admit that we are mere spectators at this play of our ideas and let nature have its way.[65]

When we separate the mind from the body we do not further, but hinder our ability to act; in this case, speculation on memory does not increase or stimulate memory "in order to increase its scope or efficiency."[66] Pragmatic anthropology concerns those observations on human nature that can be used. In another passage, Kant maintains that it is futile to explain the law of association in physiological terms or "as Descartes' so-called material ideas in the brain" because the principle "will always remain a hypothesis."[67] This explanation is not pragmatic because "we cannot use it in practising the art of association."[68] Mind and body are in harmony and working together in Kant's notion of pragmatic anthropology. In the *Anthropology*, Kant is critical of mechanistic explanation insofar as it does not further our ability to act. He is not in general critical of mechanistic theory, but only when it is applied to the living organism.

In a passage on analogy in the *Critique of Teleological Judgement*, Kant expresses his disagreement with Descartes's opinion that animals are machines. He argues that "what we can quite correctly infer *by analogy*, from the similarity between animal behavior [*Wirkung*] (whose basis we cannot perceive directly) and man's behavior (of whose basis we are conscious directly), is that animals too act according to *presentations* (rather than being machines, as Descartes would have it)."[69] When we compare human beings and animals and classify them according "to the same general kind,"[70] we are judging both based on their acts. Kant called the faculty of judgment that evaluates observable acts and compares and contrasts these acts, teleological judgment. When we use this judgment the normative dualisms of mind/body and human being/animal do not arise.

Teleological judgment is not directed toward explaining efficient causes, but rather is concerned with understanding the organization of living beings and the interconnections of living beings. Teleological judgment is the kind of judgment Kant is employing in his *Anthropology*. I have shown this already in how Kant characterizes the connection between women and nature. Kant could be said to agree with ecofeminism that mind/body dualism is inherently misguided when applied to the organic realm. It does not further our ability to act. For Shiva, indigenous knowledge is the basis of indigenous strategies of living with the complex organization of a regional ecosystem, and is connected intimately with preserving biodiversity. Indigenous knowledge is theory that is intimately connected to practice.[71]

Human beings, because they are living organisms, are also dependent on ecosystems. They cannot simply distinguish themselves from the environment and other animals and then justify unproblematically strategies of domination. Vandana Shiva argues for the interconnection of the various sectors; animal management is related to crop cultivation, and that is related to biodiversity of the ecosystem, and biodiversity is related to human spiritual connection to the earth. For Kant, too, we are animals that are dependent on ecosystems. Kant rejects the simple dualism between humans and animals, when he writes, that human beings are "so dependent on the other creatures on earth, . . . even though [their] understanding was able to rescue [them] (for the most part at least) from these devastations."[72]

Kant advocates our indirect duties toward animals, because "animal nature has analogies to human nature, and by doing our duties to animals in respect of manifestations which correspond to manifestations of human nature, we indirectly do our duty towards humanity."[73] We too have an animal nature, and hence cruelty toward animals encourages cruelty toward human beings. Kant believes that "tender feelings toward dumb animals develop humane feelings towards mankind."[74] And he praises Leibniz for having treated a worm with care:

> The more we come in contact with animals and observe their behavior, the more we love them, for we see how great is their care for their young. It is then difficult for us to be cruel in thought even to a wolf. Leibnitz used a tiny worm for purposes of observation, and then carefully replaced it with its leaf on the tree so that it should not come to harm through any act of his.[75]

The facts that we have feelings for animals and that animals can be harmed is relevant to moral consideration of them. The fact that animals care for their young is relevant to moral consideration of them. Kant expresses the moral consideration they have due as an indirect duty, but it is a duty: we ought not to use animals indiscriminately. There is a distinction between human beings and other animals, but this does not seem to be a basis for claiming superiority over other animals. Normative dualism, hence, cannot be located in Kant's understanding of the relationship between human beings and other living beings, because human beings share animality and/or organic life with all other organic creatures. There is yet the possibility that normative dualism can be found in human nature, that is, with respect to the different capacities human beings have that animals and plants do not have.

KANT'S THEORY OF HUMAN NATURE

Kant began his theory of human nature in the *Universal Natural History and the Theory of the Heavens*, which appeared anonymously in March 1755. Here Kant argued for human co-membership in the natural realm: "Human beings, standing immensely removed from the uppermost rank of beings, are indeed bold to flatter themselves in a similar delusion about the necessity of their own existence. [But] the infinity of nature includes within herself with the same necessity all beings which display her overwhelming richness."[76] In this early account, human beings have no more worth than any other species. In early 1756, in his three articles on the Lisbon earthquake, Kant criticized the belief that human beings can control nature and organize it better according to their arbitrary choices: "we flatter ourselves that we could manage everything better to our advantage, if providence had asked our opinion. Thus we wish, for example, to have the rain in our power, so that we could apportion the year according to our comfort, and could always have pleasant days between the overcast ones."[77]

In 1757, Kant introduced for the first time his lectures on physical geography, on which he then lectured nearly every year for the next forty years; twenty-three of those years he offered his anthropology lectures in the alternate semester. Kant argues in the "Announcement" that human beings will be viewed comparatively with the animal kingdom and "with regard to the differences of their natural form and color in different regions of the earth," because he believes that the prejudices and ways of thinking of people are connected to "the inclinations of human beings as they grow out of the particular region in which they live."[78] Human beings are first of all natural beings, with a natural character grounded in regional existence. Kant views human beings as being part of a system of nature whose organization extends well beyond human control.

Kant's *Anthropology* characterizes human beings as animals in the system of nature. Kant refers to human beings as living earth-dwellers or beings *(lebenden Erdbewohner, Erdwesen)*.[79] He characterizes them in terms of their animality *(Tierheit)*,[80] and as having natural predispositions *(Naturanlagen)*.[81] Kant designates them as the human species *(Menschen-gattung)*, as human beings in the system of organic nature *(Mensch[en] im System der lebenden Natur)*.[82]

Much of the feminist criticism of Kant depends on establishing that Kant's theory of the rational subject is defective in a number of ways, but most primarily because the rational subject is isolated and autono-mous. This criticism can only stand if we continue to ignore the enormous amount of literature Kant has on physical and pragmatic anthropology. In these works, it is the whole human species that is central and the individual must orient herself or himself from that per-spective.

In each of these works the human being is presented as an organic being. Kant neither assumes the superiority of the human species nor advocates it. It wasn't until the *Critique of Teleological Judgement*, that Kant was able to argue that human beings do have a special role in nature construed as a system of purposes; this is so because it is only in human beings that we can locate the final end of nature viewed in its purposive organization.

We have already discussed the concept of intrinsic purposiveness and extrinsic purposiveness, and found no normative dualism there. There is yet, however, the concept of a teleological system of nature, and this concept complicates the discussion.[83] We can, Kant argues, conceive of a system of nature or nature as a whole organization on analogy with the organization of a living organic being, because what we find in the part we should expect in the whole. Once, Kant writes, "we have discovered that nature is able to make products that can be thought of only in terms of the concept of final causes, we are then entitled to go further; we may thereupon judge products as belonging to a system of purposes."[84] Kant views nature as a producer, and as engaging in an activity of production. Without asserting that this is intentional activity, Kant nonetheless understands natural production on analogy with human production.

Human producers make products for ends outside those products. Likewise, nature may be viewed as producing natural products for some end outside of those products. This view of nature does not replace the other view of nature in which there are organic beings that have intrinsic purposiveness, but we cannot extend that model of nature beyond the living organism, as the whole of nature is not given in intuition or sensibly.

In order to conceive of nature as a whole, then, we have to have a concept of the final end of nature, modeled on the concept of human production. No being as merely natural can be the final end of nature, as we have already seen that any being can be viewed as a means to some other organic being. However, since the whole of nature will have to be conceived of as supersensible, it is only possible to locate the final end of nature in human beings and in analogy with human production, as human beings are the only beings that can conceive of purposes. Kant makes his argument in the paragraph entitled "On the Ultimate Purpose That Nature Has as a Teleological System" in the *Critique of Teleological Judgement.*

Kant argues that we cannot find the final end of nature or the whole of nature in the inner pragmatic predisposition of human beings. Nature is not organized to produce happiness for human beings. We see in the system of nature as extrinsic purposiveness that the human species is not marked out for special treatment but must suffer "natural disasters" and natural laws like any other species.[85] Even the inner predispositions of the species, or the intrinsic purposiveness of the species, are conflicting: "What is more, man's own absurd natural predispositions land him in further troubles that he thinks up himself, oppressive domination, barbaric wars, etc., and [so] man himself does all he can to work for the destruction of his own species."[86] The technical predisposition to develop the skills of the arts and sciences leads to inequality among people and those who develop those skills "keep the majority in a state of oppression, hard labor, and little enjoyment, even though some of the culture of the higher class does gradually spread to the lower also."[87] The culture that emerges is self-defeating and dysfunctional because the refinement of taste and the "luxury of [treating] sciences as food for our vanity, shower on us by producing in us so many insatiable inclinations."[88] We produce our own unhappiness in producing insatiable inclinations, and the class division that thereby arises creates a "shining misery."[89]

It is only from the point of view that human beings have a moral destiny and must develop in that direction then, that the distinctive character of the human species in the system of nature emerges. Kant concludes that "it is only as a moral being that we acknowledge man to be the purpose of creation. Thus we now have, in the first place, a basis, or at least the primary condition, for regarding the world as a whole that coheres in terms of purposes, and as a system of final causes . . . a kingdom of purposes."[90] Hence, in neither the technical nor the pragmatic capacities can we locate a superior faculty in the human species. These capacities are so conflicting that human beings end up creating dysfunctional societies. Animals, which are guided by instincts, do not develop skills that are dysfunctional. Human beings have reason and that informs the dysfunctional development of their skills. Reason, for Kant, leads to unhappiness and dysfunction, if it is used only technically and pragmatically. Kant cannot be said to be a normative dualist about reason and nature. Nature teaches human beings that their reason has a greater capacity than mere instrumental value.[91]

Ecofeminists have criticized other strands of the philosophical tradition (Aristotelian and Cartesian) for having located reason as the specific difference between animals and human beings, and for having accorded human beings superiority over animals and over the whole natural realm.[92] Aristotle's theory of immanent teleology makes nature into a totality of organic beings whose souls differ in terms of specifying differences: animal souls differ from plant souls because they have mobility; human souls differ from animal souls because they have intellect. Intellect is a higher capacity; hence, human beings are superior to animals.

In contrast to Aristotelian essentialist tradition, Kant is arguing for a subtle alternative. Human beings are naturally different from other animals, but this is not the basis for any claim to natural superiority. Any claim to superiority can only be imputed to human beings in terms of moral worthiness. Technical and pragmatic uses of reason, which in part differentiate human animality from other animality, do not elevate human beings, unless these uses are in the service of morally worthy action.[93] Morally worthy action is always action that occurs in relation to the sensible realm, and that means in relation to the human being as a natural organic animal that is developing into a rational being.[94]

For the human animal to become rational the four natural predispositions must be developed (animal, technical, pragmatic, and moral).[95]

All require the development of skills (means) that help achieve their ends.[96] The end (intent) of becoming technically skilled requires the use of specific means for some arbitrary purpose. Happiness is the end of the pragmatic predisposition and that requires a certain degree of social skill that allows one to harmonize with other human beings. Achieving moral ends requires the development of skills in judgment and also the recognition of the equal moral worth of all human beings.

The human species, hence, has the unique species characteristic that it can make of itself a rational animal through education and the development of its natural predispositions. In the *Anthropology*, Kant characterizes the human being as *animal rationabile* (animal capable of rationality) rather than as *animal rationale* (rational animal) and this reflects a point of view on human nature and nature that is not normatively dualistic. It is simply impossible to be human and not be a part of nature. Becoming rational means that the kinds of skills that human beings have naturally, have to be developed and actualized in nature. This point is relevant to ecofeminism and sustainability, because human beings cannot develop their skills unless they have means to do so. When natural resources are stripped, the means for sustainability (natural and livelihood) are also taken from future generations.

Kant has a theory of human nature and a theory of nature as a purposive system that is nondualistic. Human culture cannot be opposed to nature since culture arises out of the natural predispositions for technical and pragmatic skills. At the same time, nature and culture are not the same; culture is a conscious response to natural tendencies. It is freedom, not culture, that is opposed to nature in Kant. Culture, however, is not the realm of freedom, since anything one can find in culture can be traced back to some preceding state of affairs. Culture is a result of the interaction of freedom and nature. The freedom-nature dichotomy, on the other hand, does not permit any unproblematic according of superiority to human beings, as human autonomy from natural laws means that human beings have moral obligations and responsibility. We have a responsibility to other animals because we have feelings toward them, because they can be harmed, and because they care for the preservation of their own young. We have a responsibility to larger wholes, or ecosystems, because it is in these wholes that human beings can develop into rational beings by reproducing themselves, preserving themselves and their progeny, maintaining themselves safe from harm, having feelings for each other, and relating to one another morally.

Notes

1. I am grateful to the National Endowment for the Humanities for a travel grant (1991) awarded in order to research the German Enlightenment (biological and pedagogical) influence on Kant. I became more aware of the importance of Kant's works in physical geography and biology through my research. I am grateful to Werner Flach of the Universität Würzburg for his guidance in interpreting these works scientifically. I am also thankful for the helpful comments, critiques, and encouragement I received from the women attending the Midwest Society for Women in Philosophy (Washington University, 9 April 1993). Special thanks to Kari Anderson and Robin Schott for their extensive comments on various versions of this essay.

2. Karen J. Warren, "Feminism and Ecology: Making Connections," *Environmental Ethics* (Winter 1987): 3–20; Val Plumwood, *Feminism and the Mastery of Nature* (New York: Routledge, 1993); Maria Mies and Vandana Shiva, *Ecofeminism* (London: Zed Books, 1993); Ynestra King, "Healing the Wounds: Feminism, Ecology, and Nature/Culture Dualism," in *Gender/Body/Knowledge*, ed. Alison M. Jaggar and Susan Bordo (New Brunswick: Rutgers University Press, 1989).

3. Karen J. Warren, "Feminism and Ecology," 18–19.

4. I shall use the term transformation as this reflects more of the literature that discusses the interconnections of all types of oppression, and because it conveys the view that feminism is about transforming society. See bell hooks, "Feminism: A Movement to End Sexist Oppression," in her *Feminist Theory: From Margin to Center* (Boston: South End, 1984), 17–31.

5. Naturism assumes that human beings are unproblematically and naturally superior to "nature" or other organisms, and that human beings may then dominate nature.

6. See Kristin Waters, "Women in Kantian Ethics: A Failure in Universality" in *Modern Engendering: Critical Feminist Readings in Modern Western Philosophy*, ed. Bat-Ami Bar On, 117–25 (Albany: State University of New York Press, 1994).

7. Robin May Schott, *Cognition and Eros: A Critique of the Kantian Paradigm* (University Park: Pennsylvania State University Press, 1993). In particular see chaps. 8–10.

8. See the discussion of Kant in Nancy Tuana, *Woman and the History of Philosophy* (New York: Paragon, 1992), 57–70.

9. See Jane Flax, "Postmodernism and Gender Relations in Feminist Theory," in *Feminism and Postmodernism*, ed. with an Introduction by Linda J. Nicholson (New York: Routledge, 1990), 39-62. And Jane Flax, "Is Enlightenment Emancipatory?" in *Disputed Subjects: Essays on Psychoanalysis, Politics, and Philosophy* (New York: Routledge, 1993), 75–91.

10. See Elizabeth Fee, "Women's Nature and Scientific Objectivity," in *Woman's Nature: Rationalizations of Inequality*, ed. M. Lowe and R. Hubbard (New York: Pergamon, 1980). See Maria Mies, "Feminist Research: Science, Violence, and Responsibility," in *Ecofeminism*, 52.

11. Immanuel Kant, *Kritik der Urteilskraft*, in *Kants Gesammelte Schriften*, ed. Königlich Preussische [now Deutsche] Akademie der Wissenschaft, vols. 1–29 (Berlin: G. Reimer [now de Gruyter], 1902–), 429–30; *Critique of Judgement*, trans. Werner S. Pluhar (Indianapolis: Hackett, 1987), 317; now Akadamie-Ausgabe or AA, KU, 429-30; 317, I shall give the AA pagination first and then the pagination of the translation when available. Kant writes, "what

is it, within man himself, that is a purpose and that he is to further through his connection with nature."

12. Steven Vogel, "Nature, Science, and the Bomb," *Tikkun* 3, no. 4 (July–August 1988): 88.

13. Ibid., 88.

14. Michael Zimmerman, "On Autonomy and Humanity's Relation to Nature," *Tikkun* 4, no. 2 (March–April 1989).

15. Immanuel Kant, *Critique of Pure Reason*, trans. Norman Kemp Smith (New York: St. Martin's, 1965), B, xxxiii. Kant is critical of the "arrogant pretensions of the Schools, which would fain be counted the sole authors and possessors of such truths . . . reserving the key to themselves, and communicating to the public their use only."

16. Evelyn Fox Keller, *Reflections on Gender and Science* (New Haven: Yale University Press, 1985); Carolyn Merchant, *The Death of Nature: Women, Ecology, and the Scientific Revolution* (San Francisco: Harper and Row, 1980); Susan Griffin, *Woman and Nature: The Roaring inside Her* (New York: Harper and Row, 1978).

17. Ynestra King, "The Ecology of Feminism and the Feminism of Ecology," in *Healing the Wounds*, ed. Judith Plant (Philadelphia: New Society of Publishers, 1989), 18–28.

18. Karen J. Warren and Jim Cheney, "Ecological Feminism and Ecosystem Ecology," *Hypatia* 6, no. 1 (Spring 1991): 180. Maria Mies and Vandana Shiva, "Introduction: Why We Wrote this Book Together," in *Ecofeminism*, 15.

19. Karen J. Warren and Jim Cheney, "Ecological Feminism and Ecosystem Ecology," 182.

20. Vandana Shiva, "Reductionism and Regeneration," and "Women's Indigenous Knowledge and Biodiversity Conservation," in *Ecofeminism*, 25 and 164.

21. See Nancy Tuana's discussion in *Woman and The History of Philosophy*, 116–18.

22. Patricia Hill Collins, *Black Feminist Thought: Knowledge, Consciousness, and the Politics of Empowerment* (New York: Routledge, 1991), 70–77.

23. Warren has worked with Jim Cheney to develop a hierarchy theory with respect to the environment, but this is less concerned about how we view nature, than with how we view our theories about nature. Karen J. Warren and Jim Cheney, "Ecological Feminism and Ecosystem Ecology," 183.

24. bell hooks, "Feminism: A Transformational Politic," in *Talking Back: Thinking Feminist–Thinking Black* (Boston: South End, 1989), 19. See also many articles reprinted in Paula S. Rothanberg, *Race, Class and Gender in the United States: An Integrated Study*, 3d ed. (New York: St Martin's, 1995).

25. Maria Mies and Vandana Shiva, "Introduction," 6; and Karen J. Warren, "Feminism and Ecology," 19.

26. Vandana Shiva, "Women's Indigenous Knowledge," 166.

27. Ibid., 165.

28. Ibid., 167.

29. Vandana Shiva, "Reductionism and Regeneration," in *Ecofeminism*, 24. See also the evidence given by Carolyn Merchant in the section entitled "Women in the Third World," in *Radical Ecology: The Search for a Livable World* (New York: Routledge, 1992), 200–207.

30. Maria Mies and Vandana Shiva, "Introduction," 12.

31. Ibid., 19.

32. Val Plumwood, *Feminism and the Mastery of Nature*, 65.

33. Immanuel Kant, *Anthropologie im pragmatischer Hinsicht*, in AA, 7:305; *Anthropology from a Pragmatic Point of View*, trans. Mary Gregor (Martinus Nijhoff: The Hague, 1974), 169.

34. AA, *Anth* 7:306; 169.

35. Ibid.

36. AA, *Anth* 7:119; 3.

37. Immanuel Kant, *Critique of Pure Reason*, trans. Norman Kemp Smith (New York: St. Martin's, 1965), B 561ff. Kant writes, "By freedom, on the other hand, in its cosmological meaning, I understand the power of beginning a state spontaneously. Such causality will not, therefore, itself stand under another case determining it in time, as required by the law of nature."

38. AA, *KU*, 5:176; 15.

39. Carolyn Merchant, *The Death of Nature: Women*, 190. Kant refers to nature as the teacher of the human species. "It is only from Providence that man anticipates the education of the human race, taking the species as a whole" (AA, *Anth* 7:328; 188).

40. Nel Noddings, *Women and Evil* (Berkeley and Los Angeles: University of California Press, 1989), 112.

41. Immanuel Kant, *Grundlegung zur Metaphysik der Sitten*, in AA, 4:417; *Grounding for the Metaphysics of Morals*, trans. James Ellington (Indianapolis: Hackett, 1983), 27; now AA, Gr 4:417; 27. Kant writes, "Whoever wills the end, wills (so far as reason has decisive influence on his actions) also the means that are indispensably necessary to his actions and that lie in his power."

42. AA, *Anth* 7:325; 186.

43. AA, *Anth* 7:323–24; 185.

44. Immanuel Kant, *Education*, trans. Annette Churton (Ann Arbor: University of Michigan Press, 1964).

45. Kant, *Education*, 90–92.

46. Kant, *Education*, 88. Here Kant speaks of natural punishment, that is, punishment administered by nature. His example is of a child getting ill from overeating.

47. AA, *Anth* 7:303; 167. This could be criticized as a false dichotomy: women are weak; men are strong.

48. AA, *Anth* 7:325; 186.

49. AA, *Anth* 7:325; my translation.

50. AA, *Anth* 7:303; 167.

51. AA, *Anth* 7:323; 185.

52. AA, *Anth* 7:303; 167.

53. AA, *Anth* 7:201; 72.

54. AA, *Anth* 7:273; 140.

55. Ibid.

56. AA, *Anth* 7:306; 169.

57. Teleology does not mean "goal-directedness" for Kant. This Aristotelian understanding of teleology is often what is presupposed in most uses of the word 'teleology.' See, for example, Harley Cahen, "Against the Moral Considerability of Ecosystems," *Environmental Ethics* (Fall 1988): 195–216. For Kant, teleological judgment is a type of judgment that evaluates the relation between means and ends, and is comparative. It compares what something is with what it ought to be. Teleology is a critique of a faculty of judgment.

58. AA, *Anth* 7:303; 167.

59. AA, *KU* 5:376; 255.

60. AA, *KU* 5:376; 255.

61. AA, *KU* 5:371; 249–50.

62. AA, *KU* 5:425; 312.

63. AA, *KU* 5:427; 314.

64. AA, *KU* 5:427; 314.

65. AA, *Anth* 7:119; 3.

66. AA, *Anth* 7:119; 3.

67. AA, *Anth* 7:176; 51.

68. AA, *Anth* 7:176; 52.

69. AA, *KU* 5:464 n; 356 n.

70. AA, *KU* 5:464 n; 357 n.

71. Karen Warren, "The Power and Promise of Ecological Feminism," *Environmental Ethics* 12 (Summer 1990): 143.

72. AA, *KU* 5:428; 316.

73. Immanuel Kant, *Lectures on Ethics*, trans. Louis Infield (Indianapolis: Hackett, 1963), 239.

74. Ibid., 240.

75. Ibid.

76. Immanuel Kant, *Allgemeine Naturgeschichte und Theorie des Himmels*, in AA, 1:353–54; *Universal Natural History and Theory of the Heavens*, trans. and introd. Stanley L. Jaki (Edinburgh: Scottish Academic Press, 1981), 185; now AA, *UnH* 1:353–54; 185.

77. Immanuel Kant, "Geschichte und Naturbeschreibung der merkwürdigsten Vorfälle des Erdbebens, welches an dem Ende des 1755sten Jahres einen grossen Theil der Erde erschüttert hat," in AA, 1:454.

78. Immanuel Kant, "Entwürf und Ankündigung eines Collegii der physischen Geographie nebst dem Anhange einer kurzen Betrachtung über die Frage: Ob die Westwinde in unsern Gegenden darum feucht seien, weil sie über ein grosses Meer streichen," in AA, 2:9; *Kant's Pre-Critical Ethics*, trans. Paul Arthur Schilpp (Evanston: Northwestern University Press, 1938), 20.

79. AA, *Anth* 7:322 and 331; 183 and 191.

80. AA, *Anth* 7:327f.; 188f.

81. AA, *Anth* 7:285, 321–27, and 329; 151, 182–87, and 189.

82. AA, *Anth* 7:321; 183.

83. AA, *KU* 5:sect. 83.

84. AA, *KU* 5:380; 260–61.

85. AA, *UnH* 1:353–54; 185.

86. AA, 5:430; 318.

87. AA, 5:432; 320.

88. AA, 5:433; 321.

89. AA, 5:432; 320.

90. AA, 5:444; 333.

91. AA, *KU* 5:433–34; 321. See also AA, *Anth* 7:329–30; 190.

92. AA, *Anth* 7:119 and 321; 3 and 183.

93. AA, *Gr* 4:396; 14. Kant writes, "For as reason is not competent to guide the will with certainty in regard to its objects and the satisfaction of all our wants . . . this being an end to which an implanted instinct would have led with much greater certainty." In other words, humans are naturally at a disadvantage by reason, and therefore have a claim to inferiority.

94. AA, *Gr* 4:450 and 453; 52 and 54. Kant writes, "But now we see that when we think of ourselves as free, we transfer ourselves into the intelligible world as members and know the autonomy of the will together with its consequence, morality; whereas when we think of ourselves as obligated, we consider ourselves as belonging to the world of sense and yet at the same time to the intelligible world." Obligation does not arise unless we conceive ourselves as free and sensible at the same time.

95. In the AA, *Anth* 7:322ff.; 183ff., Kant lists the predispositions as the technical, the pragmatic, and the moral. In *Die Religion innerhalb der Grenzen der bloßen Vernunft*, AA, 6:26; *Religion Within the Limits of Reason Alone*, trans. Theodore M. Greene and Hoyte H. Hudson (New York: Harper & Row, 1960), 21 [now AA, *Rel* 6:26; 21], the three predispositions discussed are the predispositions to animality, humanity, and personality. The account of the

predisposition to animality is missing in the *Anthropology*. In the *Religion*, the account of the technical predisposition is missing. This does not necessarily represent a conflicting account of the four original predispositions, since the descriptions are given with respect to different purposes. In the *Religion*, Kant is attempting to uncover if evil is rooted in our natural predispositions, and it is relevant to discuss if it is rooted in animality. Kant does not discuss the predisposition to animality in the *Anthropology*, because there he wants to discuss the differences between human beings and animals.

96. AA, *Anth* 7:322–25; 183–85.

Select Bibliography

Alcoff, Linda, and Elizabeth Potter, eds. *Feminist Epistemologies*. New York: Routledge, 1993.

Anderson-Gold, Sharon. "Kant's Rejection of Devilishness: The Limits of Human Volition." Manuscript. New York: Rensselaer Polytechnic Institute, 1982.

Annas, Julia. "Personal Love and Kantian Ethics in 'Effi Briest.' " *Philosophy and Literature* 8 (1984): 15–31. Reprinted in *Friendship: A Philosophical Reader*, edited by Neera Kkapur Badhwar. Ithaca: Cornell University Press, 1993.

Arendt, Hannah. *Lectures on Kant's Political Philosophy*. Edited by Ronald Beiner. Chicago: University of Chicago Press, 1982.

Baier, Annette. "Trust and Antitrust." *Ethics* 96 (January 1986): 231–60.

Bar-on, Bat Ami, ed. *Modern Engendering: Critical Feminist Readings in Modern Western Philosophy*. Albany: State University of New York Press, 1994.

Baron, Marcia. "The Alleged Moral Repugnance of Acting from Duty." *Journal of Philosophy* 81, no. 4 (April 1984).

———. "Was Effi Briest a Victim of Kantian Morality?" *Philosophy and Literature*, 12 (1988): 95–113. Reprinted in *Friendship: A Philosophical Reader*, edited by Neera Kkapur Badhwar, 197–22. Ithaca: Cornell University Press, 1993.

Bartky, Sandra. *Femininity and Domination: Studies in the Phenomenology of Oppression*. New York: Routledge, Chapman and Hall, 1990.

Beauvoir, Simone de. *The Second Sex*. Translated by H. M. Parshley. New York: Vintage, 1952.

Beck, Lewis White, ed. *Kant on History*. New York: Macmillan, 1963.

———, ed. *Kant: Selections*. New York: Macmillan, 1988.

Benhabib, Seyla. "The Generalized and the Concrete Other: Visions of the Autonomous Self." *Praxis International* 5, no. 4 (1986): 402–24.

———. *Situating the Self: Gender, Community and Postmodernism in Contemporary Ethics*. New York: Routledge, 1992.

Benhabib, Seyla, and Drucilla Cornell. *Feminism as Critique: Essays on the Politics of Gender in Late-Capitalist Societies*. Cambridge: Polity, 1987.

Blum, Lawrence. *Friendship, Altruism and Morality*. London: Routledge and Kegan Paul, 1980.

———. "Gilligan and Kohlberg: Implications for Moral Theory." *Ethics* 98, no. 3 (April 1988): 472–91.

————. "Kant's and Hegel's Moral Rationalism: a Feminist Perspective." *Canadian Journal of Philosophy* 2, no. 2 (1982): 95–110.

Bordo, Susan R. *The Flight to Objectivity: Essays on Cartesianism and Culture.* Albany: State University of New York Press, 1987.

Calhoun, Cheshire. "Justice, Care, and Gender Bias." *Journal of Philosophy* 85, no. 9 (September 1988): 451–63.

Card, Claudia. "Caring and Evil." *Hypatia* 5, no. 1 (1990): 101–8.

————, ed. *Feminist Ethics.* Lawrence: University of Kansas Press, 1991.

Chodorow, Nancy. *The Reproduction of Motherhood: Psychoanalysis and the Sociology of Gender.* Berkeley and Los Angeles: University of California Press, 1978.

Code, Lorraine. *Epistemic Responsibility.* Hanover: University Press of New England, 1987.

————. *What Can She Know?: Feminist Theory and the Construction of Knowledge.* Ithaca: Cornell University Press, 1991.

Cohen, Ted, and Paul Guyer, ed. *Essays in Kant's Aesthetics.* Chicago: University of Chicago Press, 1982.

Collins, Patricia Hill. *Black Feminist Thought: Knowledge, Consciousness, and the Politics of Empowerment.* New York: Routledge, 1991.

Cornell, Drucilla. *Transformations: Recollective Imagination and Sexual Difference.* New York: Routledge, 1993.

David-Ménard, Monique. *La Folie dans la raison pure: Kant, lecteur de Swedenborg.* Paris: Librairie Vrin, 1990.

————. *Hysteria from Freud to Lacan: Body and Language in Psychoanalysis.* Ithaca: Cornell University Press, 1981.

Dillon, Robin. "Toward a Feminist Conception of Self-Respect." *Hypatia* 7, no. 1 (1992): 52–69.

Felski, Rita. *Beyond Feminist Aesthetics: Feminist Literature and Social Change.* Cambridge: Harvard University Press, 1989.

Flanagan, Owen, and Kathryn Jackson. "Justice, Care and Gender: The Kohlberg-Gilligan Debate Revisited." *Ethics* 97 (April 1987): 622–37.

Flax, Jane. *Disputed Subjects: Essays on Psychoanalysis, Politics, and Philosophy.* New York: Routledge, 1993.

Foot, Philippa. *Virtues and Vices and Other Essays in Moral Philosophy.* Berkeley and Los Angeles: University of California Press, 1978.

Fraser, Nancy. *Unruly Practices.* Minneapolis: University of Minnesota Press, 1989.

Fraser, Nancy, and Sandra Lee Bartky, eds. *Revaluing French Feminism: Critical Essays on Difference, Agency, and Culture.* Bloomington: Indiana University Press, 1992.

Friedman, Marilyn. "Feminism and Modern Friendship: Dislocating the Community." *Ethics,* 99, no. 2 (January 1989): 275–90.

Gadamer, Hans-Georg. *Philosophical Hermeneutics.* Translated by David E. Linge. Berkeley and Los Angeles: University of California Press, 1976.

Garry, Ann, and Mary Pearsall, eds. *Women, Knowledge, and Reality: Explorations in Feminist Philosophy.* Boston: Unwin Hyman, 1989.

Gatens, Moira. *Feminism and Philosophy: Perspectives on Difference and Equality.* Cambridge: Polity, 1991.

Gerhard, Ute. *Gleichheit ohne Angleichung: Frauen im Recht.* Munich: Beck, 1990.

Gewirth, Alan. *Reason and Morality.* Chicago: University of Chicago Press, 1978.

Gilligan, Carol. *In a Different Voice; Psychological Theory and Women's Development.* Cambridge: Harvard University Press, 1982.

Gilligan, Carol, Jenny Victoria Ward, and Jill McLean Taylor, eds. *Mapping the Moral*

Domain: A Contribution to Psychological Theory and Education. Cambridge: Harvard University Press, 1988.

Ginsborg, Hannah. "On the Key to Kant's Critique of Taste." *Pacific Philosophical Quarterly* 72, no. 4 (December 1991): 290–313.

Goldmann, Lucien. *Immanuel Kant.* London: New Left Books, 1971.

Gould, Carol C., ed. *Beyond Domination: New Perspectives on Women and Philosophy.* Totowa, N.J.: Rowman and Allanheld, 1983.

Gregor, Mary J. *Laws of Freedom: A Study of Kant's Method of Applying the Categorical Imperative in the "Metaphysik der Sitten."* Oxford: Basil Blackwell, 1963.

Griffin, Susan. *Woman and Nature: The Roaring inside Her.* New York: Harper and Row, 1978.

Grimshaw, Jean. *Philosophy and Feminist Thinking.* Minneapolis: University of Minnesota Press, 1986.

Gunew, Sneja, ed. *Feminist Knowledge: Critique and Construct.* New York: Routledge, 1990.

Heller, T., M. Sosna, and D. Wellberg, eds. *Reconstructing Individualism: Autonomy, Individuality and the Self in Western Thought.* Stanford: Stanford University Press, 1986.

Herman, Barbara. "Could It Be Worth Thinking About Kant on Sex and Marriage?" In *A Mind of One's Own; Feminist Essays on Reason and Objectivity,* edited by Louise M. Antony and Charlotte Witt, 49–67. Boulder: Westview, 1993.

———. "Integrity and Impartiality." *Monist* 66, no. 2 (April 1983): 233–50.

———. "On the Value of Acting from the Motive of Duty." *Philosophical Review* 90 (1981): 363–66.

———. "The Practice of Moral Judgement." *Journal of Philosophy* 82, no. 8 (August 1985): 414–36.

———. *The Practice of Moral Judgment.* Cambridge: Harvard University Press, 1993.

Hill, Thomas. *Autonomy and Self-Respect.* New York: Cambridge University Press, 1991.

Hinman, Lawrence M. "On the Purity of Our Moral Motives: A Critique of Kant's Account of the Emotions and Acting for the Sake of Duty." *Monist* 66, no. 2 (1983): 251-67.

Hippel, Theodor Gottlieb von. *Über die bürgerliche Verbesserung der Weiber.* Berlin, 1791; repr., Frankfurt: Syndikat, 1977.

Hirsch, Marianne, and Evelyn Fox Keller, eds. *Conflicts in Feminism.* New York: Routledge, 1990.

Hoagland, Sarah Lucia. "Some Concerns about Nel Noddings's Caring." *Hypatia* 5, no. 1 (1990): 109–14.

Horkheimer, Max, and Theodor Adorno. *The Dialectic of Enlightenment.* New York: Herder and Herder, 1972.

Houston, Barbara. "Caring and Exploitation." *Hypatia* 5, no. 1 (1990): 115–19.

Hull, Gloria T., Patricia Bell Scott, and Barbara Smith, eds. *All the Women are White, All the Blacks are Men, but Some of us are Brave: Black Women's Studies.* Old Westbury, N.Y.: Feminist Press, 1982.

Hulme, Peter, and Neil L. Whitehead, eds., *Wild Majesty: Encounters with Caribs from Columbus to the Present Day.* Oxford: Clarendon, 1992.

Irigaray, Luce. *This Sex Which is Not One.* Translated by Catherine Porter and Carolyn Burke. Ithaca: Cornell University Press, 1985.

Jaggar, Alison M. "Feminist Ethics: Some Issues for the Nineties." *Journal of Social Philosophy* 20 (1989): 91–107.

———. *Feminist Politics and Human Nature.* Totowa, N.J.: Rowman and Allanhead, 1983.

Jaggar, Alison M., and Susan R. Bordo, eds. *Gender/body/knowledge*. New Brunswick: Rutgers University Press, 1989.

Jauch, Ursula Pia. *Immanuel Kant zur Geschlechterdifferenz. Aufklärerische Vorurteilskritik und bürgerliche Geschlechtsvormundschaft*. Vienna: Passagen, 1988 and 1993.

Joeres, Ruth-Ellen B., and Mary Jo Maynes, eds. *German Women in the Eighteenth and Nineteenth Centuries*. Bloomington: Indiana University Press, 1986.

Kant, Immanuel. *Anthropology from a Pragmatic Point of View*. Translated by Victor Lyle Dowdell. Carbondale: Southern Illinois University Press, 1978.

———. *The Conflict of the Faculties*. Translated by Mary J. Gregor. New York: Arabis Books, 1979.

———. *The Critique of Judgement*. Translated with Analytical Indexes by James Creed Meredith. Oxford: Clarendon Press, 1928; repr. 1964.

———. *Critique of Pure Reason*. Translated by Norman Kemp Smith. New York: St. Martin's, 1965.

———. *The Doctrine of Virtue*. Translated by Mary J. Gregor. New York: Harper and Row, 1964.

———. *Education*. Translated by Annette Churton. Ann Arbor: University of Michigan Press, 1964.

———. *The Educational Theory of Immanuel Kant*. Translated by Edward F. Buckner. Philadelphia: J. B. Lippincott, 1904.

———. *Foundations of the Metaphysics of Morals*. Translated by Lewis White Beck. Indianapolis: Bobbs-Merrill, 1959.

———. *Gesammelte Schriften*. Berlin: Königliche Preussische Akademie der Wissenschaften, 1902–83.

———. *Groundwork of the Metaphysics of Morals*. New York: Harper and Row, 1964.

———. *Grundlegung zur Metaphysik der Sitten*. Edited by Karl Vorlander. Hamburg: Felix Meiner, 1965.

———. *Kant's Critique of Practical Reason and Other Works*. Translated by T. K. Abbott. 6th ed. London: Longmans, Green, 1948.

———. *Kritik der Reinen Vernunft*. Edited by Raymund Schmidt. Hamburg: Felix Meiner, 1976.

———. *Kritik der Urteilskraft: Kants gesammelte Schriften*. Vol. 5. Berlin: Königliche Preussische Akademie der Wissenschaften, 1913.

———. *Lectures on Ethics*. Translated by Louis Infield. New York: Harper Torchbooks, 1963.

———. *The Metaphysical Elements of Justice*. Translated by John Ladd. Indianapolis: Bobbs-Merrill, 1959.

———. *The Metaphysical Principles of Virtue*. Indianapolis: Bobbs-Merrill, 1964.

———. *Metaphysics of Morals*. Translated by Mary Gregor. New York: Cambridge University Press, 1991.

———. *Observations on the Feeling of the Beautiful and the Sublime*. Translated by John T. Goldthwait. Berkeley and Los Angeles: University of California Press, 1965.

———. *On History*. Edited by Lewis White Beck. Translated by Lewis White Beck, Robert E. Anchor, and Emil L. Fackenheim. New York: Bobbs-Merrill, 1963.

———. *Perpetual Peace and Other Essays*. Translated by Ted Humphrey. Indianapolis: Hackett, 1983.

———. *Philosophical Correspondence, 1759–99*. Edited by Arnulf Zweig. Translated by Victor Lyle Dowdell. Chicago: University of Chicago Press, 1967.

———. *Prolegomena to Any Future Metaphysics*. Translated by Lewis White Beck. New York: Bobbs-Merrill, 1950.

———. *Religion Within the Limits of Reason Alone.* Translated by Theodore M. Green and Hoyt H. Hudson. New York: Harper and Row, 1960.

———. *Universal Natural History and Theory of the Heavens.* Translation and introduction by Stanley L. Jaki. Edinburgh: Scottish Academic Press, 1981.

Keller, Evelyn Fox. *Reflections on Gender and Science.* New Haven: Yale University Press, 1985.

Kennedy, Ellen, and Susan Mendus. *Women in Western Political Philosophy: Kant to Nietzsche.* Hempstead, Great Britain: Wheatsheaf Books, 1987.

Kittay, Eva Feder, and Diana T. Myers, eds. *Women and Moral Theory.* Totowa, N.J.: Rowman and Littlefield, 1987.

Kofman, Sarah. *L'Enigme de la femme.* Paris: Galilée, 1980.

———. *Les Fins de l'homme.* Paris: Galilée, 1981.

———. *Le Respect des femmes.* Paris: Galilée, 1982.

Korsgaard, Christine. "Creating the Kingdom of Ends: Reciprocity and Responsibility in Personal Relations." *Philosophical Perspectives* 6 (1992): 305–32.

———. "Kant's Formulation of Universal Law." *Pacific Philosophical Quarterly* 66 (1985): 24–27.

———. "Scepticism About Practical Reason." *Journal of Philosophy* 83 (1986): 5-25.

Kuhn, Thomas. *The Structure of Scientific Revolutions.* Chicago: University of Chicago Press, 1971.

Lahar, Stephanie. "Ecofeminist Theory and Grassroots Politics." *Hypatia* 6, no. 1 (1991): 28–45.

Langton, Rae. "Duty and Desolation." *Philosophy* 67 (1992): 481–505.

Lawrence, Joseph. "Logos and Eros: the Underlying Tension in Kant's third Critique." *Idealist Studies* 22, no. 2 (May 1992): 130–43.

Lloyd, Genevieve. *The Man of Reason: "Male" and "Female" in Western Philosophy.* Minneapolis: University of Minnesota Press, 1984.

Lorde, Audre. *Sister Outsider.* Trumansburg, N.Y.: Crossing Press, 1984.

Lower, M., and R. Hubbart, eds. *Woman's Nature: Rationalization of Inequality.* New York: Pergamon, 1980.

Mohowald, Mary Briody, ed. *Philosophy of Woman: An Anthology of Classic and Current Concepts.* 2d ed. Indianapolis: Hackett, 1983.

Makkreel, Rudolf. *Imagination and Interpretation in Kant: The Hermeneutical Import of the Critique of Judgment.* Chicago: University of Chicago Press, 1990.

Marks, Elaine, and Isabelle de Courtivron, eds. *New French Feminisms.* Amherst: University of Massachusetts Press, 1980.

Merchant, Carolyn. *The Death of Nature: Women, Ecology and the Scientific Revolution.* San Francisco: Harper and Row, 1980.

———. *Radical Ecology: The Search for a Livable World.* New York: Routledge, 1992.

Meyers, Diana T. "Personal Autonomy and the Paradox of Feminine Socialization." *Journal of Philosophy* 84, no. 11 (November 1987): 619–28.

Mies, Maria, and Vandana Shiva. *Ecofeminism.* London: Zed Books, 1993.

Mills, Patricia Jagentowicz. "Feminism and Ecology: On the Domination of Nature." *Hypatia* 6, no. 1 (Spring 1991): 162–78.

Mills, Sara. *Discourses of Difference: An Analysis of Women's Travel Writing and Colonialism.* New York: Routledge, 1992.

Moi, Toril, ed. *French Feminist Thought.* Oxford: Basil Blackwell, 1987.

Nagl-Docekal, Herta, and Herlinde Pauer-Studer, eds. *Jenseits der Geschlechtermoral: Beiträge zur feministischen Ethik.* Frankfurt am Main: Fischer, 1993.

Nails, Debra. "Social-Scientific Sexism: Gilligan's Mismeasure of Man." *Social Research,* no. 50 (1983): 643–63.

Nicholson, Linda J., ed. *Feminism/Postmodernism*. New York: Routledge, 1990.

Nietzsche, Friedrich. *The Birth of Tragedy and the Genealogy of Morals*. Translated by Francis Golffing. New York: Doubleday, 1956.

Noddings, Nel. *Caring: A Feminine Approach to Ethics and Moral Education*. Berkeley and Los Angeles: University of California Press, 1984.

———. *Women and Evil*. Berkeley and Los Angeles: University of California Press, 1989.

Nunner-Winkler, Gertrud, ed. *Weibliche Moral: Die Kontroverse um eine geschlechtsspezifische Ethik*. Frankfurt am Main: York: Campus, 1991.

Nussbaum, Martha, "Feminists and Philosophy." *New York Review of Books*, 20 October 1994.

O'Neill, Onora. *Constructions of Reason: Explorations of Kant's Practical Philosophy*. New York: Cambridge University Press, 1989.

———. "Kant After Virtue." *Inquiry* 26 (1983): 387–405.

Okin, Susan Moller. *Justice, Gender, and the Family*. New York: Basic Books, 1989.

Ouden, Barnard den, and Marcia Moen, eds. *New Essays on Kant*. New York: Peter Lang, 1987.

Pearsall, Marilyn, ed. *Women and Values: Readings in Recent Feminist Philosophy*. 2d ed. Belmont: Wadsworth, 1993.

Piper, Adrian M. S. "Impartiality, Compassion and Modal Imagination." *Ethics* 101, no. 4 (July 1991): 726–57.

———. "Moral Theory and Moral Alienation." *Journal of Philosophy* 84, no. 2 (February 1987): 102–18.

———. "Two Conceptions of the Self." *Philosophical Studies* 48, no. 2 (September 1985): 173–97.

Plant, Judith, ed. *Healing the Wounds: The Promise of Ecofeminism*. Santa Cruz: New Society, 1989.

Plumwood, Val. *Feminism and the Mastery of Nature*. New York: Routledge, 1993.

Pries, Christine, ed. *Das Erhabene. Zwischen Grenzerfahrung und Grössenwahn*. Weinheim: VCH acta humaniora 1989.

Rawls, John. "Kantian Constructivism in Moral Theory: The Dewey Lectures 1980." *Journal of Philosophy* 78 (1980): 515–72.

———. *A Theory of Justice*. Cambridge: Harvard University Press, 1971.

Reiter, Rayna R., ed. *Toward an Anthropology of Women*. New York: Monthly Review, 1975.

Rorty, Amalie O., and Owen Flanagan, eds. *Identity, Character and Morality*. Cambridge: MIT Press, 1990.

Rorty, Amelie O., and Brian McLoughlin, eds. *Perspectives on Self-Deception*. Berkeley and Los Angeles: University of California Press, 1988.

Rosaldo, Michelle Z., Nannerl O. Keohane, and Barbara C. Gelpi, eds. *Feminist Theory: A Critique of Ideology*. Chicago: University of Chicago Press, 1982.

Schott, Robin May. *Cognition and Eros: A Critique of the Kantian Paradigm*. Boston: Beacon, 1988. (Paperback, University Park: Pennsylvania State University Press, 1993).

Schröder, Hannelore. "The Declaration of Human and Civil Rights for Women (Paris, 1791), by Olympe de Gouges." In *History of European Ideas* (Oxford: Pergamon, 1989), 11:263–72.

Schwickert, Eva Maria. "Gerechtigkeit und Fürsorge." *Ethik und Sozialwissenschaften* 3, no. 4 (1992): 569–71.

Spelman, Elizabeth. *Inessential Woman: Problems of Exclusion in Feminist Thought*. Boston: Beacon, 1988.

Spencer, Samia I., ed. *French Women and the Age of Enlightenment.* Bloomington: Indiana University Press, 1984.

Tong, Rosemarie. *Feminine and Feminist Ethics.* Belmont, Calif.: Wadsworth, 1993.

Trinh, Minh-Ha T. *Woman, Native, Other.* Bloomington: Indiana University Press, 1989.

Tronto, Joan. "Beyond Gender Difference to a Theory of Care." *Signs* 12, no. 4 (1987): 644–63.

Tuana, Nancy. *Woman and the History of Philosophy.* New York: Paragon, 1992.

Warren, Karen J. "Feminism and Ecology: Making Connections." *Environmental Ethics* (Winter 1987): 3–20.

———. "The Power and Promise of Ecological Feminism." *Environmental Ethics* 12 (Summer 1990): 125–46.

Warren, Karen J., and Jim Cheney. "Ecological Feminism and Ecosystem Ecology." *Hypatia* 6, no. 1 (Spring 1991): 179–97.

Young, Iris Marion. *Justice and the Politics of Difference.* Princeton: Princeton University Press, 1990.

———. *Throwing Like a Girl and Other Essays in Feminist Philosophy and Social Theory.* Bloomington: Indiana University Press, 1990.

Contributors

ANNETTE CLAIRE BAIER was Distinguished Service Professor of Philosophy at the University of Pittsburgh. She was educated at the University of Otago, New Zealand, and at Oxford University. She has published many articles on the philosophy of mind, ethics, and the history of philosophy, some of which are collected in *Postures of the Mind* (Minneapolis: University of Minnesota Press, 1985; London: Methuen, 1986). More recently she has published *A Progress of Sentiments: Reflections on Hume's Treatise* (Cambridge: Harvard University Press, 1991) and *Moral Prejudices: Essays on Ethics* (Cambridge: Harvard University Press, 1994). Her current work in ethics is on trust, and she is working on a commentary on Descartes's *Meditations*.

MARCIA BARON is associate professor of philosophy at the University of Illinois at Urbana-Champaign. She teaches courses in contemporary ethics, the history of ethics, and feminist issues. She is especially interested in Kantian ethics and has recently published *Kantian Ethics Almost Without Apology* (Ithaca: Cornell University Press, 1995).

MONIQUE DAVID-MENARD is a philosopher and psychoanalyst in Paris. She is now vice president of the Collège International de Philosophie in Paris, and member of the Société de Psychanalyse Freudienne. She has published *Hysteria from Freud to Lacan: Body and Language in Psychoanalysis* (Ithaca: Cornell University Press, 1989) and *La folie dans la raison pure: Kant, lecteur de Swedenborg* (Paris: Librairie Vrin, 1990). She is now preparing one book on the concept of the universal in psychoanalysis and philosophy, and another book on fantasy and metaphysics.

KIM HALL is currently a visiting assistant professor of philosophy at Michigan State University. Her areas of specialization include feminist philosophy, postcolonial theory, Continental philosophy, multicultural studies, and ethics. She is currently completing a book entitled *Writing with a Woman in Mind* in which she considers methods of feminist theorizing located at the intersections of gender, race, class, and sexuality.

SARAH KAUFMAN (1934–94) was a philosopher of psychoanalysis and feminist theory, and teacher, senior lecturer, and professor (1991–94) at the University of Paris. Psychoanalytic approaches to creativity inform her readings of Freud, Nietzsche, Kant, and other thinkers. Some of her main publications include *Nietzsche et la métaphore* (Paris: Galilée, 1972), *Nietzsche et la scène philosophique* (Paris: Galilée, 1979), *L'Enigme de la femme* (Paris: Galilée, 1980), *Le Respect des femmes* (Paris: Galilée, 1982), *Lectures de Derrida* (Paris: Galilée, 1984), *Mélancolie de l'art* (Paris: Galilée, 1985), *Socrate(s)* (Paris: Galilée, 1989), and *Séductions, de Sartre à Héraclite* (Paris: Galilée, 1991). She is listed in the *Biographical Dictionary of Twentieth-Century Philosophers* (ed. Stuart Brown, Diane Collinson, and Robert Wilkonson [London: Routledge, 1995]).

CORNELIA KLINGER earned a Ph.D. in philosophy from the University of Cologne (1981) and her *Habilitation* in philosophy from the University of Tübingen (1992). She has been a permanent fellow of the Institut für die Wissenschaften vom Menschen in Vienna since 1985. Her fields of special interest include political and aesthetic theory of the nineteenth and twentieth centuries, feminist issues in philosophy, and history of ideas from romanticism to postmodernism. Her publications include *Flucht—Tors—Revolte: Die Moderne und ihre aesthetischen Gegenwelten* (Munich: Hanser, 1995). She has also published a wide range of articles on feminist philosophy, German idealism and romanticism, and related subjects.

JANE KNELLER is assistant professor of philosophy at Colorado State University. She also teaches and serves on the executive board of the Women's Studies Program at Colorado State and is currently vice president of the North American Kant Society. Her publications include numerous articles and essays on Kant's aesthetic theory, the relationship between Kant's ethics and aesthetics and between Kantian aesthetics and feminism.

MARCIA MOEN is associate professor of philosophy at the University of Hartford. She teaches also in the Women's Studies Program and in the interdisciplinary All-University Curriculum.

HERTA NAGL-DOCEKAL is a professor of philosophy at the University of Vienna, and was a visiting professor for feminist philosophy at the Universities of Utrecht, Frankfurt am Main, and Konstanz, as well as at the Free University of Berlin. Her publications include the books *Feministische Philosophie* (editor, Vienna: Oldebourg, 1990 and 1994), *Denken der Geschlechterdifferenz* (co–editor, Vienna: Wiener Frauenverlag, 1990), *Jenseits der Geschlechtermoral: Beitrage zur feministischen Ethik* (co-editor, Frankfurt am Main: Fischer, 1993), and *Politische Theorie— Differenz und Lebensqualität* (co-editor, Frankfurt am Main: Suhrkamp, 1996).

ADRIAN M. S. PIPER is professor of philosophy at Wellesley College and a non-resident fellow of the New York Institute for the Humanities at New York University. Her primary research publications are in metaethics and Kant's metaphysics, and her three-volume *Rationality and the Structure of the Self* is nearing completion. Her two-volume art-related collection, *Out of Order, Out of Sight*, vol. 1, *Selected Writings in Meta-Art, 1968–92;* vol. 2, *Selected Writings in Art Criticism, 1967–1992*, has recently been published (Cambridge: MIT Press, 1996).

JEAN P. RUMSEY is associate professor of philosophy at Clarion University of Pennsylvania. Her research interests range from Kantian and feminist theory to topics in health care ethics, and she is currently involved in the University of Pittsburgh's Consortium for Medical Ethics in Western Pennsylvania.

ROBIN MAY SCHOTT was formerly associate professor of philosophy at the University of Louisville, and is currently associate professor of philosophy at the University of Copenhagen. Her publications include *Cognition and Eros: A Critique of the Kantian Paradigm* (Boston: Beacon, 1988; paperback, Penn State Press, 1993), and *Forplantning, Køn og Teknologi* (co-editor, Copenhagen: Museum Tusculanums Forlag, 1995). Her research interests include both feminist interpretation of the history of philosophy as well as contemporary feminist debates; she is currently focusing on questions of nationalism, war, and women.

HANNELORE SCHRÖDER, Dr. Phil., was born in eastern Germany. She has taught Women's Studies at the Universities of Frankfurt,

Göttingen, Hamburg, and Groningen. In 1978 she became the first lecturer in Women's Studies/Political Philosophy at the University of Amsterdam. Among her publications are "The Economic Impoverishment of Mothers is the Enrichment of Fathers" (in *Concilium*, no. 194, Edinburgh, 1987); "The Declaration of Human and Civil Rights for Women (Paris, 1791) by Olympe de Gouges" (in *History of European Ideas*, vol. 11, Oxford, 1989); "Reflections on an Anti-Patriarchal Declaration of Women's Human Rights" (in *Against Patriarchal Thinking*, ed. M. Pellikaan-Engel, Amsterdam, 1992); "Anti-Semitism and Anti-Feminism again: The Dissemination of Otto Weininger's Sex and Character in the Seventies and Eighties" (in *Empirical Logic and Public Debate*, ed. E. C. W. Krabbe, R. J. Dalitz, P. A. Smit, Amsterdam/Atlanta, 1993).

SALLY SEDGWICK is associate professor of philosophy at Dartmouth College. Her main interests are Kant and Hegel (moral and political philosophy, epistemology, and metaphysics) and she has published articles on Kant and Hegel in *Kant-Studien*, the *Monist*, *Philosophy and Phenomenological Research*, *Zeitschrift für Philosophische Forschung*, and other philosophical journals.

HOLLY WILSON is an adjunct professor of philosophy at Mundelein Seminary and Marian College. She is mainly interested in Kant and hermeneutical philosophy (Gadamer and Dilthey). Her article "Kant's Integration of Morality and Anthropology" is forthcoming in *Kantstudien* (1997). She is currently working on a book-length manuscript on Kant's anthropology.

Index

www.ingramcontent.com/pod-product-compliance
Lightning Source LLC
Chambersburg PA
CBHW021843020426
42334CB00013B/169